KT-590-963

Participants

Editors

H. M. Chapel
Department of Immunology, Nuffield Department of Medicine, John Radcliffe Hospital, Headington, Oxford OX3 9DU, UK

R. J. Levinsky
Hugh Greenwood Department of Immunology, Hospital for Sick Children, Great Ormond Street, London WC1N 3JH, UK

A. D. B. Webster
Immunodeficiency Diseases Research Group, Clinical Research Centre, Watford Road, Harrow HA1 3UJ, UK

Contributors

M. Abinun
Department of Clinical Immunology, and Allergy, Mother and Child Health Institute, R. Dakića 8, 11070 Belgrade, Yugoslavia

M. Baer
Department of Paediatrics and Division of Clinical Immunology, University Central Hospital of Tampere, SГ-33520 Tampere, Finland

G. J. Bancroft
Department of Clinical Sciences, London School of Hygiene and Tropical Medicine, Keppel Street, London WC1E, UK

P. Bartmann
Department of Paediatrics, University of Ulm, Prittwitstrasse 43, D-7900 Ulm, Germany

E. Bernatowksa-Matusziewicz
Department of Clinical Immunology, Children's Memorial Hospital, Ave Dzieci Polskich 20, 04-736 Warsaw, Poland

D. W. Beatty
Institute of Child Health, Red Cross War Memorial Children's Hospital and University of Cape Town, Rondebosch 7000, Cape Town, South Africa

A. G. Bird
HIV Immunology Unit, Department of Medicine, Edinburgh University, Edinburgh, Scotland

J. Björkander
Immunodeficiency Unit, Asthma and Allergy Research Centre and Department of Clinical Immunology, Sahlgrenska Hospital, University of Göteborg, S-41345 Göteborg, Sweden

C. Bordignon
Istituto Scientifico H S Raffaele, Milan, Italy

R. G. M. Bredius

Laboratory for Experimental and Clinical Immunology (CLB) and Clinical Immunology Laboratory (AMC), Meibergdreef 9, 91-109 1105 AZ Amsterdam, The Netherlands

C. Brémard-Oury

INSERM U 132, Hôpital des Enfants-Malades, 75730 Paris, France

V. M. Brennan

Immunology Department, John Radcliffe Hospital, Oxford OX3 9DU, UK

A. J. Cant

Department of Immunology, Institute of Child Health and the Hospital for Sick Children, London WC1N 3JH, UK

S. Caspar

CRPG-CNRS de Toulouse, CHU Purpan, Place du Docteur Boylac, F-31300 Toulouse, France

C. Cunningham-Rundles

Mount Sinai Medical Center, One Gustave Levy Place, New York, NY 10029-6574, USA

E. G. Davies

Department of Child Health and Haematology, St George's Hospital Medical School, Cranmer Terrace, London SW17 0RE, UK

K. A. Davies

Rheumatology Unit, Department of Medicine, Royal Postgraduate Medical School, Du Cane Road, London W12 0NN, UK

Ch. Diener

Institute of Clinical Immunology, Freidrich-Schiller-University, Humboldstrasse 3, 6900 Jena, Germany

J. J. M. van Dongen

Department of Immunology, Erasmus University, 3000 DR Rotterdam, The Netherlands

R. Dopfer

Department of Haematology and Oncology, Children's University Hospital, Ruemelinstraße 23, 7400 Tübingen, Germany

M. Duse

Department of Paediatrics, University of Brescia, Spedali Civili, 25100 Brescia, Italy

M. M. Eibl

Institute of Immunology, University of Vienna, Borschkegasse 8A, A-1090 Vienna, Austria

T. Español

Immunology Unit and Paediatric Haematology, R S Valle Hebrón, 08035 Barcelona, Spain

C. M. Farber

Department of Immunology, Hôpital Erasme, Université Libre de Bruxelles, Route de Lennik 808, Brussels 1070, Belgium

J. Farrant

Immunodeficiency Diseases Research Group, Clinical Research Centre, Watford Road, Harrow HA1 3UJ, UK

Editor-in-Chief: **Lord Walton of Detchant**

Progress in Immune Deficiency III

*Proceedings of a meeting of the European
Group for Immunodeficiencies held in Oxford
26–29 September 1990*

Edited by

H. M. Chapel
R. J. Levinsky
A. D. B. Webster

ROYAL SOCIETY OF MEDICINE SERVICES
LONDON · NEW YORK
1991

Royal Society of Medicine Services Limited
1 Wimpole Street   London W1M 8AE
7 East 60th Street   New York NY 10022

©1991 Royal Society of Medicine Services Limited

All rights reserved. No part of this book may be reproduced in any form by photostat, microfilm, or any other means, without written permission from the publishers.

This publication is copyright under the Berne Convention and the International Copyright Convention. All rights reserved. Apart from any fair dealing under the UK Copyright Act 1956, Part 1, Section 7, no part of this publication may be reproduced, stored in a retrieval system or transmitted in any form or by any means without the prior permission of the Honorary Editors, Royal Society of Medicine.

These proceedings are published by Royal Society of Medicine Services Ltd with financial support from the sponsor. The contributors are responsible for the scientific content and for the views expressed, which are not necessarily those of the sponsor, of the editor of the series or of the volume, of the Royal Society of Medicine or of Royal Society of Medicine Services Ltd. Distribution has been in accordance with the wishes of the sponsor but a copy is available to any Fellow of the Society at a privileged price.

British Library Cataloguing in Publication Data
European Group for Immunodeficiencies (Meeting, 1990,
  Oxford, England)
  1. Humans. Immune deficiency diseases
  I. Chapel, H. M.   II. Levinsky, R. J.   III. Webster, A. D.
  B.   IV. Series
  616.079

ISBN 1-85315-147-5

Phototypeset by Dobbie Typesetting Limited, Tavistock, Devon
Printed in Great Britain at the Alden Press, Oxford

A. Fasth

Department of Paediatrics, Gothenburg University, East Hospital, S-416 85 Göteborg, Sweden

G. Ferrari

Istituto Scientifico H S Raffaele, Milano, Italy

A. Finn

Department of Immunology, Institute of Child Health, 30 Guilford Street, London WC1N 1EH, UK

M. Fischer

Institute of Immunology, University of Vienna, Borschkegasse 8A, A-1090 Vienna, Austria

G. Fontán

Immunology Unit, Hospital La Paz, Paseo de la Castellana 261, 28046 Madrid, Spain

W. Friedrich

Department of Paediatrics and of Transfusion Medicine, University of Ulm, Prittwitstrasse 43, Ulm, Germany

M. A. H. French

Department of Clinical Immunology, Royal Perth Hospital, Sir Charles Gairdner Hospital and The University of Western Australia, Perth, Western Australia

V. Friman

Department of Infectious Disease, University of Gothenburg, East Hospital, S-41685 Gothenburg, Sweden

M. Gahr

University-Kinderklinik Göttingen, Robert-Koch-Strasse 40, D-3400 Göttingen, Germany

R. A. Gatti

Department of Pathology, UCLA School of Medicine, Los Angeles, California 90024, USA

E. J. A. Gerritsen

Department of Pediatrics, Leiden University Hospital, Rijnsburgerweg 10, 233 AA, Leiden, The Netherlands

E. A. Goddard

Department of Paediatrics and Child Health, University of Cape Town, Red Cross War Memorial Children's Hospital, Rondebosch 7000, Republic of South Africa

J. Goodship

Department of Human Genetics, 19 Claremont Place, Newcastle-upon-Tyne NE2 4AA, UK

D. Goldblatt

Department of Immunology, Institute of Child Health, University of London and The Hospital for Sick Children, 30 Guilford Street, London WC1N 1EH, UK

M. Goodall

Immunology Department, The Medical School, Birmingham B15 2TJ, UK

H. C. Gooi

Yorkshire Regional Transfusion Centre and St James's University Hospital, Leeds LS15 7TW, UK

E. de Graeff-Meeder   *Department of Immunology, University Hospital for Children and Youth, Het Wilhelmina Kinderziekenhuis, PO Box 18009, 3501 CA Utrecht, The Netherlands*

H. Griffiths   *Department of Immunology, John Radcliffe Hospital, Oxford OX3 9DU, UK*

C. Griscelli   *Hôpital Necker–Enfants Malades, 149 rue de Sèvres, 75015 Paris, France*

M. R. Hadam   *Kinderklinik, Medizinische Hochschule Hannover, 3000 Hannover 61, Germany*

L. Hammarström   *Centre for Biotechnology, Department of Clinical Immunology, Huddinge Hospital, S-14186, Huddinge, Sweden*

L. Å. Hanson   *Department of Clinical Immunology Guldhedsgatan 10, S-413 46, Göteborg, Sweden*

T. Hansel   *Department of Immunology, East Birmingham Hospital, Birmingham, B9 5ST, UK*

Z. T. Handzel   *Clinical Immunology Unit, Kaplan Hospital, Rehovot 76100, Jerusalem, Israel*

A. Haraldsson   *Department of Paediatrics, University of Nijmegen, 6500 HB Nijmegen, The Netherlands*

A. R. Hayward   *University of Colorado Health Sciences Center, 4200 E Ninth Avenue, Denver, Colorado 80262, USA*

M. Hazlewood   *Immunology Department, Medical School, Birmingham B15 2TJ, UK*

R. W. Hendriks   *Division of Immunobiology & Genetics, University Hospital, PO Box 9600, Rijnsburgerweg 10, 2300 AA Leiden, The Netherlands*

J. Heras   *Medical Department, Instituto de Hemoderivados, Immuno SA, 08028 Barcelona, Spain*

H. S. Howe   *Rheumatology Unit, Department of Medicine, Royal Postgraduate Medical School, Du Cane Road, London W12 0NN, UK*

M. R. Jacyna   *Department of Medicine, St Mary's Hospital Medical School, London W2 1NY, UK*

C. M. Jol-van der Zijde   *Department of Paediatrics, Leiden University Hospital, 2300 AA Leiden, The Netherlands*

C. Kinnon   *Department of Immunology, Institute of Child Health, 30 Guilford Street, London WC1N 1EH, UK*

N. J. Klein   *Infectious Disease Unit, Hospital for Sick Children and Institute of Child Health, Great Ormond Street, London WC1N 3JH, UK*

T. Klemola   *Childrens Hospital, University of Helsinki, Helsinki, Finland*

C. Koch   *Department of Paediatrics, Rigshospitalet, University of Copenhagen, Copenhagen, Denmark*

A. Kondyle   *Department of Immunology and Histocompatibility, Saint Sophie's Children's Hospital, Goudi, Athens, Greece*

K. Kouvalainen   *Department of Paediatrics, University of Oulu, Oulu, Finland*

D. S. Kumararatne   *Department of Immunology, Dudley Road Hospital, Birmingham, B18 7QH, UK*

P. Lachmann   *Molecular Immunopathology Unit, MRC Centre, Hills Road, Cambridge CB2 2QH, UK*

M. Lambert   *Department of Immunohaematology and Bloodbank, University Hospital, PO Box 9600, Leiden, The Netherlands*

Y. L. Lau   *Department of Paediatrics, Queen Mary Hospital, Pokfulam Road, Hong Kong*

F. Le Deist   *INSERM U 132, Hôpital des Enfants-Malades, 149 rue de Sèvres, 75015 Paris, France*

S. Le Moli   *Laboratory of Immunology, DASRS, Italian Air Force, 00040 Pratica de Mare, Rome, Italy*

J. Levy   *Ben-Gurion University of the Negev, Barzilai Medical Centre, Ashkelon, Israel*

Y. Levy   *Soroka Medical Centre, Beer Sheva, Israel*

D. Lilić   *Institute for Experimental Medicine, Military Medical Academy, Belgrade, Yugoslavia*

D. R. McCluskey   *Department of Immunology, Queen's University and Royal Victoria Hospital, Belfast, Northern Ireland*

J. W. Mannhalter   *University of Vienna, Borschkegasse 8A, A-1090 Vienna, Austria*

L. Maródi   *Department of Paediatrics, University School of Medicine, Debrecen, Hungary*

N. Matamoros   *Immunology Section and Department of Medicine, Son Dureta Hospital, Palma de Mallorca, Spain*

E. Mazzolari   *Department of Paediatrics, University of Brescia, 25100 Brescia, Italy*

S. Misbah   *Department of Immunology, John Radcliffe Hospital, Oxford OX3 9DU, UK*

V. Monafo   *Department of Paediatrics, University of Pavia, Policlinico S Matteo, P. le Golgi 2, Pavia, Italy*

G. Morgan   *Medical Research Council Laboratories, Institute of Child Health, London WC1N 3JH, UK*

F. Müller   *Laboratory for Immunohistochemistry and Immunopathology, University of Oslo, The National Hospital, Oslo, Norway*

K. Nagy   *Department of Paediatrics and Central Laboratory of Postgraduate Medical School, L Eotvos University, Gyek, Hungary*

D. E. Nilssen   *Laboratory for Immunohistochemistry and Immunopathology, University of Oslo, The National Hospital, Oslo, Norway*

M. North   *Immunodeficiency Diseases Research Group, Clinical Research Centre, Watford Road, Harrow HA1 3UJ, UK*

L. D. Notarangelo *Department of Paediatrics, University of Brescia, 25123 Brescia, Italy*

K. Nydahl-Persson *Department of Paediatrics, Gothenburg University, S-41685 Göteborg, Sweden*

R. Paganelli   *Department of Allergy & Clinical Immunology, University La Sapienza, 0185 Rome, Italy*

M. L. Palma-Carlos *Centre for Clinical Immunology and CHIUL-INIC, Immunology Institute, Faculty of Medicine, Lisbon, Portugal*

J. H. Passwell   *Department of Paediatric Immunology, Chaim Sheba Medical Center, Tel-Hashomer 52621, Israel*

A. L. Pawlak   *Institute of Human Genetics, Polish Academy of Sciences, Strzeszynska 32, 60-479 Poznan, Poland*

A. Pelham   *Department of Immunology, Institute of Child Health, 30 Guilford Street, London WC1N 1EH, UK*

M. von Planta   *University Children's Hospital, Zurich, Switzerland*

A. Plebani   *Department of Paediatrics, University of Brescia, 25123 Brescia, Italy*

O. Porras   *Paediatric Immunology Unit, National Children's Hospital, San José, INCIENSA, Tres Rios, Costa Rica*

I. Quinti   *Department of Allergy and Clinical Immunology, University, 'La Sapienza' Rome, Italy*

J. R. Regueiro	*Department of Paediatrics, University of Valladolid, Valladolid, Spain*
D. M. Roberton	*Department of Paediatrics and Immunology, Royal Children's Hospital, Melbourne, Victoria, Australia*
F. S. Rosen	*Center for Blood Research, Children's Hospital, Department of Pediatrics, Harvard Medical School, Boston, Massachusetts, USA*
J. A. Rump	*Department of Rheumatology and Clinical Immunology, Medical Clinic of the University of Freiburg, D-7800 Freiburg, Germany*
G. de Saint-Basile	*INSERM U 132, Hôpital des Enfants-Malades, 149 rue de Sèvres, 75015 Paris, France*
Ö. Sanal	*Department of Immunology, Hacettepe University Children's Hospital, Hacettepe, Ankara, Turkey*
E. A. M. Sanders	*Department of Immunology, Het Wilhelmina Kinderziekenhuis, University Hospital for Children and Youth, Postbus 18009, 3501 CA Utrecht, The Netherlands*
E. Scala	*Department of Allergy & Clinical Immunology, University La Sapienza, V. le Università 37, 00185 Rome, Italy*
K. Schwarz	*Section of Molecular Biology, Department of Paediatrics II, University of Ulm, D-7900 Ulm, Germany*
R. A. Seger	*Department of Paediatrics, University of Zürich, Zürich, Switzerland*
S. Singh	*Department of Immunology, Institute of Child Health and The Hospital for Sick Children, London WC1N 3JH, UK*
C. I. E. Smith	*Department of Clinical Immunology and Centre for Biotechnology, Karolinska Institute at Huddinge Hospital and at NOVUM, S-141 86 Huddinge, Sweden*
R. Söderström	*Sahlgren's Hospital, University of Götenborg, Sweden*
G. P. Spickett	*Department of Immunology, John Radcliffe Hospital, Oxford OX3 9DU, UK*
S. Strobel	*Department of Immunology, Institute of Child Health and The Hospital for Sick Children, London WC1N 3JH, UK*
L. Szenborn	*Clinic for Infectious Diseases of Children, Medical Academy, Wroclaw, Poland*
G. Thoenes	*INSERM U 132, Hôpital des Enfants-Malades, 149 rue de Sèvres, 75015 Paris, France*

M. W. Turner   Department of Immunology, Institute of Child Health, 30
                                 Guilford Street, London WC1N 1EH, UK

D. Valerio   Institute of Applied Radiology and Immunology, PO Box
                                 5815, 2280 HV Rijswijk, The Netherlands

J. E. Volanakis   Department of Medicine, University of Alabama at
                                 Birmingham, Birmingham, Alabama 35294, USA

J. M. Vossen   Department of Paediatrics, Leiden University Hospital, 2300
                                 AA Leiden, The Netherlands

S. Vukmanović   Institute of Microbiology and Immunology, School of Medicine,
                                 Mother and Child Health Institute, Belgrade, 11000
                                 Yugoslavia

T. B. Wallington   South Western Regional Tranfusion Centre, Southmead Road,
                                 Bristol BS10 5ND, UK

N. Watts   University College and Middlesex School of Medicine, London,
                                 UK

C. Weemaes   Department of Paediatrics, University of Nijmegen, Nijmegen,
                                 The Netherlands

K. Welte   Department of Paediatric Haematology, and Oncology, Medical
                                 School, D-3000 Hannover 61, Germany

C. B. S. Wood   Joint Academic Department of Child Health of St Bartholomew's
                                 and the London Hospital Medical Colleges, London, UK

P. L. Yap   Clinical Immunology Laboratory, Edinburgh & SE Scotland
                                 Regional Transfusion Centre, Edinburgh EH3 9HB, Scotland

B. J. M. Zegers   Department of Immunology, University Hospital for Children
                                 and Youth 'Het Wilhelmina Kinderziekenhuis', PO Box 18009,
                                 3501 CA Utrecht, The Netherlands

Contents

HUMORAL IMMUNE DEFICIENCIES

ANTIBODY DEFICIENCIES INCLUDING IgG SUBCLASSES

IgA DEFICIENCY

COMPLEMENT

IgG DEFICIENCIES AND MHC

Foreword

The European Group for Immunodeficiencies has a combined scientific/clinical meeting to discuss major advances in the field every two years. The proceedings are published rapidly in order to provide an up-to-date account of progress in many aspects of primary immune deficiencies. Subjects aired at the meeting held in Oxford in September 1990 included possible aetiologies, molecular genetics of receptor deficiencies, clinical features and new therapeutic options for all primary immune deficiencies.

The aim of these meetings is to provide an informal basis for discussion between basic scientists and clinicians and the high standard of presentations at this meeting reflected this excellent combination. These proceedings provide up-to-date information on many clinical and basic aspects of a variety of conditions.

Until now, the focus for EGID has been limited to primary immune deficiencies. The Council of Country Representatives decided in Oxford in September to broaden the scope of the meetings to include all aspects of immune dysregulation relating to primary immunological diseases. Thus primary autoimmune diseases will be included at the next meeting in 1992.

We, the Organising Committee for 1990, would like to thank all the very generous sponsors, listed below, who helped to make the meeting so successful. We also thank Conference Associates, without whose professional help the meeting would not have been possible, and Mrs Angela Welby who remained a cheerful and calm influence throughout.

The next EGID meeting is to be held in Switzerland in 1992 and we wish the organisers every success.

Dr Helen Chapel
Professor Roland Levinsky
Dr David Webster

Alpha Therapeutic UK Ltd.
Baxter Healthcare Ltd.
Becton Dickinson UK Ltd.
Biotest Pharma GmbH
Boehringer Ingelheim Ltd.
British Society for Immunology

Cutter Biological, Bayer UK Ltd.
Eurocetus BV
Immuno Ltd.
Sandoz AG
Sandoz Pharmaceuticals
Wellcome Biotech

Update on IgA and IgG subclass deficiency

L. Å. Hanson[1], R. Söderström[1], V. Friman[2], M. Hahn-Zoric[1],
C. Czerkinsky[3], M. Quiding[3], F. Cardinale[1], S. Beres Castrignano[5],
K. Theman[4], J. Björkander[4], A. Kilander[4], T. Söderström[1], B. Carlsson[1],
L. Mellander[1], M. Carneiro-Sampaio[5] and J. Holmgren[3]

Departments of [1]Clinical Immunology, [2]Infectious Diseases, [3]Medical Microbiology and Immunology
and Internal Medicine I, [4]University of Göteborg, Göteborg, Sweden and [5]Department of Pediatrics,
Faculty of Medicine of the University of São Paulo, São Paulo, Brazil

IgA DEFICIENCY

It is 25 years since IgA deficiency (IgAd) was described in healthy individuals [1] yet we still cannot explain how it is possible to remain in good health lacking the antibodies which make up about 60% of all Ig produced. This is especially remarkable since it has been clearly demonstrated that IgA antibodies on mucous membranes in the form of secretory IgA, which are also lacking in IgAd, protect against a number of microbes infecting via mucous membranes [2].

Population studies have shown the prevalence of IgAd to vary between 1/300–1/3000, with the most common figure being around 1/600 [3]. Nevertheless we do not know from unselected cases of IgAd how common it is to remain healthy, or to have frequent infections, malabsorption, autoimmune diseases, allergy or gastrointestinal malignancies; all diseases reported to be common in IgAd.

Are there compensatory host defence mechanisms in IgAd?

Numerous studies have searched for compensatory mechanisms in IgAd which could help to explain why some IgAd individuals are healthy. Brandtzaeg et al. have shown that there is an increased number of IgM immunocytes in the mucosae of a proportion of IgAd cases [4]. It was actually noted that frequent respiratory tract infections occurred in those who showed no compensatory increase in IgM in the nasal mucosa, or showed elevated numbers of IgD immunocytes. In contrast, those with an increase in IgM immunocytes did not have frequent infections [5]. These observations agree with the report by Mellander et al. where significantly elevated levels of IgM antibodies to Escherichia coli and poliovirus were found in the nasal secretion and saliva of healthy IgA-deficient compared with normal individuals [6]. However, the increase in IgAd patients with frequent infections was not significant. Norhagen et al. [7] recently reported significantly higher levels of salivary IgG and IgM in IgAd compared with normal individuals,

Progress in immune deficiency III, edited by H. M. Chapel, R. J. Levinsky and A. D. B. Webster, 1991; Royal Society of Medicine Services International Congress and Symposium Series No. 173, published by Royal Society of Medicine Services Limited.

but regardless of clinical status. There was no correlation between HLA antigens and salivary IgM or IgG levels, nor proneness to infection.

The complexity in compensatory Ig production in mucosae has been illustrated by recent studies. Savilahti found in children with IgAd that there was a striking increase in IgM, but not in IgG production in the gut [8]. However, immunizing adults with IgAd perorally with a cholera toxin B subunit-whole cell vaccine gave a predominant IgG response in those with IgAd, according to the results with ELISPOT on intestinal biopsies, which permitted studies of the antigen-specific response in the mucosa ([9], Friman *et al.* in this publication). The healthy controls had mainly IgA but also IgG immunocytes in their response. The IgG immunocytes were significantly more numerous in the IgAd patients with frequent infections than in the healthy IgAd individuals ($p < 0.01$). Only 5/14 symptomatic IgAd patients, 1/9 healthy IgAd individuals and 2/14 controls responded with IgM-producing cells in the gut. In the healthy controls both the expected predominant IgA, and also an IgG response were seen. Similar results were obtained with ELISPOT on blood lymphocytes, although at a lower level. The IgG immunocyte increase in the blood of the symptomatic IgAd patients was not significantly higher than in the healthy IgAd individuals. There was less of an IgM response in the blood than in the gut. The capacity to respond in the gut in IgAd is variable and may occasionally be inadequate; for example, oral vaccination with live poliovirus in IgAd is followed by prolonged excretion of the vaccine virus [10].

Other mucosal surfaces have been studied. Determinations of IgM and IgG antibodies against poliovirus type 1 antigen and a pool of *E. coli* O antigens in the milk and saliva of mothers with IgAd showed a quite variable pattern (Hahn-Zoric *et al.* unpublished observations). Comparing the levels in these mothers' milk and saliva with levels in normal milk using ELISA showed that one mother had massively increased (2–14 times) IgM and IgG antibody levels in her secretions (Table 1). Two others showed a compensatory increase in IgM antibody levels, but not in IgG antibody levels in milk. One of these showed increases in saliva above the normal standard for both IgM and IgG antibodies to poliovirus but not to the *E. coli* antigens. One mother showed no compensatory increases in milk or saliva. These different patterns may help to explain the variable clinical

Table 1 *Compensatory increases of IgM and IgG in milk and saliva from IgA deficient mothers are variable. Increase of antibody titres in ELISA compared with a normal milk standard*

Mother	standard:	Milk IgM milk	Milk IgG milk	Saliva IgM milk	Saliva IgG milk	Serum IgM serum	Serum IgG serum
1.	Anti-polio[a]	7.5	14.4	2.0	2.2	0.6	0.95
	Anti-coli[b]	5.6	11.4	3.8	2.7	0.4	0.4
2.	Anti-polio	6.0	0.05	3.8	9.5	0.9	0.9
	Anti-coli	2.9	0.12	0.7	0.4	0.4	0.3
3.	Anti-polio	1.5	0.17	—	—	0.9	1.0
	Anti-coli	3.3	0.04	—	—	—	—
4.	Anti-polio	0.02	0.02	<0.01	<0.01	<0.01	1.0
	Anti-coli	0	0	0	0.3	0	0

[a] Antibodies to poliovirus type 1
[b] Antibodies to a pool of 10 *E. coli* antigens

expression of infections in IgAd. It was notable that compensatory increases were seen in the secretions, but not in serum (Table 1).

Determination of titres and avidities and serum IgM and IgG antibodies to a bacterial, a viral and a food antigen in Swedish IgAd individuals showed some differences from normal controls (Cardinale *et al.* unpublished results). The IgG antibody titres against *E. coli* O antigens and poliovirus type 1 antigen, but not against β-lactoglobulin, were higher than in the controls ($p<0.01$ and $p<0.03$). The IgG antibody avidities did not differ, but the IgM antibody avidities were significantly higher ($p<0.007$ and $p<0.001$) using the bacterial and viral, but not the food antigen. These observations may be taken to indicate an increased immune response to microbial antigens in IgAd; this may be a consequence of less protection of mucosal membranes, or of dysregulation of antibody production. Whilst increased mucosal exposure could be considered for the *E. coli*, it is unlikely to explain the high titres to the poliovirus, since wild or vaccine strains are not found in Sweden. Poliovirus antibodies originate from previous vaccination and the higher titre and lower avidity may be a sign of primary dysregulation.

Brazilian IgAd children and adolescents with frequent infections and a heavy microbial exposure had significantly higher levels of serum IgM and IgG antibodies to the *E. coli* and poliovirus antigens ($p<0.05$ and $p<0.005$), but, as in the Swedish IgAd individuals, not to food protein (Beres Castrignano *et al.* unpublished results). Their salivary IgM antibodies to the two microbial antigens were also increased compared with the reference group ($p<0.05$ and $p<0.002$). Total IgG and IgM or secretory IgM in saliva were not increased in this IgAd group.

In another study we noticed that many IgAd patients had striking increases of goblet cells in the nasal mucosa [11]. It is not known whether this is a compensatory mechanism helping to protect the IgAd mucosa, or is secondary to frequent mucosal infections due to the lack of IgA. An interesting illustration of the capacity to compensate the lack of mucosal defence normally provided by secretory IgA is the fact that IgAd is no less common in a country like Brazil (1/965) where the large poor population is heavily exposed to microbes [15].

Dysregulation of vaccine responses in IgA deficiency

Another set of findings based on vaccinations of IgAd individuals may also contribute to our understanding of the variability of the clinical presentation in IgAd. Thus it was noted that vaccination of 17 IgAd individuals with the meningococcus A and C capsular polysaccharides gave a clearly deficient response in IgAd compared with controls [12]. However, a few IgAd patients responded with titres well above the controls. In another study we noticed that IgAd was accompanied by higher responsiveness of IgG3 antibodies to polysaccharide no. 14 in a pneumococcus vaccine compared with controls [13]. The pre- and postvaccination levels of IgG1 and IgG3 antibodies against polysaccharide no. 1 were also increased compared to the controls.

Such an aberrant regulation of various isotypes in IgAd may also relate to the over-representation of allergy, autoimmune phenomena and autoimmune diseases in this condition. The fact that IgAd may occur together with various IgG subclass deficiencies may be another example of dysregulation of isotypes other than IgA in IgAd. What used to be called selective IgAd does not seem to be so selective after all.

Further abnormalities which may add to the complexity of IgAd include the deficient production of interferon (IFN)-α by some IgAd individuals [14]. By contrast a good response of IFN-γ-producing cells in gut biopsies was seen in IgAd individuals after an oral booster with the cholera toxin B subunit—whole cell cholera vaccine, which was equal to that in healthy controls (Czerkinsky *et al.* unpublished data).

IgG SUBCLASS DEFICIENCY

Low levels of one or other of the IgG subclasses can be linked to increased problems with infections, especially in the respiratory tract [16]. At the same time, however, many instances of healthy individuals with IgG subclass deficiency have been described [16]. We have even seen three individuals with isolated IgG2 deficiency but without overt infectious problems in a slum area of São Paulo, Brazil (Beres Castrignano *et al.* unpublished observations).

Normal levels and ranges of IgG 1–4 at different ages have not really been settled [16–18], and we do not know the level below which an IgG subclass deficiency is of clinical relevance [17]. Varying normal ranges are given by different laboratories and methodological problems add to the fact that it is not always easy to compare data between laboratories. Although the use of monoclonal antibodies for IgG subclass quantification has given useful results, these antibodies must still be used with caution [16].

Differences in the selection of patients also add to the difficulties in comparing results of many studies. Further problems stem from the fact that IgG subclass levels can vary with time; levels in an individual may normalize or develop into more severe antibody deficiency [16]. Temporary influences such as surgical operations may decrease IgG1 and increase IgG2 [19]. Furthermore, there are changes with age so that in childhood IgG2 deficiency is most common and after puberty IgG3 deficiency is more common. In parallel there is a change in sex ratio of IgG subclass deficiency from about three boys per girl in childhood to three females per male among adults [19].

Immunoglobulin prophylaxis of IgG subclass deficiency

One way of determining the clinical relevance of IgG subclass deficiency in patients with frequent infections would be to test the response to immunoglobulin prophylaxis in a blind study. We have recently completed a double-blind cross-over two-year prophylaxis study of 43 adults with IgG subclass deficiency and recurrent respiratory tract infections (Söderström R. *et al.* unpublished results, [20]). Smokers were excluded. The patients were below the lower normal range of IgG1, IgG2 and/or IgG3 according to Oxelius [21] and were each given Ig intramuscularly in a dose of 25 mg/kg/week or saline for a total of one year.

During the study our own material for normal ranges was completed and 12 patients turned out to be above the new lower ranges; the analysis of the data was performed on the material with and without these 12 patients. Ig prophylaxis in the whole group of 43 patients resulted in a significantly decreased number of days with infections ($p < 0.05$). Excluding the 12 patients with higher IgG subclass levels the protection was also significant ($p < 0.035$).

In the small group of 10 IgG1 deficient patients a significant reduction in the number of days with infections was also noted ($p < 0.04$). The groups of patients deficient in IgG2 or IgG3 were too small to be evaluated separately. However, 11 of the excluded 12 patients had IgG3 levels below the lower range of Oxelius (0.41 g/l), but above the presently used value of 0.14 g/l. Adding these 11 to the five with IgG3 below the latter range, the whole group of 16 patients showed a significant decrease in the numbers of attacks of bronchitis ($p=0.036$) during prophylaxis. This observation illustrates how difficult it is to define a cut-off point below which clinically relevant deficiencies occur [17].

In a continued, but open, prophylactic study of 19 of the 43 IgG subclass deficient patients, a double dose of 50 mg/kg/week was given [20]. Over six months the number of days with infection was reduced by 6.2 days/month, which is highly significant, suggesting that this higher dose is better.

COMBINED IgA AND IgG SUBCLASS DEFICIENCY

Since the initial description of this combined deficiency [22] a number of patients have been studied [16,23]. In some studies it has been claimed that the combined deficiency increases the problems with infections, even the risk of developing lung function impairment [24]. In other studies no evidence is found of such a risk; some individuals with the combined deficiency are even healthy [16]. Recently we have seen three such individuals with combined IgA and IgG subclass deficiency who had no obvious infectious problems even though they lived in the slums of São Paulo, under heavy microbial exposure (Beres Castrignano *et al.* unpublished data).

These differences illustrate the problems alluded to, e.g. differences in selection of the patients, methodological variability, and differences in standards used.

In a series of 25 consecutive patients with combined deficiency attending our clinic for allergic and infectious problems, severe clinical manifestations were seen [17]. All but one had frequent infections, mainly in the respiratory tract. Thus lung function impairment was found in 12, five had bronchiectasies, three had undergone surgery for chronic sinusitis and four had diarrhoea.

Clearly we need epidemiological studies based on defined diagnostic criteria, standards and methods for IgG subclass quantification. Such studies should be followed by controlled trials of the effects of Ig prophylaxis in those with deficiencies of IgG subclasses ± IgAd and problems with infections. Although we cannot yet define the clinical role of these deficiencies, it seems that some patients improve strikingly when given antibodies prophylactically.

ACKNOWLEDGMENTS

These studies were supported by the Swedish Medical Research Council (Nos 215 and 88), the Swedish Institute, the Ellen, Lennart and Walter Hesselman Foundation and AB Kabi, Stockholm, Sweden.

REFERENCES

(1) Rockey JH, Hanson LÅ, Heremans JF, Kunkel IG, Beta-2 A aglobulinemia in two healthy men. *J Lab Clin Med* 1964; **63**: 205–12.
(2) Hanson LÅ, Brandtzaeg P. The mucosal defense system. In: Stiehm RT, ed. *Immunologic diseases in infants and children*. 3rd ed. Philadelphia: WB Saunders, 1989: 116–55.
(3) Hanson LÅ, Björkander J, Oxelius V-A. Selective IgA deficiency. In: Chandra RK, ed. *Primary and secondary immunodeficiency disorders*. Churchill Livingstone: Edinburgh, 1983: 62–84.
(4) Brandtzaeg P, Fjellanger I, Gjeruldsen ST. Immunoglobulin M: local synthesis and selective secretion in patients with immunoglobulin A deficiency. *Science* 1968; **160**: 789–91.

(5) Brandtzaeg P, Karlsson G, Hansson G, Petrusson B, Björkander J, Hanson LÅ. The clinical condition of IgA-deficient patients is related to the proportion of IgD- and IgM-producing cells in their nasal mucosa. *Clin Exp Immunol* 1988; **67**: 626–36.

(6) Mellander L, Björkander J, Carlsson B, Hanson LÅ. Secretory antibodies in IgA-deficient and immunosuppressed individuals. *J Clin Immunol* 1986; **6**: 284–91.

(7) Norhagen G, Engström P-E, Hammarström L, Söder P-Ö, Smith CIE. Immunoglobulin levels in saliva in individuals with selective IgA deficiency: compensatory IgM secretion and its correlation with HLA and susceptibility to infections. *J Clin Immunol* 1989; **9**: 279–86.

(8) Savilahti E, Pelkonen P, Verkasalo M, Koskimies S. Selective deficiency of immunoglobulin A in children. *Klin Pädiat* 1985; **197**: 336–40.

(9) Czerkinsky C, Quiding M, Nordström I, *et al*. Lymphoid cell population dynamics and the mucosal immune response in humans. In: MacDonald TT, Challacombe SJ, Bland PW, Stokes CR, Heatly RV, Mowat AM, eds. *Advances in mucosal immunology* London: Kluwer Academic Press, 1990: 326–31.

(10) Savilahti E, Klemola T, Carlsson B, Mellander L, Stenvik M, Hovi T. Inadequacy of mucosal IgM antibodies in selective IgA deficiency: Excretion of attenuated polioviruses is prolonged. *J Clin Immunol* 1988; **8**: 89–94.

(11) Karlsson G. Hansson H-A, Petrusson B, Björkander J, Hanson LÅ. Goblet cell number in the nasal mucosa relates to cell-mediated immunity in patients with antibody deficiency syndromes. *Int Arch Allergy Appl Immunol* 1985; **78**: 86–91.

(12) Hanson LÅ, Brandtzaeg P, Björkander J, *et al*. IgA deficiency with and without mucosal infections. In: McGhee JR, Mestecky J, Ogra PL, Bienenstock J, eds. *Recent advances in mucosal immunology. Part B. Effector functions*. New York: Plenum Press, 1987: 1449–53.

(13) Roberton D, Björkander, J. Henrichsen J, Söderström T, Hanson LÅ. Enhanced IgG1 and IgG3 responses to pneumococcal polysaccharides in isolated IgA deficiency. *Clin Exp Immunol* 1989; **75**: 201–5.

(14) Strannegård Ö, Björkander J, Hellstrand K, Pacsa A, Hermodsson S, Hanson LÅ. Interferon and β2-microglobulin in patients with common variable immunodeficiency or selective IgA deficiency. *Int Arch Allergy Appl Immunol* 1987; **84**: 217–22.

(15) Carneiro-Sampaio MMS, Barros Carbonara S, Beti Rozentraub R. Torres de Aranjo MN, Alves Ribeiro M, de Oliveira Porto MH. Frequency of selective IgA deficiency among Brazilian blood donors and healthy pregnant women. *Allergol Immunopathol* 1989; **4**: 213–6.

(16) Preud'homme J-L, Hanson LÅ. IgG subclass deficiency. *Immunodef Rev* 1990; **2**: 129–49.

(17) Hanson LÅ, Söderström R, Nilssen DE, *et al*. IgG subclass deficiency with or without IgA deficiency. In: Cunningham-Rundles C, Mayer L, eds. *Immunodeficiency diseases* 1990: in press.

(18) Beard LJ, Ferrante A, Hagedorn JF, Leppard P, Kiroff G. Percentile ranges for IgG subclass concentrations in healthy Australian children. *Pediatr Inf Dis J* 1990; **9**: S9–15.

(19) Söderström T, Söderström R, Andersson R, Lindberg J, Hanson LÅ. Factors influencing IgG subclass levels in serum and mucosal secretions *Monogr Allergy* 1988; **23**: 236–43.

(20) Söderström T, Söderström R, Hanson LÅ. Immunoglobulin subclasses and prophylactic use of immunoglobulins in IgG subclass deficiency. *15th Int Cancer Congress, Hamburg*, Aug. 1990; abstract.

(21) Oxelius V-A. IgG subclass levels in infancy and childhood. *Acta Paediatr Scand* 1979; **68**: 23–9.

(22) Oxelius V-A, Laurell A-B, Lindqvist B, *et al*. IgG subclasses in selective IgA deficiency: importance of IgG2-IgA deficiency. *N Engl J Med* 1981; **304**: 1476–7.

(23) Roberton D, Colgan T, Ferrante A, Jones C, Mermelstein N, Sennhauser F. IgG subclass concentrations in absolute, partial and transient IgA deficiency in childhood. *Pediatr Inf Dis J* 1990; **9**: S41–5.

(24) Björkander J, Bake B, Oxelius V-A, Hanson LÅ. Impaired lung function in patients with IgA deficiency and low levels of IgG2 or IgG3. *N Engl J Med* 1985; **313**: 720–4.

Intestinal and blood antibody-secreting cells in normal and in IgA deficient individuals after oral cholera vaccination

V. Friman[1], M. Quiding[2], C. Czerkinsky[2], I. Nordström[2], L. Larsson[2], D. Ericson[3], J. Björkander[3], A. Kilander[4], J. Holmgren[2] and L.Å. Hanson[5]

Departments of [1]Infectious Diseases, [5]Clinical Immunology, [2]Medical Microbiology and Immunology, [3]Internal Medicine II, [4]Asthma and Allergy Research Centre, University of Göteborg, Sweden

INTRODUCTION

Individuals with IgA deficiency (IgAd) may suffer from frequent upper or even lower respiratory tract infections. However, many IgA-deficient individuals cannot be distinguished from the normal healthy population. The reasons for this difference are not understood [1].

The present study was aimed at disclosing possible differences between frequently infected and healthy IgAd individuals with respect to their antibody responses and production of interferon-γ (INF-γ) in peripheral blood and intestinal mucosa after enteric immunization with cholera vaccine.

SUBJECTS

Fourteen IgA-deficient patients with frequent upper and/or lower respiratory tract infections (12 females and two males, mean age 38.9 years, range 23–65) and nine IgA-deficient healthy individuals (all males, mean age 38.5 years, range 26–59) were included in the study. Fourteen healthy individuals with a normal level of IgA (nine females and five males, mean age 36.7 years, range 26–55) served as controls. None of the individuals included in the study had previously been vaccinated against cholera. IgA deficiency was defined as serum IgA less than 0.05 g/l and IgM, IgG and IgG1–4 above the lower limit of the normal range (0.5; 7.0; 4.22; 1.17; 0.41; 0.01 g/l respectively) [2].

Patients having at least four respiratory tract infections per year requiring antibiotic treatment were defined as having frequent infections. All the patients were referred to our hospital because of their infections. The healthy IgA-deficient individuals were found when screening blood donors.

METHODS

Oral cholera vaccine, consisting of the purified B subunit of cholera toxin and killed

Progress in immune deficiency III, edited by H. M. Chapel, R. J. Levinsky and A. D. B. Webster, 1991; Royal Society of Medicine Services International Congress and Symposium Series No. 173, published by Royal Society of Medicine Services Limited.

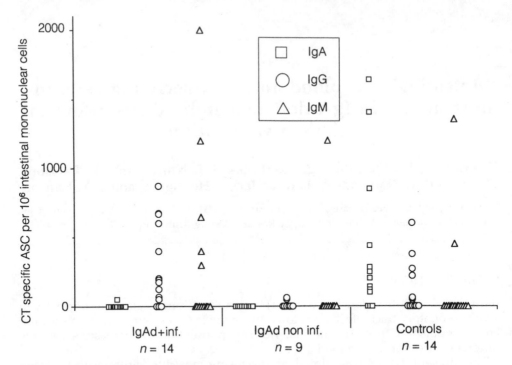

Figure 1   *Cholera toxin (CT) specific antibody-secreting cells (ASC) in the intestinal mucosa seven days after the second oral cholera vaccine dose.*

whole cell vibrios, was used (B+WCV) [3]. All subjects received two oral doses of B+WCV with an interval of 14 days.

Peripheral blood and biopsy specimens from the duodenal mucosa were collected before and seven days after vaccination.

Cholera toxin (CT)-specific antibody-secreting cells (ASC) and cells secreting IFN-γ were detected using micromodified enzyme-linked immunospot (ELISPOT) assays [4].

RESULTS

The IgAd patients had very few or no IgA-secreting cells in biopsy specimens.

The CT-specific ASC response in the intestinal mucosa of the IgAd patients with symptoms was predominantly of the IgG isotype. In contrast, low IgG ASC responses were seen in healthy IgAd individuals ($p < 0.05$) (Fig. 1). A similar pattern was seen in blood, but there the difference in IgG immunocytes between symptomatic and healthy IgAd individuals was not significant (Fig. 2).

The control group responded as expected with predominantly IgA both in blood and mucosa, but also with IgG production.

CT-specific IgM responses in blood were rarely noted. A higher intestinal IgM response was noted when comparing IgAd patients with symptoms and normal subjects or healthy IgAd individuals (not significant).

The frequency of IFN-γ-producing cells was increased after a booster dose of B+WCV, and this increase was confined to the intestinal mucosa. However, the frequency of intestinal IFN-γ-producing cells did not differ between the three groups, at least at the times examined.

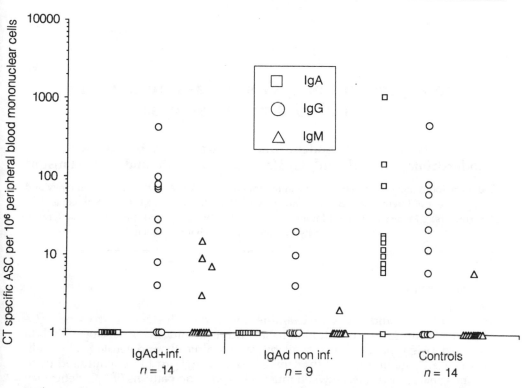

Figure 2   *CT specific ASC responses in peripheral blood seven days after the second oral cholera vaccine dose.*

CONCLUSION

Increased IgG production in the intestinal mucosa, and also in peripheral blood, appears to be a feature of IgA-deficient individuals with frequent infections. It is not clear whether this is a primary phenomenon or secondary to the frequent infections.

REFERENCES

(1) Hanson LÅ, Björkander J, Carlsson B, Roberton D, Söderström T. The heterogeneity of IgA deficiency. *J Clin Immunol* 1988; **8**: 159–62.
(2) Oxelius V-A. IgG subclass levels in infancy and childhood. *Acta Paediatr Scand* 1979; **68**: 23–7.
(3) Holmgren J, Svennerholm A-M, Lönnroth I, Fall-Persson M, Markman B, Lundbäck H. Development of improved cholera vaccin based on subunit toxoid. *Nature* 1977; **269**: 602–4.
(4) Czerkinsky C, Moldoveanu Z, Mestecky J, Nilsson L-Å, Ouchterlony Ö. A novel two colour ELISPOT assay. *J Immunol Methods* 1988; **115**: 31–7.

The expression of IgG subclass deficiencies in nasal and rectal mucosa

D. E. Nilssen[1,2], R. Söderström[3], K. Kett[1,2], P. Brandtzaeg[1], T. Söderström[4], G. Karlsson[5], G. Hansson[6], S. Fasth[7] and L. Å. Hanson[4]

[1]Laboratory for Immunohistochemistry and Immunopathology (LIIPAT), Institute of Pathology and [2]Department of Internal Medicine A, University of Oslo, Rikshospitalet, Oslo, Norway and [3]Departments of Medicine, [4]Clinical Immunology, [5]ENT, [6]Pathology, and [7]Surgery II, Sahlgren's Hospital, University of Göteborg, Göteborg, Sweden

INTRODUCTION

The aim of this study was to examine by immunohistochemistry the IgG-immunocyte subclass distribution in nasal and rectal mucosa of serologically IgG subclass-deficient patients. The availability of a clinically and serologically well-characterized patient group at the University of Göteborg [1] encouraged us to study possible associations between mucosal expression patterns of IgG-deficiency and different clinical manifestations in groups of patients with various serological IgG subclass deficiencies. A preliminary study had suggested that the nasal expression of IgG subclass deficiency does not necessarily conform with that in serum [2].

MATERIAL AND METHODS

Biopsy specimens of nasal and rectal mucosa were obtained in 18 adult patients; only a nasal *or* a rectal sample was available from a further nine similar subjects. Chronic lung disease was common in the patient groups with selective serum IgG1 deficiency (both patients) or combined IgG1 and IgG3 deficiency (four of six patients), whereas only two of four in the group with selective IgG2 deficiency suffered from this serious disease. The other categories of patients had mostly upper airway and other mild infections; thus only one of 10 with selective serum IgG3 deficiency suffered from chronic lung disease.

Paired immunofluorescence staining was performed on serial tissue sections by applying subclass-specific murine monoclonal antibodies followed by fluorescein-labelled conjugate to murine IgG and rhodamine-labelled conjugate to human IgG; the proportion of immunocytes belonging to each subclass could thereby be determined in relation to the total number of mucosal IgG-producing cells [2]. This method showed an excellent intra- and inter-observer reproducibility.

Progress in immune deficiency III, edited by H. M. Chapel, R. J. Levinsky and A. D. B. Webster, 1991; *Royal Society of Medicine Services International Congress and Symposium Series No. 173, published by Royal Society of Medicine Services Limited.*

RESULTS

Serum IgG2 or IgG3 deficiency was usually expressed also at the cellular level in rectal mucosa, and the proportion of rectal IgG1 cells was significantly correlated ($r = 0.90$, $p < 0.001$) with the IgG1 subclass level. Similarly, there tended to be a decreased isotype expression at the cellular level in the nasal mucosa of patients with serum IgG1 or IgG2 subclass deficiency. Conversely, the median nasal proportion of IgG3 cells was remarkably unaffected by a deficiency of this subclass in serum and rectal mucosa. Interestingly, these patients rather seemed to have raised IgG3 and reduced IgG2 cell proportions in nasal mucosa; this apparent local IgG3 compensation was nevertheless strongly correlated with the serum IgG3 subclass level ($r = 0.87$, $p < 0.002$).

DISCUSSION

The observed discrepancies between the expression of IgG3 subclass deficiency at the two mucosal sites might reflect different antigenic and mitogenic loads, for example a persistent protein bombardment (virus) of the nasal mucosa that could locally override a B cell maturation defect. Such stimulatory differences might explain the disparity between the rectal and nasal mucosa.

A fairly intact humoral defence afforded by IgG3 compensation in the upper respiratory tract of patients with selective serum IgG3 subclass deficiency might explain the relatively low incidence (10%) of chronic lung disease in this group. Clinicopathological evaluation of the patient material showed that the group with single or combined serum IgG1 deficiency suffered most from chronic lung disease. Absence of IgG1 is usually associated with hypogammaglobulinaemia, since IgG1 makes up the largest proportion (60–70%) of total IgG. Consequently, these patients often have a history of lung disease and increased susceptibility to pyogenic infections [3].

Genetic factors may additionally influence the IgG subclass response. Immunoglobulin deficiencies may occur as a result of defects in heavy chain genes or in the regulation of heavy chain gene switching on chromosome 14 where the genes for $\gamma 3$ and $\gamma 1$ and those for $\gamma 2$ and $\gamma 4$ are closely linked [4]. In several clinical situations the IgG isotypes appear to be regulated or expressed in patterns reflecting this gene arrangement.

Further studies of the mucosal IgG subclass distribution in relation to clinico-pathological features may contribute to a better understanding of the distinctive pathogenetic mechanisms interacting in these immunodeficient patients.

REFERENCES

(1) Söderström R, Söderström T, Lindholm B, Hanson LÅ. Effect of immunoglobulin prophylaxis in infection-prone adults with low IgG subclass levels, a double blind crossover study. In preparation.
(2) Brandtzaeg P, Kett K, Rognum TO, et al. Distribution of mucosal IgA and IgG subclass-producing immunocytes and alterations in various disorders. Monogr Allergy 1986; 20: 179–94.
(3) Schur PH, Borel H, Gelfand EW, Alper CA, Rosen FS. Selective gamma-G globulin deficiencies in patients with recurrent pyogenic infections. N Engl J Med 1970; 283: 631–4.
(4) Flanagan JG, Rabbits TH. Arrangement of human immunoglobulin heavy-chain constant region genes implies evolutionary duplication of a segment containing γ, ϵ and α genes. Nature 1982; 300: 709–13.

IgG subclass concentrations in absolute, partial and transient IgA deficiency in childhood

D. M. Roberton[1,2], T. Colgan[2], A. Ferrante[1], C. Jones[2], N. Mermelstein[2] and F. Sennhauser[2]

[1]Departments of Paediatrics and Immunology, Adelaide Children's Hospital, Adelaide, Australia and [2]Royal Children's Hospital, Melbourne, Australia

(POSTER)

IgA deficiency (IgAd) in early childhood often resolves spontaneously [1]. IgA deficiency is also frequently associated with IgG subclass deficiencies. This study was performed to determine the outcome of IgAd presenting in early childhood and the association of transient IgAd and IgG subclass abnormalities.

PATIENTS

Samples were collected on two occasions each from children referred during the 10 year period 1977–1987 for investigation of recurrent infections. The median interval for sample collection was 3.0 years (range 0.6–10.7 years). Symptomatic IgAd was defined as recurring infections in the presence of an IgA concentration below the fifth centile for 12 months of age (0.185 g/l) when total IgG and IgM concentrations were above the fifth centile for age [2]. No children were receiving anticonvulsants or had autoimmune disease. Children presenting under the age of one year were excluded.

METHODS

Immunoglobulin concentrations were measured by nephelometry or enzyme immunoassay (EIA) [3]. IgG subclass concentrations were measured by EIA, and were expressed as age-related centile values using values derived by the study of Beard et al. [4]. Absolute IgAd (aIgAd) was defined as a serum IgA concentration below 0.005 g/l; partial IgAd (pIgAd) was defined as a serum IgA concentration between 0.005 g/l and 0.185 g/l.

RESULTS

Sixty-seven children were enrolled (39 males; 28 females). All children had normal lymphocyte and phagocytic cell function using tests described previously [5]. At presentation, 18 had aIgAd and 49 had pIgAd. At the time of second testing (median 3.2 years later for aIgAd; 3.0 years for pIgAd), IgA concentrations had risen to be within the normal range for 22.2% presenting with aIgAd and 77.6% presenting with pIgAd.

Sufficient sample collected at presentation was available to measure IgG subclass concentrations in 34 children (aIgAd 12; pIgAd 22). IgG2 and IgG4 concentrations in these 34 children were below the fifth centile for age more frequently than expected (IgG2, $p < 0.025$; IgG4, $p < 0.0005$), with these deficiencies tending to be present more frequently in pIgAd than aIgAd. IgG1 and IgG2 concentrations at presentation were greater than the ninety-fifth centile in 50% and 42% respectively of children with aIgAd (IgG1, $p < 0.0005$;

Progress in immune deficiency III, edited by H. M. Chapel, R. J. Levinsky and A. D. B. Webster, 1991; Royal Society of Medicine Services International Congress and Symposium Series No. 173, published by Royal Society of Medicine Services Limited.

IgG2, $p < 0.001$), but this was not seen in pIgAd. Thirty-eight children with pIgAd had IgG subclass measurements performed on samples collected at the time of second testing. Those with persisting IgAd ($n = 7$) and those with resolved pIgAd ($n = 31$) continued to have IgG2 concentrations below the fifth centile more frequently than expected ($p < 0.005$ and $p < 0.05$ respectively).

CONCLUSIONS

In children with IgAd, there is frequently an associated defect of IgG2 and IgG4 production as described by others previously. Normal IgA concentrations are achieved in the majority of young children presenting with pIgAd when followed longitudinally. New findings from this study are that IgG2 deficiency is still more frequent than expected in resolved partial IgA deficiency, when re-studied at a median interval of 3.0 years after presentation, and that IgG1 and IgG2 concentrations are above the ninety-fifth centile for age more frequently than expected at presentation in absolute IgA deficiency but not in partial IgA deficiency.

ACKNOWLEDGMENTS

This study was supported by grants from the Royal Children's Hospital Research Foundation, the Swiss National Research Foundation and the Swiss Academy of Medical Sciences.

REFERENCES

(1) Plebani A, Ugazio AG, Monafo, V, Burgio GR. Clinical heterogeneity and reversibility of selective immunoglobulin A deficiency in 80 children. *Lancet* 1986; i: 829–31.
(2) Shelton MJ, Meek F, Goller I, Hosking CS. Serum immunoglobulin levels in children. *Aust J Med Technol* 1974; 5: 113–17.
(3) Roberton DM, Forrest PJ, Frangoulis E, Jones CL, Mermelstein N. Early induction of secretory immunity in infancy: specific antibody in neonatal breast milk. *Arch Dis Child* 1986; 61: 489–94.
(4) Beard LJ, Ferrante A, Hagedorn JF, Leppard P, Kiroff G. Percentile ranges for IgG subclass concentration in healthy Australian children. *Pediatr Inf Dis J* 1990; 9: S9–15.
(5) Hosking CS, Fitzgerald MG, Shelton MJ. The immunological investigation of children with recurrent infections. *Aust Paediatr J* 1977; 13 (suppl): 1–107.

Frequency of autoantibodies in children with IgA deficiency

V. Monafo, C. Furci, M. A. Avanzini, A. Plebani,
M. Massa and A. Ascione

Department of Pediatrics, University of Pavia, Policlinico S. Matteo, Pavia, Italy

(ABSTRACT)

The incidence of three organ-specific and six non-organ specific autoantibodies (AA) was assessed in 100 children from seven months to 18 years old with severe (serum IgA < 5 mg/dl) or partial (IgA > 5 mg/dl < −2 SD of age-normal mean) IgA deficiencies (IgAd). Anti-double stranded DNA ab (dsDNA) were assessed by a *Crithidia luciliae* assay and all other AA by indirect immunofluorescence. The frequency of positive results was compared to that in healthy children determined previously in our laboratory [1]. Twenty-nine of the 33 positive responses were of low titre; four patients (one JRA, three non-autoimmune disease) were positive for two AA. The only organ-specific positivity was for anti-parietal cell ab and was significantly higher in patients with severe IgAd (30%) than in partial IgAd (12%) or in controls (5%, $p < 0.01$). Among the non-organ-specific AA, dsDNA ab were always negative, while the most frequently positive were anti-nuclear ab (ANA), significantly higher in IgAd patients (severe 17%, partial 12%) than in controls (3%, $p < 0.05$). Next most frequent was positivity for anti-smooth muscle ab, present in 2.5% of controls, 6% of severe and no partial IgAd patients (ns). Incidence of the other non-organ-specific AA tested was lower with no significant differences between the three groups.

REFERENCE

(1) Martini A, Lorini R, Zanaboni D, Ravelli A, Burgio RG. Frequency of autoantibodies in normal children. *Am J Dis Child* 1989; **143**: 493–6.

Progress in immune deficiency III, edited by H. M. Chapel, R. J. Levinsky and A. D. B. Webster, 1991; Royal Society of Medicine Services International Congress and Symposium Series No. 173, published by Royal Society of Medicine Services Limited.

New aspects in inherited complement deficiencies

P. J. Lachmann

Molecular Immunopathology Unit, MRC Centre, Cambridge, UK

Since C2 deficiency in man was first discovered [1], genetic deficiencies of virtually all the components have been discovered in man. Of the serum components only factor B deficiency has not been described in homozygous form although two heterozygotes are known. Table 1 gives an overview of the deficiencies of complement components that have been described. The incidence of individual deficiencies is very different in different ethnic populations. C2 deficiency is found almost exclusively in Caucasians where it is seen almost invariably in the context of a single HLA haplotype. This haplotype is reasonably common and presumably has or had some survival advantage (although this may not have necessarily been for the C2 deficiency gene). Even more strikingly, C9 deficiency in the Japanese is extremely common, a point discussed further in a later section.

THE RELATIONSHIP OF COMPLEMENT DEFICIENCY TO ANTIBODY DEFICIENCY

It has been known for many years that animals that are depleted or deficient in complement activity make reduced antibody responses to low concentrations of antigen, especially when given without adjuvants. The best explanation for this difficulty was advanced by Klaus and Humphrey [2] who demonstrated that the localization of antigen on the follicular dendritic cells in the germinal follicles of lymph nodes requires the presence of both antibody and complement (as far as C3). The localization of antigen at this site is necessary for the development of efficient B cell memory. This phenomenon is not obviously replicated in humans with complement deficiency who have generally been found to have normal overall levels of immunoglobulin and normal levels of antibodies to the organisms with which they are infected. It has, however, recently been shown that patients with deficiencies of C1, C4, C2 and particularly C3, do have significantly reduced levels of IgG4. This is unlikely to be an adaptation to complement deficiency since IgG4 is the non-complement fixing IgG sub-class. It probably reflects the fact that IgG4 is at the 3' end of the IgG genes and is the last to be formed during the generation of an immune response. To this extent patients with these early classical pathway deficiencies and C3 deficiencies do seem to have some difficulty in generating IgG memory.

Progress in immune deficiency III, edited by H. M. Chapel, R. J. Levinsky and A. D. B. Webster, 1991; Royal Society of Medicine Services International Congress and Symposium Series No. 173, published by Royal Society of Medicine Services Limited.

Table 1 *Complement Deficiencies*

Complement component	Total patients	Pedigrees (if reported)	Clinical associations	Comments
C1q	11	7	Skin and renal lesions— SLE or SLE-like syndrome; Infections	Total deficiency
C1q	7	3	Skin and renal lesions— SLE or SLE-like syndrome; Infections	Dysfunctional protein
C1r/C1s	10	6	Skin and renal lesions— SLE or SLE-like syndrome; Infections	
C4	17	11	SLE +/− infections. Two normal	
C2	>77		SLE; other i/c disease; some infections; about 30% healthy	Caucasians only; ?incidence 1/10,000 of population
C3	18		Pyogenic infections; glomerulo-nephritis	
Factor I	12	0	Pyogenic infections; neisserial infection; i/c disease; healthy	
Factor H	5	2	Haemolytic uraemic syndrome; SLE; healthy	
Properdin	25	16	Infections, particularly Neisserial	
Factor D	1	1	Neisserial infection (NB patient is thin)	Factor D = adipsin
C5	18	10	Neisserial + some other infections; SLE (rare); can be healthy	
C6	56	12	Neisserial infections predominate; often healthy	
C7	28	11	Neisserial infections predominate; often healthy	
C6 + C7	2	2	Candidiasis; healthy	
C8 α-γ	6		Predominantly Neisserial infection; occasional SLE; some healthy	Gene found so far only in US blacks
C8β	25		Predominantly Neisserial infection; occasional SLE; some healthy	
C9	Many		Predominantly healthy; occasional Neisserial infection but rare in Caucasians; affects c 1/1000 Japanese	
DAF	rare		INAB phenotype of Cromer blood group; healthy	
C1-ina	Many		Hereditary angioedema; 5% have immune complex disease. NB patients are heterozygotes	

C1 INHIBITOR DEFICIENCY AND HEREDITARY ANGIOEDEMA (HAE)

HAE is a dominantly inherited disease that is due to deficiency of C1 inhibitor. It is unusual for enzyme deficiencies to give rise to disease in heterozygotes and this gave rise to ideas that C1 inhibitor deficiency might be due to some transacting mutation affecting C1 inhibitor synthesis on both chromosomes. It is, however, now clearly known that this is not the case and these patients are true hetero-zygotes for abnormalities in the structural gene. The mean level of C1 inhibitor is less than 50% due to the increased rate of catabolism of C1 inhibitor when complexed with one of the enzymes with which it reacts. For this reason there is an element in its catabolism which depends on the rate of enzyme activation *in vivo* rather than on the inhibitor concentration. This catabolic compartment is increased in conditions where enzyme activation is enhanced as indeed occurs in HAE. It has been shown by suitable turn-over studies that the synthetic rate in the patients is indeed approximately half of the normal rate and that the excess catabolism accounts for the fact that their plasma concentration is on average only 20% of the normal level. The mutations giving rise to HAE result in the failure to form a protein (Type 1) in approximately 85% of pedigrees and in about 15%, in the formation of a dysfunctional protein (Type 2). A variety of different mutations account for Type 1 HAE. It has been shown by Stoppa-Lyonnet *et al.* [3] that there are frequent Alu repeats within the introns of the C1 inhibitor gene which predispose to the elimination of a particular exon (Exon 4) by unequal crossing over. The nature of the abnormality in Type 2 HAE has been investigated by protein chemical techniques especially for those (approximately half) mutants that occur at the binding site or 'bait residue' of the inhibitor. Aulak and Harrison [4] have developed an ingenious technique where the inhibitor is immobilized on an affinity column and then cleaved, either at the normal bait residue arginine with trypsin; or, if this arginine is absent, by Pseudomonas elastase which cleaves a few amino acids at the N-terminal. The peptide so produced is then sequenced and the abnormal bait residue determined. It is found that there are frequent mutations from the bait residue arginine, histidine or cysteine. This reflects the existence of a CpG codon at this site. One serine mutant has so far been identified at this site but not the other four possible mutants resulting from single base changes. The occurrence of cysteine mutants is of interest since it explains those pedigrees of HAE that apparently have greatly increased amounts of C1 inhibitor. It is now recognized that this is an artefact due to the detection of the covalent complex between cysteine-containing C1 inhibitor mutants and mercaptalbumin.

COMPLEMENT DEFICIENCY AND SYSTEMIC LUPUS ERYTHEMATOSUS (SLE)

One of the unexpected clinical associations of complement deficiency was the high incidence of SLE and related autoimmune immune complex diseases seen in homozygous deficiencies of C1, C4 and C2. Heterozygous deficiency, particularly of C4, shows a similar association, more than half of patients with lupus having a C4AQO allele. This is true both for Caucasian populations where most of C4AQO occurs on a HLA background with A1, B8 and DR3 but also in oriental populations where this haplotype does not occur. This association is due to a functional deficiency of complement and reflects an inability to handle immune complexes properly. A schema is shown in Fig. 1 and has been discussed at length elsewhere [5]. Its essential features are that in the absence of an adequate supply

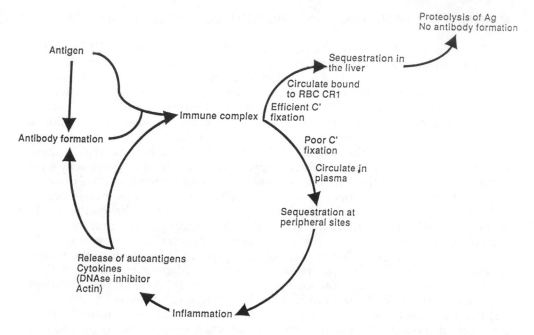

Figure 1   *Fate of immune complexes following complement activation*

of complement, immune complexes fail to get cleared adequately in the liver and are sequestered at other sites where they can give rise to inflammation. On the basis of this type of explanation, the low levels of CR1 that are found on the red cells of patients with this disease are explained by the proteolysis of CR1 in the reticulo-endothelial system at the time that immune complexes are transferred to macrophages and proteolyzed. A polyclonal antibody has been raised to the peptide that is left on the outside of the erythrocyte after the complement receptor has been cleaved off. This antibody recognizes a neoantigen on trypsin-treated erythrocytes which has been shown to correspond to the number of CR1 molecules per red cell. Using this antibody it has been possible to demonstrate that in patients with cold haemolytic antibody disease—who have the lowest CR1 numbers and the highest degree of complement activation on their cells—an appreciable portion of their CR1 occurs *in vivo* in the cleaved form. A sample of patients with SLE also have a statistically higher mean percentage of cleaved CR1 on their red cells, which supports the explanation given above.

DEFICIENCY OF THE TERMINAL COMPLEMENT COMPONENTS AND NEISSERIAL INFECTIONS

The major clinical association of deficiency of the late complement components is infection with Neisseria, predominantly meningococcal meningitis. While such deficiencies are relatively uncommon in Caucasian populations they are strikingly more common in other parts of the world. It has already been mentioned that C9 deficiency is extremely common among Japanese [6]. C9 deficiency seems to have a relatively minor effect, both on the haemolytic titre and on the incidence of Neisserial infection and it seems that *in vivo* increased concentrations of the other terminal components, notably C8, can substantially compensate for C9 deficiency. However the persistence of C9 in other populations would suggest that there is some penalty we pay for not having C9 and it may be that the high incidence of C9 deficiency in Japan does have some balancing advantage. What this may be is quite unknown, though speculatively it may be pointed out that the Japanese have a much lower incidence of multiple sclerosis than would be expected from their geographical latitude and there is a suggestion that complement is involved in the pathogenesis of this disease!

There is a substantial study of C6 deficiency among the coloured population in Cape Town [7] and of patients with more than one attack of meningococcal meningitis, the majority are C6 deficient. It is particularly interesting that in the families of these patients there is an unexpected excess of homozygous C6-deficient subjects, suggesting that there must be a powerful selective pressure in favour of C6 deficiency. The nature of the selective advantage of C6 deficiency in this population may be guessed at from their high incidence of infantile gastroenteritis and death from endotoxin shock. It is known from the studies on C6 deficient rabbits [8] that C6 deficiency provides substantial, though incomplete, protection against endotoxin shock, and although species vary in the extent to which complement is involved in endotoxin shock, it is likely that in man some protection will be afforded by C6 deficiency. This may then be the balance against the disadvantage produced by the increased incidence of meningococcal infection.

A rather similar high incidence of terminal component deficiency among patients with meningococcal meningitis has been described in Israel [9] where the deficiency most commonly found is that of C7 rather than C6. Among their population of patients with just one attack of meningitis, approximately 10% were complement deficient. The patients deficient in C7, C8 and properdin were all Moroccan Jews and the only complement-deficient Ashkenazi Jew had a C2 deficiency.

REFERENCES

(1) Silverstein AM. Essential hypercomplementemia. Report of a case. *Blood* 1960; **16**: 1338–41.
(2) Klaus GGB, Humphrey JH. The generation of memory cells. 1. The role of C3 in the generation of B memory cells. *Immunology* 1977; **33**: 31–40.
(3) Stoppa-Lyonnet D, Carter PE, Meo T, Tosi M. Clusters of intragenic Alu repeats predispose the human C1 inhibitor locus to deleterious rearrangements. *Proc Natl Acad Sci USA* 1990; **87**: 1551–5.
(4) Aulak KS, Harrison RA. Rapid and sensitive technique for identification and analysis of reactive centre P1 residue mutant C1-inhibitor proteins contained in type II HAE plasmas. *Biochem J* 1990; **271**: 565–9.
(5) Lachmann PJ. In: Ishizaka K, Lachmann PJ, Lerner R, Waksman BH, eds. *1939–1989: Fifty years progress in allergy. A tribute to Paul Kallos.* Chemical Immunology **49**. Basel: Karger, 1990.
(6) Inai S, Kitamura H, Hiramatsu S, Nagaki K. Deficiency of the ninth component of complement in man. *J Clin Lab Immunol* 1979; **2**: 85–7.
(7) Orren A, Potter PC, Cooper RC, du Toit E. Deficiency of the sixth component of complement and susceptibility to *Niesseria meningitidus* infections: studies in ten families and five isolated cases. *Immunology* 1987; **62**: 249–53.
(8) Brown DL, Lachmann PJ. The behaviour of complement and platelets in lethal endotoxin shock in rabbits. *Int Arch Allergy* 1973; **45**: 193–205.
(9) Schlesinger M, Nave Z, Levy Y, Slater PE, Fishelson Z. Prevalence of hereditary properdin, C7 and C8 deficiencies in patients with meningococcal infections. *Clin Exp Immunol* 1990; **81**: 423–7.

Complement deficiencies and meningococcal infections

M. Schlesinger, Y. Levy[1] and Z. Fishelson[2]

Barzilai Medical Center, Ashkelon, [1]Soroka Medical Centre, Beer Sheva and
[2]The Weizmann Institute of Science, Rehovot, Israel

INTRODUCTION

The association of meningococcal infections with congenital deficiency of one of the late complement (C) components C5-C8 is well documented [1]. A high incidence (10%) of C7 or C8 deficiency was recently reported in Israeli patients who survived meningococcal disease [2]. Similarly, meningococcal infections have been described in individuals with properdin deficiency [3,4]. However, the overall incidence of properdin deficiency in such patients has not been determined yet and only few families with absence or dysfunction of properdin have been so far detected. To evaluate the association between meningococcal disease and hereditary deficiency of complement components further, we analysed the activity and concentration of components of both the alternative and classical pathways of complement in patients who had one or more episodes of meningococcal infection.

PATIENTS AND METHODS

This study included 101 patients who recovered from meningococcal infections at the age of two months to 60 years. They were all examined for haemolytic activities of both the classical pathway (CH50) and the alternative pathway (AP50). Patients with low CH50 and AP50 in repeated examinations were also tested for the concentration of several C components by radial immunodiffusion in agarose (RID). Serum samples taken from family members (siblings, parents and children) of the C-deficient propositi were also tested. Each sample was tested together with a sample of the pooled normal serum. CH50, AP50, RID and Western blotting were performed by standard methods.

RESULTS AND COMMENTS

Eleven of the 101 patients enrolled in the study were found to be complement-deficient; five were deficient in C7, three in C8, two in properdin and one in C2.

Progress in immune deficiency III, edited by H. M. Chapel, R. J. Levinsky and A. D. B. Webster, 1991; Royal Society of Medicine Services International Congress and Symposium Series No. 173, published by Royal Society of Medicine Services Limited.

Ten additional C-deficient patients (eight in C7, one in C8 and one in properdin) were found among close relatives. Analysis by Western blotting revealed a selective deficiency of the C8 β subunit and reduced α, τ subunit in these patients. The C7/C8-deficient patients originated from Morocco (6/8) or from Yemen (2/8) and the properdin-deficient patients from Tunisia (2/2). They were not related and came from different parts of their original countries. The only C deficiency found among the 22 Ashkenazi Jews examined was a C2 deficiency.

The average age ($\pm$ SE) at infection of the 11 C-deficient patients was 14.2$\pm$2.9 (median: 13.5) years and that of the C-sufficient patients was 6.4$\pm$0.9 (median: 4) years. This further supports previous indications that meningococcal disease occurs in C-deficient patients at a later age than in C-sufficient patients. Similar results in the Israeli population were found by Zimran et al. However, they have not found properdin-deficient patients. Our results suggest that properdin deficiency occurs more frequently than suspected. C7 and C8 deficiencies appear to be associated in Moroccan and Yemenite Jews with susceptibility to meningococcal infection. These, as well as previous findings, indicate that certain populations or ethnic groups have characteristic complement deficiencies which can serve in them as risk factors for meningococcal disease.

REFERENCES

(1) Ross SC, Densen P. Congenital deficiency states and infections. Epidemiology, pathogenesis and consequences of Neisserial and other infections in an immune deficiency. *Medicine* 1984; **63**: 243–73.
(2) Zimran A, Rudensky B, Kramer MR, et al. Hereditary complement deficiency in survivors of meningococcal disease: high prevalence of C7/C8 deficiency in Sephardic (Moroccan) Jews. *Quart J Med* 1987; **240**: 349–58.
(3) Fijen CAP, Kuijper EJ, Hannema AJ, Sjoholm AG, van Putten JPM. Complement deficiencies in patient over ten years old with meningococcal disease due to uncommon serogroups. *Lancet* 1989; **ii**: 585–8.
(4) Editorial. Properdin deficiency. *Lancet* 1988; **i**: 95–6.

Does low C1q level always differentiate acquired from hereditary angioedema?

M. Abinun and M. Mikuška

Department of Clinical Immunology and Allergy, Mother and Child Health Institute,
Belgrade, Yugoslavia

(POSTER)

In hereditary angioedema (HAE) caused by inherited deficiency of C1 inhibitor (C1INH), uncontrolled activation of the classical complement pathway is found, leaving C1q levels normal. By contrast, in acquired angioedema, C1INH deficiency results from increased consumption of C1INH caused by increased activation of C1q due to underlying autoimmune and/or lymphoproliferative disorders, leading to decreased C1q levels. A low C1q level is therefore postulated to be a differential finding between these two forms of C1INH deficiency [1].

We report two patients with associated lupus disease and HAE, one with normal and one with low C1q levels. No 1. Systemic lupus erythematosus (SLE) was diagnosed at age 13 (polyarthralgias, fever, 'butterfly' rash, photosensitivity, leucopenia, C4 low, C3 normal, positive rheumatoid factor, no antinuclear antibodies (ANA)). Raynaud's phenomenon, alopecia, and oral ulcers occurred at age 20, with a negative lupus band test (LBT) and no signs of renal disease. Type 1 HAE (spontaneous mutation) was diagnosed at age 23 (life threatening laryngeal angioedema after dental surgery). It was noted that she had had recurrent attacks of abdominal pain since age 3 and episodic angioedema of extremities and face since age 16. C4 = 0 (0.2–0.5 g/l), C1INH = 0.06 g/l (0.19–0.58 g/l), no C1INH function, C3 and C1q normal. Follow-up revealed a low C1q 0.03 g/l (0.1–0.25 g/l) over two years, with the current C1q level being 0.084 g/l. She has a healthy son with normal complement levels. No 2. Type 2 HAE was diagnosed at age 16 (life threatening angioedema of upper airway; attacks of abdominal pain in early childhood; episodic angioedema of extremities and face since age 13). C4 = 0.028 g/l, C1INH = 0.94 g/l, C1INH function = 3 U/ml (18–28 U/ml), C1q and C3 normal. Father died aged 35 years, suggestive of HAE. Lupus-like disease diagnosed at age 19 ('butterfly' rash, Raynaud's phenomenon, photosensitivity, transient Coombs' positivity, ANA and LBT negative, no renal disease). C1q always normal. There are two children; one has type 2 HAE but no clinical disease at present.

SLE and lupus disease occur in 0.6–2% of patients with HAE, possibly associated with failure of solubilization of immune complexes [2,3]. At least two of these 16 reported patients, as well as our patient No 1, showed markedly reduced C1q levels. These findings demonstrate that C1q level cannot be taken as the only criterion to differentiate acquired from hereditary C1INH deficiency.

REFERENCES

(1) Davis III AE. Hereditary and acquired deficiencies of C1 inhibitor. *Immunodef Rev* 1989; **1**: 207–26.
(2) Agnello V. Lupus disease associated with hereditary and acquired deficiencies of complement. *Springer Semin Immunopathol* 1986; **9**: 161–78.
(3) Brickman CM, Tsokos GC, Chused TM, *et al*. Immunoregulatory disorders associated with hereditary angioedema. *J Allergy Clin Immunol* 1986; **77**: 749–57; 758–67.

Progress in immune deficiency III, edited by H. M. Chapel, R. J. Levinsky and A. D. B. Webster, 1991; Royal Society of Medicine Services International Congress and Symposium Series No. 173, published by Royal Society of Medicine Services Limited.

Shared genetic associations in different forms of humoral immunodeficiency

L. Hammarström[1], O. Olerup[1], J. Björkander[2] and C. I. E. Smith[1]

[1]Department of Clinical Immunology and Centre for Biotechnology, Huddinge Hospital, Huddinge, and [2]Department of Allergology, Sahlgrenska Hospital, Gothenburg, Sweden

INTRODUCTION

IgA deficiency is among the most common forms of humoral deficiency observed, with an estimated prevalence of one in 600 healthy individuals. Most cases of IgA deficiency appear to occur sporadically but familial clustering has been described in a number of cases, suggesting a genetic component in the susceptibility to the disorder.

Both drug-induced IgA deficiency and the sporadic form of IgA deficiency are often associated with particular major histocompatibility complex (MHC) genes, the former exhibiting an A2 association whereas the latter is thought to be associated primarily with HLA-B8 and HLA-DR3 [1]. Recently, a primary association with Class III genes was suggested [2,3]. However, it is likely that these observations are due to linkage disequilibrium. Isolated IgA deficiency has recently been shown to be strongly associated with alleles of the HLA-DQB1 locus [4] where, in analogy with findings in juvenile onset diabetes mellitus [5], the amino acid at position 57 of the DQβ chain is associated with susceptibility and resistance to IgA deficiency. Thus, the presence of aspartic acid (Asp) in this position is associated with resistance whereas the presence of other amino acids (non-Asp) is found more frequently than expected among IgA-deficient individuals.

IgG2 subclass deficiency is thought to be a distinct form of humoral immunodeficiency often, but not always, associated with susceptibility to bacterial infections. The defect is frequently found in combination with deficiency of IgA. It is still not clear whether there is a common genetic background shared between these two disorders or whether they reflect different facets of the same underlying basic defect.

Common variable immunodeficiency is again yet another form of deficiency where serum levels of all classes and subclasses of immunoglobulin may be affected. Although rare families have been described where relatives of the proband have suffered from either IgA deficiency or common variable immunodeficiency [6], a common genetic marker, linking the two disorders, has not been described to date in these instances.

Progress in immune deficiency III, edited by H. M. Chapel, R. J. Levinsky and A. D. B. Webster, 1991; Royal Society of Medicine Services International Congress and Symposium Series No. 173, published by Royal Society of Medicine Services Limited.

The purpose of the work described in this paper was to extend our previous findings of a strong DQB1 association in IgA deficiency and to investigate whether this association could also be demonstrated in IgG2 subclass-deficient individuals and in families where multiple cases of IgA deficiency and common variable immunodeficiency could be observed.

MATERIALS AND METHODS

Patients

DNA was extracted from heparinized blood from patients diagnosed as having IgA deficiency, IgA-IgG2 deficiency or common variable immunodeficiency according to established criteria.

Tissue typing

HLA-A, -B and -C typing was performed by conventional serological technique. HLA-DR and -DQ typing was performed by Taql RFLP analysis. For references on methodology and probes used see ref. 4.

RESULTS

HLA types of individuals with combined IgA-IgG2 deficiency

Typing of individuals with a combined IgA-IgG2 deficiency revealed the presence of DR3, DQw2 in six of the nine tested individuals (67%), compared to a frequency of 17.2% in 250 normal controls ($p < 0.001$) (Table 1). Non-Asp homozygosity in position 57 of the DQβ chain was seen in four of the tested patients (patients, 1, 2, 3 and 5); patient 5 displayed a DQw6 variant that does not carry Asp in position 57 [5]. This frequency is higher than the frequency found in a recently tested control material in our laboratory (33%) [4]. An additional four patients were heterozygous for this marker (DQw2,w5 or w8) as compared to 45% in the control material [4]. One patient was Asp homozygous and the frequency of Asp homozygosity is thus less than the frequency found in controls (22%).

HLA sharing in familial clustering of humoral immunodeficiencies

Three families where multiple cases of IgA deficiency and common variable immunodeficiency occurred were investigated for the pattern of HLA sharing

Table 1   *HLA typing of IgA,IgG2-deficient individuals*

No.	IgA (g/l)	IgG2 (g/l)	HLA-A	HLA-B	HLA-C	HLA-DR	HLA-DQ
1	<0.01	<0.2				3,3	w2,w2
2	<0.01	<0.2	1,11	8	—	3,3	w2,w2
3	<0.01	<0.2	1,3	8,16	—	3,4	w2,w8
4	<0.01	<0.2				3,7	w2,w9
5	<0.01	<0.2	2	35,40	3,4	w13,w13	w6,w6
6	<0.01	<0.2	2	12,22	1,5	4,7	w7,w9
7	<0.01	0.4	2,3	15,27	3	3,w11	w2,w7
8	<0.01	0.5	28	35	—	1,w14	w5,w7
9	0.08	0.5				3,4	w2,w7

Table 2 *HLA sharing in individuals from families exhibiting both IgA deficiency and common variable immunodeficiency*

Family	Defect	Relation	HLA-A	HLA-B	HLA-C	HLA-DR	HLA-DQ
1	CVI	Mother	1,2	8,18	—	3,4	w2,w8
	CVI	Daughter	1	8	7	3,3	w2,w2
	IgA	Daughter	1,2	8,18	—	3,4	w2,w8
2	CVI	Mother	2,9	8,17	6	3,7	w2,w9
	IgA	Sister	2,9	8,17	6	3,7	w2,w9
	IgA	Daughter	2,10	17,18	6	1,7	w5,w9
	IgA	Niece	2,9	7,8	—	3,4	w2,w8
3	CVI	Mother	2,28	12	5	1,w12	w5,w7
	IgA	Son	2,3	12,35	4	1,w12	w5,w7
	IgA	Daughter	2,3	12,35	4	1,1	w5,w5

(Table 2). In the first family the non-Asp DQB1 allele is present in a homozygous state in all afflicted family members. In the remaining two families, the pattern of inheritance is less clear although at least a heterozygous 'susceptibility' gene is present in all individuals with a humoral deficiency, homozygosity being present in two individuals (DQw2,w8 and w5,w5 respectively).

DISCUSSION

The strong association between the amino acid at position 57 of the DQβ chain and deficiency of IgA is hitherto the strongest genetic susceptibility found for any humoral immunodeficiency [4]. The association with the non-Asp phenotype in individuals with a combined IgA-IgG2 deficiency is almost as strong as in isolated IgA deficiency. This finding may reflect that the two disorders are indeed related. Drug-induced deficiencies on the other hand may not be associated with the tissue type most commonly seen in the 'idiopathic' form of deficiency. This has been noted previously in hydantoin-induced IgA deficiency which is associated with HLA-A2. It still remains to be determined whether patients with drug-induced immunoglobulin deficiency, as induced by drugs such as sulfasalazine [7] or diclofenac [8], shows the same genetic pattern as that observed in the 'idiopathic' form.

Sharing of 'susceptibility' genes was noted in families with multiple cases of IgA deficiency and common variable immunodeficiency. Thus, a greater than expected degree of sharing of the non-Asp carrying haplotype was observed. This may suggest that these two forms of humoral immunodeficiency are also related. This supposition is supported by recent work in our laboratory demonstrating a similar, although less pronounced, association between common variable immunodeficiency and the presence of non-Asp at position 57 of the DQβ chain. Thus, different forms of humoral immunodeficiencies may actually be facets of the same underlying genetic 'defect'. If substantiated further, these findings may necessitate a re-evaluation of the current nomenclature on humoral immunodeficiencies. Furthermore, it raises questions as to the biological relevance of the shared DQB1 sequences. We have previously postulated that humoral immunodeficiencies may be due to infection with a relatively common virus where a 'susceptibility' gene is required for the expression of the disease phenotype [9]. The finding of a common genetic denominator in various forms of humoral immunodeficiency may then suggest that a similar type of infectious agent is involved in all these diseases.

ACKNOWLEDGMENT

This work was supported by the Swedish Medical Research Council.

REFERENCES

(1) Hammarström L, Smith CIE. HLA A,B,C and DR antigens in immunoglobulin A deficiency. *Tissue Antigens* 1983; **21**, 75–9.
(2) Schaffer FM, Palmerson J, Zhu ZB, Barger BO, Cooper MD, Volanakis JE. Individuals with IgA deficiency and common variable immunodeficiency share polymorphisms of major histocompatibility complex class III genes. *Proc Natl Acad Sci USA* 1989; **86**: 8015–19.
(3) French MAH, Dawkins RL. Central MHC genes, IgA deficiency and autoimmune disease. *Immunol Today* 1990; **11**: 271–4.
(4) Olerup O, Smith CIE, Hammarström L. The amino acid at position 57 of the HLA-DQβ chain is associated with susceptibility and resistance to IgA deficiency. *Nature* 1990; **347**: 289–90.
(5) Todd JA, Bell JI, McDevitt HO. HLA-DQβ gene contributes to susceptibility and resistance to insulin-dependent diabetes mellitus. *Nature* 1987; **329**: 599–604.
(6) Asherson GL, Webster ADB. *Diagnosis and treatment of immunodeficiency diseases.* London: Blackwell Scientific Publications, 1980.
(7) Leickly FE, Buckley RH. Development of IgA and IgG2 subclass deficiency after sulfasalazine therapy. *J Pediatr* 1986; **108**: 481–2.
(8) Farr M, Struthers GR, Scott DGI, Bacon PA. Fenclofenac-induced selective IgA deficiency in rheumatoid arthritis. *Br J Rheumatol* 1985; **24**: 367–9.
(9) Hammarström L, Jonsson M, Smith CIE, Smolowicz A, Widner H. Regulation of antibody synthesis in hypogammaglobulinemia. *J Immunol Immunopharmacol* 1990, in press.

MHC Class III gene(s) endow(s) susceptibility to both IgA deficiency and common variable immunodeficiency

J. E. Volanakis[1], Z. B. Zhu[1], F. M. Schaffer[1], J. Palermos[1], B. O. Barger[1], R. D. Campbell[2], H. W. Schroeder, Jr.[1] and M. D. Cooper[3]

[1]Departments of Medicine, Pediatrics, Microbiology, and Pathology, University of·Alabama at Birmingham, the [2] MRC Immunochemistry Unit, University of Oxford, and the [3]Howard Hughes Medical Institute

IgA deficiency (IgAd) and common variable immunodeficiency (CVI) are the most frequent primary immunodeficiencies recognized in individuals of European ancestry [1]. These two immunodeficiencies have been considered to be unrelated entities on the basis of differences in laboratory findings and clinical presentations. However, IgAd and CVI have several features in common. The cellular defect in both syndromes consists of a failure of surface immunoglobulin-positive B cells to undergo differentiation into antibody-secreting plasma cells [2,3]. Although the arrest in B-cell differentiation is more extensive in CVI than in IgAd, considerable overlap between the two exists. Certain CVI individuals are not panhypogammaglobulinaemic but produce substantial amounts of IgM and, conversely, some IgAd individuals are also deficient in IgG_2 and IgG_4 [4]. In addition, IgAd and CVI have been reported to occur in the same family [5]. These considerations led us to suggest that the two immunodeficiencies share a common genetic defect. To test this hypothesis, we originally investigated [6] HLA serotypes and RFLPs of the genes encoding 21 hydroxylase, C4, and C2 in 19 CVI and 11 IgAd individuals. This study showed shared HLA antigens and a high incidence of C4A and 21-hydroxylase A gene deletions as well as the presence of rare C2 gene haplotypes in both immunodeficiencies, findings supporting our hypothesis. The presence of a susceptibility gene for both IgAd and CVI within the MHC complex was also suggested by these data [6,7].

We have extended these studies by defining extended MHC haplotypes of IgAd and CVI individuals and of their immediate relatives. MHC haplotypes were defined by analysing RFLPs for seven Class III genes and serotyping HLA-A, -B, and -DR. The results support the existence of a common recessive gene for IgAd and CVI. They further suggest that the putative gene imparts susceptibility to both immunodeficiencies and is probably located within the Class III region of the MHC gene complex.

Progress in immune deficiency III, edited by H. M. Chapel, R. J. Levinsky and A. D. B. Webster, 1991; Royal Society of Medicine Services International Congress and Symposium Series No. 173, published by Royal Society of Medicine Services Limited.

METHODS

Thirty-two immunodeficient individuals (13 IgAd and 19 CVI) from 22 families and 76 of their first degree relatives were included in the study. All immunodeficient individuals were Caucasian and the clinical, immunological, and serological parameters of all but five of them have been reported previously [6]. Genomic DNA was isolated from EDTA blood as described [6]. Procedures for restriction enzyme digestion and Southern blotting have also been described previously. The *Taq* I, *Hind* III, and *Bam* Hl RFLPs [8,9] were used to evaluate C4 gene deletions and duplications, and C4B gene length. The *Bgl* II RFLP of the G11 gene [10], resulting in 15 or 4.5 kb polymorphic fragments, the *Pst* I RFLP of the HSP 70 gene [11], resulting in 9 or 7.5 kb polymorphic fragments, and the *Nco* I RFLP of the TNFα gene [12], resulting in 9 or 5 kb polymorphic fragments, were analysed by Southern blotting. The *Msp* I RFLP of the factor B gene [13] was analysed by a PCR method. Polymorphic fragments of 0.6 or 0.4 kb were detected by agarose gel electrophoresis. Four RFLPs of the C2 gene were analysed by using *Sst* I, *Bam* Hl, or *Taq* I restricted genomic DNA. The combined results allow for the definition of nine distinct haplotypes of the C2 gene, termed a to i [14]. HLA-A, -B, and -DR typing was carried out by the microdroplet lymphocytotoxicity assay [15].

RESULTS AND DISCUSSION

Seventeen of the 22 families studied had one immunodeficient member each, while the remaining five families had multiple immunodeficient members. Of the five families, one had five immunodeficient members, two had three each, and another two had two each. Characteristically, all five families included both IgAD and CVI members, a finding lending further support to the hypothesis of a common genetic basis for these defects.

The use of polymorphic markers for 10 MHC genes or their products allowed for the definition of extended MHC haplotypes in the study population. The most remarkable finding of our initial analysis of the resulting data was that a relatively small number of MHC haplotypes were shared by all immunodeficient individuals. Three of these haplotypes were encountered most frequently (Table 1).

Not all families had the complete haplotypes conserved, but in all cases five or more contiguous polymorphic markers were present. These three haplotypes accounted for 77% of the MHC haplotypes displayed by the immunodeficient individuals. No differences in the distribution of these haplotypes were noted between IgAd and CVI. Importantly, six immunodeficient individuals (three IgAd and three CVI) were homozygous for one of the three haplotypes (one for haplotype I, two for II, and three for III). An additional 12 individuals displayed two of the three haplotypes, while 13 had one. Our preliminary analysis indicates

Table 1 *Haplotypes encountered in the patient group*

Haplotype	HLA DR	C4B	C4A	G11	Bf	C2	HSP 70	TNF α	HLA B	HLA A
I	3	Sf	0	15	0.4	a	7.5	5	8	1
II	7	S	L	4.5	0.6	b	9	9	44	29
III	4	L	L	15	0.4	a	9	9	40	24

that at least one additional, not as well-defined, haplotype is present in the population. Inclusion of this additional haplotype would increase the number of immunodeficient individuals sharing common haplotypes. These results suggest that a recessive gene(s) within the MHC underlies both immunodeficiencies.

Analysis of the haplotypes of family members demonstrated that some relatives, including siblings, displayed identical MHC haplotypes with IgAD and CVI individuals. Serum IgA concentration in these relatives was more than 50 mg/dl, but tended to be lower than those in family members with different MHC haplotypes. In addition, among 10 healthy unrelated individuals, selected on the sole basis of homozygosity for haplotype I, two were found to be IgAD. These combined results indicate that the presence of the putative gene(s) is a necessary but not sufficient condition for expression of immunodeficiency.

No informative crossovers were observed within the MHC in the study population. However, as mentioned, in some families not all polymorphic markers defining each haplotype were conserved. This finding suggests that crossover events between each of the shared haplotypes and unrelated MHC haplotypes had taken place in the past. If this assumption is correct, inspection of the conserved regions of the three haplotypes indicates that the putative susceptibility gene(s) is located within the Class III region of the MHC, probably between the C4A and the TNFα genes.

REFERENCES

(1) Rosen FS, Cooper MD, Wedgewood RJP. The primary immunodeficiencies. *N Engl J Med* 1984; **311**: 235–42.
(2) Conley ME, Cooper MD. Immature IgA B cells in IgA-deficient patients. *N Engl J Med* 1981; **305**: 495–97.
(3) Cooper MD, Lawton AR, Bockman DE. Agammaglobulinaemia with B lymphocytes. Specific defect of plasma-cell differentiation. *Lancet* 1971; **ii**: 791–94.
(4) Oxelius VA, Laurell AB, Lindquist B, Golebiowska H, Axelsson U, Björkander J, Hanson LÅ. IgG subclasses in selective IgA deficiency: importance of IgG2-IgA deficiency. *N Engl J Med* 1981; **304**: 1476–77.
(5) Wollheim FA, Belfrage S, Coster C, Lindholm M. Primary "acquired" hypogamma-globulinaemia; clinical and genetic aspects of nine cases. *Acta Med Scand* 1964; **176**: 1–16.
(6) Schaffer FM, Palermos J, Zhu ZB, Barger BO, Cooper MD, Volanakis JE. Individuals with IgA deficiency and common variable immunodeficiency share polymorphisms of major histocompatibility complex class III genes. *Proc Natl Acad Sci USA* 1989; **86**: 8015–19.
(7) Schaffer FM, Palermos J, Zhu ZB, Barger BO, Cooper MD, Volanakis JE. Genotypic studies of MHC class III genes in individuals with IgA deficiency and common variable immunodeficiency. *Progr Immunol* 1989; **VII**: 544–46.
(8) Carroll MC, Palsdottir A, Belt KT, Porter RR. Deletion of complement C4 and steroid 21-hydroxylase genes in the HLA class III region. *EMBO J* 1985; **4**: 2547–52.
(9) Yu CY, Campbell RD. Definitive RFLPs to distinguish between the human complement CHA/C4B isotypes and the major Rodgers/Chido determinants: application to the study of C4 null alleles. *Immunogenetics* 1987; **25**: 383–90.
(10) Sargent CA, Dunham I, Campbell RD. Identification of multiple HTF-island associated genes in the human major histocompatibility complex class III region. *EMBO J* 1989; **8**: 2305–12.
(11) Sargent CA, Dunham I, Trowsdale J, Campbell RD. Human major histocompatibility complex contains genes for the major heat shock protein HSP70. *Proc Natl Acad Sci USA* 1989; **86**: 1968–72.

(12) Dawkins RL, Leaver A, Cameron PU, Martin E, Kay PH, Christiansen FT. Some disease-associated ancestral haplotypes carry a polymorphism of TNF. *Hum Immunol* 1989; **26**: 91–7.
(13) Morley BJ, Campbell RD. Internal homologies of the Ba fragment from human complement component Factor B, a class III MHC antigen. *EMBO J* 1984; **3**: 153–7.
(14) Zhu ZB, Volanakis JE. Allelic associations of multiple RFLPs of the gene encoding complement protein C2. *Am J Hum Genet* 1990; **46**: 956–62.
(15) Teresaki PI, Bernoco D, Park MS, Ozturk G, Iwaki Y. Microdroplet testing for HLA-1, -B, -C, and -D antigens. The Phillip Levine Award Lecture. *Am J Clin Pathol* 1978; **69**: 103–20.

Central major histocompatibility complex genes and IgA deficiency

M. A. H. French, D. Townend and R. L. Dawkins

Departments of Clinical Immunology, Royal Perth Hospital, Sir Charles Gairdner Hospital and the University of Western Australia, Perth, Western Australia

BACKGROUND AND INTRODUCTION

IgA deficiency is the most common manifestation of arrested B cell differentiation which results in impairment of immunoglobulin isotype maturation. The underlying immunoregulatory abnormality causing this and the other immunological abnormalities and diseases which are sometimes associated with IgA deficiency, remains poorly understood. It appears that T cell function is normal in most, if not all individuals, but there is increasing evidence that the products of major histocompatibility complex (MHC) genes are of major importance.

During the last thirteen years many studies have demonstrated an association between IgA deficiency and particular HLA antigens (Table 1). Certain HLA antigen associations have been repeatedly demonstrated and these data, and data from family studies indicate that particular combinations of MHC alleles, rather than individual alleles, are implicated. Such combinations of alleles are considered to reflect ancestral haplotypes (AHs) which represent conserved segments of DNA with a specific genomic arrangement; these include deletions, duplications and insertions [1,2]. Approximately 30 AHs have been identified in caucasoid populations (Table 2). It has also been demonstrated that recombinations occur between AHs and that these recombinant AHs are particularly valuable in 'mapping' disease susceptibility regions of the MHC.

A small number of AHs have been associated with IgA deficiency (Table 3). There may also be others. The prevalence of these AHs can be different in different racial groups and also amongst individuals of the same racial group from different geographical regions. This could explain different HLA associations with IgA deficiency in different populations and the rarity of IgA deficiency in some racial groups (Table 4), for example those from parts of Asia [7,8]. Furthermore, the absence of IgA deficiency in the majority of individuals with these AHs indicates that the products of genes outside the MHC are also involved in the production of the immunoregulatory defect which leads to impaired immunoglobulin isotype maturation.

Analysis of MHC AH associations with IgA deficiency are continuing in an attempt to demonstrate the important susceptibility region of the MHC and the gene products of that region which contribute to the regulatory defect of B cell

Progress in immune deficiency III, edited by H. M. Chapel, R. J. Levinsky and A. D. B. Webster, 1991; Royal Society of Medicine Services International Congress and Symposium Series No. 173, published by Royal Society of Medicine Services Limited.

Table 1 *HLA antigen associations with IgA deficiency*

Study	A					B					DR			Disease
	1	2	11	19	28	8	13	14	17	40	1	3	7	
Ambrus *et al.* (1977)	+					+								Autoimmune disease
Van Thiel *et al.* (1977)		+				+						+		IDDM
Seignalet *et al.* (1978)			+	+					+					Infections
Cleland & Bell (1978)	+							+						SLE
Fontana *et al.* (1978)		+												Epilepsy
Oen *et al.* (1982)	+					+			+					
Hammarstrom & Smith (1983)	+				+	+						+		
Cobain *et al.* (1983)	+				+	+		+						
Jersild (1983)						+								
Heikkila *et al.* (1984)	+					+								
Hammarstrom *et al.* (1984)										+				Infections
Strothman *et al.* (1986)	+							+						
Klemola *et al.* (1988)	+					+	+					+	+	
Cuccia-Belvedere *et al.* (1989)						+		+			+			

Table 2 *The more frequent AHs found in Australian caucasoids*

B	Bf	C4A	C4B	DR	AH
8	S	0	1	3	8.1
7	S	3	1	2	7.1
44	S	3	0	4	44.1
57	S	6	1	7	57.1
44	F	3	1	7	44.2
13	S	3	1	7	13.1
62	S	3	3	4	62.1
65	S	2	1+2	1	65.1
18	F1	3	0	3	18.2
60	S	0	2	6	60.3
60	S	3	1	4	60.1
55	S	4	5	6	55.1
18	S	4	2	2	18.1
35	S	3	0	1	35.3
35	S	3	1	5	35.1
18	S	3	1	5	18.3
35	F	3+2	0	1	35.2
14	S	3	1	7	14.2
14	F	3	1	6	14.3
60	S	3	0	8	60.2
62	S	4	2	4	62.2

After Cameron *et al.* [3]

Table 3 *MHC ancestral haplotypes (AHs) associated with IgA deficiency*

HLA-B	TNF[a]	Bf	C2	C4A	C4B	HLA-DR	AH
8	S	S	C	Q0	1	3	8.1
65(14)	L	S	C	2	1+2	1	65.1
57(17)	L	S	C	6	1	7	57.1
44(12)	L	F	C[b]	3	1	7	44.2

[a] NCo1 RFLP polymorphism
[b] This AH probably contains a rare RFLP allelic form of C2
Data from Wilton *et al.* (1985), Cuccia-Belvedere *et al.* (1989) and Schaffer *et al.* (1989).

differentiation underlying IgA deficiency. Genotyping of IgA-deficient individuals by family studies has been particularly informative.

METHODS

Sixty-five IgA-deficient blood donors and hospital patients were allotyped for HLA antigens by conventional lymphocyte microcytotoxicity assays and for C4 and Bf by gel electrophoresis. C4 null alleles were assigned if there was complete absence of C4A or C4B (homozygous deficiency) or if there were two alleles at the C4A or C4B locus and the ratio of C4A to C4B by densitometry was less than 0.6 or greater than 1.4 (heterozygous deficiency). An ancestral haplotype was assigned if a complotype was present with the appropriate HLA-B and DR alleles. A recombinant AH was assigned if the complotype was present with the appropriate HLA-B *or* DR alleles.

Genotyping was performed from family studies in 37 IgA-deficient individuals, including 18 individuals from seven multicase (two or more) families.

RESULTS

All of 18 IgA-deficient individuals from seven multicase families had a C4A null allele or duplicated C4B allele (Table 5). In most cases this was due to the presence

Table 4 *Prevalence of IgA deficiency and HLA-B8 and B14 in different populations*

	Prevalence (%)		
	IgA deficiency	HLA-B8	HLA-B14
Caucasian			
a) Northern European			
i) Helsinki	0.25	17.5	0
b) Western European			
i) Bristol	0.19	25.1	6.9
ii) Paris	0.05	17.3	9.0
c) Southern European			
i) Milan/Turin	⩾0.18	12.5	6.4
ii) Rome	⩾0.2	7.5	7.9
d) West Australian	0.15	30.3	3.9
Japanese	0.004	0.2	0.2
Chinese	0	0	0
Malays	0	0	0

HLA-B8 and B14 (65) are characteristic of the 8.1 and 65.1 AH

Table 5 *MHC haplotypes in IgA deficient individuals from multicase families*

Family		Haplotype 1					Haplotype 2				
		B	Bf	C4A	C4B	DR	B	Bf	C4A	C4B	DR
AND	I1a	8	S	Q0	1	3	51	F	3	1	9
	II1	8	S	Q0	1	3	35	S	3	1	5
	II2	8	S	Q0	1	3	22	S	3	Q0	8
	II3	8	S	Q0	1	3	22	S	3	Q0	8
ADL	I1	8	S	Q0	1	3	40	S	3	1	4
	II2	8	S	Q0	1	3	14	S	2	1+2	3
	II3	14	S	2	1+2	3	40	S	3	1	4
HOG	I1	8	S	Q0	1	3	5	S	3	1	7
	II1	8	S	Q0	1	3	13	S	3	1	7
	II2	8	S	Q0	1	3	13	S	3	1	7
SMI	I1a	8	S	Q0	1	3	51	F	3	1	9
	II1	8	S	Q0	1	3	7	S	3	1	2
COO	I1	60	S	Q0	2	6	17	S	6	1	6
	II2	60	S	Q0	2	6	44	S	3	1	7
MIT	I1	14	S	2	1+2	1	37	F	1	1	1
	II1	14	S	2	1+2	1	44	S	Q0	1	3
FIS	II1	14	S	2	1+2	1	14	S	Q0	1	7
	II2	14	S	Q0	1	7	44	F	3	1	7

Table 6 *MHC haplotypes in individuals with 'sporadic' IgA deficiency genotyped from family studies*

	Haplotype 1					Haplotype 2				
	HLA-B	Bf	C4A	C4B	HLA-DR	HLA-B	Bf	C4A	C4B	HLA-DR
A0448371	8	S	Q0	1	3	14	S	2	1+2	1
B2055054	8	S	Q0	1	3	44	F	3	1	7
G0444186	8	S	Q0	1	3	44	F	3	Q0	4
E4202345	8	S	Q0	1	3	17	S	6	1	7
G5242914	8	S	Q0	1	3	8	S	6	1	7
A0347094	14	F	Q0	1	3	22	S	4	5	6
L0589060	35	S	Q0	1	5	49	S	Q0	5	4
K0450184	51	S	Q0	1	5	14	F	3	1	6
F3140131	7	F	Q0	1	7	7	S	3	1	2
G4154827	40	S	Q0	2	6	14	F	3	1	6
C0304669	14	S	2	1+2	1	35	F	3+2	1	1
D0254994	14	S	2	1+2	1	41	F	6	1	4
H0450237	14	S	2	1+2	5	17	S	6	1	7
H0276019	14	S	2	1+2	5	44	S	3	1	5
B0457546	44	F	3	Q0	1	35 or 53	F	2	Q0	4
H0533199	62(15)	S	3	3	4	7	S	3	1	2
C4057088	15	S	3	1	8	38	S	2	1	6
C0450012	7	S	3	1	2	7	S	3	1	2
E4070939	7	S	3	1	2	7	S	3	1	2

of the 8.1 and/or 65.1 AH, but in one family (Coo) the C4 null allele was part of the 60.3 AH and in another (Fis) it was part of a recombinant AH including B14.

In other families, the IgA deficiency was 'sporadic' (Table 6). Genotyping of IgA-deficient individuals from these families again demonstrated the common occurrence of C4 null alleles and duplicated C4B alleles. In almost 60% of cases these were part of the full 8.1 or 65.1 AH. Of the remainder, one individual (G4154827) had a C4 null allele as part of the 60.3 AH but the others had recombinants of 8.1 or 65.1 with other haplotypes. 'Gene mapping' of these recombinant AHs (see Table 6) clearly indicates that the HLA-B and HLA-DR alleles are not as constant as the C4 alleles, and by inference that the region containing the C4 genes is a more important disease susceptibility region. One third of individuals in this group also had a complete or recombinant 57.1 or 44.2 AH but, with one exception, this was always associated with a complete or recombinant 8.1 or 65.1 AH. The exceptional case (B0457546) had the interesting combination of a recombinant 44.2 AH and homozygous C4B deficiency. Only three individuals within this group did not have all or part of an AH which has been associated with IgA deficiency. Of these, one had an AH containing HLA-B15 and the other two were homozygous for the 7.1 AH.

Genotyping from family studies has not yet been performed in 28 individuals, but from the phenotype data it has been demonstrated that 46% have C4 null alleles compared with 31% of non-IgA-deficient controls. Furthermore, a C4A null allele has been excluded in only four individuals of whom three have the 65.1 or 57.1 AH.

SUMMARY AND CONCLUSIONS

It is now clear that the well-documented association of IgA deficiency with particular HLA antigens reflects an association with a small number of MHC supratypes [4–6] which we consider to be ancestral haplotypes. We have suggested that the genomic arrangement in the central region (between HLA-B and DR) of the AHs associated with IgA deficiency results in the production of gene products which are necessary for the development of the immunoregulatory defect underlying IgA deficiency and many of the diseases associated with it [9]. The data presented here provide additional evidence that the central MHC region is the region of the MHC conferring susceptibility to IgA deficiency and, furthermore, that the products of complement genes are at least some of the relevant gene products.

Genotyping of IgA-deficient individuals by family studies has demonstrated the common occurrence of C4A null alleles and/or duplicated C4B alleles, particularly in multicase families, where this was a finding in all individuals. These complotypes were often part of a complete 8.1, 60.3 or 65.1 AH but in some individuals they were part of a recombinant haplotype which did not include the expected HLA-B and/or HLA-DR alleles.

The other AHs which have less commonly been associated with IgA deficiency also contain aberrant MHC complement genes. The C4A6 gene present in the 57.1 AH has a unique RFLP on Southern blot analysis and the C4 product of that gene has a low haemolytic activity [4,10]. Similarly, the 44.2 AH appears to contain an uncommon RFLP allelic form of C2 [6].

Not all of the IgA-deficient individuals genotyped from family studies had all or part of an AH which has been associated with IgA deficiency. However, it was of interest that of the three individuals without one of these AHs, two were homozygous for the 7.1 AH, suggesting the presence of a relevant allele on this AH which is recessive. This AH may contain allelic forms of other central MHC genes relevant to the immunoregulatory defect in IgA deficiency.

Thus, we propose that particular genomic arrangements in the central MHC region of AHs associated with IgA deficiency, or recombinants of them, give rise to one or more gene products, including complement, which act alone or in combination, and with the products of non-MHC genes to produce an immunoregulatory defect which results in impaired immunoglobulin isotype maturation, particularly of IgA.

Publication No. 9042 of the Departments of Clinical Immunology, Royal Perth Hospital, Sir Charles Gairdner Hospital and the University of Western Australia, Perth, Western Australia.

REFERENCES

(1) Dawkins RL, Christiansen FT, Kay PH, *et al*. Disease associations with complotypes, supratypes and haplotypes. *Immunol Rev* 1983; **70**: 5.
(2) Zhang WJ, Degli-Esposti MA, Cobain TJ, Cameron PU, Christiansen FT, Dawkins RL. Differences in gene copy number carried by different MHC ancestral haplotypes: quantitation after physical separation of haplotypes by pulsed field gel electrophoresis. *J Exp Med* 1990; **171** (in press).
(3) Cameron PU, Mallal SA, French MAH, Dawkins RL. MHC genes influence the outcome of HIV infection: ancestral haplotypes with C4 null alleles explain diverse HLA associations. *Hum Immunol* 1990 (in press).
(4) Wilton AN, Cobain TJ, Dawkins RL. Family studies of IgA deficiency. *Immunogenetics* 1985; **21**: 333.
(5) Cuccia-Belvedere M, Monafo V, Martinetti M, Plebani A, dePaoli F, Burgio GR. Recurrent extended HLA haplotypes in children with selective IgA deficiency. *Tissue Antigens* 1989; **34**: 127.
(6) Schaffer FM, Palermos J, Zhu ZB, Bargert BO, Cooper MD, Volanakis JE. Individuals with IgA deficiency and common variable immunodeficiency share polymorphism of major histocompatibility complex class III genes. *Proc Natl Acad Sci USA* 1989; **86**: 8015.
(7) Yadav M, Iyngkaran N. Low incidence of selective IgA deficiency in normal Malaysians. *Med J Malaysia* 1979; **34**: 145.
(8) Kanoh T, Uchino H. Selective IgA deficiency in Japan: Frequency among 18,200 hospital patients and 22,522 blood donors. *Acta Haematol Jpn* 1982; **45**: 929.
(9) French MAH, Dawkins RL. Central MHC genes, IgA deficiency and autoimmune disease. *Immunol Today* 1990; **11**: 271.
(10) Kay PH, Dawkins RL, Williamson J, Tokunaga K, Christiansen FT, Charoenwong P. Coexistence of an MHC chromosomal segment marked by HLA B17, BfS, C4A6, B1, DR7 and DQw9 in different ethnic groups. *Hum Immunol* 1988; **23**: 27.

Polymorphic markers in the human major histocompatibility complex in CVI

H. S. Howe[1], A. K. L. So[1], J. Farrant[2] and A. D. B. Webster[2]

[1]Rheumatology Unit, Royal Postgraduate Medical School, London and [2]Immune Deficiency Diseases Research Group, Clinical Research Centre, Harrow, UK

INTRODUCTION

There is an increasing interest in the possibility that common variable immunodeficiency (CVI) is a genetically determined disease. However, the disease is clearly not inherited in classical Mendelian fashion, since families with more than one affected relative are very rare. When this does occur it is usually a pair of first degree relatives who develop CVI. The analysis of genetic data on CVI patients is further complicated by the possibility that there is more than one disease within the CVI syndrome.

The association of selective IgA deficiency (IgAd) with a variety of autoimmune diseases, and the possibility that both conditions might reflect a defect in immune regulation, has prompted an analysis of the MHC region on chromosome 6. An HLA B8 DR3 association with IgAd was observed first [1], and more recently this has been extended using molecular probes to genes in the Class III region. Some workers have suggested that IgAd may be part of the spectrum of CVI, because there are examples of first degree relatives having either CVI or IgAd, and there are some patients who develop IgAd before developing CVI (personal observation—unpublished). Shaffer et al. [2] have recently shown that both IgAd and CVI patients share polymorphisms of certain genes in the MHC Class III region, and came to the conclusion that there may be a single gene within this region that predisposes to both conditions. We have extended their study to further genes in a larger group of Caucasian CVI patients in the United Kingdom.

SUBJECTS AND METHODS

DNA was extracted from 20 ml of heparinized venous blood by standard methods obtained from 40 Caucasian patients with CVI (mean age 37 years, range 17–78) and 100 healthy control subjects. Nearly all the patients had IgG levels at diagnosis below 3.0 g/l and unrecordable serum IgA levels. IgM levels were more variable, with 28 having a level <0.2 g/l.

Progress in immune deficiency III, edited by H. M. Chapel, R. J. Levinsky and A. D. B. Webster, 1991; Royal Society of Medicine Services International Congress and Symposium Series No. 173, published by Royal Society of Medicine Services Limited.

MHC Class II typing

HLA-DR, DQA and DQB typing was performed by RFLP analysis of Southern blots of *Taq* I digested genomic DNA from patients and controls. The DRB probe was a 520bp *Pst* I fragment of a full length cDNA clone of the HLA-DR4DRB1 gene, which encodes the $\beta2$ and transmembrane domains of DRβ. The DQA probe was a full-length cDNA clone of the DQA gene from the same cell line. The DQB probe was a full-length cDNA clone of the DQB gene.

C4 RFLP

This was performed using a 500bp *BamH* I to *Kpn* I genomic fragment probe which spans the 5' end of the C4 gene [3]. DNA samples were digested with *Taq* I.

TNF RFLP

This was analysed using a 2.9 kb *EcoR* 1 genomic fragment which spans the TNFα gene (gift of Dr Duncan Campbell) to hybridize Southern blots digested with *Nco* I.

Southern blotting

7 μg of genomic DNA from each subject was digested with restriction endonuclease in the recommended buffer. Southern transfer was performed using standard techniques on to nylon membranes (Hybond-N, Amersham). Filters were prehybridized in 6×SSC, 0.1% SDS, 10×Denhardt's, 10% dextran sulphate and 50 μg/ml sheared salmon sperm DNA for >2 h at 65°C, then hybridized with the radiolabelled probe (1×10^6 cpm/ml of hybridization buffer) overnight. Filters were washed to high stringency, the final wash being 30 min at 65°C in 0.2×SSC, 0.1% SDS.

Statistical analysis

This was performed using the chi-squared statistic with Yates correction.

RESULTS

HLA-DR3 antigen frequency in the patients was 40% as compared to 30.5% in the controls ($\chi^2=3.54$, $p>0.05$). The frequency of other DR alleles was not statistically different in the two groups.

The frequency of C4A gene deletions was significantly raised in the patients ($\chi^2=4.93$, $p<0.05$) (Table 1). We have shown that HLA DR3 is significantly associated with C4A gene deletion in CVI patients ($\chi^2=21.5$, $p<0.0005$) (Table 2),

Table 1   *Frequency of C4A gene deletions in patients and normal controls*

	No.	C4A deletion +	C4A deletion −
Patients	39	18 (46%)	21 (54%)
Controls	100	25 (25%)	75 (75%)

Table 2 *HLA-DR3 association with C4A gene deletion in CVI patients*

	C4A deletion	
	+	−
DR3+	16	2
DR3−	2	19

Table 3 *Allelic association between HLA-DR3 and TNFα RFLP*

	TNF (10.5kb) Upper	+	−	TNF (5.5kb) Lower	+	−
DR3+		12	6		15	3
DR3−		19	2		9	12

as has been shown previously in IgAd patients [2]; furthermore, DR3 was also associated with a 5.5 Kb TNFα gene fragment ($\chi^2=5.11$, $p<0.025$) (Table 3).

DISCUSSION

We have shown an increased frequency of HLA-DR3 and deletions affecting the C4A gene in CVI patients. The C4A gene deletion is most frequently found as part of an extended haplotype which contains HLA-DR3 and HLA-B8. The increased frequency of HLA-DR3 in our patients suggests that the frequency of this haplotype is increased in CVI, although we have not formally demonstrated this by family studies or typing of HLA Class I antigens. This haplotype extends to the TNFα gene.

Because of strong linkage disequilibrium between the different MHC loci, it is not possible to predict whether the primary association with CVI is with an entire haplotype or a single gene within this region. However, the calculated relative risks of HLA-DR3 and C4A deletion were 1.99 and 2.57 respectively, suggesting a secondary association of CVI with HLA-DR3. HLA-DR3 and C4Q*O commonly occur as an extended haplotype which is present in about 5% of the caucasoid population. Studies of patients from ethnic groups which have a lower frequency of this haplotype may help to define the gene which is primarily associated with CVI. The same haplotype has been implicated by others in the rapid decline of CD4+ T cells in HIV-1 infection [4] and in SLE [5].

Our data add further support to the view that both selective IgA deficiency and CVI have similar pathogenic mechanisms, but throw no new light on what other factors determine the disease phenotype. There are many more genes to be cloned within the Class III region on chromosome 6, and it is possible that deletions or mutations within genes close to the C4A region may have a direct influence on the development of CVI. Our data do not support the suggestion that the disease is closely associated with a specific DQβ amino acid substitution as recently claimed by a Swedish group [6], as we found no difference in frequency of DQβ alleles with or without aspartic acid at position 57 between patients and controls. However, it is equally plausible that the ancestral haplotype HLA B8, C4*QO, DR3 is a determining factor for CVI [7]. This haplotype must have some survival advantage for healthy Caucasian individuals from Northern Europe. One possibility is that the haplotype contains genes which promote inflammation, which may have been an advantage in containing tuberculosis in our ancestors. The common occurrence of multiple granulomas in CVI patients, which are very rare in X-linked agammaglobulinaemia patients, suggests that chronic inflammation involving macrophages may be central to the pathogenesis of CVI [8].

REFERENCES

(1) Hammarström L, Smith CIE. HLA-A, -B, -C and DR antigens in immunoglobulin A deficiency. *Tissue Antigens* 1983; **21**: 75.
(2) Shaffer FM, Palermos J, Zhu ZB, Barger BO, Cooper MD, Volanakis JE. Individuals with IgA deficiency and common variable immunodeficiency share polymorphisms of major histocompatibility complex class III genes. *Proc Natl Acad Sci USA* 1989; **86**: 8015.
(3) Schneider PM, Carroll MC, Alper CA, *et al*. Polymorphism of the human complement C4 and steroid 21-hydroxylase genes. *J Clin Invest* 1986; **78**: 650.
(4) Kaslow RA, Duquesnoy RJ, Van Raden M, *et al*. A1, Cw7, B8, DR3 HLA antigen combination associated with rapid decline of T-helper lymphocytes in HIV-1 infection. *Lancet* 1990; **335**: 927.
(5) Fielder AHL, Walport MJ, Batchelor JR. A family study of the MHC of patients with SLE. Null alleles of C4A and C4B may determine disease susceptibility. *B M J* 1983; **28**: 425.
(6) Olerup O, Smith CIE, Hammarstrom L. Different amino acids at position 57 of the HLA-DQβ chain associated with susceptibility and resistance to IgA deficiency. *Nature* 1990; **347**: 289.
(7) French MAH, Dawkins RL. Central MHC genes, IgA deficiency and autoimmune disease. *Immunol Today* 1990; **11**: 271.
(8) Asherson GL, Webster ADB. *Diagnosis and treatment of immunodeficiency diseases*. Oxford: Blackwell Scientific Publications, 1980.

Demonstration of abnormalities of major histocompatibility complex Class III genes in a family with IgA deficiencies

A. Plebani[1], L. D. Notarangelo[1], O. Parolini[1], M. Duse[1], D. Nelson[2] and A. G. Ugazio[1]

[1]Department of Pediatrics, University of Brescia, Brescia, Italy and [2]National Institutes of Health, Bethesda, USA

(POSTER)

IgA deficiency (IgAd) is the most frequent form of primary immunodeficiency. Although the pattern of inheritance of IgAd is variable, genetic factors clearly influence IgA levels in humans. Association with alleles at loci in the major histocompatibility complex (MHC) on chromosome 6 has been demonstrated. Furthermore a high incidence of specific MHC supratypes containing C4A null alleles was found [1].

Recently it has been observed that one-third of patients with sporadic IgAd are heterozygous for C4A gene deletion usually associated with 21 hydroxylase A gene deletion [2]. We performed a genotypic evaluation of the genes encoding C4A, C4B, and 21

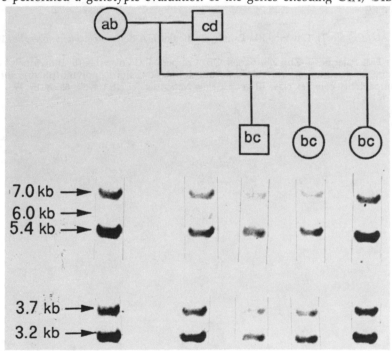

Figure 1 *Pedigree and analysis by Southern blots of the C4 and 21OH genes in the family studied. All the three children were affected by IgA deficiency. The C4 (7.0, 6.0, 5.4 kbp) and 21-OH ase A (3.2 kbp), 21-OH ase B (3.7 kbp) restriction fragment group combinations are shown respectively at the top and the bottom of each line. The haplotypes indicated are: a) 24(9), B18, CW7, DRW11(5), DRW52, DQW7(W3); b) AW33(W19), BW65(14), CW-, DR1, DQW1; c) A23(9), B44(12), CW4, DR7, DRW53, DQW2; d) A31(W19), BW65(14), CW-, DR-, DQW7(W3).*

Progress in immune deficiency III, edited by H. M. Chapel, R. J. Levinsky and A. D. B. Webster, 1991; Royal Society of Medicine Services International Congress and Symposium Series No. 173, published by Royal Society of Medicine Services Limited.

hydroxylase genes (21-OH ase A, 21-OH ase B) in a family with IgAd in three different siblings.

Genomic DNA was digested with Taq I and a 0.8 kbp kpn I/Pst I fragment of the C4A gene (pATA, Dr Campbell) was used to identify the 5′ end of the C4A and C4B genes. It can potentially yield fragments of 7.0, 6.0, 5.4 and/or 6.4 kbp respectively associated with a long C4A gene, a long C4B gene, a short C4B gene and a deletion of C4A gene with fusion to a short C4B gene. A 0.5 kbp Sst I/Pst I genomic probe (pC 21/3c Dr White) was used to identify the steroid 21-OH ase A pseudogene (3.2 kbp) and the 21-OH ase B (3.7 kbp).

Results of the study (Fig. 1) demonstrate that in all family members the C4B and 21-OH ase A bands are of higher intensity as compared to C4A and 21-OH ase B respectively. The absence of a 6.4 kbp Taq. I fragment rules out a deletion of C4A gene and suggests a duplication of C4B and 21-OH ase A genes. In particular, in the father the duplication is likely to involve the chromosome which carries the short C4B gene and is typed as A23(9), B44(12), CW4, DR7, DRW53, DQW2. All siblings have inherited this chromosome from the father. In the mother duplication of C4B short gene is also present.

The demonstration of a familial occurrence of IgAd associated with inheritance of specific duplications of C4B and 21-OH ase A genes strongly suggests an autosomal recessive trait contributed to by a yet unknown gene lying within the MHC gene region.

REFERENCES

(1) Wilton AN, Cobain TJ, Dawkins RL. Family studies of IgA deficiency. *Immunogenetics* 1985; **21**: 333–42.
(2) Schaffer FM, Palermos J, Zhu ZB, Barger OB, Cooper MD, Volanakis JE. Individuals with IgA deficiency and common variable immunodeficiency share polymorphisms of major histocompatibility complex class III genes. *Proc Natl Acad Sci USA* 1989; **86**: 8015–19.

Family analysis of immunoglobulin G2 (IgG2) subclass deficiencies

C. Brémard-Oury[1,2], C. Jouan Flahault[3], P. Aucouturier[4], N. Godfroid[3], N. Feingold[3], J.-L. Preud'Homme[4] and C. Griscelli[2]

[1]CNTS, R&D Protéines Plasmatiques, B.P. 100, 91943 Les Ulis Cedex, [2]INSERM U 132 Paris, [3]INSERM U 155 Paris and [4]CNRS URA 1172 Poitiers, France

One of the main features of IgG2 subclass deficiencies appears to be heterogeneity, which suggests that several mechanisms could be responsible for this deficiency. A previous study [1] of 41 IgG2 deficient patients belonging to 38 families emphasized this heterogeneity and described the family history in seven. However, although some family histories are suggestive of autosomal recessive transmission, coexistence in the same family of various immunodeficiencies, including IgG2 deficiencies, remains difficult to explain. In order to understand the genetic mechanisms involved in the determination of IgG2 levels, and to raise the question of the existence of a major gene, we have performed a complex segregation analysis of the trait for IgG2 levels among families identified through IgG2-deficient probands.

MATERIALS AND METHODS

IgG2 measurement

IgG2 level was measured in patients with recurrent respiratory infections by indirect competitive immunoenzymatic assay previously described [2]. Since a study of 328 controls had previously demonstrated significant effect of age, IgG2 level was adjusted for age. The final estimated IgG2 level (IgG2 c) was calculated according to the following equation:

$$IgG2_c = Log\ IgG2 + 0.53479 - 0.11532 \times age + 0.992921 \times age^2 - 0.00002199 \times age^3$$

All the subjects with IgG2 below 1.28 were defined as IgG2 deficient.

Family study

In IgG2-deficient probands and their relatives (parents, siblings), IgG2 levels were measured and adjusted for age. The possible existence of several probands in the same family led us either to duplicate nuclear families or to designate the proband randomly.

Progress in immune deficiency III, edited by H. M. Chapel, R. J. Levinsky and A. D. B. Webster, 1991; Royal Society of Medicine Services International Congress and Symposium Series No. 173, published by Royal Society of Medicine Services Limited.

Table 1 *Maximum likelihood parameter estimates and chi-square test statistics for segregation analysis of 20 nuclear families using the mixed model*

Model hypothesis	Parameter estimates						Statistics tests			
	d	q	t1	t2	t3	H	Test	Chi square	df[a]	p
1 Sporadic	0	0				0				
2 Polygenic	0	0				0.884	1 vs 2	7.74	1	<0.01
3 No transmission of major effect										
3a Recessive	0	0.33	0.628	0.628	0.628	0				
3b Codominant	0.5	0.05	0.930	0.930	0.930	0				
3c Dominant	1	0.05	0.928	0.928	0.928	0				
4 General transmission of major effect										
4a Recessive	0	0.33	0.34	1	0	0	3a vs 4a	7.1	2	<0.05
4b Codominant	0.5	0.05	1	0.437	0	0	3b vs 4b	4.93	2	NS[b]
4c Dominant	1	0.03	1	1	0	0	3c vs 4c	0.54	2	NS[b]
5 Recessive major gene transmission	0	0.318	1	0.5	0	0.053	2 vs 5	13	1	<0.001
6 Monogenic Mendelian (recessive)	0	0.33	1	0.5	0	0	6 vs 5	13	1	<0.001
							6 vs 4a	0.6	2	NS[b]

[a] df = Degree of freedom
[b] NS = Non-significant

Genetic analysis

Complex segregation analysis was performed under the unified mixed model in nuclear families as formulated and implemented in the computer program POINTER [3]. This model postulates that a phenotype is composed of the independent and additive contributions from a major transmissible effect, a multifactorial background and a residual which is supposed to be unique for every individual. Various parameters are taken into account in the unified mixed model and estimated by maximizing overall likelihood:

d = degree of dominance at the major locus,
q = gene frequency at the major locus,
H = multifactorial heritability in children.

And transmission probabilities are defined:

t_1 = probability that a homozygous AA individual transmits A to an offspring
t_2 = probability that a heterozygous Aa individual transmits A to an offspring
t_3 = probability that a homozygous aa individual transmits A to an offspring.

RESULTS

Results of segregation analysis of data on 20 nuclear families (including 70 individuals) are shown in Table 1. The sporadic model was rejected ($\chi^2 = 7.74$, df = 1, $p < 0.01$) suggesting a genetic transmission of IgG2 level. The hypothesis of absence of transmission of major effect was rejected ($\chi^2=7.1$, df$=2$, $p<0.05$) in the d$=0$ hypothesis, suggesting a recessive transmission. Under the mixed model, the presence of a recessive major gene was highly significant ($\chi^2=44.6$, df$=1$, $p<0.001$). Addition of a residual multifactorial component was necessary under the recessive hypothesis ($\chi^2=13$, df$=1$, $p<0.001$). The Mendelian transmission of the recessive major effect was consistent with the data ($\chi^2=0.6$, df$=2$, NS). These data support a recessive major gene hypothesis with possibly a residual multifactorial background in the aetiology of IgG2 deficiency.

CONCLUSION

This segregation analysis performed on 20 informative nuclear families suggests a recessive major gene contributing to the aetiology of IgG2 subclass deficiency. Furthermore these data support the hypothesis previously propounded [4] that common variable hypogammaglobulinaemia (CVH), IgA deficiency and IgG subclass deficiency could be related disorders, susceptibility to which is determined by common gene(s) in association with environmental mechanisms (virus or others). However, these data have to be verified by another model of segregation: the regressive model.

REFERENCES

(1) Brémard-Oury C, Aucouturier P, Le Deist F, Debre M, Preud'homme JL, Griscelli C. The spectrum of IgG2 deficiencies. In: Vossen J, Griscelli C, eds. *Progress in immunodeficiency research and therapy II*. Amsterdam: Excerpta Medica, 1986: 235–9.
(2) Aucouturier P, Berthier M, Bonneau D, Preud'homme JL. Concentration sérique des sous-classes d'IgG chez l'enfant normal. *Arch Fr Pédiatr* 1988; 45: 225–58.
(3) Lalouel JM, Morton NE. Complex segregation analysis with pointers. *Hum Hered* 1981; 31: 312–21.
(4) Cooper MD, Schaffer FM, Palermos J, Zhu ZB, Barger BO, Volanakis JE. A possible common genetic basis for common variable immunodeficiency and IgA deficiency. *Proceedings of the international symposium on common variable immunodeficiency*. Pisa, 1989.

IgG subclass distribution of the increased IgG immunocyte population in gut mucosa of patients with selective IgA deficiency

D. E. Nilssen[1,2], P. Brandtzaeg[1], K. Kett[1,2], O. Fausa[2] and S. Frøland[2]

[1]Laboratory for Immunohistochemistry and Immunopathology (LIIPAT), Institute of Pathology and [2]Department of Internal Medicine A, University of Oslo, The National Hospital, Rikshospitalet, Oslo, Norway

INTRODUCTION

The aim of this study was to evaluate the 'compensatory' local IgG response in IgA deficiency in order to obtain information about regulatory mechanisms involved in mucosal humoral immunity. The availability of clinically and serologically well-characterized patient material encouraged us to examine by immunohistochemistry the mucosal B cell expression patterns in IgA deficiency. Previous studies from different sites of the gastrointestinal mucosa [1,2] had suggested that when the final B cell differentiation step is blocked, as in IgA deficiency, the precursors develop locally to Ig-producing cells of the IgM and IgG classes.

MATERIAL AND METHODS

Fourteen infection-prone patients with selective serum IgA deficiency (below the lower limit of the 95 percentile range) provided the following biopsy material: gastric ($n=1$); jejunal ($n=10$); colonic ($n=2$); and rectal ($n=3$). Coeliac disease was observed in seven of the patients, mostly children ($n=5$). The jejunal IgG subclass distribution was compared with that in immunologically normal subjects ($n=10$). Gastric mucosa with slight gastritis ($n=8$) and normal large bowel mucosa ($n=10$) were also examined. The subclass distribution of IgG-producing cells was mapped by two-colour immunofluorescence staining performed on serial tissue sections with subclass-specific monoclonal antibodies followed by fluorescein-labelled anti-murine IgG and rhodamine-labelled anti-human IgG. Polyclonal fluorochrome-labelled antibody reagents were used to determine the mucosal IgG-, IgA- and IgM-immunocyte class distribution. For co-staining of cytoplasmic isotype and J chain, adjacent de-waxed tissue sections were alternatively incubated with a mixture of fluorescein-labelled isotype specific conjugate and rhodamine-labelled anti-J chain, either directly or after pretreatment with 6 M urea (pH 3.2–3.5) for 1 h at 4°C as described previously [3].

Progress in immune deficiency III, edited by H. M. Chapel, R. J. Levinsky and A. D. B. Webster, 1991; Royal Society of Medicine Services International Congress and Symposium Series No. 173, published by Royal Society of Medicine Services Limited.

RESULTS

A raised gastrointestinal IgG (34%) and especially IgM (65%) cell number was noted in IgA deficiency as reported previously by our laboratory [1]. The IgG1-immunocyte proportion in the proximal gut (median 88%) was higher than that in the biopsies from comparable controls (gastric 69%, jejunal 65%), significantly so for the jejunal mucosa ($p < 0.001$). The same trend was seen in the limited number of specimens from the distal gut compared with controls from the large bowel mucosa (55%). Conversely, IgG2 and IgG3 cells were significantly decreased ($p < 0.01$ and $p < 0.03$) compared with the comparable controls from the proximal gut. The same was true for IgG4, which also was significantly reduced ($p < 0.01$) in jejunal mucosa (0.3% vs 5.6%).

IgG-producing cells showed 71% J-chain positivity in IgA deficiency, which tended to be reduced ($p < 0.07$) compared with normal small intestinal mucosa (89%) [4]. J chain seemed to be preferentially expressed by the IgG1 cells (82%), but was also found in IgG2 (60%), IgG3 (33%) and IgG4 cells (50%), although their small numbers made the evaluation uncertain. IgM-producing cells showed a median J-chain positivity of 99% in IgA deficiency, virtually the same as in normal jejunal mucosa (100%).

DISCUSSION

This study confirms and extends previous information about the so-called compensatory B cell population in the gastrointestinal mucosa of patients with selective IgA deficiency. In addition to a predominant mucosal IgM response, there was a substantial IgG response preferentially including IgG1 cells. These results suggested that the block in differentiation to IgA is mainly located immediately upstream to the CHα1 gene, giving excessive terminal maturation of IgG1-expressing B cells in the proximal gut. Accordingly, there was no overactivation of the more distally located CHγ2 and CHγ4 genes. This might reflect the fact that vectorial switching is a major regulatory pathway leading to the normally predominant IgA1 immunocyte population seen in the proximal gut.

Since most of the compensatory IgG cells after terminal maturation in the proximal gut mucosa-expressed J-chain, they probably belonged to relatively early memory clones derived from gut-associated lymphoid tissue. These immunocytes may be considered a 'spin off' from clones that through CH gene switching ($5' \rightarrow 3'$) are on their way to polymeric IgA expression [5], which never takes place in patients with selective IgA deficiency. However, J-chain expression tended to be reduced compared with that seen in the small IgG-cell fraction normally present in the intestinal mucosa. The reason for this could be that half of the specimens were from patients with coeliac disease; some of the IgG cells might hence belong to an inflammatory immunocyte population with down-regulated J-chain [4].

REFERENCES

(1) Brandtzaeg P, Gjeruldsen S, Korsrud F, Baklien K, Berdal P, Ek J. The human secretory immune system shows striking heterogeneity with regard to involvement of J-chain positive IgD immunocytes. *J Immunol* 1979; **122**: 503–10.
(2) André C, André F, Fargier M. Distribution of IgA1 and IgA2 plasma cells in various normal human tissues and in the jejunum of plasma IgA-deficient patients. *Clin Exp Immunol* 1978; **33**: 327–31.

(3) Brandtzaeg P. Immunohistochemical characterization of intracellular J-chain and binding site for secretory component (SC) in human immunoglobulin (Ig)-producing cells. *Mol Immunol* 1983; **20**: 941–66.
(4) Brandtzaeg P, Korsrud F. Significance of different J chain profiles in human tissues: generation of IgA and IgM with binding site for secretory component is related to the J chain expressing capacity of the total local immunocyte population, including IgG- and IgD-producing cells, and depends on the clinical state of the tissue. *Clin Exp Immunol* 1984; **58**: 709–18.
(5) Bjerke K, Brandtzaeg P. Terminally differentiated human intestinal B cells. J chain expression of IgA and IgG subclass-producing immunocytes in distal ileum compared with mesenteric and peripheral lymph nodes. *Clin Exp Immunol* 1990; in press.

Intravenous IgG treatment in patients with severe chest disease and IgG3 subclass deficiency

E. Bernatowska-Matuszkiewicz[1], M. Pac[1], H. Skopczynska[1], M. Pum[2] and M. M. Eibl[2]

[1]Department of Clinical Immunology, Children's Memorial Hospital, Warsaw, Poland and [2]Institute of Immunology, University of Vienna, Vienna, Austria

INTRODUCTION

The most common complication in patients with antibody deficiency syndromes is chronic chest disease [1,2]. While some patients with chronic chest disease can be shown to be antibody-deficient, either agammaglobulinaemic or hypogammaglobulinaemic, other patients have severe chest disease and normal serum immunoglobulin levels. Several studies have demonstrated that IgG subclass deficiency and impairment of antibody production are frequent findings in this group of patients [3–9]. Intravenous IgG (IVIg) treatment has been shown to improve both the clinical situation and lung function in controlled clinical trials in patients with antibody deficiency syndromes [10–14].

A clinical study was performed at the Children's Memorial Hospital in Warsaw in patients with severe chest disease who had normal concentrations of serum IgG, IgA and IgM. Nine patients were identified as having serum IgG3 levels below 0.17 g/l.

These nine patients were entered into a prospective, controlled clinical trial with IVIg (manuscript submitted). The objective of this clinical trial was to determine whether patients with severe inflammatory lung disease who are not hypogamma-globulinaemic, but have low levels of IgG3, will show clinical improvement if treated with IVIg. Furthermore, this group of patients appeared suitable for addressing the question of whether replacement of the respective isotype is important for efficacy in such patients, or whether other biological properties (antibody activity and/or anti-inflammatory activity) might be of greater relevance.

The results obtained indicate that IVIg treatment in these patients is clinically efficacious.

THE STUDY, RESULTS AND DISCUSSION

Nine patients with serum IgG3 levels below the normal range, five boys and four girls were studied. Five of the children were below six years of age. All the children

Progress in immune deficiency III, edited by H. M. Chapel, R. J. Levinsky and A. D. B. Webster, 1991; Royal Society of Medicine Services International Congress and Symposium Series No. 173, published by Royal Society of Medicine Services Limited.

included in the study had severe chest disease with pneumonia and/or upper and lower respiratory tract infections with bronchitis and fever and/or severe asthma (steroid-dependent) and/or prolonged hospitalization.

Each patient was followed for two years and seen every other month. During the first year patients received conventional treatment with antibiotics and anti-asthmatics. During the second year IVIg treatment was added to conventional therapy at a dose level of 400 mg/kg bodyweight per month. The IVIg product used throughout the study (Iveegam) contains 5 g/100 ml native IgG but only trace amounts of IgG3.

The age of the patients, their diagnosis (recurrent upper and lower respiratory tract infections, asthma) and serum concentrations of IgG subclasses are given in Table 1.

Clinical symptoms, hospitalization and antibiotic and steroid treatment in all patients are shown in Table 2. Children are grouped by age (below and above six years of age during the first year of observation). The results are given for the first observation year and the second year when IVIg was added to the treatment regimen (Table 2).

The group of children involved in this study had severe chest disease as demonstrated by the average length of hospitalization (37.4 days in children below six years of age and 7.3 days in children above six years of age respectively) and number of days with clinical symptoms (upper and lower respiratory tract infections, wheezing) as well as by the need for antibiotic and/or steroid treatment.

IVIg treatment led to a significant improvement in these patients' conditions. Hospitalization decreased from 37.4 days in the first year to 4.2 days during the second year in the children below six years of age and from 7.3 in the first year to zero days during the second year in the older children. Upper and lower respiratory tract infections, the need for antibiotics and the need for steroids were significantly reduced during the second year, when the patients received intravenous immunoglobulin therapy (Table 2). Since the product used in the treatment of these IgG3 deficient patients contains only trace amounts of IgG3, replacement of the respective isotype was not the mechanism underlying its effect.

The mechanisms leading to the rapid improvement of lung function observed in patients with severe inflammatory lung disease after treatment with IVIg are not yet fully clear. A partial explanation may be that the immunoglobulin

Table 1 *Clinical symptoms and IgG subclass concentrations*

Pat.	Age (years)	Clinical diagnosis [a]	IgG1[b]	IgG2[b]	IgG3[b]	IgG4[b]
A	2 5/12	1	561	141	12	20
B	3 2/12	2	898	113	16	24
C	3 8/12	1	770	100	9	< 10
D	4	2	557	324	9	15
E	4 2/12	1	611	120	12	19
F	7 6/12	1	830	183	12	80
G	7 6/12	1	889	146	16	95
H	8 4/12	1	1029	145	14	67
I	9 4/12	1	604	279	10	90

[a]1: Asthma
2: Upper and lower respiratory tract infections
[b]Concentration mg/dl in patients' sera

Table 2 Children with IgG3 and IgG3+IgG4 subclass deficiency: Mean number of days with clinical symptoms, treatment or hospitalization

Age groups	No. of patients	Upper and lower respiratory tract infections				Asthma				Hospitalization	
		1st year[a]		2nd year[a]		1st year[a]		2nd year[a]		1st year[a]	2nd year[a]
		Clinical disease	Anti-biotics	Clinical disease	Anti-biotics	Wheezing	Steroids	Wheezing	Steroids		
<6 years	5(3[b])	173.2 (120–140)	129.6 (98–100)	41.0 (14–74)	26.2 (10–62)	55.3 (30–100)	28.7 (0–84)	10.0 (0–30)	0	37.4 (0–77)	4.2 (0–21)
≥6 years	4(4[b])	132.0 (120–144)	115.3 (96–140)	68.5 (49–89)	44.8 (20–71)	80.0 (40–160)	47.8 (2–120)	5.5 (0–12)	0	7.3 (0–15)	0

[a] 1st year: observation period before the initiation of IVIg treatment; during the 2nd year of the study all children received IVIg
[b] Number of children with asthma

eliminates micro-organisms at the site of infection and prevents bacterial and viral pulmonary infections. As high-dose IVIg treatment of a group of patients with Kawasaki syndrome [15] was found to have a marked anti-inflammatory effect, an anti-inflammatory mechanism of IVIg may also contribute significantly to improving lung function in patients with humoral antibody deficiencies.

REFERENCES

(1) Gelter-Bernstein C, Zur S, Kahane P, *et al.* Serum immunoglobulins in children with asthma associated with severe respiratory tract infections. *Ann Allergy* 1976; **37**: 126.
(2) Björkander J, Bake B, Oxelius V-A, Hanson L. Impaired lung function in IgA deficiency and low levels of IgG2 or IgG3. *N Engl J Med* 1985; **313**: 720–4.
(3) Loftus B, Price J, Lobo-Yeo A, Vergani D. IgG subclass deficiency in asthma. *Arch Dis Child* 1988; **63**: 1434–7.
(4) Leibl H, Liszka K, Bernatowska E, Mannhalter J, Eibl M. Serum IgG subclass concentration in patients with undue susceptibility to infections. In press.
(5) Ochs H, Wedgwood R. IgG subclass deficiencies. *Ann Rev Med* 1987; **38**: 325–40.
(6) Oxelius V-A, Hanson L, Björkander J, Hammarström L, Sjöholm A. IgG3 deficiency: common in obstructive lung disease. *Monogr Allergy* 1986; **20**: 106–15.
(7) Umetsu D, Ambrosino D, Quinti I, Siber G, Geha R. Recurrent sinopulmonary infection and impaired antibody response to bacterial capsular polysaccharide antigen in children with selective IgG subclass deficiency. *N Engl J Med* 1985; **313**: 1247–51.
(8) Schur P, Borel H, Gelfand E, Alper C, Rosen F. Selective gamma-G globuline deficiencies in patients with recurrent pyogenic infections. *N Engl J Med* 1970; **283**: 631–4.
(9) Shackelford P, Polmar S, Mayus J, Johnson W, Corry J, Nahm M. Spectrum of IgG2 subclass deficiency in children with recurrent infections: prospective study. *J Pediatr* 1986; **108**: 647–53.
(10) Hazer B, Giclas P, Gelfand E. Immunomodulatory effects of intravenous immunoglobulin in severe steroid-dependent asthma. *Clin Immunol Immunopathol* 1989; **53**: 5156–63.
(11) Roifman C, Lederman H, Lavi S, Stein L, Levison H, Gelfand E. Benefit of intravenous IgG replacement in hypoglobulinemic patients with chronic sinopulmonary disease. *Am J Med* 1985; **79**: 171–4.
(12) Roifman C, Levison H, Gelfand E. High-dose versus low-dose intravenous immunoglobulin in hypogammaglobulinaemia and chronic lung disease. *Lancet* 1987; **i**: 1075–7.
(13) Bernatowska E, Madalinski K, Janowicz W, *et al.* Results of a prospective controlled two-dose crossover study with intravenous immunoglobulin and comparison (retrospective) with plasma treatment. *Clin Immunol Immunopathol* 1987; **43**: 153–62.
(14) Hanson L, Björkander J, Wadsworth C. Intramuscular and intravenous administration of immunoglobulin to patients with hypogammaglobulinemia. In: Wedgwood R, Rosen F, Paul N, eds. *Primary immunodeficiency diseases; birth defects*. March of Dimes Birth Defects Foundation. New York: Alan R Liss, 1983: 205–7.
(15) Newburger J, Takahashi M, Burns J, *et al.* The treatment of Kawasaki syndrome with intravenous gamma globulin. *N Engl J Med* 1986; **315**: 341–7.

Complement activation by normal IgG2 antibacterial antibodies

R. G. M. Bredius[1], R. S. Weening[2] and T. A. Out[1]

[1]Clinical Immunology Laboratory, Academic Medical Centre, and Laboratory for Experimental and Clinical Immunology (CLB), Amsterdam and [2]Emma Children's Hospital, Department of Paediatrics, Academic Medical Centre, Amsterdam, The Netherlands

(POSTER)

Decreased concentrations of IgG2 have been associated with a varied pattern of immunological dysfunction, some of which may be responsible for recurrent bacterial infections in children [1]. A causal relationship is unclear, especially since properties of IgG2 with respect to complement activation and binding to Fc-γ receptors on leukocytes are poorly defined. IgG2 antibodies are generally considered to be less effective in complement activation than IgG1 antibodies [2].

In this study, we purified serum IgG1 and IgG2, including G2m(n) positive and negative allotypes, from normal individuals to analyse the complement activating properties of polyclonal antibodies against *Staphylococcus aureus*, (protein A deficient strain Wood (Sta)) and of anti-*Haemophilus influenzae* type b (Hib).

We separated IgG1 and IgG2 from sera from five normal individuals, who had IgG1 and IgG2 anti-Sta and anti-Hib. Two individuals were IgG2 G2m(n) allotype positive, the other three were negative. IgG was separated from other serum proteins by gel-filtration on a Sephacryl S-300 column. The IgG pool was applied on Sepharose protein A and IgG2 and IgG1 antibodies were eluted with a pH gradient. The mean recovery was 54% (range 36–87%) per subclass. IgG1 pools contained less than 9% IgG2. IgG2 pools contained less than 7% IgG1.

IgG subclass antibodies to freshly cultured Sta and Hib were assayed by ELISA, using enzyme-labelled monoclonal anti-subclass antibodies. Complement activation, also measured with ELISA, was assayed as follows. Bacteria were coated and incubated with antibodies, followed by agammaglobulinaemic serum. C3 deposition was then measured using HRP labelled rabbit anti-human C3c. Five different sources of complement, obtained from patients with agammaglobulinaemia, were compared.

IgG2 anti-Sta was found to activate complement equally well as IgG1 anti-Sta, indicating that IgG2 is an effective antibody in the defence against Sta. IgG2 anti-Hib showed individual differences: some IgG2 anti-Hib antibodies showed better complement activation than IgG1 anti-Hib, some worse (see figure). Complement activation by IgG2 could possibly be affected by the IgG2 G2m(n) immunoglobulin allotype, since complement component C1q binding is designated to the same CH2 domain [2]. However, no marked differenced in complement activation was seen between G2m(n) positive and negative IgG2.

Different human complement sources did show different background levels, probably due to low antibody activity still present in the sera. The antibodies from different individuals reacted similarly with all five complement sources tested.

Progress in immune deficiency III, edited by H. M. Chapel, R. J. Levinsky and A. D. B. Webster, 1991; Royal Society of Medicine Services International Congress and Symposium Series No. 173, published by Royal Society of Medicine Services Limited.

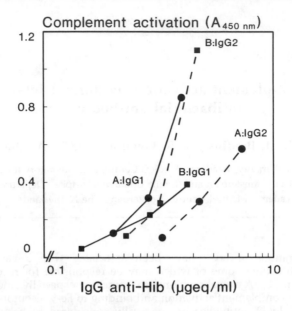

Figure 1 *Complement activation by IgG1 and IgG2 anti-*Haemophilus influenzae *types to Complement activation by IgG1 and IgG2 anti-bacterial antibodies, expressed in absorbance signals obtained with ELISA. Individual differences in complement activation by IgG1 anti-Hib and IgG2 anti-Hib were seen; results from 2 individuals A and B.* ●━━━━● *IgG1 from person A,* ■━━━━■ *IgG1 from person B* ●━━● *IgG2 from person A,* ■━━━■ *IgG2 from person B.*

We conclude that IgG2 anti-Sta and anti-Hib may have an important role in the defence against these bacteria.

Furthermore, it will be of interest to analyse IgG2-mediated phagocytosis.

REFERENCES

(1) Shackelford PG, Granoff DM, Polmar SH, *et al.* Subnormal serum concentrations of IgG2 in children with frequent infections associated with varied patterns of immunologic dysfunction. *J Pediatr* 1990; **116**: 529–38.
(2) Burton DR. Immunoglobulin G: functional sites. *Mol Immunol* 1985; **22**: 161–206.

IgG subclass findings over a three year period and their clinical significance

M. Baer and E. Soppi

Department of Paediatrics and Division of Clinical Immunology, Tampere University Central Hospital, Tampere, Finland

(POSTER)

We performed 504 IgG determinations employing end-point radial immunodiffusion with monoclonal antibodies; the majority were done in 262 infants and children with recurrent respiratory and middle ear infections, severe bacterial infections, severe atopic dermatitis, and severe or prolonged diarrhoea. Patients whose serum was 50% or more below the age-determined lower limit for a given subclass, were described as 'deficient'. Deficiency of at least one IgG subclass was present in 24% of the 262 children (Table 1).

Table 1 *Distribution of IgG subclass deficiency in different age groups*

Age (years)	0.5 to 2	2 to 7	7 to 15
No. of patients	78	122	62
IgG1 deficiency	0	1 (0.8%)	3 (5%)
IgG2 deficiency	3 (4%)	7 (5%)	6 (10%)
IgG3 deficiency	1 (1.3%)	6 (5%)	4 (6%)
IgG4 deficiency	26 (33%)	6 (5%)	0 (0%)
Total	30 (38%)	20 (17%)	13 (21%)

Nine of 32 with IgG4 deficiencies had subnormal concentrations of one or two other subclasses. Two of 11 with IgG3 deficiency had subnormal concentrations of one or two other subclasses. Six of 16 with IgG2 deficiency had additional IgG4 deficiency. Seven of 16 had subnormal concentrations of one or two other subclasses. All four with IgG1 deficiency had at least one other subclass deficiency and common variable immuno-deficiency. Two of the four patients with common variable immunodeficiency had IgG4 deficiency, both were older than seven years.

We studied the records of 63 children with IgG subclass deficiency for correlation of IgG subclass findings with clinical course. An isolated IgG4 deficiency in infancy was commonly associated with increased susceptibility for infections, particularly for viral respiratory tract infections with middle ear infection. Nine of 11 patients with septicaemia had IgG4 deficiency. On the other hand, only nine of 40 patients with IgG4 deficiency (22%) suffered from an attack of septicaemia. Five of them had an isolated IgG4 deficiency, in four others this was associated with IgG2 deficiency. Seven of these nine children were younger than two years at the time of having septicaemia. 37% of children with IgG2 deficiency (n=6) had suffered from septicaemia, three of them under two years of age. IgG3 deficiency was most often associated with chronic middle ear infection (in 73%) frequently concurrent with bronchitis and viral pneumonia. In 25% of patients with IgG2 or IgG3 deficiency severe atopic dermatitis was the problem.

CONCLUSIONS

1. Isolated IgG4 deficiency in infancy is a frequent finding in our patients. IgG4 deficiency is associated more often with septicaemia than any other IgG subclass deficiency.
2. IgG subclass deficiency is a common finding in children with recurrent or severe infections.
3. 25% of patients with IgG2 or IgG3 deficiency had severe atopic dermatitis.

Progress in immune deficiency III, edited by H. M. Chapel, R. J. Levinsky and A. D. B. Webster, 1991; Royal Society of Medicine Services International Congress and Symposium Series No. 173, published by Royal Society of Medicine Services Limited.

The clinical importance of combined IgA and IgG subclass deficiencies

N. Nagy[1], E. Sintar[2], E. Rajnavolgyi[2], J. Zsiros[1] and L. Velkey[1]

[1]Department of Paediatrics of the Postgraduate Medical School and [2]Department of Immunology of L Eotvos University, Gyek, Hungary

(POSTER) .

IgA deficiency has been reported in patients with primary humoral immunodeficiencies [1], autoimmune diseases and in patients with recurrent sinopulmonary infections [2], but it may also be present in asymptomatic subjects. In our study we examined the clinical importance of IgA and IgG subclass deficiencies by measuring the serum IgG subclass levels in IgA-deficient patients (all of them had a lower level than 2SD) with and without severe respiratory tract infections.

The patients were divided into two groups. In the first group, there were 22 children, aged 2.5–6 years (mean±SD 3.4±1.2) who had IgA deficiency with recurrent lower respiratory tract infections. In the second group there were seven children with IgA deficiency without respiratory tract infections, aged 2–6 years (mean±SD 4.1±1.2). Controls were 10 healthy children aged 2–6 years (mean±3.1±1.1). We determined diphtheria and tetanus antitoxin levels in patients with combined IgA and IgG subclass deficiencies.

For the determinations of IgG subclasses, we used well-characterized and easily standardizable mouse monoclonal antibodies specific for human IgG isotypes and we established a solid phase competitive EIA system to quantitate IgG subclasses in human body fluids. The results were expressed as a percentage of the WHO immunoglobulin standard. Diphtheria and tetanus antitoxin levels were determined by the method of haemolytic titration.

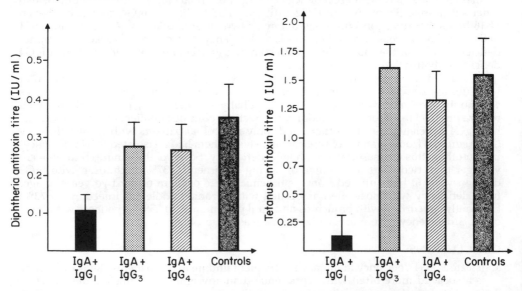

Figure 1 *Diphtheria and tetanus antitoxin titres in patients with combined IgA and IgG subclass deficiencies.*

Progress in immune deficiency III, edited by H. M. Chapel, R. J. Levinsky and A. D. B. Webster, 1991; Royal Society of Medicine Services International Congress and Symposium Series No. 173, published by Royal Society of Medicine Services Limited.

RESULTS

1. Patients with IgA deficiency without infections have significantly higher IgG1, 2, 3, 4 subclass levels than those patients with severe respiratory tract infections.
2. Patients with IgA deficiency and with severe respiratory tract infections have significantly lower IgG3 levels than healthy controls.
3. There are no significant differences in the serum IgG1, IgG2, IgG4 subclass levels between the patients with severe respiratory tract infections and healthy controls.
4. Patients with combined IgA and IgG1 deficiencies have significantly lower diphtheria and tetanus antitoxin levels than healthy controls (Fig. 1).

CONCLUSIONS

In the case of IgA deficiency, the increase of IgG subclasses in the sera can be regarded as compensatory; it may be a protection against the severe infections. The combined IgA and IgG3 deficiencies may have a principal role in the development of recurrent respiratory tract infections. In our material IgG2 deficiency was combined with other subclass deficiencies and it did not appear alone. The patients with both IgA and IgG1 deficiencies have significantly lower antibody production after vaccination. These patients should be followed up.

REFERENCES

(1) Oxelius V-A. Immunoglobulin G subclasses and human disease. *Am J Med* 1984; **76** (suppl): 7–18.
(2) Björkander J, Bake B, Oxelius V-A, *et al*. Impaired lung functions in patients with IgA deficiency and low levels of IgG2 or IgG3. *N Engl J Med* 1985; **313**: 720–4.

IgG subclass deficiencies in allergic diseases

P. Bartmann[1], H. Jaeger[1] and I. Grimm[2]

[1]Department of Paediatrics, University of Ulm, Ulm, and [2]Staedt. Kliniken, Darmstadt, Germany

(POSTER)

Allergic diseases may be associated with immunodeficiency and *vice versa*. IgG subclass deficiencies—especially of IgG2 and IgG3—can contribute to the aetiology of repeated bacterial infections. The clinical courses of patients with allergic diseases is often worsened by infections. We were thus interested in answering the question whether IgG subclass deficiency might contribute to a higher susceptibility to infections in some patients with allergic disease.

Thirty-nine children (2–18 years) with bronchial asthma were investigated for IgG subclass deficiency. Two patients with IgG2- and one with IgG2–IgG3-deficiency were identified. Yet the clinical course of these three patients did not reveal any significant differences compared with the histories of the other members of the group investigated.

Fifty adults with a large spectrum of allergic diseases (type I 33 patients, type IV 11 patients, type I + IV 5 patients, type II one patient) were screened for IgG subclass deficiency. Five IgG subclass-deficient patients were identified: one patient with IgG2-, two with IgG2-/IgG3-deficiency and two with IgG3-deficiency. Notably mean IgG3 serum levels of all 50 patients were significantly low with 0.42 ± 0.38 g/l (95% reference range 0.41–1.29 g/l). No increased susceptibility to infections compared with the whole group was observed in the five patients with IgG subclass deficiency.

CONCLUSIONS

IgG2- and/or IgG3-subclass deficiency was observed in 3/39 children with bronchial asthma as well as in 5/50 adults with different allergic diseases. Analysis of the clinical history of these patients did not reveal any indication that patients with an additional IgG subclass deficiency are more prone to infections than the others. A possible benefit of immunoglobulin substitution therapy can thus not be deduced from these data.

Progress in immune deficiency III, edited by H. M. Chapel, R. J. Levinsky and A. D. B. Webster, 1991; Royal Society of Medicine Services International Congress and Symposium Series No. 173, published by Royal Society of Medicine Services Limited.

Deletions in the IgCH locus: New forms, functional consequence and suggested nomenclature

C. I. E. Smith, P.-E. Engström, P. G. Olsson and L. Hammarström

Department of Clinical Immunology and Centre for Biotechnology, Karolinska Institute at Huddinge Hospital and at NOVUM, Huddinge, Sweden

(POSTER)

Nine different deletions in the IgCH locus have so far been reported (Table 1). Various nomenclatures have been used based on the chronological description [1] or by denoting all genes deleted. Inasmuch as there are nine structural genes and two pseudogenes in this locus, the description may be quite complex although none of the deletions so far identified encompasses more than six gene segments. The preliminary mapping of this locus [2] has recently been confirmed and established by the isolation of overlapping genomic clones [3]. A complete physical map now exists and it would seem reasonable to use a more simplified nomenclature. We thus propose that the deletion haplotypes be designated according to the most J_H proximal and J_H distal gene encompassed. Furthermore we suggest that the homozygous deletions be designated similarly but with the prefix *hom*. In accordance, duplications could be designated using the prefix *dupl*. Table 1 lists the nine different deletions as well as the corresponding designation according to this nomenclature.

Table 1 *Deletions in the immunoglobulin heavy chain locus*

Deletion	Designation	Reference
γ1	*del G1*	Smith *et al. J Immunol* (1989)
γ1 ψε1-α1-ψγ-γ2	*del G1-G2*	Smith *et al. J Immunol* (1989)
γ1-ψε1-α1-ψγ-γ2-γ4	*del G1-G4*	Lefranc *et al. Nature* (1982)
ψε1-α1-ψγ	*del PE1-PG*	Lefranc *et al. Mol Biol Med* (1983)
ψε1-α1-ψγ-γ2-γ4	*del PE1-G4*	Migone *et al. PNAS* (1984)
α1-ψγ-γ2-γ4-ε	*del A1-E*	Migone *et al. PNAS* (1984)
ψγ-γ2-γ4-ε-α2	*del PG-A2*	Bottaro *et al. Immunogenet* (1989)
γ2	*del G2*	Bottaro *et al. Immunogenet* (1989)
γ4	*del G4*	Bottaro *et al. Hum Genet* (1990)

Using Southern blotting, we have recently obtained evidence for two new deletion haplotypes corresponding to the *del G2-G4* (Olsson PG, Hofker MH, Walter MA *et al.* unpublished) and the *del G1-A1* (Hammarström L, Olsson PG, Smith CIE, unpublished). Furthermore, we have recently completed the first quantitative analysis of the effect on immunoglobulin levels of such deletions [4]. Today there are too few known cases of IGHG gene deletions to permit a detailed analysis of the influence on the individual IgG subclass levels. However, we have studied 10 individuals with *hom del A1* and one with a *hom del A2*. Normal IgA levels were noted in both serum and saliva of all these donors, except for two individuals with a *hom del A1*. Both these donors had inherited the same deletion haplotypes. Thus, in the majority of these donors an increased IgA2 production compensated for the lack of IgA1, in spite of the fact that only 10% of serum IgA is IgA2 in normal individuals.

However, when specific antibodies directed against a number of different polysaccharides as well as protein antigens were studied, decreased levels of specific IgA were noted in

Progress in immune deficiency III, edited by H. M. Chapel, R. J. Levinsky and A. D. B. Webster, 1991; Royal Society of Medicine Services International Congress and Symposium Series No. 173, published by Royal Society of Medicine Services Limited.

the eight *hom del A1* donors with a normal total IgA concentration. Antibodies to polysaccharide antigens were more severely impaired, constituting only one fifth or less of the amount found in normal healthy individuals. Specific antibodies directed against protein antigens were decreased by a factor of three. However, normal levels of specific antibodies were found in saliva. This may indicate that the secretory immune system is differently regulated, or alternatively, it could reflect the higher proportion of IgA2 normally found in the secretory system. However, the low level of specific IgA2 antibodies in the serum of donors with *hom del A1* clearly extends previous observations on IgG subclasses, and demonstrates that although other isotypes may compensate for deleted genes, this compensation is only partial.

REFERENCES

(1) Lefranc M-P, Hammarström L, Smith CIE, Lefranc G. Gene deletions in the human immunoglobulin heavy chain constant region locus: molecular and serological analysis. *Immunodef Rev* 1990; in press.
(2) Flanagan JG, Rabbitts TH. Arrangement of human immunoglobulin heavy chain constant region genes implies evolutionary duplication of a segment containing γ, ϵ and α genes. *Nature* 1982; **300**: 709–13.
(3) Hofker MH, Walter MA, Cox DW. Complete physical map of the human immunoglobulin heavy chain constant region gene complex. *Proc Natl Acad Sci USA* 1989; **86**: 5567–71.
(4) Engström PE, Norhagen EG, Bottaro A *et al*. Subclass distribution of antigen-specific IgA antibodies in normal donors and individuals with homozygous Cα1 or Cα2 gene deletions. *J Immunol* 1990; **145**: 109–15.

Potential use of polyethylene glycol-conjugated IL-2 in common variable immunodeficiency

C. Cunningham-Rundles and L. Mayer

Mount Sinai Medical Center, New York, NY, USA

Common variable immunodeficiency (CVI) represents a collection of deficiencies, in which patients have either primary B cell defects, or B cell defects due to inadequate T cell or macrophage functions [1–4]. Since both macrophage and T cell interactions are needed for most antibody responses, the extent to which a given patient has an exclusively B cell defect, or whether T cell or macrophage deficiencies are the more central abnormality is still uncertain.

In vitro, the B cells of many hypogammaglobulinaemic patients can be caused to secrete immunoglobulin by a variety of stimulators: phorbol myristate acetate [5], various B cell differentiation factors derived from allogeneic T cells [6,7] or anti-CD3 antibodies [7]. The crucial issues are whether these immunoglobulins are polyclonal, the nature of the isotype (IgG as well as IgM) and if antibody secretion is detectable. In general, most classifications of CVI include a stratification of patients into groups: those for whom more or less normal amounts of immunoglobulin secretion can be detected after stimulation *in vitro*, those for whom moderate levels of immunoglobulin secretion can be detected, and a final group for whom no immunoglobulin secretion is detectable. In most such analyses, patients who have normal or near normal levels of serum IgM are found in the first group, and patients who have little or no serum immunoglobulin in the last group.

The nature of the T cell deficiency in CVI remains unknown, but lymphokine (IL-2, IL-4, IL-5 and γ-interferon) secretion after activation is clearly deficient. While the genes for these lymphokines are expressed, expression of IL-2 mRNA of CIV cells may be lower than normal [5,8,9]. The reduced production of IL-2 may underlie the relative deficiency of γ-interferon produced after mitogen stimulation in CVI. Addition of IL-2 to cultures of T cells from patients with CVI can improve lymphocyte proliferative capacities to mitogens in many patients [8], and has been shown to restore interferon production for cells of 4/4 patients to the levels expected of antigen-stimulated normal T cells [9].

Since IL-2 can apparently exert a direct effect on activated normal B cells to promote secretion of immunoglobulin [10–12], the relative deficiency of IL-2 in CVI may be a possible factor in the lack of immunoglobulin secretion to T independent antigens. In this regard, the effects of IL-2 on *Staphylococcus aureus* Cowan I (SAC) activated B cells in CVI have been investigated by ourselves and others [13]. These data show that IL-2 and SAC can stimulate the B cells of a proportion of patients with CVI to produce immunoglobulin *in vitro*.

Progress in immune deficiency III, edited by H. M. Chapel, R. J. Levinsky and A. D. B. Webster, 1991; *Royal Society of Medicine Services International Congress and Symposium Series No. 173*, published by Royal Society of Medicine Services Limited.

In current studies we are investigating the state of relative IL-2 deficiency in CVI and are exploring the possibility that the use of a new polyethylene glycol-conjugated human recombinant IL-2 (PEG-IL-2) could be used to enhance T cell, and potentially B cell function in such patients.

MATERIALS AND METHODS

Patients and leukocyte analyses

Patients with CVI who were previously well characterized, were the subjects of the current investigation. Peripheral blood was collected from the patients in heparinized tubes and peripheral mononuclear leukocytes (PBL) were isolated by density gradient centrifugation in Ficoll-Hypaque (Pharmacia Chemicals, Piscataway NJ) [14]. Cells were washed three times in RPMI 1640 (GIBCO, Grand Island, NY) supplemented with 2 mM glutamine, 50 µg/ml penicillin, 50 µg/ml streptomycin and 10% heat-inactivated fetal calf serum. Immunofluorescence analyses were performed on a fluorescence-activated cell sorter (FACS/IV, Becton-Dickinson, Mountain View, CA) using monoclonal antibodies to CD4, CD8, and CD3 (purchased from Ortho Pharmaceuticals, Raritan New Jersey). B cells were isolated from the PBL preparations by rosette-depleting T cells and removal of monocytes and macrophages by adherance to plastic [7].

Proliferation studies

The proliferative capacities of PBL to a mitogenic concentration of CD3 (OKT3) antibody was determined by culturing 10^6 cells/ml in triplicate microwell cultures in the complete media described above with the addition of 2.5 ng/ml of OKT3 antibody [5]. Similar cultures were stimulated with PHA, (1% v/v). After 24 h, 100 µl of supernatant was removed and assayed for IL-2 activity (see below). Identical cultures were incubated for three days and then pooled for 4 h with [^{3}H]-thymidine. Cells were then harvested into glass fibre filter papers with an automated multi-sample harvester and counted in a liquid scintillation counter. Uptake of radioactivity by proliferating cells was then assessed.

In parallel experiments, the degree of proliferation produced by OKT3 or PHA was assessed when 10 U/ml (a concentration previously found optimal) of IL-2 had been added to the cultures. Results were expressed as counts per minute (cpm) (average for triplicate cultures).

To determine if the new conjugated form of recombinant IL-2, PEG-IL-2, could also be used to stimulate cells of CVI patients *in vitro*, PEG-IL-2 (Cetus Corp. Emeryville, CA) was added to cultures of 10^6 PBL cells/ml to provide 1, 10, 10^2, 10^3, or 10^4 U/ml as a final concentration of PEG-IL-2 with or without the addition of PHA (1% v/v). Cultures of cells were then incubated for three, five or seven days, at which time [^{3}H]-thymidine was added. After 6 h, cultures were terminated and the amount of incorporated [^{3}H] determined.

IL-2 determination

The IL-2 content of supernatants of cells cultured in the presence of PHA or OKT3 was determined by bioassay using the IL-2 dependent murine T cell line, CTLL-2 (American Type Culture Collection, Rockville, MD). For this, dilutions of culture supernatants or a standard amount of IL-2, were incubated with 1×10^4 CTLL-2 for 47 h. Six hours prior to terminating the cultures, 1 µCi of [^{3}H]-thymidine was added to each well. Cells were harvested and the cpm incorporated was determined. From the known IL-2 concentrations, a standard curve was constructed; and the amount of IL-2 secreted by the cultures could be determined.

IL-2 and SAC stimulation of B cells

IL-2 and SAC present a potent combination for B cell differentiation in normal subjects; the effects of these agents in CVI was also investigated. For this 10 U/ml of IL-2 was added to cultures of isolated B cells containing 0.001% of SAC (Calbiochem Behring, Lajolla, CA). After seven days of incubation, the cells were removed from culture media by centrifugation and the amount of immunoglobulin secreted into the culture media determined by ELISA.

RESULTS

In the presence of either PHA or CD3, peripheral mononuclear cell cultures of almost all CVI patients secreted subnormal amounts of IL-2 (Fig. 1). The range for IL-2 secretion for normal cells under these conditions is given.

When IL-2 was added to cell cultures incubated with mitogens, the T lymphocyte proliferation responses to PHA or anti-CD3 antibody were enhanced for many, but not all CVI patients (Fig. 2). Three patient groups appeared to emerge, especially for results to PHA: those who responded with a marked proliferative increase, those who responded to IL-2 only modestly, and those who did not have a change in proliferative responses after the addition of IL-2. Addition of IL-2 to cultures of B cells from patients with CVI was performed to determine

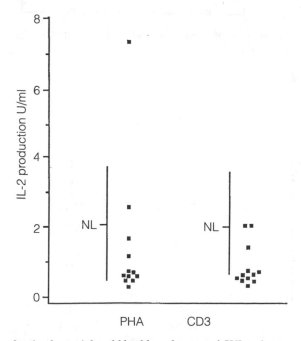

Figure 1 *IL-2 production by peripheral blood lymphocytes of CVI patients or normal subjects was stimulated in vitro with PHA or OKT3 antibody. The amount of IL-2 secreted into the culture supernatant at the end of 24 h was determined. NL = normal levels.*

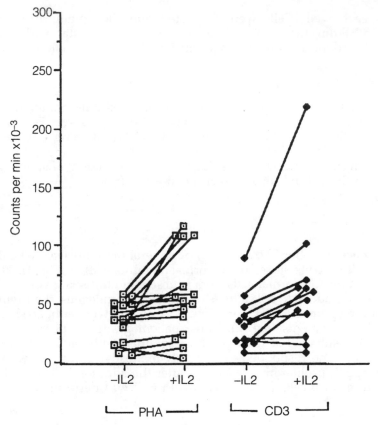

Figure 2 *The proliferation of lymphocytes when cultured with PHA or OKT3 was determined in the presence, or absence, of IL-2.*

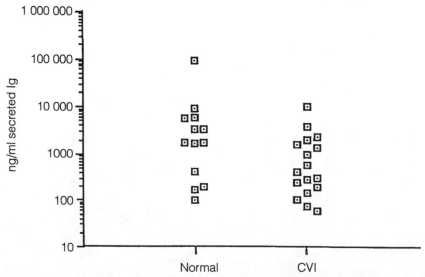

Figure 3 *IL-2 and SAC were used in concert to stimulate purified B cells of CVI patients to secrete immunoglobulin, as compared to normal controls. While CVI patients produced less Ig overall than normals, many secreted Ig in amounts similar to that produced by normals.*

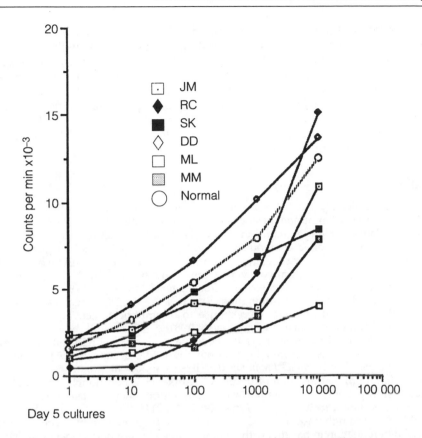

Day 5 cultures

Figure 4 *PEG-IL-2 was used to stimulate peripheral blood lymphocytes of patients with CVI in the presence or absence of PHA (the latter is shown here). The proliferative results for normal controls is indicated by a dashed line.*

the degree to which this lymphokine could act upon B cells to cause differentiation and immunoglobulin secretion, as compared to B cells isolated from normal donors. Figure 3 shows that while the overall secretion of Ig was reduced as compared to normals, about half the patients tested produced immunoglobulin in the range of 500 ng/ml or more. To determine if the conjugated form of IL-2 could stimulate alone, or in combination with PHA, the PBL of six patients with CVI were cultured with PEG-IL-2 at various concentrations. While stimulation clearly varied, the degree of proliferation produced for most patients was comparable to that found for normals (Fig. 4).

DISCUSSION

While CVI is clearly a heterogeneous disease, and intrinsic B cell defects are usually cited as the major reason for lack of immunoglobulin secretion, about half of all patients have B cells capable of responding normally or almost so to exogenous T cell-derived differentiation signals. These observations suggest that given an appropriate stimulus, the B cells of these patients could be caused to function more or less normally [2, 3, 5–8].

In severe combined immunodeficiency (SCID) failure of IL-2 production, an impaired IL-2/IL-2 receptor system due to a defect in IL-2 receptor expression, or IL-2 secretion or both, have been documented [15–17]. In a few cases of SCID or closely related phenotypes of severe T cell deficiency, therapy with recombinant IL-2 has been shown to exert a beneficial effect [15–17]. Recently a conjugated form of IL-2, PEG-IL-2, has been shown to have an extended half life as compared with IL-2, with no apparent alteration in biological capacities. PEG-IL-2 is quite soluble, and appears less immunogenic than unconjugated recombinant IL-2. This agent has been well tolerated in initial *in vivo* trials. Since specific deficiencies of IL-2 and IL-2 receptor expression have been documented in CVI, we are now turning to an *in vivo* investigation of PEG-IL-2 in CVI.

REFERENCES

(1) Cunningham-Rundles C. Clinical and immunologic analyses of 103 patients with common variable immunodeficiency. *J Clin Immunol* 1989; **9**: 22–23.
(2) Saiki O, Ralph P, Cunningham-Rundles C, Good RA. Three distinct stages of B cell defects in common varied immunodeficiency. *Proc Natl Acad Sci USA* 1982; **79**: 6008–12.
(3) Ralph P, Jeong G, Nakuinz I, Saiki O, Cunningham-Rundles C. Rescue of IgM, IgG, and IgA production in common varied immunodeficiency by T cell independent stimulation with Epstein-Barr virus. *J Clin Immunol* 1985; **5**: 122–9.
(4) Cunningham-Rundles S, Cunningham-Rundles C, Ma DI, Siegal FP, Kosloff C, Good RA. Impaired proliferative response to B lymphocyte activators in common variable immunodeficiency. *J Clin Immunol* 1981; **1**: 65–71.
(5) Fielder W, Sykora KW, Welte K, et al. Defective T cell activation in common variable immunodeficiency is restored by phorbol myristatic acetate (PMA) or allogenic macrophages. *Clin Immunol Immunopathol* 1987; **44**: 206–18.
(6) Mayer L, Fu SM, Cunningham-Rundles C, Kunkel HG. Polyclonal immunoglobulin secretion in patients with common variable immunodeficiency using monoclonal B cell differentiation factors. *J Clin Invest* 1984; **74**: 2115–20.
(7) Stohl W, Cunningham-Rundles C, Mayer L. *In vitro* induction of T cell dependent B cell differentiation in patients with common varied immunodeficiency. *Clin Immunol Immunopathol* 1989; **49**: 273.
(8) Kruger G, Welte K, Ciobanu N, et al. Interleukin-2 correction of defective *in vitro* T cell mitogenesis in patients with common varied immunodeficiency. *J Clin Immunol* 1984; **4**: 295–303.
(9) Sneller MC, Strober W. Abnormalities of lymphokine gene expression in patients with common variable immunodeficiencies. *J Immunol* 1990; **144**: 3762–9.
(10) Ralph P, Jeong G, Welte K, et al. Stimulation of immunoglobulin secretion in human B lymphocytes as a direct effect of high concentrations of IL-2. *J Immunol* 1984; **133**: 2442–5.
(11) Romagnani S, Prete GL, Giudizi MG, et al. Direct induction of human B cell differentiation by recombinant interleukin-2. *Immunology* 1986; **58**: 31–5.
(12) Mingani MC, Gerosa F, Carra G, et al. Human interleukin-2 promotes proliferation of activated B cells via surface receptors similar to those of activated T cells. *Nature (Lond)* 1984; **312**: 641–3.
(13) Ariga T, Okano M, Takahashi Y, Sakiyama Y, Matsumoto S. Analysis of B cell dysfunction in patients with common variable immunodeficiency by using recombinant interleukin-2. *Tohoku J Exp Med* 1987; **152**: 53–61.
(14) Boyum A. Separation of lymphocytes, lymphocyte subgroups and monocytes: a review. *Lymphology* 1977; **10**: 71–6 (Review).
(15) Buckley R, Schiff S, Markert L, Gerber P, Paradise C. Recombinant human interleukin-2 (rIL-2) therapy in primary immunodeficiency. *J Allergy Immun* 1989; **83**: 296.
(16) Pahwa R, Paradise C, Good RA. Management of a novel immune deficiency with IL-2 therapy. *Cancer Treat Rev* 1989; **16**: (suppl A); 143–9.
(17) Weinberg K, Parkman R. Severe combined immunodeficiency due to a specific defect in the production of IL-2. *N Engl J Med* 1990; **322**: 1718–20.

Further studies on the impairment of antigen-induced T cell activation in CVI patients

M. B. Fischer, E. Vogel, H. M. Wolf, J. W. Mannhalter and M. M. Eibl

Institute of Immunology, University of Vienna, Borschkegasse 8a, A-1090 Vienna, Austria

In previous studies performed in our laboratory, a defect in the early phase of the immune response in patients with common variable immunodeficiency (CVI) was observed [1,2]. This defect was expressed by the inability of the patients' peripheral blood T cells to respond to an antigenic stimulus presented by autologous monocytes (deficient macrophage–T cell interaction (MTI)). MTI is initiated by internalization of the antigen by the antigen-presenting cell (APC). Following uptake, antigen must be transported to a protease-containing compartment where it is processed. Processed antigen binds to MHC class II molecules, and these complexes are re-expressed on the cell surface, where they are recognized by antigen-specific T cells [3,4]. Thus at the level of the monocyte, defective MTI could be due to deficient antigen processing or re-expression as well as to inadequate coupling of the antigen to the MHC class II molecules. The T cells, on the other hand, might be unable to recognize the antigen because of insufficient priming, functional inadequacy of the T cell antigen receptor (TcR), or lack of TcR expression. Since MTI also requires signals provided by mediators, e.g. various interleukins [5], the defect could also be due to the cells' inability to produce or secrete mediators [6] or to an inadequate response to these signals.

Here we report on six patients in whom mitogen response was within the normal range, while their response to antigens was virtually absent. The first question we addressed was whether this defect could be due to a deficiency in antigen uptake or in antigen processing. We used ubiquitous antigens such as *Escherichia coli*, a particulate bacterial antigen, soluble antigens such as tetanus toxoid, or purified protein derivative (PPD) and the viral antigen FSME. After seven days of co-cultivation, T cells from healthy control individuals responded to the antigen presented by autologous macrophages with substantial proliferation, as determined by ^{3}H-thymidine incorporation (Fig. 1). Under the same conditions CVI patients' lymphocytes proliferated significantly less in response to antigenic stimulus. This deficiency could not be attributed to a shift in the peak of the response. Time kinetic studies over a period of three to 21 days revealed that the MTI of all CVI patients investigated remained depressed throughout co-cultivation (data not shown).

To assess antigen uptake and processing, monocyte monolayers were pulsed with ^{125}I-labelled antigen. After washing, the monocytes were gently scraped off

Progress in immune deficiency III, edited by H. M. Chapel, R. J. Levinsky and A. D. B. Webster, 1991; Royal Society of Medicine Services International Congress and Symposium Series No. 173, published by Royal Society of Medicine Services Limited.

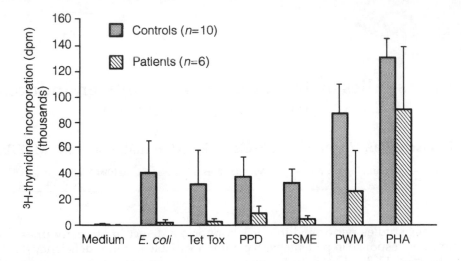

Figure 1   *T cell proliferation in response to mitogens and antigens.*

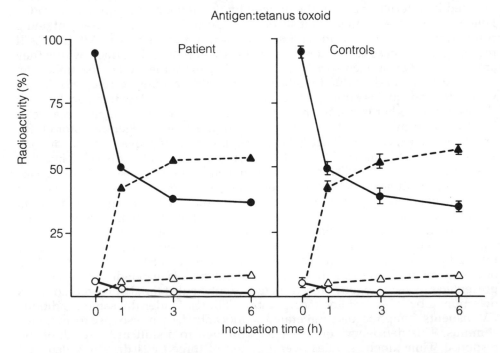

Figure 2   ●○ *Macrophage associated radioactivity* ▲ △ *Radioactivity released into the supernatant (closed symbols—TCA precipitable (10% TCA)) (open symbols—not TCA precipitable).*

with a rubber policeman, adjusted to the appropriate concentration, and incubated for the time indicated. On termination of the incubation period the supernatant was removed and the monocytes were lysed in 1% Triton X 100. Then radioactivity (precipitable and not precipitable with 10% TCA) was measured in the supernatant of the monocyte lysate. Processing and uptake were comparable in patients and controls (Fig. 2).

Table 1 *Antigen uptake and processing in monocyte monolayers*

Type of antigen added	Proliferative response to	
	E. coli	Tet. tox
Undegraded antigen	41027 ± 23975	33001 ± 25280
Antigen degraded by the controls' APC	34690 ± 19889	23927 ± 7485
Antigen degraded by the patients' APC	26048 ± 6745	28194 ± 4029
No antigen added; medium control	831 ± 103	

Monocyte monolayers from patients and controls were pulsed for 3 h with the antigen indicated and then washed thoroughly to remove antigen. After 24 h, the supernatant containing degraded antigen was removed and added to cultures containing T cells and monocytes of the controls.

Furthermore, stimulation of proliferation by antigen degraded by the patients' APC was similar to that degraded by control APC (Table 1), further indicating that antigen uptake and processing were intact.

These results suggest that the inability to mount an antigen-specific response is most likely due to a defect in T cell activation. IL-2 production was significantly lower in patients' lymphocytes than in control lymphocytes. However, when external rIL-2 was added to the patients' cultures, the expression of the IL-2 receptor and other activation markers was comparable in patients and controls (manuscript submitted).

On the basis of our investigations we conclude that the defective response to antigen observed in these patients was due to impaired production of IL-2 when T cells were activated by antigen, while IL-2 production was normal upon stimulation by mitogen.

REFERENCES

(1) Eibl MM, Mannhalter JW, Zielinksi CC, Ahmad R. Defective macrophage-T-cell interaction in common varied immunodeficiency. *Clin Immunol Immunopathol* 1982; **22**: 316–22.
(2) Eibl MM, Mannhalter JW, Zlabinger G, et al. Defective macrophage function in a patient with common variable immunodeficiency. *N Engl J Med* 1982; **307**: 803–6.
(3) Lanzavecchia A. Receptor-mediated antigen uptake and its effect on antigen presentation to class II-restricted T lymphocytes. *Ann Rev Immunol* 1990; **8**: 773–93.
(4) Harding CV, Leyva-Cobian F, Unanue ER. Mechanisms of antigen processing. *Immunol Rev* 1988; **106**: 77–92.
(5) Ullman KS, Northrop JP, Verweij CL, Crabtree GR. Transmission of signals from the T lymphocyte antigen receptor to the genes responsible for cell proliferation and immune function: the missing link. *Ann Rev Immunol* 1990; **8**: 421–52.
(6) Weinberg K, Parkman R. Severe combined immunodeficiency due to a specific defect in the production of interleukin-2. *N Engl J Med* 1990; **322**: 1718–23.

Defective T cells in common variable immunodeficiency

M. E. North, A. D. B. Webster and J. Farrant

Immunodeficiency Diseases Research Group, Clinical Research Centre, Harrow, UK

INTRODUCTION

T cells from a minority of common variable immunodeficiency patients (CVI) have depressed DNA synthesis to mitogens (e.g. PHA) or to stimulation by OKT3 through the T cell receptor (TCR). By contrast, IL-2-induced DNA synthesis (via IL-2R) is normal [1,2].

Is the defect in the TCR itself or in activation pathways? Transmembrane signalling through the TCR involves tyrosine protein kinase [3], protein kinase C (PKC) and calcium mobilization [4]. We therefore decided to by-pass the TCR by activating PKC (with phorbol dibutyrate) and mobilizing calcium (with ionomycin) to try to overcome the defect in DNA synthesis.

We also investigated the induction of T cell activation antigens *in vitro* and measured the serum levels of shed surface T cell receptors (IL-2R and CD8) in CVI patients and normal individuals. X-linked agammaglobulinaemia (XLA) patients acted as disease controls.

MATERIALS AND METHODS

Peripheral blood (40 ml) was taken from nine CVI patients and eight normal individuals. Blood was defibrinated and the mononuclear cells separated on Ficoll-Paque. T cells were then obtained by rosetting with neuraminidase-treated sheep red blood cells. Sera were collected from 40 CVI patients, seven XLA patients and 18 normal individuals. Sera was separated from clotted blood and stored at $-70°C$ until assayed.

Cultures were done in round-bottomed NUNC tissue culture plates (50 μl/well) with 0.2×10^6 cells/well (three replicates) in Iscove's serum free medium. The stimuli used were PHA (Wellcome) 1 μg/ml, ionomycin (free acid, Calbiochem) 15.6–1000 ng/ml and phorbol 12–13 dibutyrate (PdBu:Calbiochem) 0.4 and 4 ng/ml.

DNA synthesis was measured on day 3 by the uptake of ^{3}H-TdR [1] and activation antigens assessed by flow cytometry. Soluble CD25 and CD8 was measured using ELISA kits (T Cell Sciences Inc).

Progress in immune deficiency III, edited by H. M. Chapel, R. J. Levinsky and A. D. B. Webster, 1991; Royal Society of Medicine Services International Congress and Symposium Series No. 173, published by Royal Society of Medicine Services Limited.

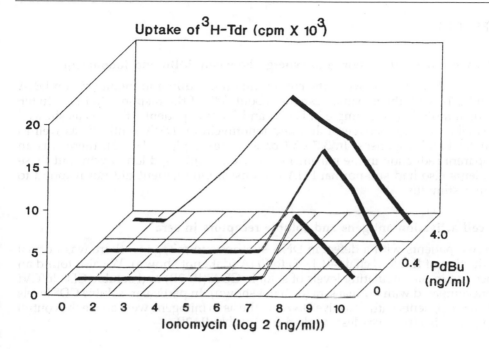

Figure 1 *Uptake of ³H-thymidine (cpm) into DNA in response to combinations of the calcium ionophore (ionomycin) and the phorbol ester (phorbol dibutyrate) by T cells from a typical normal donor.*

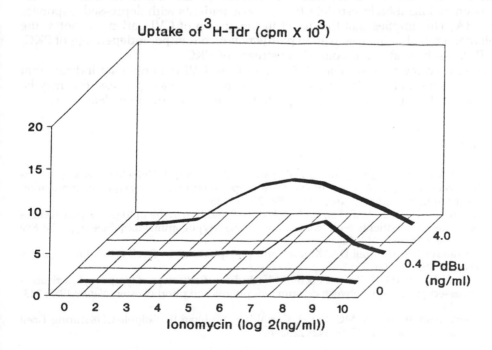

Figure 2 *Uptake of ³H-thymidine (cpm) into DNA in response to combinations of ionomycin and phorbol dibutyrate by T cells from a CVI patient with depressed responses to PHA.*

RESULTS

DNA synthesis in response to synergy between PdBu and ionomycin

We found synergy between the concentration of PdBu and ionomycin on DNA synthesis, with the maximal response about 70% of the response to PHA. In 6/6 normal individuals (example in Fig. 1) and 3/7 CVI patients, the T cells showed a similar synergy between PdBu and ionomycin on DNA synthesis as well as similar PHA responses. In 3/7 CVI patients (example in Fig. 2), there was an apparent reduction in the maximal response to PdBu and ionomycin, but these patients also had sub-normal PHA responses. One patient did not respond to either stimulus.

T cell activation antigens and soluble receptors in sera

In two patients with a defect in DNA synthesis to mitogens, there was normal induction of IL-2R (β chain—CD25) to PHA (data not shown). We also found an increase in the circulating levels of soluble CD25(IL-2R) and soluble CD8 in CVI sera compared with normal sera (data not shown). In particular, soluble CD8 levels in all the patients with defective DNA synthesis to mitogens were above the control range. This effect was less marked for soluble IL-2R.

DISCUSSION AND CONCLUSIONS

The data indicate that DNA synthesis induced by direct activation of PKC and calcium mobilization is also defective in those patients with depressed responses to PHA. This implies that the defect in this group of CVI patients is not at the cell membrane but in an activation pathway which is either independent of PKC, in PKC itself or at some point downstream of PKC.

The raised levels of soluble CD8 in sera from CVI patients may indicate that the CD8 subset of T cells is activated as part of the disease process; this may be similar to the situation recently reported in infectious mononucleosis [5].

REFERENCES

(1) North ME, Spickett, GP, Allsop J, Webster ADB, Farrant J. Defective DNA synthesis by T cells in acquired 'common–variable' hypogrammaglobulinaemia on stimulation with mitogens. *Clin Exp Immunol* 1989; **76**: 19–23.
(2) North ME, Webster ADB, Farrant J. Role of IL-2 and IL-6 in the mitogen responsiveness of T cells from patients with 'common–variable' hypogammaglobulinaemia. *Clin Exp Immunol* 1990; **81**: 412–16.
(3) Alexander DR, Cantrell DA. Kinases and phosphatases in T cell activation. *Immunol Today* 1989; **10**: 200–5.
(4) Truneh A, Albert F, Golstein P, Schmitt-Verhulst A. Early steps of lymphocyte activation bypassed by synergy between calcium ionophores and phorbol ester. *Nature* 1985; **313**: 318–20.
(5) Tomkinson BE, Brown MC, Ip SH, Carrabis S, Sullivan JL. Soluble CD8 during T cell activation. *J Immunol* 1989; **142**: 2230–6.

B cell defects in groups of patients with common variable immunodeficiency

J. Farrant, A. Franz, A. Bryant, D. Copas and A. D. B. Webster

Immunodeficiency Diseases Research Group, Clinical Research Centre, Harrow, UK

INTRODUCTION

Patients with common variable immunodeficiency (CVI) can be classified into subgroups by the secretion of IgM and IgG by their B cells *in vitro* [1–3]. In these various studies, the B cells were stimulated by 'membrane-dependent' stimuli (e.g. *Staphylococcus aureus* Cowan I (SAC) or anti-IgM with IL-2). We have now attempted to induce Ig secretion by CVI B cells by activating calcium-dependent protein kinase C (PKC) directly, using phorbol ester and ionomycin. Recent work with normal tonsil B cells by Flores-Romo *et al.* [4] shows that these stimuli induce proliferation, and when cytokines are added secretion of immunoglobulin also occurs.

MATERIALS AND METHODS

Samples of peripheral blood (40 ml) were taken from CVI patients receiving gammaglobulin therapy and from normal individuals. Tonsils from 'normal' subjects and spleens from three CVI patients were obtained after removal for therapeutic reasons. Non-T cell preparations enriched for B cells were obtained (after defibrination of blood samples) by depletion of red cells (Ficoll Paque) of macrophages (adherence), of low density accessory cells (Metrizamide) and of T cells by rosetting (using n-SRBC) [3]. With tonsil non-T cells, Percoll was used to obtain a high density preparation.

Cultures of 40000 non-T cells per well were set up in 20 μl hanging drop Terasaki plate cultures in RPMI 1640 medium with 10% FCS [3]. Stimuli used were: phorbol dibutyrate (PdBu, 1 ng/ml) with ionomycin (0.8 μg/ml) for three days, washing the cells, then adding cytokines, IL-2 (Biogen, 200 U/ml) or IL-4 (Genzyme, 100 U/ml) or IL-6 (Dr Kishimoto, Osaka, 100 U/ml). Anti-IgM on beads (Biorad) was used at 1 μg/ml.

Immunoglobulin secretion after seven days was measured by ELISA as previously described [3].

Progress in immune deficiency III, edited by H. M. Chapel, R. J. Levinsky and A. D. B. Webster, 1991; Royal Society of Medicine Services International Congress and Symposium Series No. 173, published by Royal Society of Medicine Services Limited.

RESULTS

Patient classification by B cell defects

More than 60 patients with common variable immunodeficiency have now been sub-classified by secretion of IgM and IgG *in vitro* in response to anti-IgM and IL-2. The following groups have been identified: Group A (with cells unable to secrete IgM or IgG), Group B (able to secrete IgM but not IgG) and Group C (with both IgM and IgG secreted). The findings are consistent on repeat testing, with no evidence of movement between groups.

B cell activation pathways leading to Ig secretion

With normal non-T cell preparations from peripheral blood or tonsil, or with the high density fraction of B cells from tonsil, IgM secretion in response to anti-IgM and IL-2 was markedly higher when compared to activation of PKC by PdBu and ionomycin for three days followed by IL-2 (Fig. 1a). Cells from CVI patients which were able to secrete IgM (Groups B and C) secreted less IgM with PdBu/ionomycin/IL-2 (Fig 1b). Neither stimulus induced IgM secretion from a Group A patient (Fig. 1b).

A similar pattern was seen with IgG secretion. The stimulus PdBu/ionomycin/IL-2 failed to induce IgG secretion in both Group A and Group B patients.

In general, PdBu/ionomycin reduced the unstimulated background secretion of IgM or IgG (data not shown). Subsequent addition of IL-4 or IL-6 instead of IL-2 had negligible or small effects (data not shown). Use of cell–cell contact co-signals mimicked by growing B cells on soluble CD4-coated or anti-HLA class II-coated plates also failed to induce significant Ig secretion.

Splenic B cells

In three patients, splenic B cell responses were compared with those of blood B cells on the same occasion (data not shown). In two patients, some IgM was secreted by the blood cells with anti-IgM and IL-2, but none in the other patient. However, with all three patients the splenic B cells secreted appreciable amounts of IgM. Neither the blood nor splenic B cells were able to secrete IgG in any of the patients.

DISCUSSION AND CONCLUSIONS

CVI is a complex disease of B cell differentiation, with subgroups of patients distinguished by the ability of their B cells to secrete IgM or IgG in response to crosslinking the surface receptor with anti-IgM in the presence of IL-2. Bypassing the membrane with phorbol dibutyrate and ionomycin (activating PKC), with or without the cytokines IL-2, IL-4 or IL-6, is not able to overcome the block in secretion of immunoglobulin. This suggests that the location of the block involves activation pathways independent of PKC and/or downstream of PKC. It is interesting that we have found a similar conclusion for the defect in the mitogen-induced DNA synthesis in T cells present in some CVI patients.

It appears that the CVI splenic B cell may be intrinsically different from the circulating cell, even when isolated in culture, in being able to secrete IgM.

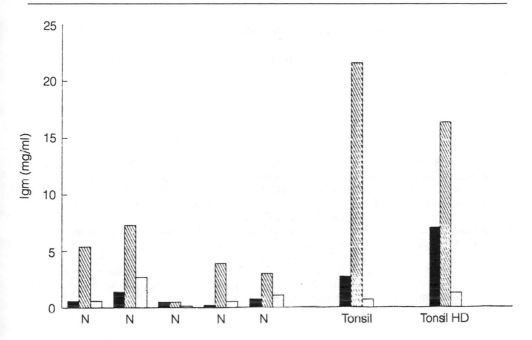

Figure 1a *IgM secretion by peripheral blood B cells from five normal donors (N) and from a normal tonsil (both a non-T preparation and a Percoll-separated high density (HD) preparation). Stimuli used were background (■), anti-IgM (1 µg/ml) with IL-2 (200 U/ml) (▨), or PdBu (1 ng/ml) and ionomycin (0.8 µg/ml) for three days before washing the cells and adding IL-2 (200 U/ml) (□).*

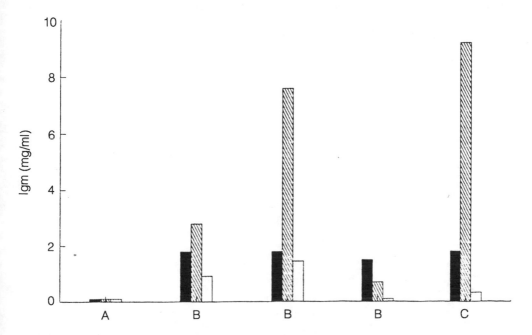

Figure 1b *IgM secretion by peripheral blood B cells from five CVI patients (one in group A, three in group B and one in group C). The stimuli used were as above.*

However, IgG secretion could not be induced in either cell type from Group A and B patients.

Each sub-group of patients described here may represent a different specific block in cellular differentiation. Further study of the cellular activation pathways in each group is planned.

REFERENCES

(1) Saiki O, Ralph P, Cunningham-Rundles C, Good RA. Three distinct stages of B-cell defects in common varied immunodeficiency. *Proc Natl Acad Sci USA* 1982; **79**: 6008–12.
(2) Ariga T, Okano M, Takahashi Y, Sakiyama Y, Matsumoto S. Analysis of B cell dysfunction in patients with common variable immunodeficiency by using recombinant interleukin 2. *Tohoku J Exp Med* 1987; **152**: 53–61.
(3) Bryant A, Calver NC, Toubi E, Webster ADB, Farrant J. Classification of patients with common variable immonodeficiency by B cell secretion of IgM and IgG in response to anti-IgM and interleukin-2. *Clin Immunol Immunopathol* 1990; **56**: 239–48.
(4) Flores-Romo L, Millsum MJ, Gillis S, Stubbs P, Sykes C, Gordon J. Immunoglobulin isotype production by cycling human B lymphocytes in response to recombinant cytokines and anti-IgM. *Immunology* 1990; **69**: 342–7.

Possible role of IL-2 deficiency for hypogammaglobulinaemia in common variable immunodeficiency (CVI) patients

J. A. Rump[1], M. Schlesier[1], W. Brugger[2], R Dräger[1], I. Melchers[3], R. Andreesen[2] and H. H. Peter[1]

[1]Department of Rheumatology and Clinical Immunology,
[2]Department of Haematology and Oncology,
[3]Clinical Research Group for Rheumatology, Medical Centre,
University of Freiburg, Freiburg iB, Germany

(POSTER)

CVI patients are unable to produce specific immunoglobulins (Ig) after antigen contact. This failure may be caused by intrinsic B cell defects, ineffective cell–cell interaction, abnormal cytokine production or increased suppressor cell activity. The aim of this study was to investigate if, in some cases of CVI, a decreased IL-2 or IL-6 *de novo* synthesis might be the cause for immunodeficiency and if this deficiency can be corrected by supplementation *in vitro*.

Mononuclear cells from the peripheral blood (PBL) (1.5×10^5 per assay) from 10 CVI patients and from six healthy controls were cultured with OKT3 (10 ng/ml), pokeweed mitogen (PWM) (0.08%) and tetanus toxoid (TT) (20 μg/ml) to stimulate IL-2 synthesis, and with *Straphylococcus aureus* Cowan I (SAC) (0.00004%) to stimulate IL-6 secretion. Cumulative IL-2 concentrations were measured in the supernatants after 0, 20, 40 and 70 h by means of an IL-2-dependent mouse cytotoxic T lymphoid line. Cumulative IL-6 concentrations were measured in the supernatants after six days by means of the IL-6-dependent B9 cell line (kindly provided by Dr L. Aarden). In addition, *in vitro* IgG and IgM synthesis was stimulated during a culture period of nine days with SAC, PWM and TT in the presence or absence of IL-2.

Eight out of 10 patients were able to synthesize normal amounts of IL-2 after OKT3 stimulation, so that the ability to synthesize IL-2 is in principle intact in these patients. Nevertheless seven of 10 patients tested were not able to synthesize normal amounts of IL-2 after stimulation with PWM, which is similar to natural antigens since six of 10 patients tested show no IL-2-production after TT-stimulation. IL-6 synthesis was normal after SAC stimulation and peaked after 72 h in culture, so that an impaired IL-6 production is not the underlying defect. Interestingly four patients could be reconstituted for TT induced IgG and IgM synthesis *in vitro*, by adding IL-2 to the culture system. After SAC stimulation five patients showed *in vitro* a normal IgM synthesis and seven patients a normal IgG synthesis when assays were supplemented with 20 U IL-2/ml.

We suppose that the defective IL2-synthesis after antigen-stimulation might be the reason for defective immunoglobulin-production in some cases of CVI. Eight patients have been enrolled for one year in a randomized, placebo controlled IL-2 therapy study for one year, in which 250 000 U n-IL-2 will be given two-weekly subcutaneously.

We conclude from this initial study:

1. IL-2 production after *in vitro* stimulation with pokeweed mitogen (PWM) or tetanus toxoid (TT) is significantly reduced or negative in most patients with CVI.
2. IgG and IgM production after *in vitro* stimulation with PWM, and with TT is reduced or negative in most CVI patients.
3. The *in vitro* immunoglobulin synthesis could be increased by IL-2 substitution in seven out of 10 CVI-patients.

Progress in immune deficiency III, edited by H. M. Chapel, R. J. Levinsky and A. D. B. Webster, 1991; *Royal Society of Medicine Services International Congress and Symposium Series No. 173, published by Royal Society of Medicine Services Limited.*

Defective *in vitro* production of interferon-γ in a patient with repeated infections and unclassified immunodeficiency

R. Dopfer, R. Handgretinger, G. Bruchelt and D. Niethammer

Department of Haematology and Oncology, Children's University Hospital, Ruemelinstr. 23, 7400 Tübingen, Germany

(POSTER)

INTRODUCTION

The role of abnormal lymphokine production in immunological disorders has been described in several patients suffering from different immunodeficiencies like severe combined immune deficiency and T-cell defects. The defect of interferon production is a rare disease and has been described only in some patients with severe or persistent virus and bacterial infections or polyclonal immunoblastic proliferation [1,6,8,9,10]. This may lead to a profound impairment of host defence against micro-organisms. Immunological investigations in our patient, suffering from recurrent bacterial and viral infection, revealed a defect in interferon-γ production. The influence of this finding on host defence and results of other immunological investigations will be discussed.

CASE REPORT

The patient, now sixteen years of age, was first seen in our outpatient department for multiple warts at the age of four years. Local treatment failed and then the boy was treated with interferon-β and interferon-α for several weeks. During that time he developed recurrent bacterial and viral infections, as summarized in Table 1. He had normal IgG, IgA and IgG subclass levels with a low IgM and an increased IgE. Initiation of immunoglobulin substitution with 7S-immunoglobulin every four weeks was started five years later and the frequency of bacterial infections decreased.

One elder brother also suffers from multiple warts and immunological investigations in the department of dermatology showed defective interferon-γ production (personal communication G. Fierbek).

Table 1 *Infective episodes in the patient*

1978	Multiple warts: hands, legs, perioral. Endogenous eczema
1983	Interferon-β and subsequently interferon-α treatment without effect. Pneumonia
1984	Pneumonia twice
1985	Mumps
1986	Haemophilus B meningitis followed by TP 1 treatment for six months
1989	Pneumococcal meningitis and immunoglobulin therapy started every four weeks. Epididymitis.

Since 1978 recurrent infections of the upper respiratory tract, bacterial skin infections and repeated paronychia of toes and fingers

Progress in immune deficiency III, edited by H. M. Chapel, R. J. Levinsky and A. D. B. Webster, 1991; Royal Society of Medicine Services International Congress and Symposium Series No. 173, published by Royal Society of Medicine Services Limited.

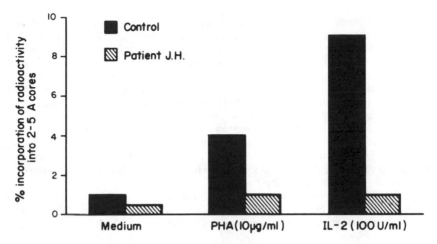

Figure 1   *2-5-A synthetase activity of PMNCs after incubation with PHA and IL-2 for 72 h.*

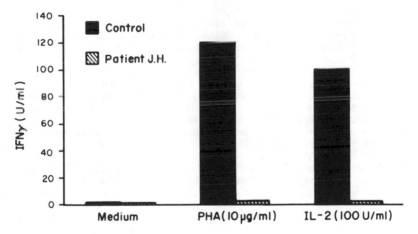

Figure 2   *Secretion of IFN-γ after incubation of PMNCs with PHA and IL-2 for 72 h. IFNγ was measured in the supernatants with an IRMA (Centocor).*

RESULTS

2-5-A-synthetase activity after stimulation with PHA or interleukin-2 is shown in Fig. 1. Compared with the control there is a significantly diminished activity. The synthetase, however, can be activated normally by interferon-β or interferon-γ (data not shown). Interferon production after stimulation with PHA or interleukin-2 is shown in Fig. 2. The mononuclear cells of the patient did not secrete interferon-γ after stimulation with PHA and interleukin-2 *in vitro*. Mitogen proliferation, however, was normal. Phenotyping of the mononuclear cells revealed slightly diminished T cells (CD3=49%) and elevated B cell numbers (CD19=38%). Only 22% of mononuclear cells were CD4 positive and 24% were CD8 positive. NK cells, as measured by CD56 were normal (10%).

DISCUSSION

Selective defects of interferon-γ production have been observed in only few patients with severe or persistent viral and bacterial infections or polyclonal immmunoblastic proliferation

[1,6,8,9,10]. The defect of interferon-γ production may result in defective NK-activity, lymphokine secretion, macrophage activation and HLA-expression [2–5,7]. This imbalance in the lymphokine network can be thought to be responsible for both the defective antiviral and antibacterial state of the patient. In our patient there is no persisting viral or bacterial infection and the defect of interferon-γ production is thought not to be the result of, but the reason for, the recurrent infections. The bacterial infections in our patient decreased after treatment with 7S-immunoglobulin every four weeks, despite the fact that the patient had normal IgG levels and normal specific antibodies against several viruses. Nevertheless, the patient is not free of recurrent viral infections of the upper respiratory tract and recurrent bacterial infections mainly of the skin and adjacent organs. The multiple warts of the hands, face and the skin are not influenced by the treatment. The patient has in addition endogenous eczema with elevation of the serum IgE level which may explain the fact that the warts are disseminated over the body.

Treatment with interferon-α and interferon-β had no effect on the warts as well as on the recurrent infections of the upper respiratory tract and the skin. DNA and RNA investigations are in progress and treatment with interferon-γ will be initiated in the patient.

REFERENCES

(1) Aiuti F, Paganelli R, Le Moli S, et al. Defects of interleukins in immunodeficiencies. In: Griscelli C, Vossen J, eds. Progress in immunodeficiency research and therapy. Amsterdam: Elsevier, 1984: 261–66.
(2) Farrar WL, Johnson HM, Farrar JJ. Regulation of the production of immune interferon and cytotoxic T lymphocytes by interleukin 2. J Immunol 1981; 126: 1120–5.
(3) Kasahara T, Hooks JJ, Dougherty SF, Oppenheim JJ. Interleukin 2-mediated immune interferon (IFN-gamma) production by human T cells and T cell subsets. J Immunol 1983; 130: 1784–9.
(4) Oppenheim JJ, Gery I. Interleukin 1 is more than an interleukin. Immunol Today 1982; 3: 113–19.
(5) Robb RJ, Munck A, Smith KA. T cell growth factor receptors. Quantitation, specificity, and biological relevance. J Exp Med 1981; 154: 1455–74.
(6) Virelizier JL, Arenzana-Seisdedos F. Role of abnormal lymphokine production in immunological disorders. In: Griscelli C, Vossen J, eds. Progress in immunodeficiency research and therapy. Amsterdam Elsevier: 1984: 271–8.
(7) Virelizier JL, Perez N, Arenzana-Seisdedos F, Devos R. Pure interferon gamma enhances class II HLA antigens on human monocyte cell lines. Eur J Immunol 1984; 14: 106–8.
(8) Virelizier JL. Les déficits de production d'interféron chez l'enfant. Presse Med 1984; 13: 495–8.
(9) Virelizier JL, Lenoir G, Griscelli C. Persistent Epstein-Barr virus infection in a child with hypergammaglobulinaemia and immunoblastic proliferation associated with a selective defect in immune interferon secretion. Lancet 1978; ii: 231–4.
(10) Virelizier JL, Griscelli C. Défaut sélectif de sécrétion d'interféron associté à un déficit d'activité cytotoxique naturelle. Arch Fr Pediatr 1981; 38: 77–81.

Analysis of T cell activation in a patient with common variable immunodeficiency

S. Vukmanović[1], S. Vučković[2] and M. Abinun[3]

[1]Institute of Microbiology and Immunology, Belgrade University School of Medicine,
[2]Department of Haematology, University Clinical Centre, and [3]Mother and Child Health Institute,
Belgrade, Yugoslavia

(POSTER)

The activation of normal peripheral T cells in response to stimulation with T cell receptor (TCR) ligands requires the presence of accessory cell-derived factors which have been identified as IL-1 and IL-6 acting synergistically [1]. Activation induces expression of IL-2 receptor on T cells and secretion of IL-2 by a proportion of T cells (mainly CD4[+]) [2,3]. The binding of IL-2 to the IL-2 receptor enables activated T cells to proliferate [4]. In some patients suffering from common variable immunodeficiency (CVI) T lymphocytes are not able to proliferate *in vitro* in response to TCR ligands. We have studied T cell activation after stimulation with mitogenic lectins in one such patient. The failure of CVI T cells to proliferate cannot be ascribed to a defect in accessory cell-derived factors as plastic adherent mononuclear cells produced IL-1 and IL-6 when stimulated with LPS, while addition of recombinant IL-1 and IL-6 could not induce proliferation of PHA stimulated mononuclear cells from a CVI patient. The inability of CVI T cells to proliferate is due to a defect in IL-2 production rather than to the defect in induction of IL-2 responsiveness since no IL-2 activity was found in supernatants of mononuclear cells stimulated with mitogenic lectins. However exogenously added IL-2 could induce proliferation of CVI T cells stimulated with mitogenic lectins. The failure of CVI T cells to secrete IL-2 is not due to the general defect in transcription or translation of the IL-2 gene as stimulation with phorbol esters and cation ionophores resulted in secretion of IL-2 and proliferation of mononuclear cells. The failure of mitogenic lectins to induce IL-2 secretion is probably due to a maturational defect in CD4[+] cells. ~50% of CD4[+] cells co-expressed the CD8 molecule, therefore resembling thymic CD4[+]CD8[+] T cells. The lower frequency of cells bearing the CD4 molecule (15%) and their immature phenotype suggest a possible defect of thymic maturation in this patient.

REFERENCES

(1) Vink A, Uyttenhove C, Wauters P, Van Snick J. Accessory factors involved in murine T cell activation. Distinct roles of interleukin 6, interleukin 1 and tumour necrosis factor. *Eur J Immunol* 1990; **20**: 1.
(2) Efrat S, Pilo S, Kaempfer R. Control of biologically active IL-2 mRNA formation in induced human lymphocytes. *Proc Natl Acad Sci USA* 1984; **82**: 2601.
(3) Grabstein K, Dower S, Gillis S, Urdal D, Larsen AD. Expression of IL-2, interferon γ, and the IL-2 receptor by human blood lymphocytes. *J Immunol* 1986; **136**: 4503.
(4) Meuer SR, Hussey RE, Cantrell DA *et al.* Triggering of the T3/Ti antigen receptor complex results in clonal T cell proliferation through an interleukin 2 dependent autocrine pathway. *Proc Natl Acad Sci USA* 1984; **81**: 1509.

Progress in immune deficiency III, edited by H. M. Chapel, R. J. Levinsky and A. D. B. Webster, 1991; Royal Society of Medicine Services International Congress and Symposium Series No. 173, published by Royal Society of Medicine Services Limited.

Analysis of lymphocyte populations in common variable immunodeficiency by flow cytometry

G. P. Spickett[1], A. D. B. Webster[2], J. Farrant[2] and H. M. Chapel[1]

[1]Department of Immunology, John Radcliffe Hospital, Oxford, and
[2]Division of Immunological Medicine, Clinical Research Centre, Harrow, UK

We have previously shown that there are three distinct populations of patients with common variable immunodeficiency (CVI), based on the response to *in vitro* stimulation of B lymphocytes from patients with anti-surface IgM+IL-2 [1]. It is also clear that defects are also found in T lymphocytes and antigen-presenting cells [reviewed in 2]. We have used an extended panel of monoclonal antibodies directly conjugated to fluorochromes to study mononuclear cells from a large group of patients in order to investigate the following questions: i) are the T and B cell phenotypes normal; ii) are activation markers expressed normally; iii) can any changes so identified be related to clinical or functional status?

Patients attending the clinics at Northwick Park Hospital and the John Radcliffe Hospital were studied. Normal controls were recruited from laboratory staff at the two institutions. A total of 40 CVI (including one patient with a thymoma and two IgG subclass deficiencies) and 20 normals were studied. Flow cytometry was performed using a lysed whole blood method. Appropriate control pairs of antibodies were used and absolute lymphocyte counts were determined.

Six patients (15%), including the patient with the thymoma, were found to lack B cells (<1% CD19+ cells) but absence of B cells did not correlate with disease severity. For those patients with B cells, the percentage distribution was similar to the normal population. Two patients had raised B cell numbers: one subsequently developed a clonal proliferation of CD5+/CD19+ cells, compatible with chronic lymphatic leukaemia. Four patients lacked the DQ antigen recognized by the antibody Leu-10, compared to only one normal control. Since Leu-10 is absent from cells expressing DQw2, which is associated with DR3 and DR7, this may indicate a disease link to MHC antigens in some patients (see Hammerström, p. 23 in this volume). There was a trend towards reduced numbers of B cells expressing the activation marker, CD23 and the EBV-receptor, CD21. However, we have not identified any patients completely lacking the CD21 antigen. We confirm previous reports that some patients have substantial reductions in Leu-8 positive B cells. Failure to express Leu 8 may prevent appropriate recirculation of lymphocytes and contribute to the immune deficit.

The T cell phenotype is markedly abnormal. Four patients have been identified with markedly reduced CD4+ T cells and two patients with markedly reduced CD8+ T cells; there is, however, very wide variation in the expression of these

Progress in immune deficiency III, edited by H. M. Chapel, R. J. Levinsky and A. D. B. Webster, 1991; Royal Society of Medicine Services International Congress and Symposium Series No. 173, published by Royal Society of Medicine Services Limited.

markers. Similarly, within the CD4$^+$ subset, there is a marked deviation in the percentage of cells expressing the CD45RO and CD45RA antigens (identifying memory and virgin T cells respectively) compared with the normal controls. Two patients have been identified with a preponderance of CD45RO$^+$CD4$^+$ T cells: both were female. One of the patients has disease characterized by marked hepatosplenomegaly and uveitis, while the other patient, who has mild antibody deficiency, presented with a localized aspergilloma of the thigh, and now has an uncharacterized interstitial lung infiltrate; her B cells are CD19$^+$/Leu-10$^-$. No differences in the expression of CD25 (Il-2R) or DR on patient T cells compared with normal cells were found, although there was a wide range of expression for both groups. An inversion of the normal proportions of CD4$^+$ and CD8$^+$ cells was seen in one of the IgG subclass-deficient patients, but the other patients had entirely normal cell markers.

REFERENCES

(1) Bryant A, Calver NC, Toubi E, Webster ADB, Farrant J. Classification of patients with common variable immunodeficiency by B cell secretion of IgM and IgG in response to anti-IgM and interleukin-2. *Clin Immunol Immunopathol* 1990; **56**: 239–48.
(2) Spickett GP, Webster ADB, Farrant J. Cellular abnormalities in Common Variable Immunodeficiency. *Immunodef Rev* 1990, in press.

Phenotypic heterogeneity of B and T lymphocytes in common variable immunodeficiency (CVI)

E. Scala, M. Fiorilli and R. Paganelli

Department of Allergy and Clinical Immunology, University 'La Sapienza', Rome, Italy

(POSTER)

We have studied the expression of T and B subset markers in a group of patients with CVI ($n=31$) attending our Day Hospital and receiving maintenance treatment with intravenous immunoglobulin infusions. The age range of the cases was 15 to 63 yrs, and M:F ratio was 1.2. Age from diagnosis was 1 to 17 yrs, and duration of treatment was a median of 4.5 yrs.

Blood samples were collected in EDTA prior to infusion, and 100 μl aliquots incubated on ice for 30 min with the following mAbs and appropriate controls, FITC or PE-conjugated: Leu4, anti-HLA-DR, Leu2a, Leu3a (Becton Dickinson); 2H4, 4B4, B1, B4 (Coulter); OKT4, OKB7 (Ortho); δ-TCS1, TCRδ1 (T cell sciences); CD23 (Immunotech). After lysis, cells were fixed in 2% formaldehyde and read on a dual parameter fluorescence analyser (Cytoron) with acquisition of 5000 gated lymphocytes.

B lymphocytes ranged from 1 to 21% (median 7.1%), as detected by CD3$^-$ DR$^+$ and CD20$^+$ cells. In two cases CD19$^+$ cells exceeded this level, perhaps due to circulating immature B lymphocytes. CD23$^+$ cells were severely reduced in 13/20 cases (0.5% or less of all lymphocytes). T lymphocytes were present in normal or increased percentage in all patients. The ratio of TCR1 to TCR2 expression was normal in 10 cases studied, however the TCR1 subset recognized by δ-TCS1 was increased two-fold compared with controls. This situation resembles that found in HIV-positive patients. Five of 18 CVI had >5% of T cells also expressing HLA-DR (activated T), despite the absence of infection or other symptoms at the time of the study. The ratio of CD4/CD8 lymphocytes was reduced, with 10/22 patients showing a ratio <1. The mean percentage of CD4$^+$ cells was 31 in this subgroup, and the relative decrease of CD4$^+$ was due selectively to the reduction of the CD45RA$^+$ subset (virgin T). The mutually exclusive CD29$^+$ subset (memory T) was detected in a normal proportion for age; therefore their relative distribution was imbalanced in 10/22 cases.

Our findings illustrate the heterogeneity of immune dysregulation in patients with CVI. B cells are present in normal percentages but they seem to be either immature or blocked in their development (perhaps due to defective expression of maturation receptors). T subset imbalances may underlie B cell inability to differentiate into Ig-producing cells. However CD4$^+$/CD29$^+$ (memory and helper cells) are normally present in CVI.

Progress in immune deficiency III, edited by H. M. Chapel, R. J. Levinsky and A. D. B. Webster, 1991; Royal Society of Medicine Services International Congress and Symposium Series No. 173, published by Royal Society of Medicine Services Limited.

Immunological parameters and clinical aspects in patients with common variable immunodeficiency

C. Diener, G. Metzner and L. Jäger

Institute of Clinical Immunology, Friedrich-Schiller-Universität, Jena, Germany

(POSTER)

Common variable immunodeficiency (CVI) is characterized by a deficiency of antibody synthesis resulting in low serum immunoglobulin levels. Additionally, disturbances of T cell populations and T cell functions have been reported in CVI patients [1,2]. This was established by means of immunophenotyping of T lymphocytes and functional assays. We were able to confirm these data in 31 patients suffering from CVI [3].

This study compares the efficacy of intravenous immunoglobulin (IVIg) replacement therapy and the immunological parameters in a group of 19 patients with CVI.

The immunoglobulin levels were severely diminished in all patients entering the study. The patients were on IVIg therapy for at least one year. According to the clinical symptoms the patients were divided into two groups. Group A consisted of 13 patients with only minor infections, without pneumonia or other severe infections. The six patients in group B were characterized by severe infections and pneumonias. The IVIg therapy was administered at three-weekly intervals. All patients received 10 g Endobulin (Immuno). No adverse reactions during the administration of Endobulin were seen.

The immunological parameters were estimated as follows. Mononuclear cells from peripheral blood were separated by density centrifugation. Surface marker studies were performed using monoclonal antibodies to CD3, CD4, CD8, CD16 and CD20 antigens. The results were expressed as relative counts of labelled cells by means of immuno-fluorescent staining. Mononuclear cells were stimulated in vitro with PHA and the proliferation was measured. Immunoglobulin trough levels were estimated serially and the median concentration was determined.

We have seen no significant differences between the groups in the total number of lymphocytes, CD3-positive cells and IgG trough levels. The data for CD4 and CD8-positive cells are shown in Table 1. Both groups are characterized by diminished CD4 counts and decreased CD4/CD8 ratios. However, we could not demonstrate a strong correlation between these immunological parameters and the clinical course of the disease. It must be emphasized that the lymphocytes of three out of six patients with ineffective replacement therapy failed to respond after PHA stimulation. CVI patients with impaired T effector

Table 1 Relative percentages of CD4 and CD8 positive peripheral blood mononuclear cells and CD4/CD8 ratio in two groups of patients with CVI

		Group A	Group B
CD4	Range	13–62	10–49
	Median	35	26
CD8	Range	16–66	26–73
	Median	35	55
CD4/CD8	Range	0.3–3.9	0.1–1.9
	Median	1.1	0.5

Progress in immune deficiency III, edited by H. M. Chapel, R. J. Levinsky and A. D. B. Webster, 1991; Royal Society of Medicine Services International Congress and Symposium Series No. 173, published by Royal Society of Medicine Services Limited.

functions are prone to serious complications in the course of the disease and such patients are susceptible to various virus infections in addition to bacterial complications.

REFERENCES

(1) Ichikawa Y, Gonzales EB, Daniels JC. Suppressor cells of mitogen-induced lymphocyte proliferation in the peripheral blood of patients with common variable hypogammaglobulinemia. *Clin Immunol Immunpathol* 1982; **25**: 252–63.
(2) Pandolfi F, Quinti I, Frielingsdorf A, Goldstein G, Businco L, Aiuti F. Abnormalities of regulatory T-cell subpopulations in patients with primary immunoglobulin deficiencies. *Clin Immunol Immunpathol* 1982; **22**: 222–30.
(3) Metzner G, Enke B, Diener C, Jäger L. Clinical and immunological aspects in patients with agammaglobulinemia *Z ges Inn Med* 1989; **44**: 687–91.

Occurrence and persistence of autoantibodies in predominantly antibody defects

G. Fontán, R. Alvarez Doforno, M. C. García Rodríguez, A. Ferreira and M. López Trascasa

Immunology Unit, Hospital La Paz, 28046 Madrid, Spain

(POSTER)

Primary immunodeficiency diseases are frequently associated with autoimmune disorders and positive tests for autoantibodies (Aab). The most frequent autoimmune diseases in these patients affect the blood cells, but a high incidence of other autoimmune diseases has also been recorded. Aab against a variety of self-antigens is a frequent finding in healthy individuals, and in a few cases precedes the appearance of the autoimmune disease.

As primary immunodeficient patients are prone to the development of autoimmune disorders, we have studied in 71 cases of predominantly antibody defects (46 males, 25 females), during a four-year follow-up, the occurrence and persistence of 14 Aab (none of them directed against blood cells), as well as the development of related autoimmune disorders. The Aab tested every six months were those directed against: ANA, ENA, dsDNA, rheumatoid factor, IgA, cytoskeleton, smooth muscle, gastric parietal cells, reticulin, mitochondria, liver–kidney microsomes, cardiolipin, thyroglobulin and thyroid microsomes. Forty-seven of the patients presented 78 Aab, detected in most cases in a single determination. The occurrence of Aab was: 28.5% in X-linked agammaglobulinaemia ($n=14$); 83% in hyper IgM syndrome ($n=8$); 66% in IgG2 deficiency ($n=9$); 90% in IgA deficiency ($n=21$) and 57.8% in common variable immunodeficiency ($n=19$). In total 66.2% of the patients presented at least one Aab during the follow-up (58.6% of the males and 80% of the females). The most frequent Aab found were against: cardiolipin (26.8% of the patients), IgA (23.9%) and thyroid microsomes (18.3%). Occurrence of Aab was similar in the different age groups. Those patients with chronic infection did not have a higher incidence of Aab. The Aab percentage was higher in patients with normal B lymphocyte numbers (81%) than in those with B lymphocyte numbers <3% (22%). Nine patients (two males and seven females) presented the same Aab throughout follow-up. Only one of them presented a possible autoimmune disorder (IgA anaphylaxis). The persistent Aab were directed against: IgA ($n=4$), cytoskeleton ($n=3$) and thyroid microsomes ($n=2$).

We conclude that Aab are a frequent phenomenon in predominantly antibody defects, especially in those that retain some antibody production. Most of the Aab are transient and the vast majority of those persistent are not related to actual autoimmune disease, at least during the four-year period studied.

Progress in immune deficiency III, edited by H. M. Chapel, R. J. Levinsky and A. D. B. Webster, 1991; Royal Society of Medicine Services International Congress and Symposium Series No. 173, published by Royal Society of Medicine Services Limited.

Kappa/lambda light chain ratio in immunoglobulins G, A, and M in some immunological disorders

A. Haraldsson, J. A. J. M. Bakkeren, G. B. A. Stoelinga and C. M. R. Weemaes

Department of Pediatrics, University of Nijmegen, Nijmegen, The Netherlands

(POSTER)

Immunoglobulin kappa (x) and lambda (λ) light chains have been studied on various occasions. The normal $x:\lambda$ ratio has been described earlier and some deviation from the normal pattern has been found in various diseases, miscellaneous infections and in some immunological disorders [1,2]. It has been pointed out that certain antigen determinants produce an antibody response primarily in either x- or λ-bearing immunoglobulins [3]. Apparently, the immune system can produce relatively more x- or λ-bearing immunoglobulins depending on different stimulation.

By using the ELISA-sandwich method we are able to measure the $x:\lambda$ light chain ratio separately in immunoglobulins G, A and M. The method has been standardized and reference values have been established for different age-groups [2]. We studied patients developing agammaglobulinaemia but who still retained some immunoglobulins and patients with dysgammaglobulinaemia.

Agammaglobulinaemia Serum samples from four patients developing late onset agammaglobulinaemia but still having some immunoglobulins were studied before start of therapy. All the patients showed deviation from our reference values of IgG, IgA and IgM as well as total $x:\lambda$ ratio. Apparently regulation of production of the light chains is disturbed as well as that of the heavy chains.

IgA deficiency Patients with IgA deficiency showed neither abnormalities in IgG or IgM $x:\lambda$ ratio, nor in total $x:\lambda$ ratio. A few of the patients demonstrated trace amounts of IgA in serum as measured with the ELISA. In these, the IgA $x:\lambda$ ratio was high.

Hyper IgE syndrome Four patients with hyper IgE syndrome had normal total and IgG $x:\lambda$ ratio. Two of these patients had a high IgA $x:\lambda$ ratio and low IgM $x:\lambda$ ratio. One patient had a low IgA $x:\lambda$ ratio.

Hyper IgD syndrome Various minimal abnormalities were found in patients with the hyper IgD syndrome.

Measuring the $x:\lambda$ ratios separately in IgG, IgA and IgM may provide a means of understanding better the function of the immunoglobulin light chains in health and disease.

REFERENCES

(1) Renckens ALJL, Jansen MJH, van Munster PJJ, Weemaes CMR, Bakkeren JAJM. Nephelometry of the kappa/lambda light chain ratio in serum of normal and diseased children. *Clin Chem* 1986; **32:** 2147–9.
(2) Haraldsson A, Kock-Jansen MJH, Jaminon M, Eck-Arts PBJM, Weemaes CMR, Bakkeren JAJM. Determination of kappa and lambda light chains in serum immunoglobulins G, A and M (submitted).
(3) Heilman C, Barington T. Distribution of x and λ light chain isotypes among human blood immunoglobulin-secreting cells after vaccination with pneumococcal polysaccharides. *Scand J Immunol* 1989; **29:** 159–64.

Progress in immune deficiency III, edited by H. M. Chapel, R. J. Levinsky and A. D. B. Webster, 1991; Royal Society of Medicine Services International Congress and Symposium Series No. 173, published by Royal Society of Medicine Services Limited.

Low immunoglobulin levels in infants with recurrent infections. Transient hypogammaglobulinaemia of infancy?

A. Kondyle, E. Vrachnou, M. Kanariou, N. Constantinidou
and K. Mandalenaki-Lambrou

Department of Immunology and Histocompatibility,
Saint Sophie's Children's Hospital, Athens, Greece

(POSTER)

This study included 41 infants, 26 boys and 15 girls, aged three to 12 months, who were hospitalized with recurrent infections. The infants presented low IgG or low IgG and IgA levels, 1–2 SD below the mean value for their age.

To clarify further the underlying immunological defect we studied their cellular immunity to confirm whether the increased susceptibility to infections was due only to hypogammaglobulinaemia and/or to possible defects of their cellular immunity. Thirteen out of the total 41 infants were examined again one or two years later for the same parameters.

Twenty-three age-matched healthy children with documented normal immunoglobulin levels, served as controls. Serum levels of IgG, IgA and IgM were determined by nephelometry. T cells (CD2, CD3), T cell subsets (CD4, CD8), B cells (CD20) and natural killer (NK) cells (CD16) were estimated in peripheral blood mononuclear cells by monoclonal antibodies and indirect immunofluorescence.

The infants were divided into two groups according to their age. Group A included 22 infants aged three to six months and group B included 19 infants, aged seven to 12 months. Two out of 22 infants in group A had such severe recurrent infections that we decided to treat with intravenous immunoglobulin (IVIg). Three out of the same group had treatment with immunoglobulin intramuscularly (IMIg). From group B one infant was given IVIg and eight were administered IMIg.

Both groups of infants in this study had normal percentages of circulating B and T cells. Decreased numbers of NK cells (CD16) were found in group A (aged three to six months) and decreased numbers of CD4 cells in group B (aged seven to 12 months).

The re-estimation of the same parameters performed one to two years later for 13 infants showed improvement in IgG levels. The percentages of CD4 and CD16 cells were in the normal range for the age, although there were no statistically significant differences between the two measurements. The children were in good physical condition without frequent or recurrent infections for the last six months.

We suppose that infants with recurrent infections and low (not below 2 SD) immunoglobulin levels might have transient hypogammaglobulinaemia.

Progress in immune deficiency III, edited by H. M. Chapel, R. J. Levinsky and A. D. B. Webster, 1991; Royal Society of Medicine Services International Congress and Symposium Series No. 173, published by Royal Society of Medicine Services Limited.

Treatment of chronic hepatitis B infection with murine monoclonal anti-HBs in patients with hypogammaglobulinaemia

M. R. Jacyna[1], J. Waters, A. M. L. Lever, A. D. B. Webster[2] and H. C. Thomas

[1]Department of Medicine, St. Mary's Hospital, and [2]Northwick Park Hospital, Watford Road, Harrow

(POSTER)

Chronic hepatitis B virus (HBV) infection is a major cause of morbidity and mortality in man. The hepatic inflammation seen in patients with this infection is not directly caused by the virus, but is believed to be mediated by cellular mechanisms. Patients with hypogammaglobulinaemia usually have normal cell-mediated immunity and their hepatitis may be severe, possibly due to a combination of failure to make specific antibodies and active cellular immunity.

Although antiviral trials using α-interferon have shown some advantage in a small minority of treated patients, no other therapy is of proven benefit. However, monoclonal antibodies directed at HBV antigens theoretically offer an attractive option for treatment, particularly in hypogammaglobulinaemic individuals who do not produce antibodies to heterologous proteins and thus can be treated repeatedly with animal-derived monoclonal antibodies. Two patients with hypogammaglobulinaemia, chronic HBV infection and chronic active hepatitis were treated with a murine monoclonal antibody specific for HBsAg. The anti-HBs antibody (RF-HBs-1) was obtained by fusion of mouse spleen cells from an animal vaccinated against HBsAg, with a mouse myeloma cell line in the presence of polyethylene glycol. The resulting fusion cell lines were cloned by limiting dilution and an anti-HBs clone was isolated and grown in mycoplasma free cell lines or mouse ascites. The RF-HBs-1 produced was purified on an HBsAg/cyanogen bromide 'Sepharose' affinity column. Monthly infusions of 0.6 mg of this antibody were given to the two patients.

A rapid loss of markers of viral replication (HBV-DNA) was noted in both patients during therapy, and by three months both patients had notable clinical and biochemical improvement and loss of HBeAg, which is usually considered the end-point of successful anti-viral therapy. In one patient, recurrence of disease and HBeAg were noted one year after the completion of therapy, but three further doses of RF-HBs-1 resulted in a further rapid serological and biochemical remission. A repeat liver biopsy in this patient at this time showed disappearance of the chronic inflammation noted at the time of a first biopsy prior to therapy. No side-effects were encountered by the patients. This small study has indicated that murine monoclonal anti-HBs may be a useful therapeutic option for chronic hepatitis B virus carriers with hypogammaglobulinaemia.

Progress in immune deficiency III, edited by H. M. Chapel, R. J. Levinsky and A. D. B. Webster, 1991; Royal Society of Medicine Services International Congress and Symposium Series No. 173, published by Royal Society of Medicine Services Limited.

Total IgE in immunodeficiencies

M. L. Palma-Carlos, M. C. Santos and A. G Palma-Carlos

Institute of Immunology, Faculty of Medicine, INIC, Lisbon, Portugal

Total serum IgE is usually increased in allergic atopic diseases, parasitosis, IgE myeloma and the immunodeficiency associated with the hyper IgE syndrome. An increase of total IgE has been reported also in some cases of IgA deficiency. However the incidence of IgE increase in immunodeficiencies, other than the hyper IgE syndrome is not well known.

We have studied the level of total IgE in a group of immunodeficiencies, 52 primary, four acquired, classified according to the last report of WHO working group [1].

MATERIALS AND METHODS

Total IgE has been evaluated by an immunoenzymatic method (PRIST–Phadezym, Pharmacia, Uppsala, Sweden). Immunodeficiencies have been studied by current methods comprising clinical history, multipuncture tests with seven antigens for cellular immunity (Multitest, IMC, Mérieux, France), assay of immunoglobulins and complement by radial immunodiffusion, study of peripheral blood cell populations with monoclonal antibodies for CD2, CD4, CD8, CD19, CD22, CD25, HLA-DR. Immunoglobulin values have been related to normal values for age and sex. The study of allergic diseases has been done by clinical history, skin prick tests for allergens and assays for specific IgE by RAST-Phadezym.

RESULTS

Twenty-seven deficiencies of IgA, 12 common variable immunodeficiencies, eight deficiencies of C1 inhibitor, one deficiency of C4, two cases of chronic mucocutaneous candidiasis, three of AIDS-related complex and one acquired deficiency of C-inhibitor have been studied. An increase of total IgE related to age has been observed in 24 patients without parasitic infection. From these 24 patients, 20 were atopic as shown by clinical data, skin prick tests to a large range of inhalants and food allergens and results of specific IgE assay by RAST Phadezym. The atopic patients were 13 children (eight males, five females) and seven adults (five males, two females). The remaining four non-atopic patients with increased serum total IgE were two common variable immunodeficiencies (one male child and one male adult) and two deficiencies of IgA (one male child and one male adult).

DISCUSSION

These results suggest that apart from the hyper IgE syndrome which was not observed in this series, an increase in total IgE not related to atopy could be seen in some patients with common variable immunodeficiency or IgA deficiency, even in the absence of allergic diseases, positive skin tests or positive assay for specific IgE to common inhalants or food allergens. In this group, an increase in total IgE has been found only in male patients, two children and two adults. Atopy is much more common in boys than in girls, usually in a 2 : 1 ratio. The organic factors contributing to the larger incidence of allergic diseases

Progress in immune deficiency III, edited by H. M. Chapel, R. J. Levinsky and A. D. B. Webster, 1991; *Royal Society of Medicine Services International Congress and Symposium Series No. 173*, published by Royal Society of Medicine Services Limited.

in male children could also probably explain the appearance of an increased IgE only in male patients in this group. A prospective study to find hidden allergy or future allergic disease in immunodeficient patients without atopy may clarify the relationship between allergy and immunodeficiency.

REFERENCE

(1) Scientific Group on Immunodeficiency of the World Health Organisation. Primary immunodeficiency diseases. *Immunodef Rev* 1989; **1**: 173–205.

HTLV-I infection and common variable immunodeficiency

M. A. Barbosa, M. Cortez, A. Parreira, L. Parreira, M. L. Palma-Carlos
and A. G. Palma-Carlos

Institute of Immunology, Department of Medicine III, CHIUL, INIC,
Lisbon School of Medicine, Portugal

(POSTER)

We report the case of a 31-year-old Caucasian woman, who was born and lived in Brazil, working as an anthropologist. She moved to Portugal in November 1988, and was admitted to Lisbon University Hospital in December 1989 with fever, nausea, vomiting and abdominal pain.

CASE REPORT

Since 20 years of age she has had multiple respiratory infections, vulval candidiasis and in 1984, *Pneumocystis carinii* pneumonia which was successfully treated in Brazil. Primary immunodeficiency was diagnosed at that time. In October, 1989, she was admitted to hospital in Brazil with abdominal pain, nausea and vomiting and a diagnosis of oedematous pancreatitis was made. From October to December 1989 she lost 10 kg in weight. A variable pattern of CD4, CD8, lymphocyte subpopulations was found in sequential blood analysis. IgG and IgA levels were either normal or decreased, in serial blood samples. Delayed hypersensitivity skin tests with multitest (IMC) were negative. At that time, HIV-1, HIV-2 and HTLV-1 tests were all negative. A diagnosis of common variable immunodeficiency (CVI) was confirmed [1,2]. The patient was admitted to our department on December 7th 1989, with fever, nausea, vomiting and abdominal pain; no diarrhoea or constipation were present. There was no history of tobacco smoking or intravenous drugs. She was heterosexual, with no promiscuous sexual activity. Family history was considered not relevant.

Physical examination showed a thin patient, slightly pale, with no jaundice. The temperature was 37.5°C; blood pressure 110/80 mmHg; pulse 82 per min; respiratory rate 18. The lungs and heart were normal. Liver was felt 3 cm below the costal margin and splenomegaly [2 cm] was present on abdominal examination. There was no lymphadenopathy and pelvic and neurological examinations were normal. Urine was normal. The white-cell count was $34 \times 10^3/\mu l$, with 71% of abnormal lymphocytes; IgG: 1230 mg/dl; IgA: 167 mg/dl; IgM: 336 mg/dl; multitest IMC was negative (score 0/0). Antibody tests to HIV-1 and HIV-2 were negative but antibodies to HTLV-1 were detected. Bone marrow examination showed hypercellularity of all series and 25% of lymphoid cells had a lobulated appearance.

The study of lymphocyte subpopulations [3] revealed CD4+, CD25+ lymphocytes with a mature appearance; the monoclonal nature of this T cell population was demonstrated by southern blot analysis of TCR rearrangements [4–6].

X-Ray of the skull and hands showed multiple, widespread osteolytic bone lesions. The abdominal CT scan showed hepatomegaly and splenomegaly, with no lymphadenopathy.

A definite diagnosis of adult T-cell leukaemia/lymphoma (ATL) was made. Presumably the longstanding immunodeficiency was associated with a chronic form of ATL which evolved to an acute form [7–9].

Progress in immune deficiency III, edited by H. M. Chapel, R. J. Levinsky and A. D. B. Webster, 1991; *Royal Society of Medicine Services International Congress and Symposium Series No. 173*, published by Royal Society of Medicine Services Limited.

REFERENCES

(1) Palma-Carlos AG. Imunodeficiencies primárias. In: Palma-Carlos AG, Palma-Carlos ML, eds. *Manual de imunologia*, vol. 2. Lisboa: Cilag, 1989: 87–106.
(2) Scientific Group on Immunodeficiency (WHO). Primary immunodeficiency disease. *Immunodef Rev* 1989; **1**: 173–205.
(3) Parreira A, Pombo de Oliveira MS, Matutes E, Foroni L, Morilla R, Catovsky D. Terminal deoxynucleotydil transferase positive acute myeloid leukaemia: an association with immature myeloblastic leukaemia. *Br J Haematol* 1988; **69**: 219–24.
(4) Flanagan JG, Rabbitts TH. The sequence of a human immunoglobulin epsilon heavy chain constant region gene, and evidence for three non-allelic genes. *EMBO J* 1982; **1**: 655–60.
(5) Foroni L, Foldi J, Matutes E, *et al*. α, β and τ T-cell receptor genes: rearrangements correlate with haematological phenotype in T cell leukaemias, *Br J Haematol* 1987; **67**: 317–9.
(6) Sims JE, Tunacliffe A, Smith WJ, Rabbitts TH. Complexity of human T-cell antigen receptor β-chain constant and variable region genes. *Nature* 1984; **312**: 541–5.
(7) Yamaguchi K, Kiyokawa T, Nakada K, *et al*. Polyclonal integration of HTLV-1 proviral DNA in lymphocytes from HTLV-1 seropositive individuals: an intermediate state between the healthy carrier state and smouldering ATL. *Br J Haematol* 1988; **68**: 169–74.
(8) Yamaguchi K, Seiki M, Yoshida M, Nishimura H, Kawano F, Takatsuki K. The detection of human T cell leukaemia virus proviral DNA and its application for the classification and diagnosis of T cell malignancy. *Blood* 1984; **63**: 1235–40.
(9) Rosenblatt JD, Chen IS, Wachsman W. Infection with HTLV-I and HTLV-II: evolving concepts. *Sem Haematol* 1988; **25**: 230–46.

Mapping of the X-linked agammaglobulinaemia locus

M. A. J. O'Reilly[1], S. Malcolm[2], R. J. Levinsky[1] and C. Kinnon[1]

[1]Departments of Immunology and [2]Genetics, Institute of Child Health, London, UK

(POSTER)

The molecular bases for the X-linked immunodeficiency diseases remain largely undetermined. We are currently attempting to identify and isolate the gene responsible for causing one of these diseases, namely X-linked agammaglobulinaemia (XLA). The gene responsible for causing this defect maps to the long arm of the X chromosome, to Xq22.

XLA is characterized by agammaglobulinaemia involving all immunoglobulin subclasses and is the direct result of a lack of mature B cells. Pre-B cells are present at normal levels in the bone marrow and the presumed defect is thought to involve a block in their differentiation. Other lymphocyte populations appear to be unaffected.

We have made substantial progress in our quest to identify the gene responsible for causing XLA through the use of genetic and physical mapping techniques. Genetic linkage analysis has revealed an overall consensus order of loci which map to this region to be; DXS3—(DXS178, 'XLA')—DXS94—DXS17, where no recombinations have been found between the XLA locus and the DXS178 locus. We have now extended this genetic map into a long-range physical map of the region using the technique of pulsed field gel electrophoresis (PFGE), incorporating both polymorphic and non-polymorphic probes.

So far, we have mapped a total of about 5mb of DNA on non-overlapping *Mlu*I fragments using 10 probes. We estimate that the Xq22 region containing the XLA locus spans about 10–12 mb of genomic DNA on the basis of high resolution cytogenetic analysis. This has allowed us to construct a preliminary map of the locus which shows that DXS83, DXS54, DXS24 and PLP, are linked on *Mlu*I fragments spanning about 1.7 mb of DNA and DXS94; DXS147, DXS87 and DXS17 are on a single *Mlu*I fragment of about 2.7 mb.

We have been unable to incorporate DXS178 into this map since by this analysis it appears to be flanked by two putative CG islands which give smaller sized fragments of DNA, of the order of 100-300 kb, on digestion with a number of rare-cutting restriction enzymes. We are currently attempting to clone these regions of DNA with the hope of generating gene probes which would be good candidates for the gene which is defective in XLA.

Progress in immune deficiency III, edited by H. M. Chapel, R. J. Levinsky and A. D. B. Webster, 1991; Royal Society of Medicine Services International Congress and Symposium Series No. 173, published by Royal Society of Medicine Services Limited.

Chronic echovirus meningoencephalitis in X-linked agammaglobulinaemia

S. A. Misbah[1], J. Hockaday[2], J. B. Kurtz[3], E. R. Moxon[2] and H. M. Chapel[1]

[1]Departments of Immunology, [2]Paediatrics and [3]Virology, John Radcliffe Hospital, Oxford, UK

(POSTER)

Chronic enteroviral meningo-encephalitis (CEMA), particularly with echoviruses, is a well-recognized complication in patients with X-linked agammaglobulinaemia (XLA) [1]. Hitherto virtually all published reports have referred to its occurrence in patients on intramuscular immunoglobulin (Ig) or on no Ig replacement. We report the development of CEMA in an 11-year-old boy on regular IVIg replacement whose serum IgG levels were maintained between 6–8 g/l.

CASE REPORT

KL, a Caucasian male child born in 1978 to unrelated patients had XLA diagnosed in 1982 (serum IgG 0.1 g/l, IgA 0.1 g/l, IgM < 0.1 g/l; absent circulating B cells) just after the death of his brother from meningitis. Regular IMIg was commenced and two years later he was converted to regular IVIg. Apart from an occasional ear or chest infection he remained well and grew normally. Behavioural problems were noted at school towards the end of 1989 and in January 1990 he was hospitalized elsewhere with acute lymphocytic meningitis of unknown aetiology; CSF-sterile; stools and throat washings—no virus isolated. He was treated empirically with IV acyclovir and after a slow initial recovery, he deteriorated steadily over a period of two months.

In May 1990, he had progressive apathy, headache, drowsiness and a shuffling gait. His serum IgG at this time was 10 g/l. On clinical examination he had a stiff neck, mild dementia, bilateral optic atrophy and a combination of pyramidal and extra-pyramidal deficits in the limbs. A cranial CT scan showed communicating hydrocephalus with mild dilatation of the entire ventricular system.

In view of ventricular dilatation and a probable diagnosis of CEMA, a CSF reservoir was inserted for sampling. Ventricular CSF analysis showed a lymphocytic pleocytosis with raised protein levels (protein 1.9 g/l, lymphocytes 146, polymorphs 4, red blood cells 8,320). A profuse growth of echovirus, type 11, was noted in CSF after 48 h culture; no virus was isolated from throat swabs, urine and stools and a muscle biopsy was normal.

Treatment with daily IVIg (2.5 g to 7.5 g) containing a 1:32 titre of neutralizing antibody against the patient's echovirus was commenced. No clinical improvement was noted until three weeks had elapsed when the serum IgG had risen to 17.5 g/l and the CSF IgG 0.3 g/l (normal CSF IgG ⩽ 0.08 g/l). Six weeks after commencement of high dose IVIg (peak serum IgG 39.8 g/l, CSF IgG 0.4 g/l) the patient was alert, had no neck stiffness, showed objective improvement on neuropsychometric tests and had flexor plantar responses. Viral growth however remained unimpeded. A progressive fall in CSF albumin levels (from 2.3 g/l to 1.2 g/l) accompanied the clinical improvement and suggested a reduction in the permeability of the blood-brain barrier. This implied that any further rise in CSF IgG was unlikely to be achieved by the venous route.

Intraventricular Ig [IVent Ig] was therefore commenced (two five-day courses of 50–150 mg, 150–250 mg respectively) but was unsuccessful in eradicating the virus, despite achieving peak CSF IgG levels of 0.9 to 1.0 g/l. No further clinical improvement was

Progress in immune deficiency III, edited by H. M. Chapel, R. J. Levinsky and A. D. B. Webster, 1991; Royal Society of Medicine Services International Congress and Symposium Series No. 173, published by Royal Society of Medicine Services Limited.

discernible during the intraventricular courses which were tolerated well. Colonization of the CSF reservoir with *Propionibacterium acnes* during the second course resulted in its removal. Simultaneous examination of both lumbar and ventricular CSF at this time demonstrated equal amounts of echovirus, 11 at both sites.

In view of the continued presence of live virus and plateauing of the clinical response, Ribavirin, a purine nucleoside analogue licensed for use in RSV infection and Lassa fever, was commenced at 11 weeks. Ribavirin has shown promising activity *in vitro* against entero-viruses [2] and crosses the blood-brain barrier after oral dosing [3]. Although Ribavirin has been well tolerated, viral growth has remained unchanged. High dose IVIg has been continued throughout (30 g/week) maintaining s.IgG levels at 28–35 g/l but examination of lumbar CSF four weeks later, by which stage adequate CSF levels of ribavirin would have been achieved, still showed live virus (>100 pfu's), in addition to a lymphocytic pleocytosis and raised protein levels. Towards the end of the six-week course of ribavirin there was a recurrence of his initial symptoms, i.e. headache, drowsiness, neck stiffness in association with inappropriate ADH secretion (SIADH).

DISCUSSION

The introduction of IVIg and its widespread acceptance as the ideal method of Ig replacement in patients with XLA was thought to have virtually eradicated CEMA. Our patient, who had achieved good maintenance levels of serum IgG with regular IVIg, nonetheless went on to develop CEMA. The virus in our patient has proved resistant to both high dose IVIg and two courses of IVent Ig containing high titres of specific neutralizing antibodies; both these modes of treatment have previously been reported to be successful in some patients with CEMA. Ribavirin, despite its promising *in vitro* activity against a range of RNA viruses including echovirus, has proved ineffective in eradicating the virus.

REFERENCES

(1) McKinney RE, Katz SL, Wilfert SM. Chronic enteroviral meningoencephalitis in agammaglobulinaemic patients. *Rev Infect Dis* 1987; 9: 334–56.
(2) Gilbert BE, Knight V. Biochemistry and clinical applications of Ribavirin. *Antimicrob Agents Chemother* 1986; 30: 201–5.
(3) Crumpacker C, Bubley G, Lucey D, *et al*. Ribavirin enters cerebro-spinal fluid. *Lancet* 1986; ii: 45–6.

Incidence of primary and acquired immunodeficiencies in an outpatient population

A. G. Palma-Carlos, M. L. Palma-Carlos

Institute of Immunology, INIC, Faculty of Medicine and Centre for Allergy and Clinical Immunology, Lisbon, Portugal

(POSTER)

Immunodeficiency diseases are probably more frequent than generally considered. Immunodeficiencies are sometimes associated with other immunological (e.g. allergy, auto-immunity) or non-immunological (e.g. cancer) diseases. The diagnosis of less severe forms of immunodeficiency is not always easy but it is possible if a systematic search is undertaken in clinical immunology departments. The occurrence of primary and acquired immunodeficiency diseases has been evaluated in 5100 outpatients at a clinical immunology centre (not AIDS oriented), consulted by patients with allergy and allergic-like diseases, repeated respiratory, digestive or cutaneous infections, collagenosis and autoimmune diseases.

MATERIAL AND METHODS

Five thousand one hundred outpatients aged from six months to 60 years, of both sexes, have been studied. Clinical history, skin prick tests for allergy, including inhalants and food allergens, intradermal tests with candida, tricophyton, streptococcus, *Escherichia coli*, *Staphylococcus aureus* and the multipuncture IMC Multitest for cellular *in vivo* responses were performed. Values for immunoglobulins G, A, M and complement fractions by radial immunodiffusion (RID) were always related to age and sex. Studies of lymphocyte sub-populations with monoclonal antibodies to CD2, CD4, CD8, CD19, CD22, CD25, HLA-DR and in some cases evaluation of phagocytosis, chemotaxis and free radical release have been performed. Immunodeficiency diseases have been classified according to WHO scientific group on immunodeficiencies [1].

RESULTS

Using the methods quoted, 57 (1.12% of total population) immunodeficiency diseases have been detected, 53 primary and four acquired. Primary immunodeficiencies diagnosed in these series were 27 deficiencies of IgA (0.53%), (18 in children, nine in adults) deficiencies of IgG in two adults (one male, one female), 12 cases of common variable immunodeficiency (CVI) (0.24%) (five in children (two males, three females), seven in adults (four males, three females)), eight primary deficiencies of C1-inhibitor (0.16%) in three families, deficiency of C4 in one male child, chronic mucocutaneous candidiasis in two adults. The smaller group of acquired immunodeficiencies comprised three cases of AIDS-related complex (ARC) in HIV-1 positive bi- or homosexual atopic male adults and one case of acquired deficiency of C1-inhibitor in a patient with an IgM monoclonal gammapathy without clinical expression of Waldenström's macroglobulinaemia.

Progress in immune deficiency III, edited by H. M. Chapel, R. J. Levinsky and A. D. B. Webster, 1991; Royal Society of Medicine Services International Congress and Symposium Series No. 173, published by Royal Society of Medicine Services Limited.

DISCUSSION

The number of immunodeficiency diseases found in this group points to a significant incidence (1%) of immunodeficiencies in overall immunological disorders, including allergy. A systematic search of clinical and laboratory patterns of immunodeficiency in allergic and other immunological diseases could give a more realistic panorama of immunodeficiency than studies done only in infected patients.

REFERENCE

(1) Scientific Group on Immunodeficiency (WHO). Primary immunodeficiency diseases. *Immunodef Rev* 1989; **1**: 173–205.

Prevalence of primary hypogammaglobulinaemia in a well defined population in the UK

D. R. McCluskey and N. A. M. Boyd

Department of Immunology, Queen's University and Royal Victoria Hospital Belfast, N. Ireland

(POSTER)

Determining the prevalence of primary immunodeficiency disorders in a British population is difficult for a variety of reasons, including the absence of an immunodeficiency register (see Gooi, p. 103 in this volume), the fact that patients are managed by a variety of specialists in both adult and paediatric clinics, and population drift. The population of Northern Ireland has remained relatively constant at 1.5 million with very little population drift or immigration. All patients with hypogammaglobulinaemia receive replacement therapy through the Northern Ireland Blood Transfusion Service or attend the Regional Immunology Clinic at the Royal Victoria Hospital.

The aim of this study was to identify all patients in Northern Ireland who suffer from hypogammaglobulinaemia. The patients were reviewed at the Immunology Clinic where a detailed history and clinical examination was recorded. The prevalence of the various forms of this disorder was then determined.

RESULTS

There are 23 patients with primary hypogammaglobulinaemia in Northern Ireland. These may be classified according to aetiology. Congenital hypogammaglobulinaemia accounted for over 50% (11 X-linked, and one autosomal recessive). There were 11 patients with acquired hypogammaglobulinaemia (seven male; four female).

The clinical features of patients with X-linked and acquired hypogammaglobulinaemia are summarized in Table 1.

The prevalence of X-linked, autosomal recessive and acquired hypogammaglobulinaemia are 7, 0.6 and 7 per million total population respectively. These results are similar to those obtained in other studies by Fasth [1] and Hosking et al. [2]. Swedish figures [1] give 8 and 6 per million population and Australian [2] 10 and 12 per million population for X-linked and acquired hypogammaglobulinaemia respectively.

Table 1 *Comparison of features of X-linked and acquired hypogammaglobulinaemia*

	X-linked	Acquired
Mean age at onset of symptoms	12 months	28 years
Mean age at diagnosis	21 months	31 years
Common presenting symptoms	Recurrent ear, sinus chest infections and gastroenteritis	Recurrent ear, sinus and chest infections
Complications prior to treatment	Meningitis, poliomyelitis, osteomyelitis	Rheumatoid arthritis, thrombocytopenia, malabsorption
Complications on treatment	Liver cirrhosis	None

Progress in immune deficiency III, edited by H. M. Chapel, R. J. Levinsky and A. D. B. Webster, 1991; Royal Society of Medicine Services International Congress and Symposium Series No. 173, published by Royal Society of Medicine Services Limited.

Previous studies in the UK [3] and in Europe and North America [4] have reported that the X-linked disease is less common than the acquired. We have found the prevalence to be approximately equal.

At present 19 out of 23 patients with primary hypogammaglobulinaemia are on intravenous replacement therapy, two are on intramuscular replacement therapy and two are on no treatment. The mean IgG level for patients on intravenous therapy was 7.5 g/l. The mean IgG level for patients on intramuscular therapy was 4.5 g/l (normal 7–19 g/l). The patients' subjective assessments of their general health on a scale from 0–10 were as follows: those on intravenous therapy tended to feel healthier with values between 8–10 while those on intramuscular treatment scored values between 3–8.

REFERENCES

(1) Fasth A. Primary immunodeficiency disorders in Sweden: Cases among children, 1974–1979. *J Clin Immunol* 1982; **2**: 286–92.
(2) Hosking CS, Robertson DM. Epidemiology and treatment of hypogammaglobulinaemia. *Birth Defects* 1983; **19**: 223–7.
(3) Hypogammaglobulinaemia in the United Kingdom. Medical Research Council Special Report Series, 1971: 310.
(4) Lever AML, Webster ADB. Immunodeficiency in children and adults. *Med Int* 1984; **2**: 245–52.

Primary immunodeficiencies in Costa Rica. Report from a hospital-based Registry

O. Porras[1,2], O. Arguedas[1], A. Fasth[3], L. Gonzalez[2] and A. Abdelnour[1]

[1]Paediatric Immunology Unit, National Children's Hospital, San Jose, [2]INCIENSA (Institute for Research and Training in Health and Nutrition) Tres Rios, Costa Rica, and [3]Department of Paediatrics, Gothenburg University, Gothenburg, Sweden

(POSTER)

In 1985 the Costa Rica Immunodeficiency Registry was organized at the National Children's Hospital (NCH) in San Jose. The hospital is a paediatric national reference centre and primary immunodeficiency was diagnosed in children attending the recurrent infections clinic. The criteria proposed by a WHO scientific group [1] were used. Ninety-three cases of ID were registered up to July 1990. Predominantly antibody deficiencies were most common, 34 cases (36.6%). Combined deficiencies were diagnosed in six children (6.5%). Other well-defined immune deficiencies made up 28 cases (30.1%) and eight cases of other syndromes with associated immune deficiencies were also found. Phagocyte defects were diagnosed in 17 children (18.2%) and one child had a complement defect.

The immune-deficient children showed a 24.7% mortality and 4.3% developed malignancy. No autoimmune diseases were found except for an autoimmune haemolytic anaemia in one IgG2 deficient girl. The sex ratio was 1.3:1 (male:female). Ataxia telangiectasia (AT) constituted 25.8% of the total number. Two families with more than one AT child were registered. The incidence of severe combined immunodeficiency was 1.2/100 000 live newborns.

REFERENCE

(1) Scientific Group on Immunodeficiency of the World Health Organization. Primary Immunodeficiency Diseases. *Immunodef Rev* 1989; **1**: 173–205.

Progress in immune deficiency III, edited by H. M. Chapel, R. J. Levinsky and A. D. B. Webster, 1991; Royal Society of Medicine Services International Congress and Symposium Series No. 173, published by Royal Society of Medicine Services Limited.

Primary immunodeficiency register—United Kingdom

H. C. Gooi (for Immunology Travellers' Club, UK)

Yorkshire Regional Transfusion Centre and St James's University Hospital, Leeds, UK

(POSTER)

The prevalence of primary immunodeficiency diseases in the UK is not clearly established. The Medical Research Council Working Party on Hypogammaglobulinaemia estimated the life-time prevalence of hypogammaglobulinaemia to be 1 in 50 000 but indicated that the true prevalence was likely to be higher [1]. More recent statistics indicate wide regional variations in prevalence [2].

DATA COLLECTION AND ANALYSIS

Basic data submitted by colleagues who manage primary immunodeficiency patients were analysed according to diagnosis, age of onset and residence.

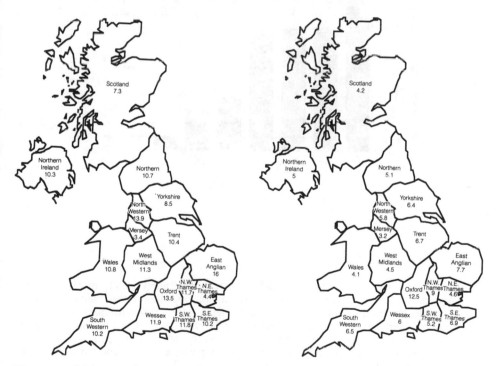

Figure 1 *Male prevalence rate of common variable immunodeficiency in different health regions of the United Kingdom 1990. (No. per million.)*

Figure 2 *Female prevalence rate of common variable immunodeficiency in different health regions of the United Kingdom 1990. (No. per million.)*

Progress in immune deficiency III, edited by H. M. Chapel, R. J. Levinsky and A. D. B. Webster, 1991; Royal Society of Medicine Services International Congress and Symposium Series No. 173, published by Royal Society of Medicine Services Limited.

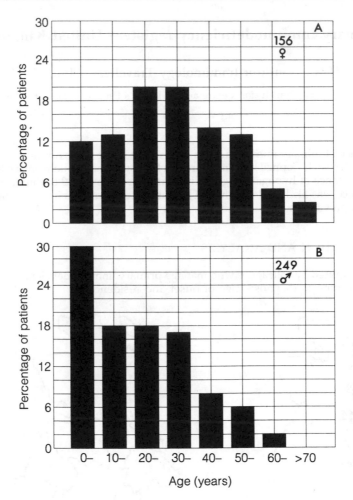

Figure 3 *Age distribution of patients with common variable immunodeficiency at diagnosis. Panel A females; Panel B males.*

RESULTS AND COMMENTS

1. The prevalence rate for common variable immunodeficiency (CVI) in the United Kingdom as ascertained so far in 1990 is 7.9 per million population, the male prevalence rate being 10 per million and the female prevalence rate 5.9 per million.
2. There are regional variations in the prevalence rate, ranging from 3.4 to 16 per million in the males (Fig. 1) and 3.2 to 12.5 per million in the females (Fig. 2).
3. CVI can present at any age and two-thirds of the patients are diagnosed before the age of 40 years (Fig. 3).
4. Eighteen per cent of humoral immunodeficiency is due to X-linked agammaglobulinaemia.
5. The above prevalence rates will underestimate the true prevalence as not all centres have yet submitted details of their patients.

ACKNOWLEDGMENT

I would like to thank all colleagues who submitted details of patients under their care; Fiona Aylott, Nicky Brennan and Sheila Cochrane for their help in the collection of the data; the Office of Population Censuses and Surveys for the population statistics; and Dr H. Chapel for her help and encouragement.

REFERENCES

(1) *Hypogammaglobulinaemia in the United Kingdom, MRC Working Party on Hypogammaglobulinaemia.* Medical Research Council Special Report Series No. 310, London: HMSO, 1971.
(2) Bird AG. Diagnosis of antibody deficiency states. In: Levinsky RJ, ed. *IgG subclass deficiencies.* Royal Society of Medicine Services International Congress and Symposium Series No. 143. London: Royal Society of Medicine Services, 1989: 3–12.

UK Register of patients on home intravenous immunoglobulin replacement therapy

V. M. Brennan, F. Aylott and H. Chapel

Department of Immunology, John Radcliffe Hospital, Oxford, UK

(POSTER)

In the UK there are a number of patients suffering from hypogammaglobulinaemia who require regular replacement therapy with intravenous immunoglobulin. A pilot study was set up in Oxford to train suitable patients to self-infuse intravenous immunoglobulin at home [1]. Thirty patients were followed for over four years to prove the safety, efficacy and compliance of self-infusing at home.

In 1986 a UK Register was set up in order to monitor the number of patients trained to self-infuse intravenous immunoglobulin at home. This register is held at the John Radcliffe Hospital in Oxford and provides useful information for hospitals wishing to set up self-infusion programmes. Guidelines for UK hospitals are also available.

The register shows that the predominant reason for patients wanting to self-infuse at home was the amount of time wasted travelling to and from the hospital or clinic, resulting in missing a day's work or, in the case of a child, missing schooling. There are 97 patients registered to the end of August 1990. Ninety-three patients have primary immune deficiency, 80 diagnosed as common variable and 13 with XLA. Two patients had hypogammaglobulinaemia secondary to chronic lymphocytic leukaemia [CLL]; one patient had immune deficiency associated with a thymoma and in one patient it was secondary to intestinal lymphangiectasia.

From the register it was noted that the duration of disease varied from one to 36 years, the average was five years. Thirty-four of the patients are female and 63 male, and their ages range from the youngest who was nine years at the time of training to the eldest of 67 years at the time of training. The register shows the varying occupations of the patients including schoolchildren, students, housewives, clerks, lecturers and some patients who are retired.

Of these 97 patients, 70 had previously received intramuscular immunoglobulin therapy; amongst these 70 patients, five were changed to intravenous therapy because of an adverse reaction to intramuscular immunoglobulin and 60 were changed in order to receive a higher dose of immunoglobulin. The register also shows that the actual time taken to train a patient to self-infuse varies considerably. It may take as short a time as five weeks or it may take as long as 36 weeks. This depends upon the method of training, and the ability and confidence of the patient. Some centres train the patient a little at each infusion, others have an extensive training course over two to three days. It is not necessarily the more intelligent who learn quicker, though older patients do take longer [1].

The UK Register shows the range of patients who can successfully infuse at home and that self-infusing intravenous immunoglobulin at home is efficacious for the patient.

After a patient has been assessed as suitable for home therapy, it is a UK legal requirement for all patients to attend a formal training course before commencing self-infusion at home.

REFERENCE

(1) Chapel HM, Brennan VM, Delson E. Immunoglobulin replacement therapy by self-infusion at home. *Clin Exp Immunol* 1988; **73**: 160–2.

Progress in immune deficiency III, edited by H. M. Chapel, R. J. Levinsky and A. D. B. Webster, 1991; Royal Society of Medicine Services International Congress and Symposium Series No. 173, published by Royal Society of Medicine Services Limited.

Cost-effectiveness analysis of IV immunoglobulin home treatment vs its hospital administration in Spain

J. Heras[1] and M. Rodriguez[2]

[1]Medical Department, Instituto de Hemoderivados Immuno SA, Barcelona, and [2]Faculty of Economics, University of Barcelona, Spain

(POSTER)

With the goal of developing a home treatment programme for hypogammaglobulinaemia in Spain, and starting from an analysis of current health practices, together with previous experience and similar precedents in our country, we have performed a prospective analysis to evaluate the cost-effectiveness of two alternatives of intravenous immunoglobulin therapy for hypogammaglobulinaemic patients: self-administration at home and hospital treatment.

The study is based on a poll taken from a sample of 38 patients or their family members, aged between four and 76 years (mean: 22 years) coming from 10 different hospitals (Table 1).

Table 1 *Characteristics of present form of treatment*

	Cases	Percentage
Circumstances of treatment		
Hospital admission	6	15.8
Day-care unit	14	36.8
Outpatient consulting	18	47.4
Frequency (weeks)		
2	3	7.9
3	27	71.1
4	8	21.1
Dosage (g) mean		13.71
Time of session (h) mean		3.17
Total time: commuting + session (h) mean		4.83
Patient school or working time loss (h) mean		2.84
Working time loss of companion (h) mean		1.89

Patients were asked about their personal and family characteristics, their health status, the characteristics of their present method of treatment and their attitudes towards self-administration at home (Table 2).

The propensity to change to home-treatment declines with the age of the patient or companion. A positive attitude towards home treatment coincides with a higher time loss of working companions. The health and stability of patients would enable 65% of them to change to home treatment. The final proportion of patients who would like to, and could, try such a method of treatment is 43%.

With respect to cost we have considered medicine, hospital stay, commuting for infusions, follow up, material, training and supervision as the direct costs, and the hours of working time lost for both the patients and the companions as the indirect cost. Home therapy is slightly less expensive, allowing a saving per patient of between 243.946 Ptas.* as minimum in the first year and 277.969 Ptas.* as maximum in successive years.

Progress in immune deficiency III, edited by H. M. Chapel, R. J. Levinsky and A. D. B. Webster, 1991; Royal Society of Medicine Services International Congress and Symposium Series No. 173, published by Royal Society of Medicine Services Limited.

Table 2 *Opinion about treatment alternatives*

	Cases	Percentage
Hospital treatment inconvenience		
Very much/A lot	10	34.2
A little/Not too much	15	65.8
The home treatment is:		
Much more/A little more convenient	24	64.9
Nearly the same	2	5.4
More inconvenient	11	29.7
Propensity to try home treatment		
Yes, now/Yes, in the future	25	67.5
No	12	32.5

Patients perceive this alternative as allowing more independence, less loss of school and working time and avoidance of frequent interaction in an unpleasant setting such as hospital. This last advantage is specially valued in the case of parents with young children. Only a third of the patients would still prefer a hospital, because it gives them more reassurance.

*Ptas. estimated in 1989

Delayed maturation of antigen-specific IgG3: Another variant of paediatric immunodeficiency?

D. Goldblatt[1,2], M. W. Turner[1] and R. J. Levinsky[1,2]

[1]Department of Immunology, Institute of Child Health, University of London and [2]The Hospital for Sick Children, Great Ormond Street, London, UK

INTRODUCTION

The description of healthy individuals with IgG subclass deficiencies [1] and the difficulty in correlating quantitative IgG subclass deficiencies with clinical syndromes [2] has increasingly led investigators to evaluate qualitative aspects of IgG subclass function. The age- and antigen-restricted nature of the IgG subclass response has been well described though the clinical significance is less certain [1,2]. In adults IgG1 and IgG3 are thought to be the subclasses produced in response to protein antigens while IgG2 has predominantly been associated with responses to carbohydrate antigens [3]. Nevertheless, a role for IgG1 in the anti-carbohydrate response of adults is now recognized [4]. The role of IgG4 is unclear although it appears to be an important part of the response to repeated stimulation with the same antigen [5]. In children the relative contribution of individual IgG subclasses are even less clear. While IgG1 is an important part of the antibody response to proteins it also appears to have an anti-carbohydrate role in younger children. This may be an important compensatory mechanism for the age-restricted IgG2 anti-carbohydrate response in children, particularly those under the age of two [6]. The inability to mount an isotype-appropriate IgG subclass response to carbohydrate antigens in childhood is thought to explain the susceptibility of young children to infection with encapsulated bacteria and limits the usefulness of vaccines containing unconjugated carbohydrate antigens in this age group. Much of the work on the antigen-restricted nature of the IgG subclass response has focused on carbohydrate antigens (T-independent antigens) and the IgG2 response and there is little information on the age-restricted nature of the anti-protein isotype response in childhood. The successful immunization of infants with tetanus and diphtheria toxoid, proteins which predominantly induce an IgG1 response, has suggested that antibody responses to protein antigens are not age-restricted.

We have previously described the recognition of the outer membrane proteins (OMP's) of a Gram-negative organism *Moraxella* (*Branhamella*) *catarrhalis* (*M. catarrhalis*) by serum antibody [7] and demonstrated the importance of IgG3 in OMP recognition. This organism is ubiquitous and lives in the moist mucous membranes of the nasopharynx. Previously thought to be a harmless commensal

Progress in immune deficiency III, edited by H. M. Chapel, R. J. Levinsky and A. D. B. Webster, 1991; Royal Society of Medicine Services International Congress and Symposium Series No. 173, published by Royal Society of Medicine Services Limited.

it is now recognized as an important cause of paediatric ear and sinus disease and may cause disease in adults with immunodeficiency or lung damage [8,9]. This pattern of infection suggests that immunity is acquired during childhood and subsequently protects the healthy adult from infection. Prior to the development of such immunity in childhood, or following the loss of such immunity in adult life, the individual is susceptible to infection. Having previously shown that healthy adults have demonstrable levels of anti-*M. catarrhalis* antibody [10] we have undertaken this study in order to analyse the IgG subclass nature of the response in healthy children and adults susceptible to recurrent infection. To characterize further the nature of the IgG subclass response we have measured the affinity of the antigen-specific antibodies directed against this organism.

METHODS

Enzyme linked immunoassays previously developed [10] were used to determine the levels and IgG subclass distribution of antibodies to both the whole bacteria and outer membrane protein antigens. Serum from 53 healthy children undergoing elective surgical procedures were used to assess the levels of naturally-occurring antibodies in childhood. Antibodies to *M. catarrhalis* were also assessed in a group of 25 adults with a diagnosis of non-allergic recurrent rhino-sinusitis (kindly provided by Dr G. Scadding, Royal Ear, Nose and Throat Hospital, London) and their antibody levels were compared to those in a group of 40 healthy adults. Statistical analysis was performed using Student's t test.

Functional affinity (avidity) of the specific anti-*M. catarrhalis* antibodies (IgG1, IgG2 and IgG3) was measured by an inhibition assay and a modification of the ELISA technique [11]. The results obtained were confirmed by analysing all sera in the presence or absence of diethylamine (DEA), a mildly chaotropic agent which inhibits low-affinity but not high-affinity antibody-antigen binding.

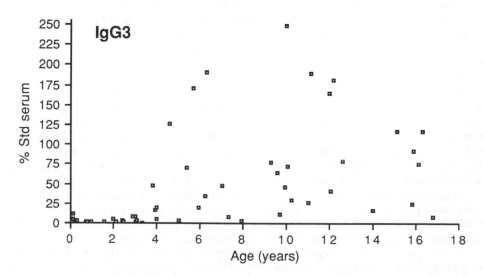

Figure 1   *Range of age-related naturally-occurring anti-*Moraxella (Branhamella) catarrhalis *IgG3 antibodies in children undergoing elective surgical procedures. Each symbol represents an individual child (n = 53) and levels (determined by ELISA [10]), are expressed as percentage of the level of antibody found in a pooled standard prepared from 60 apparently healthy adults.*

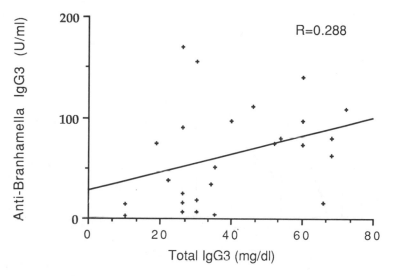

Figure 2   *Correlation between the specific anti-Moraxella (Branhamella) catarrhalis IgG3 antibody levels in a group of adult patients with chronic rhinosinusitis and their total serum IgG3. Levels of specific IgG3 are expressed as a percentage of a pooled adult standard and levels of total IgG3 are in mg/dl. (Patients kindly provided by Dr G. Scadding, Royal Ear, Nose and Throat Hospital, London.)*

RESULTS

Most healthy adults have antibodies to *M. catarrhalis*. Levels of specific IgG1 in children begin to rise during the first year of life, yet specific IgG3 antibodies cannot be measured under the age of four (Fig. 1).

The levels of specific anti-*M. catarrhalis* IgG1 and IgG2 antibodies were measured in a group of adults with recurrent URTI and compared to an adult control group; there were no significant differences. In contrast the levels of specific IgG3 antibody were significantly lower ($p=0.016$) in the patient group; as shown in Fig. 2, these lower levels of specific IgG3 were not related to the total serum IgG3 levels.

The affinity of the specific antibodies as measured by both the inhibition assay and the DEA method ranked the affinity of the specific antibodies in the following order: IgG3>IgG1>IgG2 (Figs. 3 and 4).

DISCUSSION

Structurally IgG3 is the most unusual of the four subclasses. Possessing a long hinge region it is probably more flexible than the other subclasses although it is also more susceptible to enzymatic degradation which probably accounts for its shorter half life. This extended hinge region is also thought to potentiate the binding of C1q to the C_H2 domain leading to the efficient activation of the complement cascade [12]. IgG3 is also known to bind to Fc receptors [13].

IgG3 antigen-specific responses have mostly been reported in association with anti-viral antibodies and appear to be important in the responses to various viral infections including herpes simplex, polio, rotavirus and some vaccinations [14]. The isotype distribution of anti-bacterial antibodies is dependent on the antigenic

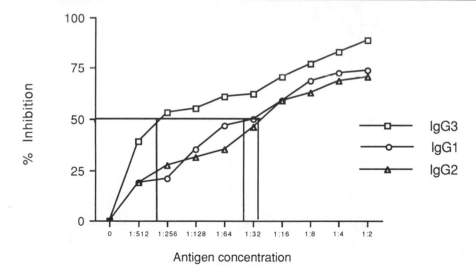

Figure 3 *Functional affinity (avidity) of anti-*Moraxella *(Branhamella) catarrhalis antibodies as measured by inhibition assay. Free antigen (live* M. catarrhalis) *in increasing concentration was added to serum of fixed concentration. The amount of antigen required to produce 50% inhibition was compared for the three subclasses. Less free antigen is required to inhibit the binding of high affinity than low affinity antibodies, and for high affinity antibodies inhibition approaches 100%.*

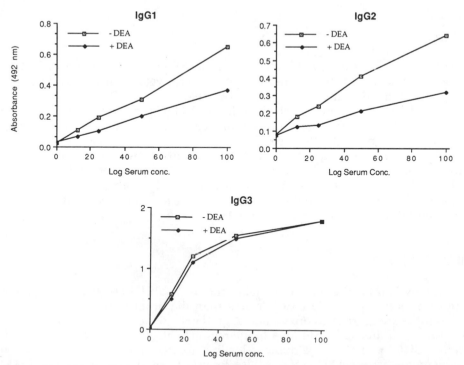

Figure 4 *Functional affinity (avidity) of anti-*Moraxella *(Branhamella) catarrhalis antibodies as measured by ELISA in the absence or presence of a chaotropic ion, diethylamine (20 mM). Low affinity antibody binding is more easily disrupted than high affinity antigen–antibody interactions* [11]. *The absence of any significant deviation in the case of IgG3 suggests higher functional affinity.*

determinants of any given bacteria and the OMP's of nontypable *Haemophilus influenzae* have previously been shown to be one of the few important bacterial targets for IgG3 [15]. It has also been shown that antibodies directed against these antigenic determinants are bactericidal and protect individuals from recurrent infection [16].

The OMP's of *M. catarrhalis* appear to be targets for serum antibodies and a rise in antibody levels to these determinants has previously been shown in patients recovering from infections with *M. catarrhalis* [17]. The importance of IgG3 in this recognition is supported by our observation that specific IgG3 antibodies are of higher affinity than IgG1 and IgG2 antibodies to this organism. High affinity responses are an essential part of the protective immune response and it is for this reason that it is likely that IgG3 has an important role.

If IgG3 does have such a role in anti-bacterial immunity the absence of specific IgG3 antibodies in the sera of children under the age of four is interesting. The mechanism for this is unclear although non-exposure to the organism is unlikely since specific IgG1 rises in the second year of life and studies have shown 50% nasal carriage in both adult and paediatric populations [18]. The epidemiological data showing that younger paediatric patients are particularly susceptible to otitis media with this organism suggests that this clinical susceptibility may be related to the lack of antibody.

The finding of lower levels of anti-Moraxella IgG3 in adults with frequent infection may also reflect an inability in some individuals to mount an adequate immune response to this organism. Convalescent rises in anti-*M. catarrhalis* antibodies have been observed in a group of children with proven upper respiratory tract viral infections and the authors have postulated that the damaged nasal mucosa subsequently became permissive to the normal bacterial flora [19]. Microbiological data from adult patients such as those described above will provide further insight into the relevance of the reduced specific IgG3 noted in this group.

Mechanisms for IgG3 production *in vivo* are poorly understood although antigen-specific IgG3 responses have not previously been shown to be age-restricted. It is possible that the V-region sequences which confer anti-*M. catarrhalis* specificity are restricted in some way from combining with the γ-3 heavy chain constant region in younger children although lower affinity IgG1 responses are not age-restricted. Alternatively, antigen presentation and accessory cell involvement may be crucial for the isotype appropriate response, perhaps through the involvement of particular cytokines (*cf* the role of IL-4 in IgE and IgG4 synthesis [20]). The fact that *M. catarrhalis* has been shown to be a B cell mitogen *in vitro* where it appears to stimulate a preferential IgG3 response [21] may provide a clue to the importance of the IgG3 contribution seen *in vivo*. Whether naive B cells are stimulated to switch to IgG3 production or whether pre-committed IgG3 cells are preferentially stimulated remains unclear and is the subject of further investigations in our laboratory.

ACKNOWLEDGMENTS

DG is a research training fellow funded by Action Research for The Crippled Child.

REFERENCES

(1) Lefranc MP, Lefranc G, Rabbits TH. Inherited deletion of immunoglobulin heavy chain constant region genes in normal human individuals. *Nature* 1982; **300**: 760–2.

(2) Ambrosino DM, Siber GR, Chilmoncyzk JB, Jernberg JB, Finberg RW. An immunodeficiency characterized by impaired antibody responses to polysaccharide. N Engl J Med 1987; **316**: 790–3.

(3) Yount WJ, Dorner MM, Kunkel HG, Kabat EA. Studies on human antibodies; VI. Selective variations in subgroup composition and genetic markers. J Exp Med 1968; **127**: 633.

(4) Makela O, Matilla P, Rautonen N, et al. Isotype concentrations of human antibodies to Haemophilus influenzae type b polysaccharide in young adults immunised with the polysaccharide as such or conjugated to a protein. J Immunol 1987; **139**: 1999–2004.

(5) Aalberse RC, Gaag R van der, Leeuwen J van. Serologic aspects of IgG4 antibody levels. I. Prolonged immunisation results in an IgG4-restricted response. J Immunol 1983; **130**: 722–6.

(6) Freijd A, Hammastrom L, Persson MAA, Smith CIE. Plasma anti-pneumococcal antibody activity of the IgG class and subclasses in otitis prone children. Clin Exp Immunol 1984; **56**: 233–8.

(7) Goldblatt D, Turner MW, Levinsky RJ. Branhamella catarrhalis: Antigenic determinants and the development of the IgG subclass response in childhood. J Infect Dis 1990; **162**: 1128–35.

(8) Bluestone C. The bacteriology of otitis media. In: Bluestone C, Klein J, eds. Otitis media in children. Philadelphia: WB Saunders, 1988: 45–58.

(9) Diamond LA, Lorber B. Branhamella catarrhalis pneumonia and immunoglobulin abnormalities: a new association. Am Rev Resp Dis 1984; **129**: 876–8.

(10) Goldblatt D, Seymour N, Levinsky RJ, Turner MW. An enzyme-linked immunosorbent assay for the determination of human IgG subclass antibodies directed against Branhamella catarrhalis. J Immunol Methods 1990; **128**: 219–25.

(11) Devey ME, Bleasdale K, Lee S, Rath S. Determination of the functional affinity of IgG1 and IgG4 antibodies to tetanus toxoid by isotype-specific solid-phase assays. J Immunol Methods 1988; **106**: 119–25.

(12) Feinstein A, Richardson N, Taussig MJ. Immunoglobulin flexibility in complement activation. Immunol Today 1986; **7**: 169.

(13) Lawrence DA, Weigle WO, Spiegelberg HL. Immunoglobulins cytophilic for human lymphocytes, monocytes and neutrophils. J Clin Invest 1975; **55**: 368.

(14) Skvaril F. IgG subclasses in Viral infections. In: Dukor P, Kallos P, Trnka Z, Waksman BH, eds. Monographs in allergy. Basel: Karger, 1986; **19**: 134–43.

(15) Hammarstrom L, Smith CIE. IgG subclasses in Bacterial infections. In: Dukor P, Kallos P, Trnka Z, Waksman BH, eds. Monographs in allergy. Basel: Karger, 1986; **19**: 122–33.

(16) Barenkamp SJ, Bodor FF. Development of serum bactericidal activity following nontypable Haemophilus influenzae acute otitis media. Pediatr Inf Dis J 1990; **9**: 333–9.

(17) Chi DS, Verghese A, Moore C, Hamatii F, Berk SL. Antibody responses to P-Protein in Patients with Branhamella catarrhalis infections. JAMA 1990; **88**(5A): S25–S27.

(18) Van Hare GF, Shurin PA, Marchant CD et al. Acute otitis media caused by Branhamella catarrhalis: biology and therapy. Rev Infect Dis 1987; **9**: 1–15.

(19) Hietala J, Uhari M, Tukko H, Leinonen M. Mixed bacterial and viral infections are common in children. Pediatr Inf Dis J 1989; **8**: 683–6.

(20) Ishizaka A, Sakiyama Y, Makinishi M, et al. The inductive effect of interleukin-4 on IgG4 and IgE synthesis in peripheral blood lymphocytes. Clin Exp Immunol 1990; **79**: 392–6.

(21) Walker L, Johnson GD, MacLennan ICM. The IgG subclass responses of human lymphocytes to B-cell activators. Immunology 1983; **20**: 106–15.

Defective anti-polysaccharide antibody response in children with recurrent respiratory tract infections

E. A. M. Sanders, G. T. Rijkers, A. J. Tenbergen-Meekes, C. C. A. M. Peeters and B. J. M. Zegers

Department of Immunology, 'Het Wilhelmina Kinderziekenhuis', University Hospital for Children and Youth, Utrecht, The Netherlands

INTRODUCTION

In recent years selective or isolated defects of antibody formation to polysaccharide (PS) antigens have been reported in patients with normal serum immunoglobulins (Ig) [1–5]. We studied the antibody response to PS antigens after pneumococcal vaccination of 44 children with recurrent respiratory tract infections.

MATERIALS AND METHODS

Patients

Forty-four patients, aged 1.7–17.1 years (geom. mean age 4.7 years) with the primary complaint of recurrent upper and/or lower respiratory tract infections with more than eight episodes during the previous two years, were investigated.

All subjects were immunized with 23-valent pneumococcal vaccine (Pneumovax; Merck, Sharp and Dohme). Serum was withdrawn before and 1, 2 and 4 weeks after vaccination and stored at $-20°C$ until analysis. The 44 patients were divided into two separate groups on the basis of their serum immunoglobulin levels.

Group I: Thirty-three patients who showed normal serum levels for IgM, IgG, and IgA-IgG subclasses. Their age varied from 1.7 to 13 years (geom. mean 3.9 years); two patients were below two years of age, six between two and three years, 25 older than three years.

Group II: Eleven patients, aged 2.8–17.1 years (geom. mean 4.9 years), were found to have various types of Ig deficiencies, varying from selective IgA deficiency to common variable hypogammaglobulinaemia. A 4.4 year old boy with normal immunoglobulins except for a low IgG4 was included in this group because both his older brother and sister (7.2 and 8.9 years respectively) showed low IgG2 and IgG4.

Progress in immune deficiency III, edited by H. M. Chapel, R. J. Levinsky and A. D. B. Webster, 1991; Royal Society of Medicine Services International Congress and Symposium Series No. 173, published by Royal Society of Medicine Services Limited.

Anti-pneumococcal antibody assays

Serum antibody titres to type-specific pneumococcal capsular polysaccharides types 3, 4, 6B, 9N, 14, 19F and 23F were measured by ELISA [6]. Capsular polysaccharides were obtained from ATCC, Rockville, MD. To correct for the presence of species-specific cell wall polysaccharide (C-PS) antibodies, all sera were preincubated with 50 μg/ml soluble C-PS, overnight at 4°C, before assay [7]. Antibody levels were calibrated using a hyperimmune plasma pool [8] as standard serum. Antibody concentrations are expressed in Units/ml. The reference serum is standardized as 100 Units/ml for each serotype.

Evaluation of responses to pneumococcal polysaccharides

Non-responders to pneumococcal vaccination were defined as those who failed to respond to five or more of the seven serotypes tested. A sufficient response to an individual capsular polysaccharide was defined as a two-fold increase in serum antibody titre, provided that the post immunization antibody concentration was greater than the geometric mean concentration of antibody before vaccination of 33 children with normal immunoglobulins (group I).

RESULTS AND CONCLUSIONS

We found that 3% of patients in group I responded insufficiently to types 3 and 9N, 9% had a poor response to type 4 and about 20% had a poor response to types 6B, 14, 19F and 23F (Table 1). On the basis of these results we found three patients who failed to respond to five or more of the seven pneumococcal serotypes. These non-responders were young children, aged 1.7, 3.2 and 3.4 years respectively. One of these three patients failed to respond to all seven antigens tested.

In group II, comprising 11 patients with various types of Ig deficiencies, seven patients were found to be non-responders and six failed to respond to any

Table 1 *Responses to Pneumovax® immunization in patients of group I and group II*

Pneumococcal serotype	Group I		Group II	
	% of children with <2-fold increase in ab	% of children with post-immunization level <GM of level in children in Group I	% of children with <2-fold increase in ab	% of children with post-immunization level <GM of level in children in Group I
3	24 (8/33)	3 (1/33)	82 (9/11)	64 (7/11)
4	39 (13/33)	9 (3/33)	55 (6/11)	64 (7/11)
6B	61 (20/33)	21 (7/33)	73 (8/11)	64 (7/11)
9N	27 (7/33)	3 (1/33)	64 (7/11)	55 (6/11)
14	67 (22/33)	21 (7/33)	82 (9/11)	73 (8/11)
19F	61 (20/33)	21 (7/33)	82 (9/11)	73 (8/11)
23F	67 (22/33)	21 (7/33)	82 (9/11)	91 (10/11)

Group I 3/33 patients failed to respond to 5–7 serotypes
Group II 7/11 patients failed to respond to 6–7 serotypes
GM = geometric mean

polysaccharide tested. The seventh patient, a 3.1 year old girl with IgG2 deficiency responded to type 3 and 9. The four patients who had sufficient antibody responses showed selective IgA deficiency (2), IgG2 deficiency (1) and common variable hypogammaglobulinaemia (1).

Three children of one family who all failed to respond to any serotype, were followed from 1988 until 1990. The older girl and boy had low IgG subclass levels (IgG2 and IgG4) at the time of vaccination. Their brother, who also failed to respond to any serotype and who is four years younger, only showed low IgG4 at the time of vaccination and during follow up. The follow up of this boy has not been long enough to see whether or not he will develop other Ig deficiencies.

We conclude that in both groups I and II of patients with recurrent respiratory tract infections, deficient antibody responses to PS antigens of pneumococci are found. In Group I, representing patients with normal serum immunoglobulins, there were three patients (about 10%) who, according to our definition, showed a selective defect in antibody formation. This result confirms and extends earlier findings of our group [1] and of others [2–5] that selective antibody deficiency to PS antigens may occur without an overt immunoglobulin deficiency.

The results in group II show that defective anti-PS responses are relatively common among patients with various types of Ig deficiencies [9,10]. The findings in the three siblings of one family suggested that defective anti-PS antibody responses may precede development of Ig isotype deficiency and thus may be an early indicator of a more severe immunodeficiency disease. The observation that a patient with a selective IgA deficiency and a defective anti-PS response gradually developed hypogammaglobulinaemia supports the hypothesis.

Defective anti-PS antibody formation may be caused by either a defect of regulatory T cells, cytokine production or of B cells. As far as the patients of group I are concerned, the defective antibody response to PS antigens may reflect a delay in the maturation of B cells and/or regulatory cells. Furthermore we and others [1–5] have found that in most patients the defect is not limited to pneumococcal PS antigens but comprises the class of so-called thymus-independent type 2 (TI-2) antigens e.g. the capsular polysaccharide polyribose phosphate (PRP) of *Haemophilus influenzae* type b. It is therefore of interest that several of our non-responder patients of both group I and II did make antibodies to PRP when vaccinated with the thymus-dependent form of the antigen i.e. the conjugate vaccine HbOC (unpublished observations and references 4,11,12). This result shows that PRP-reactive (and perhaps more general TI-2 antigen reactive) B lymphocyte precursors are present in patients with a selective antibody deficiency to PS antigens. Research in the next few years in these patients will therefore be focused on the requirements for B cell activation by TI-2 antigens, including analysis of the role of regulatory cells and cytokines. Clinical follow-up is required in these patients both to monitor the development of the defect and to institute adequate therapy.

REFERENCES

(1) Rijkers GT, Kuis W, de Graeff-Meeder ER, Peeters CCAM, Zegers BJM. Selective antipolysaccharide antibody deficiency. *N Engl J Med* 1987; **317**: 838.
(2) Ambrosino DM, Siber GR, Chilmonczyk BA, Jernberg BJ, Finberg RW. An immuno-deficiency characterized by impaired antibody response to polysaccharides. *N Engl J Med* 1987; **316**: 790–3.

(3) Herrod HG, Gross S, Insel R. Selective antibody deficiency to *Haemophilus influenzae* Type B capsular polysaccharide vaccination in children with recurrent respiratory tract infection. *J Clin Immunol* 1989; **9**: 429–34.

(4) Knutsen AP. Patients with IgG subclass and/or selective antibody deficiency to polysaccharide antigens: Initiation of a controlled trial of intravenous immune globulin. *J Allergy Clin Immunol* 1989; **84**: 640–7.

(5) Rothback C, Nagel J, Rabin B, Fireman P. Antibody deficiency with normal immunoglobulins. *J Pediatr* 1979; **94**: 250–3.

(6) Rijkers GT. Anti-pneumococcal polysaccharide ELISA. *J Immunol Methods* 1986; **88**: 285–6.

(7) Peeters CCAM, Tenbergen-Meekes AM, Evenberg DE, Poolman JT, Zegers BJM, Rijkers GT. A comparative study of the immunogenicity of pneumococcal Type 4 polysaccharide- and oligosaccharide tetanus toxoid conjugates in adult mice. Submitted.

(8) Siber GR, Ambrosino DM, McIver J, *et al.* Preparation of human hyperimmune globulin to *Haemophilus influenzae* b, *Streptococcus pneumoniae* and *Neisseria menigitides*. *Infect Immun* **45**: 248–54.

(9) Umetsu DT, Ambrosino DM, Quinti I, Siber GR, Geha RS. Recurrent sinopulmonary infection and impaired antibody response to bacterial capsular polysaccharide antigen in children with selective IgG-subclass deficiency. *N Engl J Med* 1985; **313**: 1247–51.

(10) Siber GR, Schur PH, Aisenberg AC, Weitzman SA, Schiffman G. Correlation between serum IgG2 concentrations and the antibody response to bacterial polysaccharide antigens. *N Engl J Med* 1980; **303**: 178–82.

(11) Insel RA, Anderson PW. Response to oligosaccharide-protein conjugate vaccine against *Haemophilus influenzae* b in two patients with IgG2 deficiency unresponsive to capsular polysaccharide vaccine. *N Engl J Med* 1986; **315**: 499–503.

(12) Schneider IC, Insel RA, Howie G, Madore DV, Geha RF. Response to a *Haemophilus influenzae* type b diptheria CRM$_{197}$ conjugate vaccine in children with a defect of antibody production to *Haemophilus influenzae* type b polysaccharide. *J Allergy Clin Immunol* 1990; **85**: 948–53.

An association between homozygous C3 deficiency and impaired antibody responses to PCP

M. Hazlewood[1], D. Kumararatne[1,2], P. Bird[3], M. Goodall[1] and H. Joyce[2]

[1]Immunology Department, Medicinal School, Birmingham, [2]Immunology Department, Dudley Road Hospital, Birmingham and [3]Immunology Department, Royal (Dick) School of Veterinary Science, Edinburgh, UK

INTRODUCTION

Antibodies directed against the capsular polysaccharides (PS) of certain high grade bacterial pathogens such as *Streptococcus pneumoniue*, *Haemophilus influenzae* type b and *Neisseria meningitidis* protect from invasive disease. Bacterial capsular polysaccharides often induce antibody responses restricted to the IgG2 and to a lesser extent IgG1 isotypes [1]. Patients with inherited deficiencies of complement components are known to have an increased risk of bacterial infections. It has also been reported that patients with homozygous C3 deficiency have reduced serum levels of IgG2 and IgG4. There is also experimental evidence in animal models that depletion of C3 may be associated with a decreased ability to produce antibodies though data relating to humans are incomplete.

Specific antibody levels against a panel of bacterial capsular polysaccharide antigens and tetanus toxoid were determined. These were used to assess the immune response to thymus-independent type 2 (TI-2) and thymus-dependent (TD) antigens respectively in patients with complement deficiencies encompassing the alternative, classical and terminal components of the cascade. The IgG and IgG subclass concentrations in these sera have been reported previously [2].

MATERIALS AND METHODS

Sixty-five individuals with definite severe inherited deficiency of isolated complement components were studied. One hundred normal sera obtained from healthy age-matched volunteers were used as a control group. Vaccines were used as a source of pure antigens to create the solid phase. Those used were 23 valent Pneumovax (Merck, Sharpe and Dohm); Hib poly-ribose phosphate (Merieux); Meningococcal A + C (Merieux) and Tetanus toxoid simple solution (Wellcome). The Hib and meningococcal preparations were both conjugated to poly-L-lysine prior to use. The assays were performed as described previously [3]. Briefly, polystyrene microtitre plates were sensitized overnight with the appropriate

Progress in immune deficiency III, edited by H. M. Chapel, R. J. Levinsky and A. D. B. Webster, 1991; Royal Society of Medicine Services International Congress and Symposium Series No. 173, published by Royal Society of Medicine Services Limited.

antigen diluted in a carbonate buffer (pH8.5). The following day these plates were sequentially incubated with human sera, murine anti-human monoclonal antibodies and a sheep anti-mouse antibody conjugated to horse radish peroxidase. The reaction was developed with OPD and stopped with 20% sulphuric acid. A given normal serum pool was titred on every plate in order to provide a standard. The results from the control group were not normally distributed, hence a normal range for each assay was based upon the median and 5th and 95th percentiles. Comparisons between groups of complement-deficient individuals and the controls were made, using Wilcoxon's test.

RESULTS

Control group: Anti-PCP antibody titres

One hundred normal individuals were studied and the 5th percentile values obtained for serum anti-pneumococcal capsular polysaccharide (PCP); these values were whole IgG 1:140; IgG1 1:5 and IgG2 1:50. Results below these figures for patients were taken to reflect deficiency. The scatter for whole IgG levels can be seen in Fig. 1.

Complement-deficient group: Anti-PCP antibody titres

Serum anti-PCP antibody titres (whole IgG only) are shown in Fig. 1 for all of the patients studied. Only in the C3 group is there a significant lack of specific antibodies, in that three of the four individuals had titres lower than *any* of the normals. No other group of patients with complement deficiency were found to be significantly lacking in anti-PCP antibodies when compared with the control group.

Homozygous C3-deficient individuals

The specific anti-PCP antibody subclass levels for the homozygous C3-deficient patients can be seen in Table 1. A lack of specific antibody correlates with depressed serum IgG2 levels. Patient 'Arm' was found to have no detectable antibody, whilst the low titres of patients A.V. and B.V. (1:44 and 1:47 respectively) were predominantly of the IgG1 isotype. It should be noted that the only individual in Table 1 with a normal anti-PCP response (patient Ren) produced an IgG2 anti-PCP antibody response and had normal levels of serum IgG2.

Other specific antibody results

Tetanus toxoid antibody responses were found to be normal in the patient groups when compared to the controls (data not shown). Serum antibody titres against

Table 1 *Homozygous C3-deficient individuals; their subclass responses to pneumococcal capsular polysaccharide (PCP) (For IgG and IgG subclass values see reference 1)*

Patient code	Age (yrs)	Serum IgG	Serum IgG2	Anti-PCP antibody titres		
				Whole	IgG1	IgG2
Arm	Child	Normal	Low	<1:5	<1:5	<1:5
A.V.	24	Normal	Low	1:47	1:19	<1:5
B.V.	21	Normal	Low	1:44	1:15	<1:5
Ren	8	Normal	Normal	>1:2560	1:10	1:640

Hib prp and meningococcal A + C for the patients were within the normal ranges for these assays (data not shown).

DISCUSSION

Data presented here indicate that three of four patients with homozygous C3-deficiency had significantly reduced antibodies to PCP and low serum IgG2 levels. A similar association was not seen in patients with other deficiencies of the complement components. Since two of the patients with C3 deficiency and low anti-PCP antibody levels were over 20 years old, the low specificity antibody levels could not be due to physiological deficiency of TI-2 antibody responses, characteristically seen in children below five years of age [1]. These results are even more striking as these three C3-deficient individuals have a history of recurrent pneumococcal sepsis.

Homozygous C3 deficiency may result in defective anti-PCP antibody responses due to (i) C3 genes being in linkage disequilibrium with immune-response genes to PCP; (ii) impaired processing of bacterial capsular antigen in the complete absence of C3; or (iii) a failure of accessory signal delivery to PCP antigen-specific B cells.

There is no evidence in support of the first possibility; C3 genes are located on the 19th chromosome which does not contain any members of the immunoglobulin supergene family. Secondly, it is possible that phagocytosis of pneumococci by macrophages, followed by stripping off of the capsular polysaccharide from the bacterial cell wall and the subsequent expression of this on the surface of the macrophage, may be required for initiation of anti-PCP antibody responses. Such initial phagocytosis of viable pneumococci, in a non-immune host, would require opsonization with C3b generated via the alternate pathway and will not occur in the complete absence of C3. Alternatively, C3 genes may be in linkage disequilibrium with genes coding for enzymes involved in cleaving the PCP away from the pneumococcal cell wall.

Alternatively, if the density of repeating epitopes on PCP is insufficient to cross-link surface Ig receptors of antigen-specific B cells adequately, C3 breakdown products may be required as an accessory signal. Our findings also show that cell interactions governed by the LFA family (which include the CR3 receptor) are not required for effective antibody responses to this antigen. Such accessory signals may be transmitted via CD21 surface receptors on B cells (CR2) [4]. Interestingly, the pattern of ontogeny of CD21 B cells in the spleen of human infants mirrors that of TI-2 antibody responses [6].

In contrast to PCP, Hib prp and meningococcal capsular antigens may be capable of inducing specific antibody responses despite C3 deficiency due to the following reasons: (a) the stereo-chemistry of these latter antigens may make them less dependant on accessory signals by inducing activation of specific B cells (b) the latter bacteria may elicit concomitant T cell activation through their outer membrane proteins with production of T cell-derived accessory factors which may provide a synergistic signal to the polysaccharide-responsive B cells.

Finally, one of the four individuals with C3 deficiency was found to have good specific antibody titres and normal IgG2 subclass levels. It has been documented that mononuclear phagocytes from homozygous C3-deficient humans were capable of C3 synthesis *in vitro* [5]. Therefore, although circulating C3 levels may be depressed, in such patients there may be sufficient production of C3 in the micro-environment containing PCP specific B cells, to generate adequate accessory

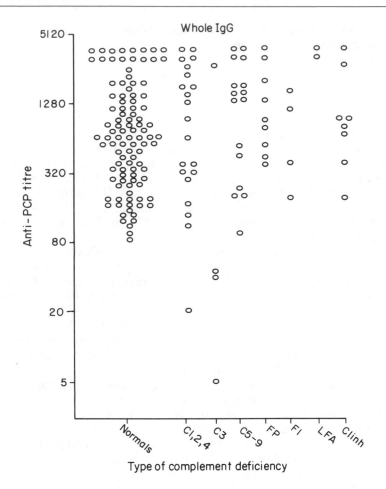

Figure 1   *Anti-pneumococcal capsular polysaccharide antibody titres of complement-deficient patients.*

signals. In this context, it is interesting that secondary deficiency of C3 caused by lack of factor I, or suboptimal C3 activation due to factor P deficiency were not accompanied by diminished responses to pneumococcal capsular polysaccharide. Taken together, our data would be consistent with the hypothesis that PCP antibody responses are greatly reduced in the complete absence of C3 within the lymphoid tissue micro-environment, but reduced levels of this component are compatible with normal antibody responses to this antigen.

REFERENCES

(1) Jefferis R, Kumararatne DS. Review: Selective IgG subclass deficiency: quantification and clinical relevance. *Clin Exp Immunol* 1990; **81**: 357–67.
(2) Bird P, Lachmann P. The regulation of IgG subclass production in man: low serum IgG4 in inherited deficiencies of the classical pathway of C3 activation. *Eur J Immunol* 1988; **18**: 1217–22.
(3) Kumararatne DS, Bignall A, Joyce H, Hazlewood HA. Antibody deficiency disorders. In: Gooi J, Chapel H, eds. *Clinical immunology: A practical approach.* Oxford: IRL Press, 1990.

(4) Klaus G, Humphrey J. A re-evaluation of the role of C3 in B-cell activation. *Immunol Today* 1986; **7**: 163–5.
(5) Einstein LP, *et al*. Biosynthesis of the third component of complement (C3) *in vitro* by monocytes from both normal and homozygous C3-deficient humans. *J Clin Invest* 1977; **60**: 963–9.
(6) MacLennan ICM, Liu YJ, Oldfield S, Zhang J, Lane PJL. The evolution of B-cell clones. *Curr Topics Microbiol Immunol* 1990; **159**: 37.

Restricted heterogeneity of IgG anti-tetanus toxoid antibodies after allogeneic bone marrow transplantation

E. J. A. Gerritsen[1], J. M. A. Wels[1], C. M. Jol-van der Zijde[1],
H. C. Rümke[2], J. M. Vossen[1], J. Radl[3] and M. J. D. van Tol[1]

[1]Department of Paediatrics, Leiden University Hospital, Leiden, [2]National Institute of
Public Health and Environmental Protections (RIVM), Bilthoven, and [3]Institute for Experimental
Gerontology, TNO, Rijswijk, The Netherlands

INTRODUCTION

Mono- and oligoclonal gammapathies of low concentration (homogeneous immunoglobulins, H-Ig) can be detected in frequencies up to 100% in sera of patients after allogeneic bone marrow transplantation (BMT) [1–6]. Studies have been done to determine the class and subclass isotypes and allotypes of these transient H-Ig [3, 7–10]. The antibody specificity of these post-BMT H-Ig is unknown. In this study we investigated whether anti-tetanus toxoid (TT) specificity was present in homogeneous immunoglobulin of IgG isotype (H-IgG) in BMT recipients, vaccinated with TT. In addition, we investigated the electrophoretic heterogeneity of IgG anti-TT antibodies in BMT patients in comparison with that in healthy infants, children and adults.

METHODS

Patients and controls

Group A: BMT recipients ($n=27$); AML 10, ALL 10, other diagnoses 7, (age four months–18 years, mean 8.3 year) were vaccinated with diphtheria-tetanus-polio (DTP, RIVM, Bilthoven, The Netherlands) at six, 10 and 14 weeks after BMT. Between six and 12 months after BMT eight patients received a DTP booster vaccination. Serum samples were taken two weeks after each vaccination and three and six months after the last vaccination.

Group B: Healthy infants and children ($n=20$, age three months, followed up to four years) were vaccinated with DKTP (RIVM, 'K' stands for Pertussis) according to the Dutch National Immunization Programme at age three, four, five and 11 months; at the age of four years they received a DTP booster vaccination. Informed consent was obtained to sample serum four weeks after each vaccination.

Progress in immune deficiency III, edited by H. M. Chapel, R. J. Levinsky and A. D. B. Webster, 1991; Royal Society of Medicine Services International Congress and Symposium Series No. 173, published by Royal Society of Medicine Services Limited.

Group C: Healthy adult volunteers ($n = 20$, age 25–40 years) received a single DTP booster vaccination. Serum samples were taken two weeks, four weeks, three months and six months after vaccination and stored at $-20°C$.

Laboratory techniques

Agar gel electrophoresis of serum was performed according to Wieme, with a modification [11]. After electrophoresis the separated proteins were transferred to Immobilon membranes (0.45 μm, Millipore) either uncoated (direct IgG pattern) or coated with TT (RIVM) (TT-specific pattern) or bovine serum albumin (BSA, Biorad) (negative control pattern). The serum samples (diluted 1:250 and 1:1000) were investigated together with a positive and a negative control (human IgG Moab anti-TT, 0.2 μg/ml and human IgG Moab anti-Hep B sAg, 20 μg/ml; these Moabs were kindly provided by Dr W. Zeylemaker, CLB, Amsterdam). Antigen coating was done overnight at 4°C with 3 μg/cm^2 TT in 0.5 M NaHCO$_3$, pH 8. The free unoccupied sites of the membrane were blocked with 1% BSA (w/v), 0.05% Tween 20 (T) (v/v) in phosphate-buffered saline (PBS) for 1 h at room temperature (RT). After blotting the membrane was developed by successive incubation with a combination of mouse anti-human IgG Moabs (NI 335 and NI 343, Nordic), alkaline phosphatase conjugated polyclonal rabbit anti-mouse Ig antiserum (RAMAP, Dakopatts) and substrate as previously described [12]. After 15 min the reaction was stopped by incubation for 10 min in 10% acetic acid (v/v). After washing in distilled water the membrane was dried and analysed. A restricted heterogeneity (of immunoglobulins or antibodies after electrophoresis) reflects deficiencies in some populations and an excess in others. In addition, the IgG anti-TT titre in each serum sample was determined with ELISA.

RESULTS

In ELISA the geometric mean anti-TT IgG titre of responders and the number of non-responders versus responders was not significantly different between BMT recipients and healthy infants. The TT-immunoblotting pattern in healthy infants was heterogeneous, with few exceptions, whereas in BMT recipients a high frequency of patterns with restricted antibody heterogeneity was observed, increasing after each vaccination. In the sera of healthy children four years of age and in healthy adults after booster vaccination, the TT antibody pattern was heterogeneous with one or few small dominant homogeneous antibody components in about half of them (data not shown). In contrast in BMT recipients, a marked increase in frequency and concentration of homogeneous antibody components was seen (see Fig. 1); this was in agreement with a significantly higher anti-TT IgG titre.

DISCUSSION

The IgG antibody response to TT in healthy infants (following the normal vaccination programme up to 11 months) is heterogeneous with respect to the electrophoretic pattern. This is in contrast with the electrophoretically restricted heterogeneity of the response to TT seen in the serum of BMT recipients in the first year after grafting. The restricted IgG antibodies in BMT recipients may be the result of a limited B cell repertoire and/or of an inadequate T cell helper

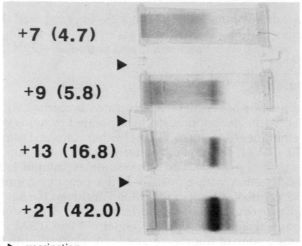

▶ = vaccination
+7, +9, +13, +21 = weeks after BMT
4.7, 5.8, 16.8, 42.0 = AU/ml anti TT-IgG in ELISA

Figure 1 *TT-specific immunoblotting pattern in serum of a BMT recipient: 1:250 diluted serum samples are blotted onto a TT-coated membrane, before and after consecutive vaccinations of a BMT-recipient.*

function. After booster vaccination of healthy persons (either of children aged four years or of adults) a heterogeneous TT-IgG pattern with small homogeneous antibody components can frequently be observed. The difference between the strictly heterogeneous response in healthy infants and the response with the appearance of homogeneous antibody after booster vaccination at a later age might be explained by selection in the course of time of the most effective B cell clones, in terms of affinity (Fab part) and with respect to antigen neutralization (Fc part). Booster vaccination six to 12 months after BMT resulted in an antibody response of restricted heterogeneity, with the presence of one or more clear cut components. This 'overshoot' of antibodies from one or few dominant B cell clones may reflect an inefficient T cell suppressor function. In a few cases the concentration of homogeneous antibody was so high that it could explain a H-IgG as detected with routine electrophoresis. Our study demonstrates that transient homogeneous immunoglobulins (H-Ig) seen in the serum of a marrow graft recipient can in part be accounted for by antibodies following antigenic stimulation of a not yet completely reconstituted immune system. It can be hypothesized that they develop due to restrictions in B cell repertoire, or more likely, due to temporary T cell regulation insufficiency, as shown in animal experiments [13].

REFERENCES

(1) Radl J, Dooren LJ, Eysvoogel VP, Went JJ van, Hijmans W. An immunological study during post-transplantation follow-up of a case of severe combined immunodeficiency. *Clin Exp Immunol* 1972; **10**: 367–82.

(2) Radl J, Berg P van den. Transitory appearance of homogeneous immunoglobulins—'paraproteins'—in children with severe combined immunodeficiency before and after transplantation treatment. In: Peters H, ed. *Protides of the biological fluids*, **20**. Oxford: Pergamon Press, 1973: 263–6.

(3) Mitis AJ, Stein R, Rappeport JM, *et al.* Monoclonal and oligoclonal gammopathy after bone marrow transplantation. *Blood* 1989; **74**: 2764–8.

(4) Gerritsen E, Vossen J, Tol M van, Jol-van der Zijde C, Weyden-Ragas R van der, Radl J. Monoclonal gammapathies in children. *J Clin Immunol* 1989; **9**: 296–305.

(5) Kent EF, Crawford J, Cohen HJ, Buckley RH. Development of multiple monoclonal serum immunoglobulins (multiclonal gammopathy) following both HLA-identical unfractionated and T cell-depleted haploidentical bone marrow transplantation in severe combined immunodeficiency. *J Clin Immunol* 1990; **10**: 106–14.

(6) Fischer AM, Simon F, Le Deist F, Blanche S, Griscelli C, Fischer A. Prospective study of the occurrence of monoclonal gammapathies following bone marrow transplantation in young children. *Transplantation* 1990; **49**: 731–5.

(7) Gerritsen EJA, Radl J, Tol MJD van, Vossen JM. Monoclonal gammapathies in children. In: Radl J, Van Camp B, eds. *Monoclonal gammapathies II—Clinical significance and basic mechanisms.* Eurage 1989: 39–44.

(8) Tol MJD van, Gerritsen EJA, Lankester AC, *et al.* Allotypes of homogeneous immunoglobulins after allogeneic bone marrow transplantation. In: Radl J, Van Camp B, eds. *Monoclonal gammapathies II—Clinical significance and basic mechanisms.* Eurage 1989: 203–6.

(9) Hammarström L, Smith CIE. Frequent occurrence of monoclonal gammopathies with an imbalanced light-chain ratio following bone marrow transplantation. *Transplantation* 1987; **43**: 447–9.

(10) Akker TW van den, Benner R, Radl J. Transient monoclonal gammapathies with lambda light chains. *Transplantation* 1987; **44**: 725–6.

(11) Radl J. Immunoglobulin levels and abnormalities in aging humans and mice. In: Adler WH, Nordin AA, eds. *Immunological techniques applied to aging research.* Boca Raton, FL: CRC Press 1981: 121–39.

(12) Jol-van der Zijde CM, Labadie J, Vlug A, *et al.* Dot-immunobinding assay as an accurate and versatile technique for the quantification of human IgG subclasses. *J Immunol Methods* 1988; **108**: 195–203.

(13) Benner R, Akker ThW van den, Radl J. Monoclonal gammapathies in immunodeficient animals—a review. In: Radl J, Hijmans W, Van Camp B, eds. *Monoclonal gammapathies I—Clinical significance and basic mechanisms.* Eurage 1985: 97–102.

Antibody isotype responses to the *Haemophilus influenzae* type B vaccine in IgA-deficient persons

T. Klemola[1], E. Savilahti[1] and O. Mäkelä[2]

[1]Children's Hospital, University of Helsinki, and [2]Department of Bacteriology and Immunology, University of Helsinki, Helsinki, Finland

(POSTER)

IgA deficient (IgAd) persons have frequent respiratory tract infections; they often have IgG subclass deficiencies [1] and some have impaired lung function [2]. Earlier studies suggest that IgAd is associated with defects in antibody isotype responses to polysaccharide antigens [3]. We tested antibody isotype responses to the components of *Haemophilus influenzae* type b (Hib) vaccine in patients with IgAd.

MATERIAL AND METHODS

Eighteen IgAd patients and 16 controls with normal immunoglobulin levels were vaccinated with Hib capsular polysaccharide/diphtheria toxoid conjugate vaccine (Connaught Lab., Inc., USA). Antibody responses were measured in serum samples before and two weeks after the vaccination. Sera were assayed for the antibody titres of IgG, IgM, IgA and four IgG subclasses with a four-layer solid phase radioimmuno-assay [4].

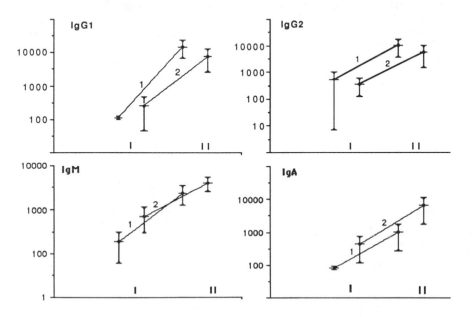

Figure 1 *Anti-Hib antibody titres (IgG1, IgG2, IgM and IgA are presented) before = I and after = II the Hib-vaccination. 1 = IgAd, 2 = controls. Mean and 95% confidence limits are shown.*

Progress in immune deficiency III, edited by H. M. Chapel, R. J. Levinsky and A. D. B. Webster, 1991; Royal Society of Medicine Services International Congress and Symposium Series No. 173, published by Royal Society of Medicine Services Limited.

RESULTS

The IgG, IgM and IgG subclass responses to vaccine did not differ between control and IgAd (Fig. 1); IgAd patients produced, naturally, significantly less ($p = 0.0004$) IgA antibodies than controls due to a low IgA response in four patients with partial IgA deficiency. We did not find any correlation between the total IgG subclass level and vaccine-specific rise of IgG subclass level in IgAd. Four patients showed abnormal responses to the vaccine. One boy produced no specific antibodies of any isotype after the vaccination; he suffered from frequent respiratory tract infections. However, he was revaccinated two years later and his antibody response was then adequate. Three IgAd patients showed poor IgG1 and IgM responses but their IgG2 responses were adequate; two of these also had frequent infections and the remaining one had coeliac disease.

DISCUSSION

Our results show that IgAd patients usually have good antibody isotype responses to polysaccharide antigens. The total levels of immunoglobulin isotypes did not correlate with the vigorousness of the responses in the same isotype. However, the response pattern is abnormal in some IgAd patients. In our study, four of the 18 with IgAd had poor IgG1 and IgM antibody response and defective antibody responses may explain susceptibility to recurrent infections.

REFERENCES

(1) Oxelius V-A, Laurell A, Lindqvist B, *et al.* IgG subclasses in selective IgA deficiency. Importance of IgG2 deficiency. *N Engl J Med* 1981; **304**: 1476–7.
(2) Björkander J, Bake B, Oxelius V-A, Hanson LÅ. Impaired lung function in patients with IgA deficiency and low levels of IgG2 or IgG3. *N Engl J Med* 1985; **313**: 720–4.
(3) Lane P, MacLennan I. Impaired IgG2 antipneumococcal antibody responses in patients with recurrent infection and normal IgG2 levels but no IgA. *Clin Exp Immunol* 1986; **65**: 427–33.
(4) Mäkelä O, Mattila P, Rautonen N, *et al.* Isotype concentrations of human antibodies to Haemophilus influenzae type b polysaccharide (Hib) in young adults immunized with the polysaccharide as such or conjugated to a protein (diphtheria toxoid). *J Immunol* 1987; **139**: 1999–2010.

The quantitation of anti-polysaccharide antibodies in human sera

M. Goodall[1], M. Hazlewood[1,2],
D. S. Kumararatne[1,2] and R. Jefferis[1]

[1]Immunology Department, The Medical School, Birmingham and
[2]Immunology Department, Dudley Road Hospital, Birmingham, UK

(POSTER)

Quantitative or absolute restriction in the IgG subclasses contributing to specific immune responses is well documented. Considerable clinical experience suggests an association between selective IgG subclass deficiencies and recurrent infection with certain micro-organisms [1]. New prophylactic and therapeutic modalities are being introduced (e.g. conjugate vaccines and the IV administration of IgG) which must be investigated to correlate clinical benefit with antibody isotype. Qualitative analysis is readily accessible but accurate quantitative data and inter-laboratory comparisons depend on the availability of appropriate standards. We have developed a preparative protocol for the isolation of IgG1 and IgG2 subclass antibodies which retain activity against pneumococcal polysaccharides (PCP) and *Haemophilus influenzae* type b polyribose phosphate (PRP). The protocol is of general applicability for the preparation of standards to be applied in quantitative assays. The antibodies isolated will also be used in vaccine immunogenicity studies.

MATERIALS AND METHODS

The starting material was Sandoglobulin; a pool of normal plasma from blood banks from which the IgG fraction was prepared by ethanol precipitation. The preparation, which was freeze dried with sucrose, was reconsituted with saline to give 5 mg/ml. Reverse passive haemagglutination (RPHA) revealed traces of IgM and IgA. IgM was removed by euglobulin precipitation and the IgA by passage over a column of sepharose 4B conjugated to anti-IgA MoAb 2D7.

The IgG fraction was dialysed against 0.01M Tris/HCl pH8.5 and passed over an affinity column of anti IgG1 (JL512) at 4°C. The bound IgG1 was eluted with 3M KSCN and dialysed against 0.01M Tris/HCl pH8.5. The dialysate was passed down a TM10 (non IgG1) affinity column which removed traces of IgG2, IgG3 and IgG4. The breakthrough, containing IgG1, was dialysed against PBS/1% trehalose and freeze dried. The unbound fraction from the JL512 column was passed over an affinity column HP6019 which bound IgG1, IgG3 and IgG4 and the IgG2 which passed through was dialysed against PBS/trehalose and freeze dried.

The purity of the products was monitored at all stages using RPHA. MoAbs specific for IgG1, IgG2, IgG3, IgG4, IgM and IgA were covalently bound to sheep red cells using chromium chloride [2]. Preparations were shown to consist of a single subclass >98% purity. The activity of the preparations was assessed in a four layer ELISA [3]. Briefly, polystyrene microtitre plates were coated with antigen; tetanus toxoid, PCP or Hib PRP. The plates were successively incubated, with human serum, then MoAb to Ig classes or IgG subclasses and finally with sheep anti-mouse Ig conjugated to HRP before developing with OPD.

Progress in immune deficiency III, edited by *H. M. Chapel, R. J. Levinsky and A. D. B. Webster*, 1991; *Royal Society of Medicine Services International Congress and Symposium Series No. 173, published by Royal Society of Medicine Services Limited.*

RESULTS

The starting material was found to be almost deficient in IgG3 and IgG4 antibodies specific for Hib PRP or PCP. Thus these isotypes were not isolated.

The IgG1 and IgG2 preparations were found to be over 98% of a single subclass and retained specific antibody activity. The anti-tetanus toxoid antibodies were exclusively IgG1. Antibodies specific for *Haemophilus influenzae* type b PRP were roughly equally divided between IgG1 and IgG2 subclasses. The antibody activity specific for pneumococcal capsular polysaccharide was predominantly found in the IgG2 preparation with only a small amount being IgG1.

REFERENCES

(1) Jefferis R, Kumararatne DS. Review: Selective IgG subclass deficiency: quantification and clinical relevance. *Clin Exp Immunol* 1990; **81**: 357–67.
(2) Ling NR, Bishop S, Jefferis R. A use of antibody-coated red cells for the sensitive detection of antigen and in rosette tests for cells bearing surface immunoglobulins. *J Immunol Methods* 1977; **15**: 279–89.
(3) Kumararatne DS, Bignall A, Joyce HJ, Hazlewood HA. Antibody deficiency disorders. In: Gooi J, Chapel H, eds. *Clinical immunology: A practical approach* Oxford: IRL Press 1990.

Selective deficiency of anti-polysaccharide antibodies as a risk factor for invasive disease caused by capsulated bacterial pathogens

D. S. Kumararatne[1,2], H. J. Joyce[1], M. Hazlewood[1,2], M. Goodall[2], R. Jefferis[2], S. Misbah[3] and H. Chapel[3].

Departments of Immunology, [1]Dudley Road Hospital, [2]The Medical School, Birmingham, and [3]John Radcliffe Hospital, Oxford, UK

(POSTER)

AIM OF STUDY

By measuring specific antibody responses to a panel of polysaccharide and protein antigens in patients with recurrent pyogenic infection, we have identified a spectrum of patients with a selective inability to respond to TI-2 antigens, most of whom had normal concentrations of serum immunoglobulin isotypes.

MATERIALS AND METHODS

Patient selection

(a) Three hundred and fifty patients with a history of invasive disease caused by capsulated bacteria (eg: *Streptococcus pneumoniae, Haemophilus influenzae*, type b) or recurrent infections especially involving the upper and lower respiratory tract, referred to the above centres during the years 1986–90 were studied. Patients with primary immunodeficiency syndromes known to cause antibody deficiency (eg: X-linked or common variable hypogamma-globulinaemia) or clinical disorders giving rise to secondary antibody deficiency (eg: myelomatosis) were excluded from the study. Children below five years were excluded as physiological deficiency of TI-2 responses is seen in this age group.

Antigen-specific antibody levels

Specific antibody levels to a panel of protein (tetanus and diphtheria toxoid) and polysaccharide (pneumococcal capsular polysaccharide, Haemophilus b polyribose ribitol phosphate (Hib PRP), *Neisseria meningitidis* types A and C capsular polysaccharide, *E. coli* J5 lipopolysaccharide) antigens were measured by a four-layer solid phase ELISA as described in detail elsewhere [1].

RESULTS

Seventeen of the 350 patients were found to have low antibody levels to capsular polysaccharide of all three bacterial species. Polysaccharide antibody-deficient patients as a group had normal anti-protein (TD) antibody levels but selective deficiency of IgG pneumococcal antibodies, when compared with healthy, age-matched control groups ($p < 0.05$ by Wilcoxon rank sum test). Two further patients each had highly selective

Progress in immune deficiency III, edited by H. M. Chapel, R. J. Levinsky and A. D. B. Webster, 1991; Royal Society of Medicine Services International Congress and Symposium Series No. 173, published by Royal Society of Medicine Services Limited.

deficiencies to a single bacterial species viz. *N. meningitidis* (types A and C) and Group B Streptococcus, respectively. Seventeen of 19 patients with TI-2 antibody deficiency had normal serum Ig isotype levels, while two had selective IgG2 deficiency. As a group they did not respond to immunization with the respective purified capsular polysaccharide vaccines. Two out of the three patients with poor response to Hib PRP vaccine developed good sustained antibody responses to Hib PRP conjugated to a protein carrier.

CONCLUSIONS

Without measuring specific antibody responses to a panel of bacterial capsular polysaccharides most of these patients would not have been accurately diagnosed as suffering from antibody deficiency. We believe that specific antibody levels should be routinely measured in patients with recurrent infection or severe invasive disease caused by capsulated bacteria and is of greater value than measuring total serum Ig levels.

Our study shows that most patients with defective TI-2 responses have normal serum IgG2 levels. Hence this study rules out the possibility that defective anti-carbohydrate antibody responses are primarily due to the inability to synthesize this isotype. Inability to respond to TI-2 antigens may be correctable using protein–polysaccharide conjugate vaccines in some patients.

REFERENCE

(1) Kumararatne DS, Bignell A, Joyce HJ, Hazlewood M. Antibody deficiency disorders. In: Gooi J, Chapel H, eds. *Clinical immunology: a practical approach*. Oxford: IRL Press, 1990: 1–22.

Antibody deficiency in allogeneic bone marrow engrafted adults

I. Quinti[1], E. Guerra[1], S. Le Moli[2], F. Aiuti[1], M. F. Martelli[3] and A. Velardi[3]

[1]Department of Allergy and Clinical Immunology, University of Rome, [2]DASRS Laboratory of Hygiene and Immunology, Pratica di Mare, [3]Division of Haematology, University of Perugia, Italy

(POSTER)

Long-term survivors after allogeneic bone marrow transplantation (BMT) may experience recurrent bacterial infections in the first months following BMT. We recently demonstrated that the humoral immune system of adults undergoing successful marrow engraftment reproduces some of the maturational steps that occur in normal B cell ontogeny during the first year of life. In particular, we found a marked IgG2 deficiency. This defect is often associated with an impaired response to polysaccharide antigens from those bacteria that represent the major pathogens of subjects with humoral immunodeficiencies and during childhood. Since the combined cellular and humoral immunodeficiency of marrow graft survivors recovers slowly and infections may be a serious problem in the months following engraftment, we analysed the repertoire of anti-polysaccharide antibodies in a population of allogeneic bone marrow engrafted adults immunized with meningococcal group A and C and pneumococcal antigens, in comparison with a group of immunized adult healthy subjects.

Normal adults had large antibody rises after the injection of meningococcal polysaccharide A, and isoelectrofocusing indicates that the antibody rises come mainly from increases of extant clonotypes.

Allogeneic bone marrow engrafted adults, immunized with meningococcal type A and C and pneumococcal type 14 polysaccharide antigens, showed only low antibody titres of the IgM class, no antibody titres of the IgG nor IgA classes and no bactericidal activity *in vitro*. The analytical isoelectrofocusing showed the appearance of a restricted pattern of clonotypes in a minority of subjects. These observations are consistent with the hypothesis that B cells in bone marrow transplant patients express some characteristics of neonatal B cells and suggest that polysaccharide-protein conjugates, rather than isolated polysaccharides might be utilized in the setting of bone marrow transplantation.

Progress in immune deficiency III, edited by H. M. Chapel, R. J. Levinsky and A. D. B. Webster, 1991; Royal Society of Medicine Services International Congress and Symposium Series No. 173, published by Royal Society of Medicine Services Limited.

Immunogenicity of *Haemophilus influenzae* type b (Hib) vaccines in patients with recurrent infections and/or immune deficiencies

C. Brémard-Oury[1], F. Veber[2], A. Barra[3], P. Aucouturier[3], P. Houmeau[4], L. Hessel[4], J. L. Preud'homme[3] and C. Griscelli[2]

[1]CNTS Paris, [2]Hôpital Necker, Paris, [3]CNRS, URA 1172, Poitiers, and [4]Pasteur Merieux—Marne la Coquette, France

(POSTER)

Impaired response to polysaccharides has been previously described in patients with low IgG2 level or recurrent infections. In order to describe these abnormalities better and to compare the immunogenicity of Hib polysaccharide (PRP) and Hib polysaccharide tetanus toxoid conjugate vaccine (PRP-T), we immunized 42 patients with recurrent infections (23) and/or known immune deficiencies (19). The patients were randomized to receive either PRP at day 0 and PRP-T at day 30 (group A:21 patients) or PRP-T at day 0 and day 30 (group B:21 patients). The anti-PRP antibodies were evaluated by the radio immune FARR assay at days 0, 30, 60, 180, 360. Class and subclass distribution of the Hib antibodies were studied by ELISA.

Our conclusions were the following:

Before immunization, 35 patients showed low anti-PRP level ($<1\,\mu g/ml$), even below the protective level ($0.15\,\mu g/ml$) in 13, emphasizing the usefulness of immunization in a large majority of patients.

No difference was found between group A and group B before immunization. No severe adverse effect was reported either after PRP (21) or after PRP-T (62) vaccines. At day 30, the total anti-PRP antibodies and IgM antibodies produced were higher in group B than in group A ($p=0.07$ and 0.03 respectively).

Anti-PRP antibody levels increased between day 30 and day 60; this was higher in group A than in group B (1.47 to $6.05\,\mu g/ml$ vs 2.34 to 8.51 respectively). 14/17 high responders ($>15\,\mu g/ml$ at day 30) showed no increase between day 30 and day 60.

All the patients with mild recurrent infections (24/24), isolated IgA deficiency (6/6) and combined immune deficiency (1/1) produced anti-PRP antibodies $>6\,\mu g/ml$ at day 60. Conversely 4/6 patients with hypogammaglobulinaemia, 3/4 with Wiskott-Aldrich syndrome and 1/1 with severe bronchiectasis produced lower titres ($<6\,\mu g/ml$), even below $1\,\mu g/ml$ in five patients.

Progress in immune deficiency III, edited by H. M. Chapel, R. J. Levinsky and A. D. B. Webster, 1991; Royal Society of Medicine Services International Congress and Symposium Series No. 173, published by Royal Society of Medicine Services Limited.

Predictors of infection in patients with low-grade B cell tumours

H. Griffiths and H. M. Chapel

John Radcliffe Hospital, Oxford, UK

(POSTER)

INTRODUCTION

Regular immunoglobulin replacement therapy has been shown to reduce the incidence of serious bacterial infection in patients with low grade B cell tumours [1,2]. However, the selection of who will benefit from replacement therapy remains uncertain. Since there is a group of patients with low serum IgG levels who do not suffer from recurrent infection we report a study on the incidence of infection in patients with low-grade B cell tumours with particular reference to indicators of infection risk.

PATIENTS AND METHODS

Patient details

The case notes of 64 patients, 61 with chronic lymphocytic leukaemia (CLL) and three with low-grade non-Hodgkin's lymphoma (NHL) were reviewed. The duration and stage of disease was recorded in addition to chemotherapy or radiotherapy administered during the course of the disease. The number and severity of infections over the preceeding two years was noted. The patients were classified into three groups according to their infection history; those who had severe or multiple infections (six or more infections over the previous two years or one life-threatening infection requiring hospital admission and intravenous anti-biotics), occasional infections (three to five infections in two years) or no infections (less than three infections in two years). Blood samples were taken at the end of the two-year period for the measurement of immunoglobulin levels and specific antibodies to tetanus, diphtheria and pneumococcal polysaccharides. A group of elderly normal volunteers acted as controls.

Methods

Serum immunoglobulins were measured by turbidimetry. Specific antibodies were measured by an enzyme-linked immunosorbent assay, using tetanus toxoid simple vaccine, diphtheria toxoid and pneumovax II as antigens.

RESULTS

Thirty percent (19) of the patients studied had a history of severe or multiple infections, 18% (12) had occasional infections and the remaining 52% (33) had no history of infection over the two-year study period. There was no relationship between infection history and duration or current stage of disease; only 52% of patients with stage IV disease had a history of multiple infection. Neither was there any association between prior treatment and infection.

Over half of the patients (33) had serum IgG levels below the lower limit of our normal range [<6.0 g/l] (Fig. 1). The majority (16/19) of patients with multiple infections had low IgG levels, though 24% (8/33) of patients with no history of infection also had low IgG levels. In relation to stage of disease, only half the patients with low IgG levels had

Progress in immune deficiency III, edited by H. M. Chapel, R. J. Levinsky and A. D. B. Webster, 1991; Royal Society of Medicine Services International Congress and Symposium Series No. 173, published by Royal Society of Medicine Services Limited.

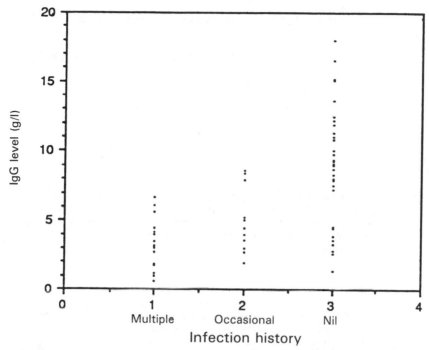

Figure 1 *Serum IgG levels in patients with multiple, occasional or nil infections.*

stage IV disease. There was a tendency for long duration of disease to be associated with low IgG levels.

Tetanus antibodies were low in 68% of patients with a history of multiple infection and 36% of patients with no infections compared with 29% of the elderly normal controls. No details were known about previous immunization history. Diphtheria antibodies were low in 89% of patients with multiple infections but in 73% of patients with no infections and 63% of elderly normal controls. Pneumococcal antibody levels were low in 79% (15/19) of patients with multiple infections and in only 12% (4/33) of patients with no infections and 8% (3/38) of elderly normal controls. There was no clear correlation between IgG and pneumococcal antibody levels.

CONCLUSION

One-third of the patients in this study had a history of multiple or serious infections. Specific antibody levels to tetanus and diphtheria were not helpful in distinguishing which patients had infection, but this is not surprising as antibody levels to tetanus and diphtheria are known to fall with increasing age [3]. In contrast, low pneumococcal antibody levels were associated with a history of serious or multiple infection. Measurement of pneumococcal antibody levels is a useful indicator of infection risk.

REFERENCES

(1) Co-operative group for the study of immunoglobulin in chronic lymphocytic leukaemia. A randomized, controlled clinical trial of intravenous immunoglobulin in chronic lymphocytic leukaemia. *N Engl J Med* 1988; **319**: 902.
(2) Griffiths H, Brennan V, Lea J, Bunch C, Lee M, Chapel H. Crossover study of immunoglobulin replacement therapy in patients with low-grade B cell tumours. *Blood* 1989; **2**: 366.
(3) Kjeldsen K, Simonsen O, Heron I. Immunity against diphtheria 25–30 years after primary vaccination in childhood. *Lancet* 1985; **i**: 900.

Immunological responses in myeloma

R. M. Hargreaves[1], J. R. Lea[1], H. Griffiths[1], J. Faux[1], M. Lee[2] and H. M. Chapel[1]

[1]Department of Immunology, John Radcliffe Hospital, Oxford, UK and
[2]Baxter Healthcare, California, USA

(POSTER)

AIMS

A group of 41 patients with myeloma at varying stages of their disease and treatment were assessed to investigate whether any relationship could be found between basic immunological measurements (immunoglobulins and IgG subclasses), immunization responses to tetanus and diphtheria toxoids and Pneumovax, results of skin testing and susceptibility to infection.

METHODS

Patients were selected from a larger group of patients who were undergoing regular follow-up for myeloma. A detailed infection history was recorded for each patient; infections were classified by severity (major, moderate and minor) and site. Baseline non-paraprotein immunoglobulin levels and pneumococcal and *Escherichia coli* antibodies were measured on all patients by an in-house ELISA method, and IgG subclasses (excluding paraprotein IgG subclass in IgG myelomas) by radial immune diffusion using a monoclonal antibody kit. The patients were skin tested with a commercial kit (Merieux CMI) containing seven commonly encountered antigens (Tetanus, Diphtheria, Streptococcus, TB, Candida, Tricophyton, Proteus) and the results graded as anergic, hypoergic or normal according to the overall response. Patients were immunized with tetanus toxoid, diphtheria toxoid and Pneumovax. Serum was taken immediately prior to and four weeks post-immunization. Sixty-two elderly normal volunteers (aged over 65 years) acted as controls for measurement of baseline specific antibody titres to tetanus and *E. coli* and IgG subclasses.

RESULTS

Thirty-seven episodes of serious infection (major and moderate) were recorded overall in the group of patients under study. Infections of the upper and lower respiratory tract (10 pneumonia and 10 secondary infection of the upper respiratory tract) were predominant comprising 54% all serious infections recorded. Baseline pneumococcal and *E. coli* titres and IgG subclasses were lower in the patients with myeloma compared to the elderly control group. The majority of patients with myeloma had IgM levels below the normal range; low titres to Pneumococci and *E. coli* correlated well with degree of this immunosuppression in these patients. Following immunization, 22 patients (55%) produced a good response to tetanus toxoid, 14 (35%) to diphtheria toxoid and 18 (45%) to Pneumovax. Patients who did not demonstrate severe humoral immunosuppression (non-paraprotein IgG > 3 g/l; IgA > 0.3 g/l and IgM > 0.2 g/l) were more likely to produce a good response to immunization. There was an association between poor response to Pneumovax immunization and occurrence of septicaemia, but no other correlations between immunization response and

Progress in immune deficiency III, edited by H. M. Chapel, R. J. Levinsky and A. D. B. Webster, 1991; Royal Society of Medicine Services International Congress and Symposium Series No. 173, published by Royal Society of Medicine Services Limited.

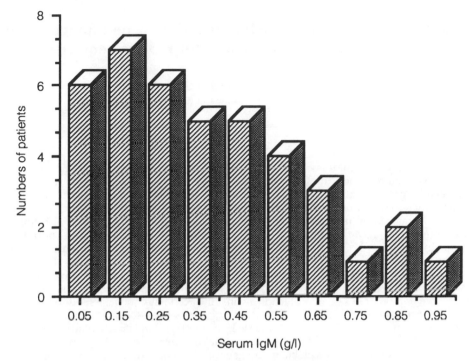

Figure 1 *Immunosuppression in myeloma.*

serious infection. Sixteen (41%) patients responded normally to skin testing, six (15%) produced a hypoergic response and 17 (44%) were anergic. There were no clear correlations between skin testing, humoral immunosuppression and serious infection.

These findings suggested that more detailed breakdown of the type of immunosuppression, i.e. specific antibody titres involved, and immunization response, particularly to Pneumovax immunization, might be useful investigations in predicting infection risk in patients with myeloma. Skin testing appeared to be less helpful.

Intravenous and intrathecal administration of immunoglobulin in purulent meningitis as a model for replacement therapy

L. Szenborn and Z. Rudkowski

Clinic for Infectious Diseases of Children, Medical Academy, Wrocław, Poland

(POSTER)

Purulent meningitis in childhood remains a very serious illness despite modern antibiotic therapy, particularly when the CNS infection is due to unusual organisms. In cases of life-threatening CNS infection and to minimize neurological sequelae, it has been recommended that humoral immune defences be supported in addition to antibiotics. We chose the human immunoglobulin preparation containing not only IgG but also highly concentrated (12%) IgM-fraction [1]. Pentaglobin® has both antibacterial and endotoxin-neutralizing action [2]. Compared with other common polyvalent immunoglobulin preparations, it achieves an antibacterial potency of eight-fold magnitude against *Escherichia coli* and *Pseudomonas aeruginosa*, 16-fold against *Klebsiella pneumoniae* and *Staphylococcus aureus* and even 32-fold against *Streptococcus pyogenes*. In the experimental studies in mice Pentaglobin demonstrates good protection against induced Salmonella, Pseudomonas and staphylococcal infection [2,3].

Due to its high content (12%) of pentameric IgM, Pentaglobin is particularly efficient in the opsonization of bacteria and subsequently in making them susceptible to phagocytosis. The very potent activity of Pentaglobin in the neutralization of endotoxins of Gram-negative bacteria was confirmed by laboratory experiments and in clinical situations among patients with septic shock [2,4].

The purpose of our randomized and prospectively controlled study was to treat purulent meningitis with antibiotics in association with Pentaglobin-immunotherapy, which might

Table 1 *Clinical and laboratory data*

	Group A ($n=10$) Antibiotics & Pentaglobin	Group B ($n=10$) Antibiotics alone
Age	Mean=6.5 month (range 4–13 months)	Mean=6.4 month (range 0.5–16 months)
Sex	5 male, 5 female	9 male, 1 female
Mean time to clinical improvement	4.2 days $\pm$ 1.9	4.4 days $\pm$ 1.35
Duration of fever	6.33 days $\pm$ 3.3	4.4 days $\pm$ 1.78
Peripheral leukocytosis	3.6 days $\pm$ 2.2	4.0 days $\pm$ 0.8
CSF granulocytes		
on day 1	85.78 $\pm$ 9.96	88.1 $\pm$ 9.5
on day 7	25.1 $\pm$ 25.7	27.3 $\pm$ 17.9
Protein (mg%)		
on day 1	387.5 $\pm$ 58.1	445.3 $\pm$ 309.9
on day 7	113.8	105.2 $\pm$ 49.3
Immunoglobulins (mg%)		
on day 3 IgG	10.24 $\pm$ 1.92	10.8 $\pm$ 6.7
IgM	2.69 $\pm$ 1.03	1.58 $\pm$ 1.53
Index GRC after 3 days (%)	93.31 $\pm$ 4.46	86.05 $\pm$ 9.52 ($p < 0.01$)

Progress in immune deficiency III, edited by H. M. Chapel, R. J. Levinsky and A. D. B. Webster, 1991; Royal Society of Medicine Services International Congress and Symposium Series No. 173, published by Royal Society of Medicine Services Limited.

be particularly useful in immunodeficient patients. Our group of infants with purulent meningitis (group A, $n = 10$) were given antibiotics such as penicillin, ampicillin or cephalosporins and we added intravenously and simultaneously intrathecal Pentaglobin in a dosage of 5 ml/kg IV and 0.5 ml/kg intrathecally every third day, for six to 12 days. Infections in this group included *Neisseria meningitidis* (4), *Strep. pneumoniae* (4), *Salmonella typhimurium* (1) and one unknown. The infants in control group B ($n = 10$) were treated only with similar antibiotics. Infections included *N. meningitidis* (1) *Strep. pneumoniae* (1), *Haemophilus influenzae* (1), *Salmonella enteritidis* (1) and three unknown.

The clinical and laboratory data are given in Table 1. To make the comparison between both groups more objective, we evaluated the results of the treatment using the GRC index (percentage global reduction of CSF cells) [5].

We conclude that early therapeutic injection of Pentaglobin IV and intrathecal in purulent meningitis enhances normalization of CSF the pattern, probably due to the highly concentrated IgM immunoglobulin which has an antitoxic, antibacterial and opsonizing properties. Our observations indicate a potential benefit of Pentaglobin therapy in the early stages of purulent meningitis in patients with immunodeficiency, characterized by severe clinical course, therapeutic difficulties and serious prognosis.

REFERENCES

(1) Weipl G. Therapie der eitrigen Meningitis mit Immunoglobulinen. *Pädiat Pädol* 1977; **12**: 209–312.
(2) Deicher H, Schoeppe W. In: *Klinisch angewandte Immunologie*. Berlin: Springer Verlag, 1988.
(3) Dichtelmüller H, Stephan W. Untersuchung zur Wirksamkeit von IgM i.v. Immunoglobulinen gegen Bakterielle Infectionen und zur Neutralisation bakterieller Toxine. *Arzneim Forsch/Drug Res* 1987; **37**: 1273–6.
(4) Kornhuber B. In: *Patient-Infection-Immunoglobulin*. Berlin: Springer Verlag, 1984: 1–2 and 128–129.
(5) Neu I. Der therapeutische Wert von Immunoglobulinen bei Infectionen des Zentralnervensystems. *Med Klin* 1980; **15**: 554–7.

Production of lymphokines during immunoglobulin replacement therapy

C. M. Farber, L. Schandene, A. Crusiaux, J. P. Van Vooren and E. Dupont

Université Libre Bruxelles and Immunology Department, Hôpital Erasme, Bruxelles, Belgium

(POSTER)

Patients receiving intravenous gammaglobulins (IVIg) often present moderate side effects, e.g. chills, fever. Those effects can usually be controlled by slowing the rate of infusion after interrupting it, and by acetylsalicylic acid or paracetamol. We thought tumour necrosing factor (TNF-α) might be involved in those reactions and evaluated TNF-α and interleukin-1 (IL-β) levels by an immunoradiometric assay (IRMA; IRE, Medgenix, Fleurus, Belgium) in an endotoxin-free system. This assay uses several different monoclonal antibodies to either substance.

We first checked *in vitro* that monomeric IgG, as present in immunoglobulin preparations for intravenous use, did not induce TNF-α or IL1-β production by human mononuclear cells; in contrast IgG coated on the polystyrene wall of the reaction tube did induce them [1]. We concluded that what we were doing was mimicking immune complexes allowing IgG molecules, close to each other, to cross-link Fcγ receptors on monocytes.

When we evaluated TNF-α in our patients during IVIg infusion, we found an increase in serum concentrations, peaking 120 min after the beginning of treatment in four out of five (Table 1). Levels reached varied from patient to patient (110–780 pg/ml). IL-β levels were not significantly elevated during treatment. The levels of TNF observed were similar to levels observed by others in septic shock, although our patients were clinically stable [2].

We could not explain the rise in TNF-α by elevation of circulating immune complex levels. It is also puzzling that IVIg treatment abolished TNF-α production in experimental animals [3].

We think that TNF-α might still be involved in reactions to immunoglobulin infusions. Different observations in the literature have obviously been made in different situations, using different experimental systems. More research is clearly needed to understand the respective role of TNF-α, its binding to inhibitors and the role of co-factors.

Table 1 *Serum TNF levels during IVIg treatment (pg/ml)*

Patient No.	T0	T30'	T60'	T90'	T120'	T150'	T180'
1	25	20	20	130	850	790	620
2	20	20	20	200	410	200	
3	20	20	25	200	320	200	200
4	0	0	75	110	90		
5	0	0	0	0	20	0	0

Patient no. 5 at 360 and 480 min and 24 h: 0 pg/ml

Progress in immune deficiency III, edited by H. M. Chapel, R. J. Levinsky and A. D. B. Webster, 1991; Royal Society of Medicine Services International Congress and Symposium Series No. 173, published by Royal Society of Medicine Services Limited.

REFERENCES

(1) Schandene L, Deviere J, Denys C, Crusiaux A, Farber CM, Dupont E. Coated IgG synergizes with E Coli LPS to induce TNF and IL-1 production. *10th meeting of the European Federation of Immunological Societies*, Edinburgh, September 1990.
(2) Calandra Th, Baumgartner JD, Grau Georges, *et al*. Prognostic values of tumor necrosis factor/cachection, interleukin-1, interferon-α and interferon-γ in the serum of patients with septic shock. *J Infect Dis* 1990; **161**: 982–7.
(3) Shimazato T, Iwata M, Tamura Z. Suppression of tumor necrosis factor alpha production by a human immunoglobulin preparation for intravenous use. *Infect Immun* 1990; **58** (5): 1384–90.

Results of a twelve-month study with TNBP/Tween-treated IV immunoglobulin

J. Björkander[1], R. Söderström[1], G. Bryntesson[1], L.Å. Hanson[1] and A. Vietorisz[2]

[1]Immunodeficiency Unit, Asthma and Allergy Research Centre and Department of Clinical Immunology, University of Göteborg and [2]Division of Biopharma, Plasma Products, Kabi, Stockholm, Sweden

(POSTER)

According to IUIS/WHO [1] and our recent data from a controlled study, patients with certain IgG subclass deficiencies can be improved by immunoglobulin (Ig) prophylaxis. A 12-month safety study has been performed in IgG subclass-deficient patients using a new virus-inactivated intravenous immunoglobulin (IVIg) preparation.

MATERIALS AND METHODS

Patients

Five female and three male infection-prone patients with IgG subclass deficiencies entered the study. They had not previously been treated with blood, plasma or other blood products, except for occasional hepatitis A prophylaxis. The eighth patient dropped out after the seventh infusion.

Ig preparation

The Ig preparation Gammonativ (KabiVitrum, Stockholm, Sweden), is a Cohn Fraction II chromatographed on DEAE Sephadex. Before pooling of plasma from more than 1000 healthy Scandinavian donors, every unit of plasma is tested for non-reactivity for hepatitis B surface antigen (HBsAg), as well as human immunodeficiency virus (HIV) antibodies. A virus inactivation step based on a solvent detergent treatment has been included [2,3]. The Fraction II solution is exposed to 0.3% tri-(n-butyl) phosphate (TNBP) and 1% Tween 80 for 6 h at 37°C. The product is later stabilized by addition of glucose and human heat-treated albumin before lyophilization.

Study plan

The clinical course during the Ig prophylaxis was documented on diary cards and immunological parameters were monitored as well. Virus safety data were collected and evaluated according to the current recommendations for viral safety studies, as outlined by the International Committee on Thrombosis and Haemostasis (ICTH) [4]. Liver function was checked every two weeks during the first four months and thereafter every four weeks. Each patient was treated with the same batch throughout the study and every batch was used for two patients. All patients were given a dose of 400 mg/kg of Ig every four weeks, and four normal production batches of Gammonativ have been studied.

RESULTS

Clinical and immunological data

Patients with low IgG1 or IgG2 serum levels showed increases after the initial infusion (Figs. 1 and 2). In contrast there was no increase of the IgG3 levels (Fig. 3). The levels of IgG4 were increased in four patients (Fig. 4).

Progress in immune deficiency III, edited by H. M. Chapel, R. J. Levinsky and A. D. B. Webster, 1991; *Royal Society of Medicine Services International Congress and Symposium Series No. 173*, published by Royal Society of Medicine Services Limited.

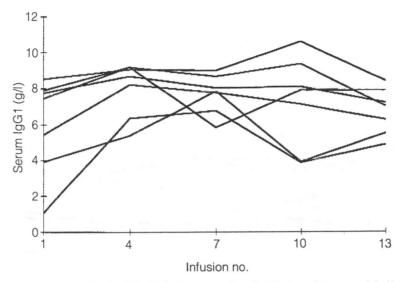

Figure 1 *Serum levels of IgG1 before every fourth infusion of immunoglobulin.*

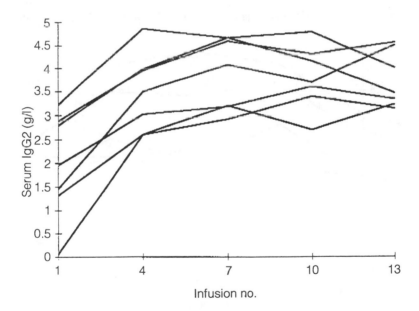

Figure 2 *Serum levels of IgG2 before every fourth infusion of immunoglobulin.*

Five of the seven patients completing the study registered improvement during treatment. This was supported by the fit of a linear trend (days = A + B × period, A = intercept, B = slope) for five of the seven patients analysing days with fever, days with infections, days with antibiotic treatment and days on sick leave.

Virus safety data

Liver function tests were all normal for the eight patients with regard to alkaline phosphatase and bilirubin. Two separate elevated alanine aminotransferase (ALT) values, 0.86 and 0.90 microkat/l, were seen in one patient in connection with an increased dose of an

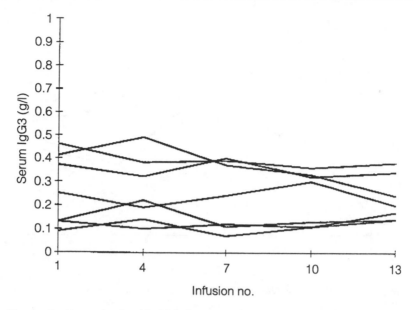

Figure 3   *Serum levels of IgG3 before every fourth infusion of immunoglobulins.*

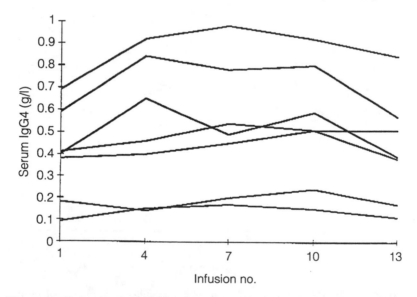

Figure 4   *Serum levels of IgG4 before every fourth infusion of immunoglobulins.*

antidepressant drug. The increment of these ALT values did not fulfil the requirement for the diagnosis of non-A, non-B (NANB) hepatitis.

CONCLUSION

This study shows that the new Gammonativ, which is produced with a virus inactivation step with TNBP/Tween, is safe as to NANB hepatitis. Subjective improvement in 5/7 patients agreed with the fit of a linear trend analysis during Ig treatment for the different disease parameters.

REFERENCES

(1) IUIS/WHO. Appropriate use of human immunoglobulin in clinical practice. *Clin Exp Immunol* 1983; **52**: 417–22.
(2) Horowitz B, Wiebe ME, Lippin A, Stryker MH. Inactivation of viruses in labile blood derivatives. *Transfusion* 1985; **25**: 516–22.
(3) Prince AM, Horowitz B, Brotman B. Sterilisation of hepatitis and HTLV-III viruses by exposure to tri-(n-butyl)phosphate and sodium cholate. *Lancet* 1986; **i**: 706–10.
(4) Schimpf K, Manucci PM, Kreutz W, *et al.* Absence of hepatitis after treatment with a pasteurized factor VIII concentrate in patients with hemophilia and no previous transfusion. *N Engl J Med* 1987; **316**: 918–22.

Can intravenous immunoglobulin therapy 'cure' common variable immunodeficiency?

A. Todd[1], P. L. Yap[1], P. E. Williams[1], G. Neill[1], C. L. S. Leen[2] and R. P. Brettle[2]

[1]Clinical Immunology Laboratory, Edinburgh and SE Scotland Regional Transfusion Centre, Edinburgh and [2]Infectious Diseases Unit, City Hospital, Edinburgh, UK

(POSTER)

Patients with common variable immunodeficiency (CVI) present with persistent hypogammaglobulinaemia and recurrent bacterial infections, particularly of the respiratory tract. Replacement therapy is generally in the form of intravenous immunoglobulin (IVIg) and is a life-long requirement. Recovery of immunoglobulin production has been described only in rare cases following hepatitis or HIV infection and occasionally in response to cimetidine or steroids. Hammarström et al. [1] have recently reported apparently spontaneous recovery in two patients with CVI.

In three out of a total of 44 patients who fulfill the criteria for the diagnosis of CVI, we have observed recovery of immunoglobulin production; transiently in one patient receiving plasma therapy and sustained in two on intravenous immunoglobulin.

All three patients presented with symptoms and immunological parameters of hypogammaglobulinaemia (Table 1). All developed rising pre-infusion levels of IgG to 7–12 g/l, the first while receiving fresh frozen plasma every three weeks and the other two while on IVIg in a dose of 200 mg/kg four-weekly. Replacement therapy was discontinued and the patients were monitored closely. Case 1 again developed hypogammaglobulinaemia 11 months later, concurrently with an episode of pneumonia and replacement therapy was recommenced; he has not repeated the pattern of rising pre-infusion IgG levels. The other two patients remain off IVIg, now 27 and 70 months respectively and remain free of serious infection with normal levels of IgG. However both show persistent deficiencies of IgA, IgG2 and IgG4 and it is of interest that this pattern of deficiency has been shown to precede panhypogammaglobulinaemia in some cases (2).

We propose that IVIg therapy may have affected the natural history of the disease although the mechanism remains unknown.

Table 1 *Details of cases 1–3 at diagnosis*

Case	Age at first symptoms (years)	Age at diagnosis (years)	Serum levels (g/l)[a]			Presenting symptoms
			IgG	IgA	IgM	
1	25	26	2.9	0.0	0.0	Giardiasis
2	44	49	1.2	0.0	0.1	Recurrent pneumonia
3	16	22	0.7	0.1	0.1	Sinusitis Otitis media Pneumonia

[a]Normal range: IgG 5–13 g/l, IgA 0.5–4.0 g/l, IgM 0.36–1.92 g/l.

Progress in immune deficiency III, edited by H. M. Chapel, R. J. Levinsky and A. D. B. Webster, 1991; Royal Society of Medicine Services International Congress and Symposium Series No. 173, published by Royal Society of Medicine Services Limited.

REFERENCES

(1) Hammarström L, Jonsson M, Smolowicz A, Widner H, Smith CIE. Regulation of antibody synthesis in hypogammaglobulinaemia. *EOS—Revista di Immunologia ed Pharmacologia* 1990; (in press).
(2) Ishizaki A, Nakanishi M, Yamada Y, *et al*. Development of hypogammaglobulinaemia in a patient with common variable immunodeficiency. *Eur J Pediatr* 1989; **149**: 175–6.

Anti-HCV antibodies in gammaglobulin for intravenous use

I. Quinti, R. Paganelli, I. Mezzaroma, G. P. D'Offizi, E. Scala, E. Guerra and F. Aiuti

Department of Allergy and Clinical Immunology, University of Rome 'La Sapienza', Rome, Italy

(POSTER)

Recently the blood-borne non-A non-B hepatitis (NANBH) agent, designated hepatitis C virus (HCV) has been isolated and the correlation of HCV with transfusion recipients in whom NANBH developed and with their donors has been well established. NANBH has also been reported in patients with X-linked agammaglobulinaemia or common variable immunodeficiency (CVI) after treatment with intravenous gammaglobulin (IVIg). In our series of 60 patients with primary antibody deficiencies who received replacement therapy with IVIg for a median of five years at a dose of 200–400 mg/kg every two to three weeks, only three presented with clinical and serological abnormalities of acute hepatitis; in two patients chronic hepatitis developed later. For these reasons, we have tested 50 lots of IVIg from 11 different sources by HCV ELISA (Ortho, Raritan, NJ). HCV antibodies were found in 26 (52%) lots. Percentages of HCV-positive lots differ according to the preparation, from 0% to 100%. A decrease in the percentage of positive lots was observed comparing lots prepared before (59%) and after 1987 (39%), the year in which the testing of anti-HIV antibodies of each single plasma unit used for the manufacture of IVIg was introduced. The three patients with acute and chronic hepatitis received different lots of a preparation with high titres of anti-HCV antibodies. Since seroconversion is not detectable in CVI patients, we followed a homosexual HIV-positive patient who developed acute hepatitis, negative for serological markers of CMV, EBV, HAV and HBV, after three months of IVIg treatment. We demonstrated an increased reactivity to HCV during the acute hepatitis. One month later, the normalization of ALT levels occurred and four months later the HCV antibody reactivity was undetectable.

We diluted anti-HCV antibodies of a serum from a positive subject in IVIg (anti-HCV negative) and found a positive reaction at very high dilution (1:1024). This suggests that even a low number of anti-HCV positive plasma units could be responsible for the HCV reactivity of a lot of IVIg prepared from a pool of one or two thousand donors. Unless clear evidence is provided that steps in IVIg preparation inactivate NANBH virus, we suggest that plasma from anti-HCV positive donors should not be used.

Progress in immune deficiency III, edited by H. M. Chapel, R. J. Levinsky and A. D. B. Webster, 1991; Royal Society of Medicine Services International Congress and Symposium Series No. 173, published by Royal Society of Medicine Services Limited.

Intravenous immunoglobulin in the management of epileptic children

M. Duse[1], A. Plebani[1], S. Tiberti[2], L. D. Notarangelo[1], E. Menegati[2] and A. G. Ugazio[1]

[1]Department of Paediatrics, University of Brescia and [2]Division of Neurology and Child Psychiatry, City Hospital, Brescia, Italy

(POSTER)

In recent years intravenous immunoglobulin (IVIg) has been employed with encouraging results for the treatment of epilepsy on the hypothesis that immunological mechanisms are involved in the pathogenesis of some epileptic disorders. In our previous experience, immunological evaluation of a group of children with intractable childhood epilepsy (ICE) defined as severe, recurrent seizures, resistant to appropriate pharmacological treatment after a period of intensive medical therapy [1], showed that 6/12 had an IgG2 subclass deficiency: five of these six children improved dramatically following treatment with high dose IVIg while none of the six children with normal IgG2 responded favourably. After discontinuing IVIg therapy, four out of five responder patients relapsed [2].

Table 1 *Clinical features of patients treated with IVIg*

Patient	Sex	Age years/ months	ICE duration months	Type of ICE	Neurologic abnormality	CT scan findings
1 A.A.	F	1/10	12	PEE	Cerebral palsy	Microcephaly
2 T.C.	F	1/3	12	West	Cerebral palsy	Diffuse cerebral atrophy
3 G.D.	F	3/0	33	PEE	Cerebral palsy	Diffuse cerebral atrophy
4 B.R.	M	1/3	11	PEE	Cerebral palsy	Diffuse cerebral atrophy
5 C.Mi.	M	4/0	43	West	Cerebral palsy	Minimal cortical atrophy
6 C.Mo.	M	4/0	35	West	Dysequilibrium	Minimal cortical atrophy
7 Z.L.	M	6/6	62	Lennox	Cerebral palsy	Diffuse cerebral atrophy
8 R.M.	M	6/9	43	Lennox	Motor disability	Intracerebral calcifications
9 V.C.	F	6/5	36	Lennox	Cognitive disorders	Negative
10 G.M.	M	4/10	11	Lennox	Cerebral palsy	Congenital hydrocephalus
11 G.N.	M	6/8	12	Lennox	Cerebral palsy	Negative
12 T.A.	F	12/0	70	Lennox	Mental retardation	Negative
13 C.E.	M	1/0	6	West	Cerebral palsy	Tuberous sclerosis
14 M.M.	M	5/2	56	West	Cerebral palsy	Minimal cortical atrophy
15 R.Ae.	F	5/7	24	Lennox	Cerebral palsy	Negative
16 R.Aa.	F	5/7	24	Lennox	Cerebral palsy	Negative
17 S.S.	F	3/9	24	Lennox	Motor disability	Negative
18 T.F.	F	3/6	36	West	Cerebral palsy	Tuberous sclerosis
19 C.M.	M	8/10	81	Lennox	Cerebral palsy	Diffuse cerebral atrophy
20 D.G.	F	7/10	83	Lennox	Cerebral palsy	Diffuse cerebral atrophy

Progress in immune deficiency III, edited by H. M. Chapel, R. J. Levinsky and A. D. B. Webster, 1991; Royal Society of Medicine Services International Congress and Symposium Series No. 173, published by Royal Society of Medicine Services Limited.

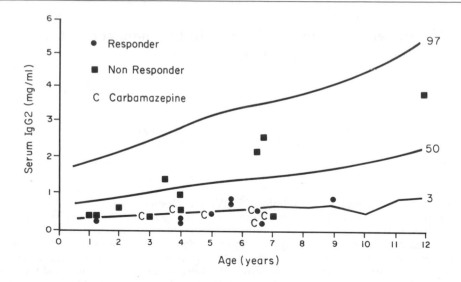

Figure 1

In the present study we report the result of IVIg treatment of a further eight children with ICE: the main clinical features are reported in Table 1. Four patients improved dramatically, with a complete disappearance of seizures in two. IgG2 deficiency was observed in one patient. Neither intrathecal synthesis or presence of Ig was observed in the CSF.

Recently it has been suggested that the high prevalence of IgG2 deficiency among epileptic children may result from treatment with carbamazepine. Eight of 20 treated patients showed low serum IgG2 levels (six responders and two no responders): of these five have been treated with carbamazepine (Fig. 1).

The susceptibility to the immunosuppressive effect of carbamazepine may identify a subgroup of ICE patients susceptible to the beneficial effect of IVIg. On the other hand, when we looked at the type of ICE, we found that seven responder patients out of nine suffered from the Lennox Gastaut Syndrome: these data have been confirmed by other authors and suggest that IVIg has a place in the treatment of the Lennox Gastaut Syndrome whether or not associated with IgG2 deficiency. The mechanism of action of IVIg is still obscure.

REFERENCES

(1) Alcardi J. *Epilepsy in children*. New York: Raven Press, 1986.
(2) Plebani A. Duse M. Tiberti S, *et al.* Intravenous gammaglobulin therapy and serum IgG subclass levels in intractable childhood epilepsy. *Monogr Allergy* 1988; **23**: 204–15.

The infection-prone child. A clinical trial comparing IV immunoglobulin, trimethoprim/sulphamethoxazole and placebo

K. Nydahl-Persson[1], A. Fasth[1,2], S. Schmeisser[3], L. Hammarström[4] and E. Smith[4]

Departments of [1]Pediatrics, [2]Clinical Immunology and [3]Clinical Bacteriology, University of Göteborg, Göteborg and [4]Department of Clinical Immunology, Karolinska Institute at Huddinge Hospital, Huddinge, Sweden

(POSTER)

In 1988 a randomized, triple-blind study on infection-prone pre-school children, living in Göteborg was initiated to compare the efficacy of intravenous immunoglobulin (IVIg, Gammagard, Baxter AB, Sweden), long term trimethoprim-sulphamethoxazole (TMP-SMX), and placebo on the rate of infection. We also looked for differences, clinical and treatment-related, between children with normal levels of IgG2 and those with low amounts, as well as studying the possibility that other immunological markers could differentiate between children that benefited from active therapy and those that did not.

All children were investigated every fourth week for a four-month period during the autumn. The parents recorded symptoms and only children with at least one bacterial infection during the observation period were entered. Investigations were repeated during therapy over the following winter and spring, as well as at follow-up the next autumn. The following tests were included: routine haematology and biochemistry, serum immunoglobulin and IgG subclass levels; IgG subclass-specific antibodies to a number of protein and carbohydrate antigens; lymphocyte subpopulations and mitogen transformation; sweat electrolytes; a consultation at the ENT department and naso-pharyngeal cultures.

After the four-month observation period the children were stratified according to the year of treatment and IgG subclass levels, followed by randomization into three groups: IVIg 400 mg/kg, four infusions at four-week intervals + oral placebo (for TMP-SMX) 5 ml b.i.d. for 16 weeks: TMP-SMX 5 ml b.i.d. for 16 weeks + placebo (for IVIg): Placebo (for IVIg) + placebo (for TMP-SMX).

RESULTS

During the first year 15 children out of 30 referred fulfilled entrance criteria; of these, 13 completed the protocol.

Active drug, IVIg or TMP-SMX, was given to nine children and only one had infections (two pneumonias) during therapy and follow up. In contrast, all four children in the placebo group continued to have bacterial infections. This difference is significant ($p < 0.02$, two-tailed four-tables test). The groups are at present too small to allow for comparison between the two groups given active drug.

Low IgG2 subclass levels were observed in seven of the 13 children; five in the active drug groups and two in the placebo group. Before therapy all children grew pathogens in their nasopharynx; only those given TMP-SMX eradicated these bacteria.

CONCLUSIONS

This study shows that in a well defined population of infection-prone children, therapy with either TMP-SMX or IVIg can markedly diminish the infection rate. A much larger cohort must be studied in order to be able to find differences in efficacy between IVIg and TMX-SMP.

Progress in immune deficiency III, edited by H. M. Chapel, R. J. Levinsky and A. D. B. Webster, 1991; *Royal Society of Medicine Services International Congress and Symposium Series No. 173, published by Royal Society of Medicine Services Limited.*

Defective mIg signalling in SCID B cells

**B. J. M. Zegers, I. Hiemstra, E. de Graeff-Meeder, W. Kuis,
A. W. Griffioen and G. T. Rijkers**

Department of Immunology, University Hospital for Children and Youth
'Het Wilhelmina Kinderziekenhuis', Utrecht, The Netherlands.

INTRODUCTION

Severe combined immunodeficiency disease (SCID) is a heterogeneous disorder characterized by defective cellular and humoral immunity. The majority of patients are severely lymphopenic and lack phenotypic and functional T and B lymphocytes. A number of SCID patients, however, are only moderately lymphopenic, in which case the majority of circulating lymphocytes are B cells. Based on analysis of surface marker expression, it has been suggested that SCID B cells represent a population of B cells present during normal B cell ontogeny [1]. This view is compatible with the finding that successful transfer of T cell function, through bone marrow transplantation, restores B cell function [2]. We have studied B cell function in two SCID patients with B cells. Our data indicate that, unlike neonatal B cells, SCID B cells fail to increase $[Ca^{++}]_i$ upon activation with anti-μ or anti-δ antibodies.

MATERIALS AND METHODS

Patients

Within a period of six months, two male patients who were diagnosed elsewhere as agammaglobulinaemic were referred to our hospital. Diagnosis was based on virtual absence of serum immunoglobulins and normal peripheral lymphocyte counts. On admission, over 75% of blood lymphocytes in both patients appeared to be B cells; phenotypical and functional T cells were completely absent. These patients therefore were classified as SCID with B cells. Severe and multiple infections of the respiratory tract (including pneumocystis and aspergillus) resulted in death of both patients from respiratory insufficiency within two weeks after admission.

Methods

Mononuclear cells were prepared from heparinized venous blood obtained from the patients and from healthy adult volunteers, from cord blood, or from splenic

Progress in immune deficiency III, edited by H. M. Chapel, R. J. Levinsky and A. D. B. Webster, 1991; Royal Society of Medicine Services International Congress and Symposium Series No. 173, published by Royal Society of Medicine Services Limited.

tissue removed at autopsy. Procedures used for loading cells with indo-1/AM and flow cytometric analysis of changes in intracellular calcium concentrations ($[Ca^{2+}]_i$) have been described [3]. Briefly, cells were loaded with $4\,\mu M$ indo-1/AM in RPMI – 1640 medium. Indo-1 loaded cells, resuspended in calcium-containing assay buffer were analysed at 37°C on an FACS Analyser equipped with a mercury arc lamp as a UV light source. Data analysis was performed using INCA software [4]. The ratio of 405 nm and 485 nm fluorescence intensities, both measured using linear amplification, was used for calculation of relative $[Ca^{2+}]_i$.

For membrane immunofluorescence, cells were washed twice in minimal essential medium (MEM) and resuspended in MEM, 1% BSA, 0.05% Na-azide. $0.5–1\times10^6$ cells were incubated for 30 min at 4°C in $10\,\mu l$ appropriately diluted CD38 (Leu 17; Becton Dickinson), CD73 (anti-ecto 5' nucleotidase, a kind gift of Dr L. Thompson, Oklahoma), or CD45 (BD). Next, cells were washed and incubated with fluoresceinated goat anti-mouse Ig (BD) for another 30 min followed by an incubation with phycoerythrin-conjugated CD20 (Leu 16). Stained cells were run on a FACS Analyser (BD). From each sample 10 000 events were stored in list-mode and analysed using Consort 30 software.

RESULTS AND DISCUSSION

Peripheral blood lymphocytes and splenic lymphocytes in both SCID patients mainly consisted of B cells. These B cells expressed surface IgM, surface IgD, Class I and II MHC molecules, CD11 adhesion molecules, and complement receptors

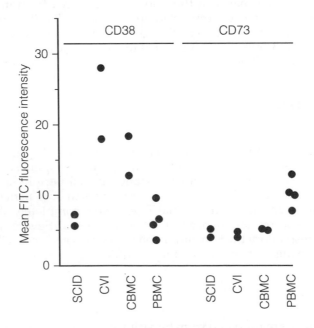

Figure 1 *Expression of CD38 and CD73. Peripheral blood mononuclear cells of SCID patients, patients with common variable immunodeficiency (CVI), or normal adult (PBMC), and cord blood MC (CBMC) were incubated with CD38 (Leu 17) or CD73 (anti-ecto-5' NT). Next cells were washed and incubated with fluoresceinated goat anti-mouse Ig followed by an incubation with phycoerythrin-conjugated CD20 (Leu 16). Mean FITC fluorescence intensity of CD20+ cells is shown.*

in a density comparable to that on normal adult B cells. SCID B cells did not, as do normal adult B cells, express CD5 (Leu 1). SCID B cells were studied for a number of other B cell differentiation antigens and compared with B cells from patients with common variable immunodeficiency (CVI) and from normal cord blood (CB). Data shown in Fig. 1 indicate that CD38, a marker for immature B cells, is expressed on CB and CVI B cells, but not on the SCID B cells.

In vitro activation of PBMC with the T cell independent polyclonal B cell mitogen *Staphylococcus aureus* Cowan I (SAC) induces IgM, IgG, or IgA containing plasma cells. In cultures of CB and CVI mononuclear cells lower numbers of (mainly IgM containing) plasma cells are generated. In both SCID patients, *in vitro* activation with SAC did not induce any plasma cell generation (data not shown).

Cross-linking of the antigen receptor on B cells initiates a series of events which lead to an elevation of the concentration of free cytoplasmic calcium ($[Ca^{2+}]_i$). In neonatal B cells lower concentrations of anti-μ are required to induce calcium mobilization. While CVI B cells mobilized calcium in response to activation with anti-μ, activation of peripheral blood or splenic B cells from both SCID patients with anti-μ or anti-δ did not lead to an increase in $[Ca^{2+}]_i$ (Fig. 2).

Recently it has been described that ligation of membrane Ig on terminally differentiated B cells does not result in a detectable Ca^{2+} mobilization response [5]. An involvement of CD45 (B220) in regulation of B cell antigen receptor-mediated signal transduction has become evident since a differentiated B cell

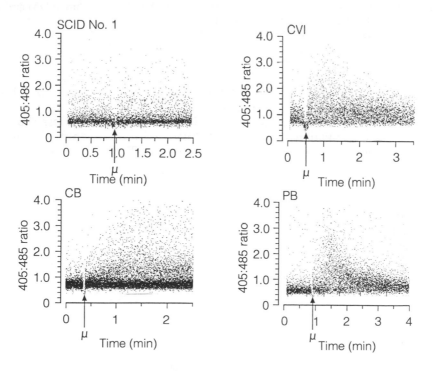

Figure 2 *Calcium response of indo-1 loaded B cells to activation with anti-μ antibodies. Non-T cells were loaded with indo-1 and resuspended in calcium-containing assay buffer. While being kept at 37°C, cells were run on a FACS Analyser to establish resting calcium levels. Anti-μ antibodies (1 μg/ml F(ab')$_2$ fragments of goat anti-human IgM) were added (indicated by an arrow) and the cells were run for an additional period of time. The relative calcium response is shown in a dot-plot format of 405:485 nm fluorescence ratio vs time.*

line lacked CD45 while transfection with CD45, which reconstituted expression, restored mIg-mediated Ca²⁺ mobilization. CD45 expression on splenic B cells was therefore studied, but found to be normal in both SCID patients.

These data indicate that an intrinsic defect exists in antigen receptor mediated signalling in B cells from these patients. Alternatively, the defect may be secondary because B cell development has taken place in the absence of T cells. Our results are not necessarily at variance with the finding that reconstitution with bone marrow induces B cell function of host origin. The presence of T cells may allow the generation of new B cells, not defective in mIg signalling.

REFERENCES

(1) Small TN, Keever C, Collins N, Dupont B, O'Reilly RJ, Flomenberg N. Characterization of B cells in severe combined immunodeficiency disease. *Hum Immunol* 1989; **25**: 181–93.
(2) O'Reilly RJ, Keever CA, Small TN, Brochstein J. The use of HLA-non-identical T-cell-depleted marrow transplants for correction of severe combined immunodeficiency disease. *Immunodef Rev* 1989; **1**: 273–9.
(3) Griffioen AW, Rijkers GT, Zegers BJM. Measurement of cytoplasmic calcium in lymphocytes using flow cytometry. *J Immunol Methods* 1988; **120**: 23–7.
(4) Rijkers GT, Griffioen AW, Gregory CD, Keij J, Zegers BJM. Calcium mobilization in B lymphocytes measured by flow cytometry. *Progress in Cytometry* 1989: 63–73.
(5) Justement LB, Wienands J, Hombach J, Reth M, Cambier JC. Membrane IgM and IgD molecules fail to transduce Ca²⁺ mobilizing signals when expressed on differentiated B lineage cells. *J Immunol* 1990; **144**: 3272–80.

Note added in proof

Recently, a second child was born in family No. 1. The diagnosis of SCID with B cells in this child, a girl, was based on the presence of more than 50% CD20 B cells in cord blood mononuclear cells and the virtual absence (less than 2%) of CD3+T cells. Activation of cord blood B cells with anti-μ antibodies in this patient did, however, lead to a normal calcium mobilization response.

Severe combined immunodeficiency (B- SCID) patients show an altered recombination pattern at the JH locus

K. Schwarz[1,2], T. E. Hansen-Hagge[2], W. Friedrich[1], E. Kleihauer[1] and C. R. Bartram[1,2]

[1]Department of Pediatrics II and [2]Section of Molecular Biology,
University of Ulm, D-7900 Ulm, Germany

INTRODUCTION

Severe, combined immunodeficiency (SCID) is a rare, heterogeneous lethal congenital disorder of the lymphatic system. The loss of enzymatic functions of the purine salvage pathway (adenosine deaminase, purine nucleoside phosphorylase), lack of signal transduction (IL-1) or interleukin-2 production (IL-2) and loss of the expression of restriction elements for the HLA loci are known causes for the disturbed humoral and cellular immune function in respective patients [1]. These deficiencies account for approximately 20–30% of SCIDs in humans.

One of the prerequisites for the development of functional lymphocytes is the correct joining of distinct gene elements (variable = V, diversity = D, joining = J elements; V(D)J joining) to generate coding sequences for immunoglobulin (Ig) and T cell receptor (TCR) variable regions [2,3].

This assembly process of the elements is tightly regulated, occurs in a preferential temporal order (For example: $D_H J_H$ prior to $V_H D_H J_H$ recombinations; subsequently $V_L J_L$ recombinations) and in a lineage specific manner (T cell receptor loci are not functionally rearranged in B cells and *vice versa*).

Rearrangement is thought to be mediated by a site-specific recombination system (the so-called VDJ recombinase). The recombinase system has not been characterized yet and V(D)J assembly is only partly understood. Each of these gene elements is flanked by a highly conserved heptamer-spacer-nonamer DNA sequence motif (recombination recognition signal) marking the ends of the DNA which is deleted during the recombination process. T and B lymphocytes make use of the same recombination machinery [4].

Recently a SCID mouse model has been described [5]. Studies of Abelson murine leukaemia virus (A-MuLV) transformed pre-B cell lines derived from homozygous SCID mice indicated that the V(D)J recombinase in SCID pre-B cells can recognize appropriate gene segments and make endonucleolytic cuts between coding and signal sequences; the defect appears to affect the terminal stages of coding joint formation at the point when the DNA ends are to be ligated [6].

Progress in immune deficiency III, edited by H. M. Chapel, R. J. Levinsky and A. D. B. Webster, 1991; Royal Society of Medicine Services International Congress and Symposium Series No. 173, published by Royal Society of Medicine Services Limited.

The failure for a productive rearrangement on either allele of an antigen receptor gene affects the developing lymphocyte, which will in turn be non-functional and will presumably die.

In contrast to the inbred SCID mouse strain(s), human SCIDs are heterogeneous in their molecular defects. B- SCIDs lack functional B and T lymphocytes indicating a mutation in a gene important for the differentiation of both cell lineages and giving rise to the question whether some subtypes of human SCIDs have analogous recombination disorders as shown for the SCID mouse model. Due to the very limited amount of patient sample DNA available, we established a polymerase chain reaction (PCR)-based assay to address these questions.

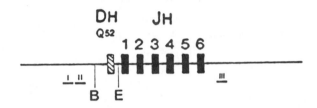

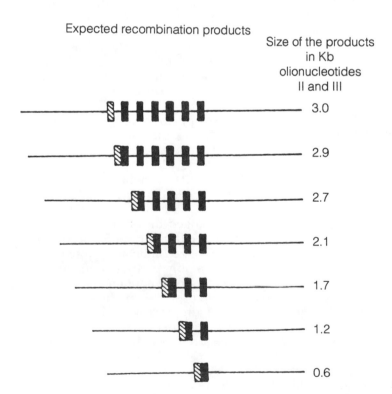

Figure 1 *Schematic drawing of the strategy used for the PCR amplification of possible D_{HQ52}-J_H recombinations in bone marrow or PBL DNA.*
The D_{HQ52}-J_H locus was amplified using either primers I/III or oligonucleotides II/III. The recombination products and their expected sizes (for primers II and III) are shown. B = Bgl II, E = EcoN I.

STRATEGY

In the early development of B cells, the majority of the rearranged alleles represent joining of the most 3' D segment (D_{HQ52}) to one of the six J_H segments, suggesting that this D segment is a preferential target for the initiation of IgH gene rearrangements [7]. Since the DNA sequence at the IgH D_{HQ52}-J_H locus has been published [8], we designed the PCR strategy [9] for the amplification of recombined D_{HQ52}-J_H loci as outlined in Fig. 1.

Briefly, DNA is isolated from bone marrow or from peripheral blood and amplified by PCR. The primers were chosen to include the D_{HQ52} as well as all

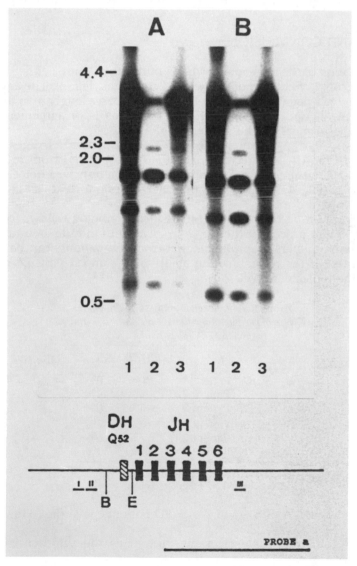

Figure 2 *Southern blot analysis (0.8% gel) of the amplification products of bone marrow DNA of healthy donors. Probe A was used for detection. The DNA was undigested (lane 1) or cut with EcoN I (lane 2) or BamH (lane 3). The amplification primers were oligonucleotides I/III (A) or II/III (B).*

six J_H elements. The amplified DNA products are used for Southern blotting and hybridized to probes of the J_H locus.

A germ-line configuration of the D_{HQ52} locus is indicated by amplified products of 3.0 kb when primers II/III are used. A rearrangement of D_{HQ52} to any of the J_H elements shows up as a distinct, yet shorter fragment, since DNA is deleted during the recombination process. (For example: $D_{HQ52}J_4$ rearrangement yields a 1.7 kb fragment.)

Amplification products with sizes different from those predicted may indicate illegitimate recombination events. To enrich for recombination events versus the germ-line product, the DNA can be digested with EcoN I prior to the amplification, since EcoN I cuts only the germ-line and not the rearranged configurations.

RESULTS AND CONCLUSIONS

The amplification of the bone marrow DNA of healthy donors, either undigested or cut with EcoN I, yields bands of the predicted sizes (Fig. 2). The amplification products of primer pair (I/III) (Fig. 2A) are about 100 bases longer than the products obtained with oligonucleotides II/III (Fig. 2B). This is in agreement with the position of the primers on the sequence map.

The D_{HQ52}-J_2 rearrangement is resolved only after EcoN I digestion of the sample DNA. The D_{HQ52}-J_1 recombination is not separated from the germ-line band in this gel system. The same amplification pattern was detected in bone marrow (Fig. 2, Fig. 4: N1, N2) and peripheral mononuclear cell DNA (Fig. 3: N1, N2) of normal donors.

This newly developed assay based on the PCR technology allows us to analyse the rearrangement process at the D_{HQ52}-J_H locus with minute amounts of DNA. The constraints of sparse sample material from the patients can be overcome. Therefore a test of the recombination ability of B+ and B− SCIDs (Table 1) is feasible at the molecular level.

Table 1 *Fluorescence analysis of the phenotype of peripheral mononuclear cells of B− and
B+ SCID patients*

		CD 20	CD 3
B− SCID	Patient 1	0%	0%
	Patient 2	0%	44%
	Patient 3	<1%	70%[a]
B+ SCID	Patient 1	65%	7%
	Patient 2	8%	0%
	Patient 3	60%	11%

[a] Maternal T cells as judged by HLA typing of cells separated by magnetic beads.

The analysis of DNA of B+ and B− SCID patients gave the following result:

B+ SCIDs recombined with the same pattern as their normal counterparts (Fig. 3: S 1–3).
All B− SCIDs had an abnormal recombination pattern (Fig. 4: S1–3) with the loss of all (Fig. 4: S 2) or some (Fig. 4: S 1, S 3) recombination fragments or with irregular sizes of some of the products (Fig. 4: S 3).

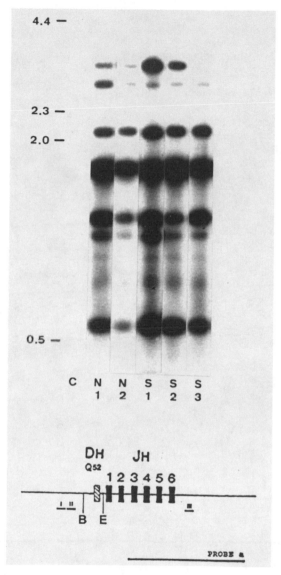

Figure 3 *Southern blot analysis (0.8% gel) of the amplification products of PBL DNA of normal donors (N1, N2) and B+ SCID patients (S1–S3). The DNA was digested with EcoN I prior to amplification with oligonucleotides II/III. The filters were hybridized to probe A.*

To our knowledge this is the first time that a difference between B+ and B− SCID has been defined at the molecular level.

The presumed mutation(s) in B+ SCID do(es) not affect the recombinase system at the level tested here. However, these results indicate that B− SCID patients apparently lack the normal recombination ability at this locus. In analogy to the SCID mouse model this is possibly due to a less efficient or even defective recombination machinery or to changes in the regulation of the V(D)J recombinase. The maturation block of the B cell compartment is most likely at the early pro-B cell level.

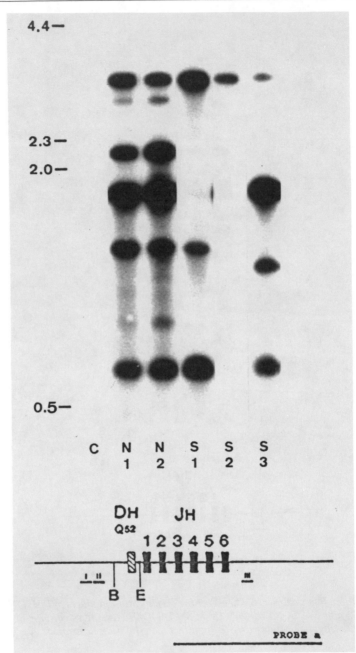

Figure 4 *Southern blot analysis (0.8% gel) of the amplification products of bone marrow DNA of normal donors (N1, N2) and B− SCID patients (S1–S3). The DNA was digested with EcoN I prior to amplification with oligonucleotides II/III. The filters were hybridized to probe A.*

The detection of some normally sized fragments in B− SCIDs can be explained either by the leakiness of the presumed recombinase defect, or by (incomplete) rearrangement in materno-fetally transfused cells or by illegitimate recombinations.

The case for a mutation affecting the recombinase system could certainly be strengthened if a similarly irregular rearrangement pattern is detected in the T cell lineage of B− SCID patients. Analysis of maternal X-chromosome inactivation in obligate carriers of the disease [10] supports the notion that an (enzymatic) machinery important for the development of both B and T cells is defective in SCID patients.

SUMMARY

The use of a newly established assay, which is based on the PCR of the D_{HQ52}-J_H locus and Southern blotting allows differentiation of B+ and B− SCID patients according to their recombination capacity.

B+ SCID patients show the pattern of healthy donors.
B− SCID patients have a grossly altered recombination pattern.

The lack of a normal recombination ability of B− SCID patients may locate the differentiation block of the B cell compartment in these patients to the stage of the early pro-B cells.

REFERENCES

(1) Gelfand EW. SCID continues to point the way. N Engl J Med 1990; **322**: 1741–3.
(2) Blackwell TK, Alt FW. In: Hames BD, Flover DM, eds. Molecular immunology. Oxford: IRL Press, 1989; 1–60.
(3) David MM. In: Hames BD, Flover DM, eds. Molecular immunology. Oxford: IRL Press, 1989: 61–79.
(4) Yancopoulos G, Blackwell TK, Suh N, et al. Introduced T cell receptor variable region gene segments recombine in a pre-B cells: evidence that B and T cells use a common recombinase. Cell 1986; **44**: 251–9.
(5) Bosma GC, Custer RP, Bosma MJ. A severe combined aminodeficiency mutation in the mouse. Nature 1983; **301**: 527–30.
(6) Lewis S, Gellert M. The mechanism of antigen receptor gene assembly. Cell 1989; **59**: 585–8.
(7) Nickerson KG, Berman J, Glickman E, Chess L, Alt FW. Early human IgH gene assembly in Epstein–Barr virus Transformed fetal B cell lines. Preferential utilization of the most JH-proximal D segment (DQ52) and two unusual VH-related rearrangements. J Exp Med 1989; **169**: 1391–403.
(8) Ravetch JV, Siebenlist U, Korsmeyer S, Waldmann T, Leder P. Structure of the human immunoglobulin μ locus: Characterisation of embryonic and rearranged J and D genes. Cell 1981; **27**: 583–91.
(9) Saiki RK, Gelfand DH, Stoffel S, Scharf SJ, Higuchi R, Horn GT, Mullis KB, Erlich HA. Primer-directed enzymatic amplification of DNA with a thermostable DNA polymerase. Science 1988; **239**: 487–91.
(10) Puck JM, Krauss CM, Puck SM, Buckley RH, Conley ME. Prenatal test for X-linked severe combined immunodeficiency by analysis of maternal X-chromosome inactivation and linkage analysis. N Engl J Med 1990; **322**: 1063–6.

A new variant of the DiGeorge syndromes

K. Kouvalainen[1], J. Leisti[2], A. Mustonen[2], R. Herva[3] and E. Herva[4]

[1]Departments of Pediatrics, [2]Clinical Genetics and
[3]Pathology, University of Oulu,
and [4]National Institute of Health, Oulu, Finland

(POSTER)

The classic DiGeorge syndrome includes absence or hypoplasia of the thymus and parathyroid glands, a typical appearance, and cardiac and great artery abnormalities. The aplasia of the thymus is associated with impaired lymphocyte functions, and the lack of parathyroids results in hypoparathyroidism.

Patients with different degrees and presentations of DiGeorge anomalies have been described. Thomas et al. have estimated that theoretically there are 38 possible variants [1].

We report here a new variant of the DiGeorge syndrome with dominantly inherited periauricular pits, ear anomalies and some new clinical and immunological findings.

A male infant was born to a 30-year-old mother and 31-year-old father who both had dominantly inherited preauricular pits. The infant had severely malformed auricles and ear canals, fistulae, an antimongoloid slant, a small nose, narrow nostrils, a peculiar mouth, a high and narrow palate, slight mandibular hypoplasia, cryptorchidism, angular clavicles, vertebral anomalies, and bilateral subluxation of the hips. A ventricular septal defect was also found in the newborn state, but it was found to have closed spontaneously later. The patient was in good condition after delivery and a BCG vaccination was carried out. The first month of life was uneventful. From the second month on the patient developed a number of pathological conditions: eczema and later erythrodermia, incurable oral candidiasis, and at five months of age fever and markedly enlarged lymph nodes. Tuberculosis was diagnosed from the lymph nodes and appropriate antibiotic therapy was started. In spite of this the patient died with clinical signs of pneumonia at 7.5 months. The results of laboratory tests were as follows: no thymus shadow in X-ray picture, Ca 1.72–1.93 mmol/l (neonatal values 1.99–2.27), Pi 1.44–1.68 mmol/l, parathormone below 0.25 µg/l, phagocytosis and NBT tests normal; IgM 0.86, IgA 0.17, IgG 2.76, and IgD 0.01 g/l, IgE 815 IU/l. The blood leucocyte count was $16.2-27.1\times10^9$/l and the percentage of lymphocytes and eosinophils 23–78 and 5–15 respectively. The percentage of T lymphocytes was 65 and that of the B cells 2. The ratio of CD4+/CD8+ T cells was 0.5. The response of peripheral blood lymphocytes to PHA was 32–100% and weak to ConA and PWM, this being seen more clearly in seven-day cultures than in three-day ones. There was no response to PPD, tetanus or diphtheria toxoids. Interestingly, a high proliferative activity of unstimulated seven-day cultures was found repeatedly (2386–2436 cpm versus 29–304 in controls). The abnormalities in the numbers and functioning of T lymphocytes explain the susceptibility of the patient to BCG tuberculosis of the lymph nodes, chronic candidiasis and Pneumocystis carinii pneumonia, diagnoses which were verified at autopsy. No thymus or parathyroids were found at autopsy. The lymphatic tissues were found to be partially hypoplastic, but the paracortical areas were even hyperplastic in some lymph nodes. Portal hepatitis was seen in autopsy samples, and the exfoliative erythrodermia and the extremely high spontaneous mitotic activity of blood lymphocytes may point to a GVH reaction. In such a case the reacting lymphocytes could have been transferred from the mother via the placenta or breast milk. The brother of the patient born two years later also has

Progress in immune deficiency III, edited by H. M. Chapel, R. J. Levinsky and A. D. B. Webster, 1991; Royal Society of Medicine Services International Congress and Symposium Series No. 173, published by Royal Society of Medicine Services Limited.

preauricular pits (T4/T8 ratio during the first year 13.7–4.1; later 2.0). Furthermore, the mother had a therapeutic abortion because of fetal hydronephrosis. The clinical and immunological findings, together with the peculiar inheritance pattern suggested by the parents' and brother's preauricular pits, make this case a new variant of the DiGeorge branchial arch syndromes.

REFERENCE

(1) Thomas RA, Landing BH, Wells TR. Embryologic and other developmental considerations of thirty-eight possible variants of the DiGeorge anomaly. *Am J Med Genet* 1987; **3** (suppl 3): 43–66.

Hypogammaglobulinaemia four years after a compatible bone marrow transplantation in a SCID girl

T. Español[1], I. Caragol[1], J. Garcia[1], S. Sauleda[1] and J. J. Ortega[2]

Departments of [1]Immunology and [2]Paediatric Haematology, R. S. Valle Hebrón, Barcelona, Spain

(POSTER)

Bone marrow transplantation (BMT) is the only effective therapy in severe combined immunodeficiency (SCID), but in cases in which T cell depleted BM is used, there is a high incidence of persistent antibody deficiency [1]. In the vast majority of patients with compatible BM full reconstitution has been observed.

In our case, antibody deficiency was detected four years after histocompatible BMT. Because of very low B cell numbers we have not been able to demonstrate if they are of host origin. The causes of antibody deficiency could be a T–B cell collaboration defect, because of donor B cell engraftment, or due to B cell failure or to subclinical GvH disease. The different pathogenic mechanisms have important therapeutic implications.

CASE REPORT

A six year old girl was diagnosed as suffering from SCID at three months of age and received a non-conditioned BMT (2.6×10^6 cells/kg) at five months of age from an HLA-compatible

Table 1 *Immunological follow-up*

Age:	4 months	BMT	8 months	1 year	1.5 years	3 years	5 years	5.5 years	IVIg	6 years
CD3 (%)[a]	2		26	55	67	64	69	66		72
CD4 (%)	3		10	31	29	23	18	26		23
CD8 (%)	12		19	32	27	41	43	42		41
CD20 (%)	0		3	14	7	2	1	1		1
CD25 (%) (PHA-stim.)	2		5	12		30	32			38
PHA resp	2		8	27	20	26	8	29		32
PWM resp (index)[b]	1			3		7				
Ig G(mg%)	135		1200	635	555	531	395	200		788
Ig M(mg%)	3		499	34	39	27	27	17		15
Ig A(mg%)	1		16	10	16	6	6	6		6
Ig G2(mg%)							32			
% of total IgG							8			
MLC[c]	8%						17%			
Ig production *in vitro*[d]: ng/ml.								299/254		

[a] using MoAb and analysis in FACS
[b] normal values PHA resp.index > 20, PWM resp.index > 10
[c] Relative response is calculated as $\dfrac{(R^i + D) - D}{(C^i + D) - D} \times 100$
[d] 12 days culture with and without PWM, control values: 954/697 ng/ml.

Progress in immune deficiency III, edited by H. M. Chapel, R. J. Levinsky and A. D. B. Webster, 1991; *Royal Society of Medicine Services International Congress and Symposium Series No. 173*, published by Royal Society of Medicine Services Limited.

brother. She was treated with four doses of MTX, corticosteroids for two weeks, ALG two days because of neutropenia and eosinophilia and IV immunoglobulin (Ig) for two months. Peripheral blood chimaerism was demonstrated 1.5 months after BMT (Table 1).

She has been in very good clinical conditions but in the last two years she has had some upper respiratory tract infections that have improved with antibiotics. She has been treated with IVIg therapy for the past six months.

DISCUSSION

B cells were present for the first two years after BMT. Since then Ig levels have been decreasing very slowly with minor clinical manifestations. Although Ig therapy will substitute the lack of antibody function, a subclinical form of GvHD may underly the present immunological status, and a different form of therapy might be required.

REFERENCE

(1) O'Reilly RJ, Keever CA, Small TN, Brochstein J. The use of HLA-non-identical T-cell depleted marrow transplants for correction of severe combined immunodeficiency disease. *Immunodef Rev* 1989; **1**: 273–309.

Prenatal diagnosis of SCID by fetal blood immunophenotyping

M. Watts[1], D. Linch[1], G. Morgan[2], R. Levinsky[2],
K. Nicolaides[3] and C. Rodeck[4]

[1]University College and Middlesex Hospital School of Medicine, [2]Institute of Child Health,
[3]Kings College Hospital and [4]Institute of Obstetrics and Gynaecology, London, UK

(POSTER)

Although some forms of severe combined immunodeficiency (SCID) can be diagnosed prenatally by enzyme analysis or genetic analysis of fetal derived tissue, these approaches cannot be applied to all cases. Phenotype analysis of fetal blood allows diagnosis of all at risk cases, provided the disease is manifest *in utero*. We have used this technique successfully to identify all nine cases of SCID in 29 consecutive cases at risk for the disease.

0.2–1.0 ml of EDTA or heparinized blood was used for analysis. This was obtained by fetoscopy-guided, or more recently ultrasound-guided, cordiocentesis. Fetal purity was proved by channelyser analysis of the red cell volume.

Haematological measurements included a total nucleated cell count (TNCC) on a Coulter analyser, with a visual differential cell count on MGG stained blood films to assess lymphocyte and nucleated red cell numbers, and thus derive an absolute lymphocyte count.

Initial immunophenotyping was by a micro-titre plate FACS method using a CD45 monoclonal to distinguish leucocytes from nucleated red cells. This was compared against a reference range from 14 normal fetal blood samples.

This method, however, involved washing, lysis, and manipulation of the data to allow for the indirect determination of nucleated red cell numbers. It was replaced by a more direct standard PAP staining method of fixed buffy coat smears for which reference values from 39 normal prenatal blood samples was determined. The mean T cell phenotype results by PAP gave approximately 25% higher readings than the FACS method. Seven monoclonal antibodies were selected for use as a diagnostic panel; CD7, CD3, CD4, CD8 and CD22.

The absolute values for mean and ranges of lymphocyte count and subtype of PAP on 39 normal (17–22 week gestation) fetal samples were in good agreement with other published values. These were ($\times 10^9$/l); lymphocytes, 1.8 (0.7–4.4); CD7 1.4 (0.5–3.4); CD3 1.4 (0.5–3.4); CD4 1.1 (0.4–2.4); CD8 0.3 (0.1–0.8); and CD22 0.2 (<0.1–0.5).

Nine of the 29 at-risk fetuses were predicted as SCID on the basis of marked lymphopenia ($<0.5 \times 10^9$/l), extremely low, or total absence of CD3 ($<0.1 \times 10^9$/l), and absence of CD4 and CD8. Parents of all predicted cases elected for termination of pregnancy. Athymia was confirmed at autopsy in every case. Interestingly, in some cases of SCID a small number of non-B lymphocytes were present which were positive with antibodies to the early T cell (CD7) antigen, though negative for CD3. In three of the 29 at-risk samples intermediate T cell values were seen with a CD3 count lower than any normal value. This could indicate that heterozygotes have low values *in utero* at mid-gestation. Of the 20 at-risk fetuses diagnosed as negative for SCID by immunophenotyping, there have been three spontaneous abortions, 15 normal pregnancies, with two pregnancies continuing.

Prenatal diagnosis of SCID by leucocyte phenotyping of fetal blood is thus highly reliable although the presence of intermediate values in possible heterozygotes indicates the need for accurate determination of absolute values. The process of obtaining fetal blood may pose a risk to the fetus, although in large series of cordiocentesis for other indications the risk is less than 2%.

Progress in immune deficiency III, edited by H. M. Chapel, R. J. Levinsky and A. D. B. Webster, 1991; Royal Society of Medicine Services International Congress and Symposium Series No. 173, published by Royal Society of Medicine Services Limited.

In an rgp 160-immunized chimpanzee challenge with HIV is not followed by an antibody response to viral core proteins

J. W. Mannhalter[1,2], M. M. Eibl[2], F. Dorner[1], B. Moss[3], R. C. Gallo[3] and G. Eder[1]

[1]Immuno AG, Vienna, Austria, [2]Institute of Immunology, University of Vienna, Vienna, Austria and [3]National Institutes of Health, Bethesda, MD, USA.

(ABSTRACT)

In order to test the potency of an HIV candidate vaccine chimpanzees received six intramuscular doses of recombinant gp160 (rgp 160, 50μg per immunization) mixed with a lipid-based adjuvant on days 0,25,55,97,120 and 147. This immunization led to a substantial and long lasting T cell memory towards rgp 160 which was observed for several months after the last booster. Serum titres of neutralizing antibodies (Ab), however, never exceeded 1:20. On day 315 of the study period two rgp 160-immunized chimpanzees (D8,E7) and one control animal (D6) were challenged by intravenous injection with 10^2TCID$_{50}$ units of HIV-1 (III B strain). At the time of challenge substantial gp 160-specific T cell proliferative responses (indicating the presence of gp 160-primed memory T cells) were observed, whereas neutralizing antibody titres were already decreased.

In immunized chimps HIV challenge was followed by a rapid and long-lasting increase in the capacity of chimpanzee lymphocytes to become activated upon stimulation with rgp 160 (activation was measured by the expression of the IL2-receptor CD25; maximal post-challenge values were 92% CD25$^+$ cells for chimp E7 and 34% CD25$^+$ cells for chimp D8; the corresponding pre-challenge data were 56% (E7) and 20% (D8)). In the control animal the capacity of lymphocytes to become activated upon gp 160 stimulation developed much more slowly and never exceeded 20%. HIV challenge also led to the generation of core specific antibodies (determined by Westerns blots) in animal D8 and in the control chimpanzee. In contrast, animal E7 remained completely negative for antibodies to HIV core and regulatory proteins, which suggests control of viral replication.

Progress in immune deficiency III, edited by H. M. Chapel, R. J. Levinsky and A. D. B. Webster, 1991; Royal Society of Medicine Services International Congress and Symposium Series No. 173, published by Royal Society of Medicine Services Limited.

Accelerated ontogeny of UCHLI (CD45RO) expression on T lymphocytes of HIV infected infants

A. G. Bird[1], K. Docherty[1], J. Whitelaw[1], R. Hague[2], J. Mok[2] and K. Froebel[1]

[1]HIV Immunology Unit, Department of Medicine, Edinburgh University, and [2]Department of Infectious Diseases, City Hospital, Edinburgh, UK

(POSTER)

The monoclonal antibody, UCHL1, recognizes the 180 KD isoform variant of the CD45 leucocyte common antigen and is thought to represent the population of human lymphocytes containing memory T cells [1]. In the cord blood of normal infants this antigen is expressed on few (<5%) T cells and the proportion rises during the first 15 years of life to reach adult levels when 40–60% of T lymphocytes express CD45RO [2]. In normal ontogeny the proportion of CD4 cells expressing CD45RO exceeds that of the CD8 population in the majority of individuals. In HIV infection, functional impairment of memory T cell responses is one of the earliest markers of the progressive immunodeficiency and we, therefore, examined the consequences of HIV vertical transmission on the ontogeny of CD45RO in infected children.

MATERIALS AND METHODS

Nine children (aged >18 months) born to HIV-infected mothers and who were consistently HIV antibody positive from birth were studied. Control samples from 10 HIV-negative children (aged >18 months) born to positive mothers and five non-risk negative children were compared. Lymphocytes were examined by dual-colour immunofluorescence for co-expression of CD45RO and CD3, CD4 or CD8 using FITC conjugated UCHL1 (DAKO) and phycoerythrin-coupled Leu 4a, 3a or 2a (Becton Dickinson) using the whole blood lysis technique.

RESULTS

The respective expression of CD45RO on CD4 and 8 populations at different ages is shown in Table 1. Accelerated expression of CD45RO was seen in both CD4 and 8 populations in HIV-infected children. The overall fall in CD4 absolute count in HIV-infected children resulted in lower absolute numbers of CD4+ CD45RO+ cells though the percentages were elevated in this group. In the CD8 population, both the percentages and absolute values for CD8+ CD45RO+ were strikingly elevated at all ages, and also in comparison with previously published data [2]. In two HIV-infected children, more than 90% of CD8 lymphocytes consistently expressed CD45RO.

DISCUSSION

This study demonstrates a consistent expansion of CD45RO-positive T cells in all HIV vertically infected children examined, preferentially involving the CD8 subpopulation. The majority of the Edinburgh HIV-infected children remain well, despite relatively long-standing infection and only one of the children studied has established AIDS. It is possible

Progress in immune deficiency III, edited by H. M. Chapel, R. J. Levinsky and A. D. B. Webster, 1991; Royal Society of Medicine Services International Congress and Symposium Series No. 173, published by Royal Society of Medicine Services Limited.

Table 1 *Expression of CD45RO on CD4 and CD8 populations at different ages*

Patient group	Age (months)	No.	CD4/CD45RO		CD8/CD45RO	
			Percent	Abs.No./mm^3	Percent	Abs.No./mm^3
Infected	19–36	2	35	330	35^a	490^a
	37–80	7	56^b	280	71^b	1370^b
Uninfected	19–36	9	15	410	18	180
	37–80	6	31	345	16	125

Patients significantly higher than controls (Mann Whitney U test);
$^a p < 0.05$
$^b p < 0.01$

that within this expanded memory population are HIV-specific CD8 T cells. Longitudinal follow-up and functional analysis of the individual populations are in progress.

REFERENCES

(1) Terry LA, Brown MH, Beverley PCL. Monoclonal antibody UCHL1 recognizes 180,000 MW component of the human leukocyte-common antigen CD45. *Immunology* 1988; **64**: 331–6.
(2) Hayward AR, Lee J, Beverley PCL. Ontogeny of expression of UCHL1 antigen on TcR-1+ (CD4/8) and TcRδ + Tr cells. *Eur J Immunol* 1989; **19**: 771–3.

Acquired immunodeficiency syndrome following mother-to-child transmission of human immunodeficiency virus type 2

G. Morgan[1,3], H. A. Wilkins[1], J. Pepin[1], O. Jobe[1], D. Brewster[2] and H. Whittle[1]

[1]Medical Research Council Laboratories and [2]Royal Victoria Hospital, The Gambia, West Africa and [3]Department of Immunology, Institute of Child Health, University of London

(POSTER)

Infection with human immunodeficiency virus type 2 (HIV2) is thought to cause less morbidity and mortality than infection with HIV1. HIV2 was initially detected in predominantly healthy individuals and the reported absence of clinical signs of immunodeficiency in a cohort of 92 HIV2 seropositive prostitutes followed since 1985 in Senegal are suggestive of a low frequency of immunodeficiency induced by HIV2 infection, even allowing for an incubation period greater than for HIV1. However, a recent study from Guinea-Bissau reported a significant excess mortality amongst HIV2 seropositive individuals.

Mother-to-child transmission of HIV1 occurs in approximately one-third of children born to HIV1 seropositive mothers. Many of these children subsequently develop AIDS following a variable incubation period.

Mother-to-child infection with HIV2 is thought to be rare, and there have been few previous reports of transmission by this route. Reports of morbidity associated with HIV2 infection in children are also rare. We are aware of only one report of morbidity associated with HIV2 transmission from mother to child: no evidence of mother-to-child transmission was found in a total of 66 children born to HIV2 seropositive mothers in Guinea-Bissau.

We describe eight children born to mothers who were infected with HIV2: five developed AIDS and three were still seropositive at 17 to 49 months of age. The only apparent route of HIV2 transmission was from mother to child, except for one child who had been transfused. Three of the children with AIDS died, all having decreased CD4+ve lymphocytes and mitogen responses.

Two factors may explain why mother-to-child transmission has been observed in this study and not in others. Firstly, the generally advanced stage of HIV2 infection in the mothers of our cases. Four mothers in our study had AIDS and a fifth had generalized lymphadenopathy, whereas previously transmission in asymptomatic mothers was studied. Secondly, there may be varying pathogenicity of HIV2 strains. Recent studies have shown that the wide genetic variation seen between isolates of HIV1 also occurs in HIV2 isolates, and that the replicative and cytopathic characteristics of HIV2 vary with the severity of infection.

Further studies are needed to determine the prevalence and natural history of mother-to-child transmission of HIV2.

Progress in immune deficiency III, edited by H. M. Chapel, R. J. Levinsky and A. D. B. Webster, 1991; Royal Society of Medicine Services International Congress and Symposium Series No. 173, published by Royal Society of Medicine Services Limited.

Both IgA subclasses are reduced in saliva from patients with AIDS

F. Müller[1], S. S. Frøland[2] and P. Brandtzaeg[1]

[1]Laboratory for Immunohistochemistry and Immunopathology, Institute of Pathology and
[2]Section of Clinical Immunology and Infectious Diseases, Medical Department A, University of Oslo,
The National Hospital, Rikshospitalet, Oslo, Norway

(POSTER)

INTRODUCTION

Many of the opportunistic infections in AIDS are related to the mucous membranes. It is therefore important to study the mucosal immune system in patients with HIV infection. The systemic B cell response seen in adult patients with HIV infection is usually characterized by a polyclonal hypergammaglobulinaemia, often comprising several immunoglobulin (Ig) classes. However, little is known about the Ig concentrations in the external secretions. The aim of this study was to examine how HIV infection influences the level of secretory IgA (SIgA) and IgM (SIgM) in parotid saliva, which is an external secretion that can be collected under acceptable and controllable conditions.

MATERIALS AND METHODS

Peripheral blood and acid-stimulated parotid saliva were obtained from 28 individuals with asymptomatic HIV infection, 16 patients with AIDS, and 19 HIV-seronegative controls. Oral infections comprised candidiasis ($n=7$), Herpes simplex ($n=2$), and ulcerative stomatitis of unknown origin ($n=2$).

Parotid total IgA, SIgA, IgA1, IgA2, and IgM were measured by catch ELISA, whereas serum Ig levels were determined by nephelometry.

RESULTS AND DISCUSSION

The parotid output of SIgA from patients with AIDS was significantly reduced compared with both the HIV-seronegative controls and the individuals with asymptomatic HIV

Table 1 *Parotid SIgA, serum IgA and CD4+ lymphocyte counts in peripheral blood from patients from HIV infection and controls*

Subject category	Parotid SIgA (mg/l)	Serum IgA (g/l)	CD4+ lymphocytes in blood ($\times 10^6$/l)
HIV-seronegative controls	23.0 (11.2–32.9)	2.8 (2.1–3.8)	810 (700–980)
Asymptomatic HIV-positive patients	17.1 (12.5–27.2)	2.9 (2.0–3.7)	400[a] (270–510)
AIDS patients	10.4[b] (7.1–15.7)	6.9[b] (5.2–9.0)	60[b] (40–80)

Data are given as medians and 25–75 percentiles.
[a]$p<0.05$ vs controls and AIDS patients
[b]$p<0.05$ vs controls and asymptomatic HIV-positive patients

Progress in immune deficiency III, edited by H. M. Chapel, R. J. Levinsky and A. D. B. Webster, 1991; Royal Society of Medicine Services International Congress and Symposium Series No. 173, published by Royal Society of Medicine Services Limited.

infection (Table 1). The reduced SIgA in the AIDS patients comprised both IgA1 and IgA2. The former subclass was reduced to 69% of the control level and the latter to 68%. Patients with a low number of CD4$^+$ lymphocytes in peripheral blood ($<200 \times 10^6$/l) had significantly lower SIgA output compared with HIV-infected patients with CD4$^+$ lymphocyte counts $>200 \times 10^6$/l (10.4 mg/l vs 17.0 mg/l).

The reduced SIgA output in AIDS patients may be of pathogenetic significance for the frequent oral infections seen in these subjects, since those with oral infections had significantly lower SIgA output than patients without such lesions (11.0 mg/l vs 17.0 mg/l).

The low parotid SIgA concentration in the AIDS patients was in striking contrast to their raised serum IgA levels (Table 1). There was a significant relationship between reduced parotid SIgA output and a low number of circulating CD4$^+$ lymphocytes.

No significant difference in the parotid IgM output was found between patient and control groups. Only a slight trend towards a compensatory IgM response was noted in patients with low parotid SIgA output.

The molecular basis of a common defect of opsonization

M. W. Turner[1], M. Super[1], R. J. Levinsky[1] and J. A. Summerfield[2]

[1]Department of Immunology, Institute of Child Health, London and [2]Department of Medicine, St Mary's Hospital Medical School, Imperial College, London, UK

INTRODUCTION

The term opsonization refers to the process of coating micro-organisms with molecules which will interact specifically with receptors on neutrophils and/or mononuclear phagocytes. When first described by Wright and Douglas [1] it was clear that more than one mechanism was involved but the extent of this heterogeneity is only just beginning to be appreciated. Most significantly, advances in our knowledge of the structure and function of phagocyte receptors have provided a more comprehensive understanding of the corresponding opsonic ligands. Antibody molecules comprise one of the two major groups of opsonins and at least four receptors are involved in these interactions (reviewed by Pound and Walker [2]). The $Fc_\gamma R1$ receptor is expressed on mononuclear cells and binds to monomeric IgG1, IgG3 and IgG4. $Fc_\gamma RII$ is a low affinity receptor expressed on many cell types including neutrophils and recognizes IgG1 and IgG3 only. Similarly $Fc_\gamma RIII$ is also low affinity, is expressed on neutrophils and macrophages and interacts with IgG1 and IgG3. More recently an IgA receptor ($Fc_\alpha R$) has been described and there is clear evidence that IgA1 and IgA2 can also behave as opsonins.

The other major opsonic molecules are those derived from complement component C3 and their interactions with membrane receptors have also been the subject of much recent investigation (reviewed by Lambris [3]). The initial major C3 cleavage product—C3b—is able to interact with CR1 receptors which are expressed on the surfaces of various cells including mononuclear phagocytes and neutrophils. The other major C3 derived opsonin is C3bi which is produced by enzymic modification of C3b. This molecule interacts primarily with two phagocyte receptors, namely CR3 and CR4 (p150, 95).

The complex interplay of all the above opsonic ligands and their corresponding receptors constitutes a major defence mechanism and plays a central role in much antimicrobial immunity. Antibody and complement exert both individual and synergistic effects and may, to some extent, be compensatory. A functional opsonic deficiency, identified in a laboratory test may, therefore, be difficult to evaluate. Miller et al. [4] were the first to describe such a 'plasma associated phagocytic defect'. The serum of an infant with severe dermatitis, recurrent infections,

Progress in immune deficiency III, edited by H. M. Chapel, R. J. Levinsky and A. D. B. Webster, 1991; Royal Society of Medicine Services International Congress and Symposium Series No. 173, published by Royal Society of Medicine Services Limited.

diarrhoea and failure to thrive was unable to opsonize baker's yeast (*Saccharomyces cerevisiae*) for phagocytosis by normal polymorphonuclear leucocytes. Subsequently Miller and colleagues [5,6] proposed that the cause of this yeast opsonization defect was a functional inadequacy of the C5 component of complement and that this was the underlying aetiology of Leiner's disease which had first been described 60 years previously [7]. The association of the yeast opsonization defect with both C5 deficiency and Leiner's disease subsequently proved to be erroneous [8,9] but variations of the original assay have, nevertheless, continued to be clinically useful for the evaluation of opsonic function. For example, the yeast opsonization defect was identified in 11 of 43 children with frequent unexplained infections [10], in association with chronic diarrhoea of infancy [11] and in a significant proportion of children developing otitis media during the first year of life [12]. In addition to these studies of defined clinical groups, there have been three studies of apparently healthy adult populations which have all shown the defect to be surprisingly frequent ($\sim 5\%$) [10,13,14].

The molecular mechanisms underlying defective yeast opsonization have been unclear; the assay systems (with phagocytosis as an end-point) were widely believed to be measuring a complement-dependent process but no functional deficiency of complement activity could ever be demonstrated in the sera. Nevertheless, we were able to show that such sera were associated with suboptimal deposition of C3b/C3bi opsonic fragments on yeast or zymosan surfaces [15,16]. Evidence was also obtained for the existence of a thermolabile zymosan binding factor able to enhance the deposition of C3 fragments derived from the classical pathway.

More recently, mannan (a major component of the yeast cell wall) has been coated on to ELISA microtitre plates and used as a substrate for binding opsonic proteins. Using dilute serum (typically 5–15%) a bimodal distribution of C3b deposition was observed in a population of 179 blood donors and this distribution profile was significantly correlated with that obtained in an earlier opsonic assay [17]. In the same study bimodal population distributions were also observed for properdin, Factor B, C4b and the serum lectin, mannose-binding protein (MBP). There was a highly significant correlation between the binding patterns of all of these moieties. In contrast the levels of mannan-binding immunoglobulins showed no correlation whatsoever. On the basis of these observations and the work of Lu *et al.* [18] (see below) we proposed that, at these low serum concentrations, the mannose-binding protein was regulating the degree of C3 cleavage and the subsequent deposition of complement-derived opsonins. In further studies we were able to demonstrate low levels of MBP ($< 30\,\mu$g/litre) in 10 serum samples from individuals previously shown to express the yeast opsonization defect [19]. Moreover, the addition of affinity purified MBP to the serum of individuals with poor opsonic function was shown to correct the defect *in vitro*.

THE STRUCTURE AND FUNCTION OF MANNOSE-BINDING PROTEIN (MBP)

MBP is a C-type (i.e. Ca^{++} dependent) animal lectin which has been shown to be secreted by the liver of several mammalian species [20]. It is composed of 32 kD subunits which have a cysteine-rich N-terminal region, a collagenous region, a 'neck' region and a carboxyterminal domain. Three such chains become closely associated through disulphide bridging in the N-terminal region and the formation of a triple helix in the collagenous domain. The associated chains of the carboxyterminal globular region represent the carbohydrate binding domain. Further polymerization of the three chain unit into trimers and tetramers results in a molecule which resembles Clq [20]. Like Clq, MBP is able to interact with the Clr and Cls components of complement [18] and activate the classical pathway of complement independent of antibody [21–23]. Through the carbohydrate recognition domains (CRD) the protein is able to bind to mannose and N-acetylglucosamine sugar groups which occur widely in the cell walls of pathogenic Gram-negative bacteria, mycobacteria and yeasts. Kuhlman *et al.* [24] have presented evidence that MBP bound to mannose-rich Salmonella organisms is able to function as an opsonin directly, presumably through interactions with the Clq receptors on the phagocyte surface. Other work from the same group (Ezekowitz *et al.* [25]) has demonstrated that MBP is also able to bind to the high mannose groups of the oligosaccharide side chains of the gp120 protein of HIV and thereby inhibit HIV infection of H9 lymphoblasts. It is of interest that although most of the assays for the common opsonic defect have used baker's yeast (*S. cerevisiae*) or its extract zymosan as the test material, similar results have also been obtained with *Candida albicans*, *Staphylococcus aureus* and *Escherichia coli*, suggesting that the defect is relevant to a range of organisms.

We believe that MBP activation of the classical pathway of complement is an example of an accessory immune system, the absence of which may become important when there is some other co-existing deficiency. In early infancy, following the decay of passively transferred maternal antibody, there is a well-documented period of vulnerability to infection. The infant has a restricted repertoire of available antibodies and will therefore have relatively low levels of IgG opsonins and a reduced capacity for classical pathway activation of complement. Low levels of MBP would be an additional risk factor at this time and many of the patients described have initially presented between six months and two years of age (e.g. the otitis media association described by Richardson *et al.* [12]). It also follows that the period of susceptibility may be transient because the infant's antibody repertoire would slowly mature and provide appropriate, efficient opsonic mechanisms.

Even within such a transient physiological window there may still be a requirement for another co-existing primary defect of the immune system if disease is to become manifest (see Fig. 1). There are several possible candidates and some occur surprisingly frequently. For example, approximately 8% of Caucasians lack two of the four possible functioning C4 genes [27] and consequently have a reduced capacity for classical pathway activation. The C4B locus products are known to be functionally four times more active than the proteins encoded at the C4A locus and to interact preferentially with carbohydrate-rich surfaces. It is therefore particularly interesting that a homozygous deficiency of the protein products of both C4B loci has been shown to predispose children to bacterial meningitis [28].

The most likely candidate for a co-existing second defect is an IgG subclass abnormality. The possibilities here include an affinity maturation defect (Hammerström [29] has proposed that early responses to carbohydrate antigens are predominantly low affinity IgG1), an isotype switching defect, a V-region restriction or the possession of a 'high risk' immunoglobulin allotype. In support of the latter there is an increasing body of data which suggests that individuals with two G2m(n-) alleles respond poorly to polysaccharide antigens [30, 31]. It is also of interest to note that Jefferis and Kumararatne [32], in a recent review of selective IgG subclass deficiencies, also made the suggestion that 'when multiple partial defects occur the individual may be compromised and disease susceptibility may manifest itself in an episodic manner'.

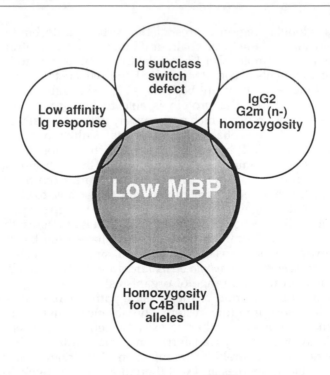

Figure 1 *Some of the possible risk factors which may, in association with a low MBP level, precipitate immunopathology. Such co-existing deficiencies may be particularly important between six and 24 months of age.*

THE MBP GENE AND POSSIBLE GENETIC BASIS OF LOW LEVELS OF THE SERUM LECTIN

The gene encoding human MBP has now been cloned and sequenced in two laboratories [33,34]. As shown in Fig. 2 each domain of the expressed protein is encoded by a separate exon. Exons 1 and 4 also encode extensive untranslated regions characterized by consensus sequences which may be involved in controlling the expression of human serum MBP. For example, in the 5' UT flanking sequence the following have been identified: a heat shock promoter sequence, three glucocorticoid responsive elements and a sequence homologous with one found in the 5' flanking sequence of the serum amyloid A gene [35]. These consensus sequences suggest that MBP is regulated as an acute phase protein synthesized by the liver as originally proposed by Ezekowitz *et al.* [36]. In the 3' UT there are seven motifs with the base sequence AUUUA [29]. These are the so-called instability sequences which have been proposed to play a role in the rapid degradation of mRNA from several short-lived proteins, e.g. cytokines and growth factors.

The underlying cause of the low serum concentrations of MBP observed in patients with the opsonic defect remains unclear. Two hypotheses are currently under consideration: either a normal protein is synthesized in low amounts due to abnormal control of MBP gene expression or the MBP gene in these patients encodes an abnormal protein.

As discussed previously the 5' and 3' sequences flanking the MBP gene indicate that MBP is an acute phase protein and likely to be produced in response to

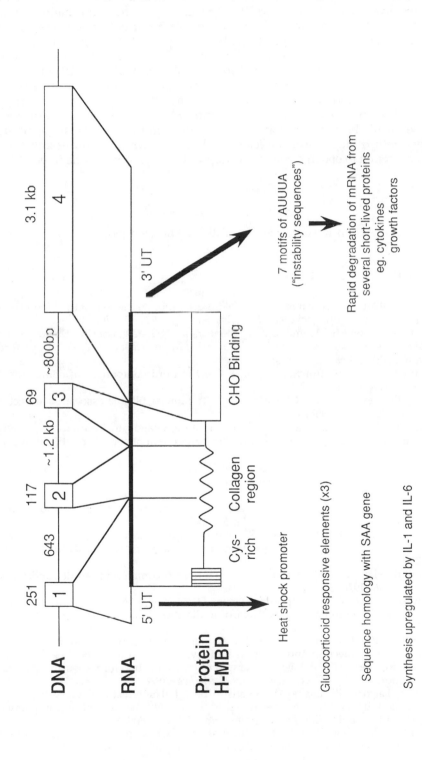

Figure 2 *The exon structure of the human MBP gene on chromosome 10 and the corresponding structural regions of the protein. Shown at the bottom are features of the 5' and 3' UT regions which are thought to be characteristic of acute phase protein control sequences. (Based on data from [33] and [34].)*

cytokines such as interleukin 1 and interleukin 6. There are several mechanisms which could account for abnormal MBP expression including abnormalities in the control sequences (which may be 5', intragenic or 3') or defective transcription factors that act on these sequences [37]. It is also possible that alterations in the putative mRNA instability sequences (the 3' AUUUA motifs) could result in very unstable MBP mRNA that would lead to low rates of MBP translation.

The second cause of low serum MBP levels could be an abnormal protein and this would imply abnormal coding sequences in the MBP gene. Such an abnormal protein might be unstable and undergo rapid intracellular degradation. Alternatively it might be unsuitable for secretion and accumulate in the hepatocyte (as occurs in patients with α_1-antitrypsin deficiency). We are currently addressing these issues in an attempt to obtain evidence in support of one or other of the hypotheses.

ACKNOWLEDGMENT

The support of Action Research is gratefully acknowledged.

REFERENCES

(1) Wright AE, Douglas SR. An experimental investigation of the role of the blood fluids in connection with phagocytosis. *Proc Roy Soc* 1903; **72**, 357–70.
(2) Pound JD, Walker MR. Membrane Fc receptors for IgG subclasses In: Shakib, F, ed. *Human IgG subclasses—molecular analysis of structure, function and regulation*. Oxford: Pergamon Press 1990: (in press).
(3) Lambris JD. The multifunctional role of C3, the third component of complement. *Immunol Today* 1988; **9**: 387–93.
(4) Miller ME, Seals J, Kaye R, Levitsky LC. A familial plasma-associated defect of phagocytosis. *Lancet* 1968; **ii**: 60–63.
(5) Miller ME, Nilsson UR. A familial deficiency of the phagocytosis-enhancing activity of serum related to a dysfunction of the fifth component of complement (C5). *N Engl J Med* 1970; **282**: 354–8.
(6) Miller ME, Koblenzer PJ. Leiner's disease and deficiency of C5. *J Pediatr* 1972; **80**: 879–80.
(7) Leiner C. Erythrodermia desquamativa (universal dermatitis of children at the breast). *Br J Child Dis* 1908; **5**: 244–51.
(8) Rosenfeld SI, Kelly ME, Leddy JP. Hereditary deficiency of the fifth component of complement in man. *J Clin Invest* 1976; **57**: 1626–34.
(9) Glover MT, Atherton DJ, Levinsky RJ. Syndrome of erythroderma, failure to thrive and diarrhoea in infancy: a manifestation of immunodeficiency. *Paediatrics* 1988; **81**: 66–72.
(10) Soothill JF, Harvey BAM. Defective opsonization. A common immunity deficiency. *Arch Dis Child* 1976; **51**: 91–9.
(11) Candy DCA, Larcher VF, Tripp JH, Harries JT, Harvey BAM, Soothill JF. Defective yeast opsonization in children with chronic diarrhoeal states. *Arch Dis Child* 1980; **55**: 189–93.
(12) Richardson VF, Larcher VF, Price JF. A common congenital immunodeficiency predisposing to infection and atopy in infancy. *Arch Dis Child* 1983; **58**: 799–802.
(13) Levinsky RJ, Harvey BAM, Paleja S. A rapid objective method for measuring the yeast opsonization activity of serum. *J Immunol Methods* 1978; **24**: 251–6.
(14) Kerr MA, Falconer JS, Bashey A, Swanson-Beck J. The effect of C3 levels on yeast opsonization by normal and pathological sera: identification of a complement independent opsonin. *Clin Exp Immunol* 1983; **54**: 793–800.
(15) Turner MW, Mowbray JF, Roberton DR. A study of C3b deposition on yeast surfaces by sera of known opsonic potential. *Clin Exp Immunol* 1981; **46**: 412–19.

(16) Turner MW, Seymour ND, Kazatchkine MD, Mowbray JF. Suboptimal C3b/C3bi deposition and defective yeast opsonization. Evidence for the absence of essential co-factor activity. *Clin Exp Immunol* 1985; **62**: 427–34.

(17) Super M, Levinsky RJ, Turner MW. The level of mannan binding protein regulates the binding of complement derived opsonins to mannan and zymosan at low serum concentrations. *Clin Exp Immunol* 1990; **79**: 144–50.

(18) Lu J, Thiel S, Reid KBM. Activation of Clr²-Cls² by mannan binding protein–zymosan complexes via a mechanism independent of antibody or Clq (Proceedings of the XIIIth International Complement Workshop) *Complement Inflamm* 1989; **6**: 363.

(19) Super M, Thiel S, Lu J, Levinsky RJ, Turner MW. Association of low levels of mannan-binding protein with a common defect of opsonisation. *Lancet* 1989; **ii**: 1236–9.

(20) Thiel S, Reid KBM. Structures and functions associated with the group of mammalian lectins containing collagen-like sequences. *FEBS Letters* 1989; **250**: 78–84.

(21) Ikeda K, Sannoh T, Kawasaki N, Kawasaki T, Yamashina I. Serum lectin with known structure activates complement through the classical pathway. *J Biol Chem* 1987; **262**: 7451–4.

(22) Kawasaki N, Kawasaki T, Yamashina I. A serum lectin (mannan-binding protein) has complement-dependent bactericidal activity. *J Biochem* 1989; **106**: 483–9.

(23) Ohta M, Okada M, Yamashina I, Kawasaki T. The mechanism of carbohydrate-mediated complement activation by the serum mannan-binding protein. *J Biol Chem* 1990; **265**: 1980–4.

(24) Kuhlman M, Joiner K, Ezekowitz RAB. The human mannose-binding protein functions as an opsonin. *J Exp Med* 1989; **169**: 1733–45.

(25) Ezekowitz RAB, Kuhlman M, Groopman JE, Byrn RA. A human serum mannose-binding protein inhibits *in vitro* infection by the human immunodeficiency virus. *J Exp Med* 1989; **169**: 185–96.

(26) Turner MW, Grant C, Seymour ND, Harvey BAM, Levinsky RJ. Evaluation of C3b/C3bi opsonisation and chemiluminescence with selected yeasts and bacteria using sera of different opsonic potential. *Immunology* 1986; **58**: 111–15.

(27) Hauptmann G, Tappeiner G, Schifferli JA. Inherited deficiency of the fourth component of human complement. *Immunodef Rev* 1988; **1**: 3–22.

(28) Rowe PC, McLean RH, Wood RA, Leggiadro RJ, Winkelstein JA. Association of homozygous C4B deficiency with bacterial meningitis. *J Infect Dis* 1989; **160**: 448–51.

(29) Hammerström L, Lefranc G, Lefranc MP, Persson MAA, Smith CIE. Aberrant pattern of anti-carbohydrate antibodies in immunoglobulin class or subclass deficient donors. In: Hanson LÅ, Söderström T, Oxelius V-A, eds. *Immunoglobulin subclass deficiencies*. Basel: Karger, 1986: 50–56.

(30) Granoff DM, Munson RS. Prospects for prevention of *Haemophilus influenzae* type b disease by immunization. *J Infect Dis* 1986; **153**: 448–61.

(31) Sarvas H, Rautonan N, Sipinen S, Makela O. IgG subclasses of pneumococcal antibodies—effect of allotype G2m(n). *Scand J Immunol* 1989; **29**: 229–37.

(32) Jefferis R, Kumararatne DS. Selective IgG subclass deficiency: quantification and clinical relevance. *Clin Exp Immunol* 1990; **81**: 357–367.

(33) Sastry K, Herman GA, Day L, et al. The human mannose-binding protein gene. Exon structure reveals its evolutionary relationship to a human pulmonary surfactant gene and localization to chromosome 10. *J Exp Med* 1989; **170**: 1175–89.

(34) Taylor ME, Brickell PM, Craig RK, Summerfield JA. Structure and evolutionary origin of the gene encoding a human serum mannose-binding protein. *Biochem J* 1989; **262**: 763–71.

(35) Woo P, Sipe J, Dinarello CA, Colten HR. Structure of a human serum amyloid A gene and modulation of its expression in transfected L cells. *J Biol Chem* 1987; **262**: 15790–5.

(36) Ezekowitz RAB, Day L, Herman G. A human manose-binding protein is an acute phase reactant that shares sequence homology with other vertebrate lectins. *J Exp Med* 1988; **167**: 1034–86.

(37) Reith W, Satola S, Herrero Sanchez C, et al. Congenital immunodeficiency with a regulatory defect in MHC Class II gene expression lacks a specific HLA-DR promoter binding protein, RFX. *Cell* 1988; **53**: 897–906.

Mechanisms of the candidacidal activity of monocytes and monocyte-derived macrophages: Implications for immunodeficiency disease

L. Maródi[1], J. R. Forehand and R. B. Johnston, Jr.

Department of Pediatrics, University of Pennsylvania, USA
[1]Present address: Department of Paediatrics, University School of Medicine, Debrecen, Hungary

INTRODUCTION

Candida sp. are frequent pathogens in patients with primary or secondary immunodeficiencies [1–4]. Systemic candidal infections occur mostly in patients with cancer or phagocytic cell defects [3,4]. Although mononuclear phagocytes are known to play a key role in the clearance of pathogens from the blood stream, the precise mechanism by which monocytes (Mo) and macrophages phagocytose and kill Candida is largely unexplored. We studied the functional characteristics of the killing of fully opsonized and unopsonized *Candida albicans* (a serious pathogen) and *C. parapsilosis* (rarely pathogenic) by Mo and monocyte-derived macrophages (MDM) from normal individuals and patients with chronic granulomatous disease (CGD). Respiratory burst and degranulation responses of Mo upon stimulation with Candida and the effects of products of the myeloperoxidase (MPO)-H_2O_2-halide microbicidal system on the killing of these fungi was also studied.

MATERIALS AND METHODS

Monocytes were isolated with a gradient of lymphocyte separation medium (Organon Technika, Durham, NC). MDM were obtained by culturing Mo for five days in Dulbeco's modified Eagle's medium supplemented with L-glutamine, penicillin-streptomycin and 10% heat-inactivated autologous serum. Normal human serum (NHS) was prepared from blood of healthy donors. Stationary phase *C. albicans* (ATCC 18804) or *C. parapsilosis* (ATCC 19019) was prepared in Sabouraud's 2% dextrose broth [5]. Preopsonization was performed by incubation of 5×10^6 Candida/ml with 10% serum for 30 min at 37°C. Killing of Candida was determined by colony counts.

Oxygen consumption by Mo was measured using a polarographic assay [5]. Release of superoxide anion by Mo or MDM was measured as the superoxide dismutase-inhibitable reduction of ferricytochrome c [6,7]. Degranulation assays were performed as described [8]. Inactivation of toxic oxygen metabolites by

Progress in immune deficiency III, edited by H. M. Chapel, R. J. Levinsky and A. D. B. Webster, 1991; Royal Society of Medicine Services International Congress and Symposium Series No. 173, published by Royal Society of Medicine Services Limited.

Table 1 *Comparison of phagocytosis and killing of* Candida *sp. by monocytes and monocyte-derived macrophages*

Cell type	*Candida* spp.	Phagocytosis[a] with serum	without serum	Killing[a] with serum	without serum
		% of inoculum ingested		*% of inoculum killed*	
Monocyte					
Normal	*C. albicans*	96±4[b]	0	40±9	0
Normal	*C. parapsilosis*	95±5	0	91±7	0
CGD	*C. albicans*	94±4	0	0	0
CGD	*C. parapsilosis*	97±2	0	0	0
Macrophage					
Normal	*C. albicans*	93±5	89±9	43±7	21±4
Normal	*C. parapsilosis*	96±3	83±6	45±5	19±3
CGD	*C. albicans*	95±2	81±7	1.2±0.8	0
CGD	*C. parapsilosis*	95±4	84±6	1.9±0.6	0

[a] Phagocytic cells were incubated with candida for 120 min in the presence of 2.5% normal serum or in the absence of serum.
[b] Data represent mean ± SEM; $n \geqslant 6$ with normal cells and $n = 2$ with CGD cells. Data adapted from references 10 and 11.
CGD = chronic granulomatous disease.

Candida was studied by determining the remaining oxidizing activity of NaOCl or NH_2Cl after incubation with washed suspensions of Candida [9].

RESULTS AND DISCUSSION

Normal serum promoted ingestion of both *Candida* species with maximal uptake occurring at concentrations of 2.5%. In the presence of serum the extent and time course of ingestion of the two *Candida* species were equivalent for Mo and macrophages (Table 1). In contrast to the lack of phagocytosis of unopsonized Candida by Mo, macrophages ingested a large number of both species by 120 min of incubation in the absence of serum. The ingestion of Candida by CGD Mo or macrophages was comparable to that of normal cells (Table 1). In the absence of serum, no killing of Candida could be detected by monocytes but normal MDM killed about 20% of both species by 120 min. NHS increased the degree of killing by both cell types (Table 1). Contrary to results with Mo, no difference was observed in the killing of the two species by MDM. No killing was detected of either *Candida* species by Mo or macrophages isolated from a CGD patient. These results confirm a requirement for the respiratory burst for effective killing of both *C. albicans* and *C. parapsilosis* by human mononuclear phagocytes.

Consumption of oxygen by monocytes upon stimulation with preopsonized Candida was comparable for the two species (data not shown). Addition of *C. albicans* or *C. parapsilosis* to Mo in the presence of 2.5% serum initiated a comparable degree of O_2^- release by these cells (Table 2). Unopsonized Candida triggered negligible release of O_2^- from Mo, and macrophages stimulated with the same number of fungi produced small amounts of this oxygen radical. Opsonized Candida elicited a vigorous respiratory burst response in both Mo and MDM, with no difference between the two *Candida* species; but Mo released about twice as much O_2^- than macrophages under the same experimental conditions. Candida-induced release of MPO and β-glucuronidase from Mo during phagocytosis of

Table 2 *Release of superoxide anion and granule enzymes by monocytes and monocyte-derived macrophages exposed to* Candida sp.[a]

Cell type	Candida spp.	Conc. of serum (%)	O_2^--release (nmol)	MPO-release (%)[b]	β-glucuronidase-release (%)[b]
Monocyte					
	C. albicans	2.5	35 ± 4^c	23 ± 4	6.8 ± 2.1
	C. parapsilosis	2.5	32 ± 5	21 ± 6	8.5 ± 3.4
	C. albicans	0	1.2 ± 1.0	0.5 ± 0.4	0.3 ± 0.3
	C. parapsilosis	0	0.8 ± 0.5	0.3 ± 0.6	0.2 ± 0.4
Macrophage					
	C. albicans	2.5	18 ± 7	0	ND
	C. parapsilosis	2.5	19 ± 5	0	ND
	C. albicans	0	2.5 ± 1.4	0	ND
	C. parapsilosis	0	3.0 ± 0.7	0	ND

[a] The release of O_2^- and granule enzymes was determined after 60 min of incubation in reaction mixtures identical to those of the killing assays using equal numbers of Candida and Mo in the presence or absence of normal serum.
[b] The results are expressed as the percentages of the total enzyme activity of Triton X-100-treated homogenates.
[c] Data represent mean ± SEM; $n \geqslant 5$. Data from reference 11.

Table 3 *Candidacidal activity of sodium hypochlorite (NaOCl) and monochloramine (NH$_2$Cl)*

Candida species	Oxidant added	Candida killed (% of inoculum)[a]	Candida required for 50% inactivation of the oxidant $(\times 10^6)$[b]
C. albicans	NaOCl (1 μM)	6 ± 4^c	—
	NaOCl (2.5 μM)	8 ± 5	—
	NaOCl (0.2 mM)	—	1.8 ± 0.8
	NH$_2$Cl (1 μM)	4 ± 3	—
	NH$_2$Cl (2.5 μM)	7 ± 4	—
	NH$_2$Cl (0.2 mM)	—	1.5 ± 0.4
C. parapsilosis	NaOCl (1 μM)	36 ± 9	—
	NaOCl (2.5 μM)	38 ± 8	—
	NaOCl (0.2 mM)	—	6.0 ± 1.6
	NH$_2$Cl (1 μM)	32 ± 7	—
	NH$_2$Cl (2.5 μM)	37 ± 9	—
	NH$_2$Cl (0.2 mM)	—	5.3 ± 0.9

[a] Candida (10^6/ml) were incubated for 60 min at room temperature in phosphate buffer (pH 6.0) containing oxidants and 2.5% serum.
[b] Inactivation of 0.2 mM oxidant by Candida was determined by measuring the remaining oxidizing activity of the supernatant after 10-min incubation at room temperature with varying numbers of Candida.
[c] Data represent mean ± SEM; $n > 6$. Data from reference 11.

opsonized *C. albicans* or *C. parapsilosis* was also comparable (Table 2). Macrophages released no MPO upon stimulation with Candida.

We suggest that the greater killing of *C. parapsilosis* than *C. albicans* by Mo, which are rich in MPO, but not by MDM, which are MPO-deficient, might be related to a different sensitivity of the two species to the products of the MPO-H_2O_2-halide system, HOCl and NH$_2$Cl. As shown in Table 3, killing of *C. parapsilosis* by both of the oxidants was significantly greater than killing of

C. albicans. We explored species differences in the ability of Candida to inactivate HOCl or NH$_2$Cl; contrary to our expectations, a significantly lower number of C. albicans was necessary to inactivate 50% of each compound (Table 3). Thus, the Candida species that is killed more easily by these oxidants (C. parapsilosis) inactivates them less effectively.

Earlier findings [12] and our observation with CGD cells here indicate that non-oxidative mechanisms are not sufficient for efficient killing of Candida species by phagocytic cells. Furthermore, MPO augments significantly the killing of these fungi by monocytes, and presumably by granulocytes. These data suggest that increased Candida infections might be expected in patients with CGD or with MPO deficiency and less commonly with antibody or complement deficiency since macrophages can ingest without a requirement for serum. In addition we propose that the resistance of C. albicans to products of the MPO-mediated candidacidal system may be a virulence factor that has contributed to the emergence of this species as the most severe pathogen of the Candida genus.

REFERENCES

(1) Kirkpatrick CH, Sohnle PG. Chronic mucocutaneous candidiasis. In: Safai B, Good RA, eds. Immunodermatology. New York: Plenum Publishing Corporation, 1981: 495.
(2) Klein RS, Harris CA, Butkins-Small C. Oral candidiasis in high-risk patients as the initial manifestation of the acquired immunodeficiency syndrome. N Engl J Med 1984; **311**: 354.
(3) Bodey GP. Candidiasis in cancer patients. Am J Med 1984; **30**: 13.
(4) Cohen MS, Isturiz RE, Malech HL. Fungal infections in chronic granulomatous disease: The importance of the phagocyte in defense against fungi. Am J Med 1981; **71**: 59.
(5) Sasada M, Johnston RB Jr. Macrophage microbicidal activity: correlation between phagocytosis-associated oxidative metabolism and the killing of candida by macrophages. J Exp Med 1980; **152**: 85.
(6) Johnston RB, Jr., Godzik CA, Cohn ZA. Increased superoxide anion production by immunologically activated and chemically elicited macrophages. J Exp Med 1978; **148**: 115.
(7) Maródi L, Kalmár Á, Karmazsin L. Stimulation of the respiratory burst and promotion of bacterial killing in human granulocytes by intravenous immunoglobulin preparations. Clin Exp Immunol 1990; **79**: 164.
(8) Brittinger G, Hirschorn R, Douglas SD, Weissmann G. Studies on lysosomes. XI. Characterisation of hydrolase-rich fraction form human lymphocytes. J Cell Biol 1968; **37**: 394.
(9) Beilke MA, Collins-Lech C, Sohnle PG. Candidacidal activity of the neutrophil myeloperoxidase system can be protected from excess hydrogen peroxide by the presence of ammonium ion. Blood 1989; **73**: 1045.
(10) Maródi L, Korchak MH, Johnston RB Jr. Mechanisms of host defense against candida: Phagocytosis by monocytes and monocyte-derived macrophages. J Immunol (in press).
(11) Maródi L, Forehand JR, Johnston RB Jr. Mechanisms of host defense against candida: Biochemical basis for killing of candida by mononuclear phagocytes (manuscript submitted).
(12) Lehrer RI. The fungicidal mechanism of human monocytes. I. Evidence of myeloperoxidase-linked and myeloperoxidase-independent candidacidal mechanism. J Clin Invest 1975; **55**: 338.

Macrophage activation syndrome after varicella

A. Fasth[1,2]**, J. Abrahamsson**[1]**, B. Andersson**[2]**, A. Enskog**[2]**, L. Mellander**[1] **and B. Ridell**[3]

Departments of [1]Pediatrics, [2]Clinical Immunology and [3]Pathology, University of Göteborg, S-416 85 Göteborg, Sweden

INTRODUCTION

Haemophagocytic histiocytic syndromes with macrophage activation and severe clinical symptoms and signs are rare complications of a number of disorders such as infections, malignancies, autoimmune disorders and benign lymphohistiocytosis syndromes such as Langerhans cell histiocytosis [1]. This disorder is an important differential diagnosis in children with fever and hepatosplenomegaly, as the disease if left untreated can be rapidly fatal.

THE PATIENT

A previously apparently healthy 10-year-old boy fell ill with varicella and developed a persistent high fever. The fever has continued for more than a year, relieved only by steroids. He twice presented with interstitial pneumonitis with pleural effusion and on the second occasion he was referred to our hospital. At admission he had hepatosplenomegaly with increased hepatic transferases, marked muscular weakness and severe pancytopenia. After investigations, prednisolone (2 mg/kg) was initiated with a prompt effect on symptoms and signs. Within days he was afebrile and X-ray showed a normalization of pulmonary findings. Attempts to discontinue steroids have resulted in recurrence of symptoms and signs.

RESULTS

Before steroids were given, profound pancytopenia was found with increased carbon monoxide haemoglobin as a sign of haemolysis. The bone marrow showed histiocytic infiltration with haemophagocytosis. In his serum high triglycerides, low fibrinogen, and very high creatine kinase were observed. All these changes, except the increased creatine kinase, normalized during steroid therapy.

Initially very high serum levels of TNF-α and INF-γ were found. During steroid treatment they decreased, but only to increase again as the therapy was

Progress in immune deficiency III, edited by H. M. Chapel, R. J. Levinsky and A. D. B. Webster, 1991; *Royal Society of Medicine Services International Congress and Symposium Series No. 173*, published by Royal Society of Medicine Services Limited.

tapered off. An antigen response was found to vaccination antigens (tetanus and polio), to varicella and cytomegalovirus, but not Epstein-Barr virus.

Severe immunological disturbances were noted at admission: CD3+ cells >85%; CD4 15–25%; CD8 60–80% with a high proportion CD8, DR+; Mitogen stimulation with PHA and ConA low; no blast transformation to varicella antigens; and no *in vitro* immunoglobulin synthesis after EBV or PWM stimulation. During therapy these parameters tended to normalize. Furthermore, a high proportion of DR+ granulocytes were observed in peripheral blood. These cells lost the DR expression during steroid therapy and were succeeded by a temporary rise in DR+ monocytes.

CONCLUDING REMARKS

Recently the name macrophage activation syndrome was proposed for the haemophagocytic histiocytic disorders [1,2]. As both the T cell and the monocyte/macrophage can be the cell primarily activated by the initiating factor, the syndrome could also be called inappropriate or hyper cytokine release syndrome. Tumour necrosing factor-α (TNF-α), IL-1 and IL-6 induce an acute phase reaction; prostaglandin PGE$_2$ causes immunodeficiency; TNF produces hypertriglyceridaemia; and plasmin activator causes hypofibrinogenaemia. The splenomegaly, interstitial pneumonia and muscle destruction can be explained by excess levels of GM-CSF [3], and the activated macrophage shows increased phagocytosis.

REFERENCES

(1) Hallé F, Seger R, Nadal B, *et al*. Pathogenetic factors in Macrophage Activation Syndrome. *Abstract of 7th Int Congress Immunol*. Stuttgart, New York: G Fischer, 1989; 278.
(2) Mazingue F. Le syndrome d'activation du monocyte-macrophage. *Pédiatrie* 1988; **43**: 297–300.
(3) Metcalf D. The consequences of excess levels of haematopoietic growth factors. *Br J Haematol* 1990; **75**: 1–3.

Flow cytometric evaluation of nitroblue tetrazolium reduction in human granulocytes

S. Le Moli, A. Fattorossi, R. Nisini, P. M. Matricardi and R. D. Amelio

Laboratory of Immunology, DASRS, Italian Air Force, Pratica di Mare, Italy

(ABSTRACT)

Oxidative metabolic burst of activated human polymorphonuclear leukocytes (PMN) is most commonly investigated in clinical practice by evaluating nitroblue tetrazolium (NBT) reduction at the single cell level. Reduced NBT precipitates where the redox reaction has taken place, and can be visualized as PMN-associated dark blue granules of formazan in light microscopy. We developed a new flow cytometry technique in which the PMN membrane was rendered fluorescent by a short incubation with fluorescein-conjugated ConA. PMN were then incubated with NBT and increasing doses of phorbol myristate acetate (PMA). Formazan has a peak of absorption at 520 nm which represents the peak of emission of fluorescein, so that it quenches the PMN-associated fluorescence. Data show that a dose-dependent reduction of fluorescence can be obtained using graded amounts of PMA in normal PMN. PMN-associated fluorescence remains unchanged in patients with chronic granulomatous disease, a disorder characterized by a selective impairment of PMN oxidative metabolism.

The present method could become a useful test for clinical purposes.

Progress in immune deficiency III, edited by H. M. Chapel, R. J. Levinsky and A. D. B. Webster, 1991; Royal Society of Medicine Services International Congress and Symposium Series No. 173, published by Royal Society of Medicine Services Limited.

Nijmegen breakage syndrome: Clinical, immunological and pathological findings

C. Weemaes[1], C. van de Kaa[2], P. Wesseling[2], A. Haraldsson[1],
J. Bakkeren[1], E. Seemanova[3], A. Schmidt[4] and E. Passarge[4]

Department of [1]Paediatrics and [2]Pathology, University of Nijmegen, The Netherlands; [3]Genetické oddĕleni Ústavu výzkumu vývoje dítéte FDL, University Karlovy, Praha, Czechoslovakia and [4]Institut für Humangenetik, Universitätsklinikum Essen, Germany

In 1981 a new chromosome instability disorder, the Nijmegen breakage syndrome (NBS), was reported [1]. The main clinical manifestations were microcephaly and short stature, but the immunological, cytogenetic and cellular findings were strongly reminiscent of those in ataxia telangiectasia (AT). Since the first description [1,2] at least 14 patients with Nijmegen breakage syndrome have been reported [3–6].

All patients have microcephaly from birth, growth retardation, a bird-like face, chromosome instability with multiple 7/14 rearrangements and X-ray hypersensitivity. They belong to two complementation groups (V1 and V2), different from the four AT complementation groups [7]. Two Mexican twin girls belonging to complementation group V1 in addition have both ataxia and telangiectasia [6].

CLINICAL SYMPTOMS

The main clinical symptoms in 14 patients are microcephaly from birth, growth retardation, and a peculiar 'bird-like' face (Table 1). Intelligence is normal in most patients, but some appear to be slightly mentally retarded (Table 1).

Most patients have repeated respiratory tract infections. Three patients died from respiratory failure. Five patients developed a malignancy (Table 2).

IMMUNODEFICIENCY

Immunodeficiency was detected in all 11 patients who could be investigated immunologically. All had defects in the B cell system. Four had an agammaglobulinaemia, three an IgA deficiency, and two an IgG2 and IgG4 deficiency. The Mexican twins have normal serum immunoglobulins.

Antibody synthesis was deficient in those patients tested and is more disturbed than in our patients with AT. The response to *Helix pommatia* haemocyanin was

Progress in immune deficiency III, edited by H. M. Chapel, R. J. Levinsky and A. D. B. Webster, 1991; *Royal Society of Medicine Services International Congress and Symposium Series No. 173*, published by Royal Society of Medicine Services Limited.

Table 1 *Clinical symptoms in the patients*

Microcephaly from birth	14/14
Growth retardation	13/14
'Bird-like' face	14/14
Receding fore head	
Receding mandible	
Large prominent ears	
Prominent mid-face	
Syndactyly	3/14
Repeated respiratory tract infections	11/14
Repeated urinary tract infections	5/14
Intelligence	
Normal	8/14
Slightly mentally retarded	6/14

Table 2 *Malignancies occurring in the patients*

Patient	Age	Malignancy
Czechoslovakian girl	2 years	Mediastinal lymphosarcoma
German girl	15 years	B-cell lymphoma
Dutch boy	4 years	B-cell lymphoma
Dutch boy	19 years	Mediastinal lymphoma
Czechoslovakian boy	8 years	Paraprotein IgM kappa type

greatly disturbed in the four patients investigated. Specific antibody response following pneumoccocal polysaccharide immunization was absent in the Mexican girls. In addition, antibody response to tetanus toxoid was impaired in some patients.

In addition, all 10 patients investigated had T cell defects. Our first patient had only a mild defect as only a decreased percentage of T cells and a slightly diminished *in vitro* response of the lymphocytes to pokeweed mitogen was found. However, severe defects were demonstrated in the other patients.

PATHOLOGICAL FINDINGS

Our youngest patient, BvH, died at the age of four years from a malignant B cell lymphoma. At autopsy, microcephaly (brain weight 500 g, normal for age 1200 g) was found. The cerebellum was of relatively normal size. Microscopically, diffuse cortical cerebellar degeneration characteristic of ΛT was not found. The dentate nucleus was normal. The thymus displayed the atrophic changes associated with severe stress (weight 3.0 g; normally 16 g) but also resembling simple dysplasia. Lymph nodes were structurally normal although follicles were sparse and paracortical areas revealed some hypocellularity. Gut-associated lymphoid tissue was poorly developed. In tonsils and small and large intestines a highly malignant diffuse large cell non-Hodgkin lymphoma (B immunoblastic type) was found. Evidence of this tumour was also found in the cerebrum, but not in the lymph nodes.

Five of the 14 patients have developed a malignancy (Table 2). In most immunodeficiencies the risk for malignancy is increased, but this is especially true for chromosome breakage disorders (Bloom's Syndrome 40%; AT 10–20%). It is important to diagnose these patients with NBS as they have an increased

X-ray hypersensitivity *in vivo*, complicating treatment of the tumour by X irradiation. As yet no solid tumours have been found in NBS.

REFERENCES

(1) Weemaes CMR, Hustinx TWJ, Scheres JMJC, van Munster PJJ, Bakkeren JAJM, Taalman RDFM. A new chromosomal instability disorder: the Nijmegen Breakage Syndrome. *Acta Paediatr Scand* 1981; **70**: 557–64.
(2) Seemanová E, Passarge E, Beneškova D, Houšték J, Kasal P, Ševčíková M. Familial microcephaly with normal intelligence, immunodeficiency and risk for lymphoreticular malignancies: a new autosomal recessive disorder. *Am J Med Genet* 1985; **20**: 639–48.
(3) Conley ME, Spinner NB, Emauel BS, Nowell PC, Nichols WW. A chromosome breakage syndrome with profound immunodeficiency. *Blood* 1986; **67**: 1251–6.
(4) Wegner RD, Metzger M, Hanefeld F, *et al.* A new chromosome instability disorder confirmed by complementation studies. *Clin Genet* 1988; **33**: 20–32.
(5) Taalman RDFM, Hustinx TWJ, Weemaes CMR, *et al.* Further delineation of the Nijmegen Breakage Syndrome. *Am J Med Genet* 1989; **32**: 425–31.
(6) Curry CJR, Tsai J, Hutchinson HT, Jaspers NGJ, Wara D, Gatti RA. AT-Fresno. A phenotype linking ataxia telangiectasia with the Nijmegen Breakage Syndrome. *Am J Hum Genet* 1989; **45**: 270–5.
(7) Jaspers NGJ, Taalman RDFM, Baan C. Patients with an inherited syndrome characterized by immunodeficiency, microcephaly and chromosomal instability: Genetic relationship with ataxia telangiectasia. *Am J Hum Genet* 1988; **42**: 66–73.

T cell responses to three HPLC-separated *Mycobacterium leprae* 12-KDA antigens in leprosy patients and healthy individuals

Z. T. Handzel[1], V. C. Buchner[2], Y. Burstein[2], A. Leviatan[3] and H. M. Dockrell[4]

[1]Clinical Immunology Unit, Kaplan Hospital, [2]Department of Organic Chemistry, Weizmann Institute of Science, Rehovot, [3]Hansen's Hospital, Jerusalem, Israel; [4]Department of Clinical Sciences, LSHTM, London, UK

(POSTER)

Lepromatous leprosy (LL) is characterized by T-cell anergy to the causative agent, *Mycobacterium leprae* (ML). ML antigens which trigger T cell help rather than suppression in patients with the less severe tuberculoid leprosy (TT), are expected to constitute important components of an *M. leprae* subunit vaccine. B and T cell epitopes are being determined on recombinant ML proteins that are known by their relative molecular weights, 65, 36, 28 and 18 K, but the 12 K proteins have just begun to be analysed in depth [1]. Sera from LL patients reacted in Western blots with the 12 K protein band resolved from sonicated ML by sodium dodecyl sulphate polyacrylamide gel electrophoresis [2,3], but T cell recognition of it by leprosy patients has not been consistent [4–6]. We used HPLC to isolate from a sonicate of *M. leprae* three native 12 K proteins, designated P12α, P12β, P12γ, and tested their ability to stimulate peripheral blood mononuclear cells from leprosy patients, healthy leprosy contacts and BCG vaccinees.

RESULTS

Among the patients, 7/10 recognized P12α (1/3 TT, 4/4 borderline, 2/4 LL); 3/4 family contacts and 5/6 BCG-vaccinees also recognized P12α. Only TT patients (2/3) and BCG-vaccinees (3/6) recognized P12β, while 2/4 contacts, 1/3 borderline patients and 1/6 BCG-vacinees recognized P12γ. Analysis by dot ELISA, using the ML 12 K-specific monoclonal antibody ML06 [7], indicated that P12α was similar or even identical to an immunoaffinity purified 12 KI ML protein that has been shown to be immunogenic for cloned *M. leprae*-reactive T cells of the helper phenotype [8].

CONCLUSIONS

Until now, *M. leprae* 12 K proteins have been shown to be ML-specific at the humoral level [7,9]; MoAb ML06 (which recognized our P12α antigen) has not been shown to react with any other mycobacterial species [7]. However, in our study, the recognition of P12α by mononuclear cells from the majority of BCG-vaccinated normal subjects implied that, at the cellular level, these proteins must contain at least one T cell epitope shared with other mycobacteria or non-related antigens. Preliminary results of an analysis of the N-terminal amino acids of P12α, revealed that the first 20 amino acids are identical to those of the 12 K proteins of BCG/*M. tuberculosis*. This result supports the conclusion that cross-reactive epitopes are indeed present in the 12 K proteins of these three mycobacterial species. It seems that the reversal of the T cell defect in LL patients by stimulation with fractionated

Progress in immune deficiency III, edited by H. M. Chapel, R. J. Levinsky and A. D. B. Webster, 1991; *Royal Society of Medicine Services International Congress and Symposium Series No. 173, published by Royal Society of Medicine Services Limited.*

M. leprae components in this and other studies [3] suggested that, in the absence of suppressor factors, such patients can respond to individual antigens, which may prove to be useful for immunotherapy.

In conclusion, we have shown that P12α contains at least one T cell epitope that is antigenically identical to the species-specific 12 K epitope of *M. leprae* previously defined by Ivanyi and his group. We have also shown for the first time not only that the N-terminal of P12α shows complete homology to the 12 K proteins of BCG/*M. tuberculosis*, but also that these 12 K proteins are cross-reactive at the cellular level. Despite the fact that ML 12 K proteins are known to elicit non-protective humoral immune responses, our results suggest that T cell epitopes of one or more of the 12 K antigens could be added to the repertoire of purified T cell reactive antigens which are already available for vaccine construction, namely P18, P30/31, P36, P65 and P70.

REFERENCES

(1) Young DB. Stress-induced proteins and the immune response to leprosy. *Microbiol Sci* 1988; **5**: 143–6.
(2) Britton WJ, Hellquist L, Garsia RJ, Basten A. Antigens of *Mycobacterium leprae* identified by immunoprecipitation with sera from leprosy and tuberculosis patients. *Clin Exp Immunol* 1988; **71**: 394–8.
(3) Vega-Lopez F, Stoker NG, Locniskar MF, Dockrell HM, Grant KA, McAdam KPWJ. Recognition of myobacterial antigens by sera from patients with leprosy. *J Clin Microbiol* 1988; **26**: 2472–9.
(4) Ottenhoff THM, Converse PJ, Gebre N, Wondimu A, Ehrenberg JP, Kiessling R. T cell responses to fractionated *Mycobacterium leprae* antigens in leprosy. The lepromatous nonresponder defect can be overcome *in vitro* by stimulation with fractionated *M. leprae* components. *Eur J Immunol* 1989; **19**: 707–13.
(5) Mendez-Samperio P, Lamb J, Bothamley G, Stanley P, Ellis C, Ivanyi JJ. Molecular study of the T cell repertoire in family contacts and patients with leprosy. *J Immunol* 1989; **142**: 3599–604.
(6) Lee SP, Stoker NG, Grant KA, *et al*. Cellular immune responses of leprosy contacts to fractionated *Mycobacterium leprae* antigens. *Infect Immun* 1989; **57**: 2475–80.
(7) Ivanyi J, Sinha S, Aston R, Cussel D, Keen M, Sengupta U. Definition of species specific and cross-reactive antigenic determinants of *Mycobacterium leprae* using monoclonal antibodies. *Clin Exp Immunol* 1983; **52**: 528–36.
(8) Ottenhoff THM, Klatser PR, Ivanyi J, Elferink DG, de Wit MYL, de Vries RRP. *Mycobacterium leprae*-specific protein antigens defined by cloned human helper T-cells. *Nature* 1986; **319**: 66–8.
(9) Chakrabarty AK, Maire MA, Lambert PH. SDS-PAGE analysis of *M. leprae* protein antigens reacting with antibodies from sera from lepromatous patients and infected armadillos. *Clin Exp Immunol* 1982; **49**: 523–33.

Effects of granulocyte colony stimulating factor (G-CSF) in children with severe congenital neutropenia

K. Welte[1], C. Zeidler[1], A. Reiter[1], J. Rösler[1], L. Souza[2] and H. Riehm[1]

[1]Department of Paediatric Hematology and Oncology, Kinderklinik der Medizinischen Hochschule Hannover, Germany, and [2]Amgen, Thousand Oaks, CA, USA

INTRODUCTION

Severe congenital neutropenia (SCN; Kostmann Syndrome), a disorder of myelopoiesis, is characterized by an impairment of myeloid differentiation in bone marrow with absolute neutrophil counts (ANC) below $200/\mu l$ in blood of affected patients [1–6]. This disorder was first described by Kostmann [1,2]. Patients with SCN experience frequent episodes of fever, pneumonitis, skin infections, perianal and liver abscesses, usually beginning in early infancy and often leading to fatal infections in spite of antibiotic therapy. Bone marrow morphological findings in these patients have been variable, but a maturation arrest of myelopoiesis at the promyelocyte stage is usually seen [1–6]. Several methods of therapy have been attempted in these patients including white cell transfusions, corticosteroids, vitamin-B6, lithium, androgens, and bone marrow transplantation (BMT). To date, only BMT has resulted in partial or complete correction of the neutropenia [7,8]. The aetiology of SCN is unknown. There is no evidence for serum inhibitors or anti-neutrophil antibodies in these patients.

Recently, granulocyte-colony-stimulating factor (G-CSF) has been purified, molecularly cloned and expressed as recombinant protein [9,10]. It has been shown to be a potent stimulus for normal myeloid proliferation and differentiation *in vitro* and *in vivo* [9–12]. Using bone marrow cells from SCN patients, CFU-GM-assays in the presence of rhG-CSF demonstrated predominantly monocyte/macrophage colonies. The growth of neutrophil colonies with G-CSF as a growth factor was significantly diminished when compared with normal marrow (own unpublished observation).

In a previous clinical trial we investigated the effects of granulocyte-macrophage-CSF (GM-CSF) in SCN patients [13] and because only one of seven patients showed any increase in circulating neutrophils, we subsequently initiated a study

Supported in part by Grant We 942/2–1 from the Deutsche Forschungsgemeinschaft

Progress in immune deficiency III, edited by H. M. Chapel, R. J. Levinsky and A. D. B. Webster, 1991; Royal Society of Medicine Services International Congress and Symposium Series No. 173, published by Royal Society of Medicine Services Limited.

with G-CSF. The objectives of this study were to determine the biological effectiveness of G-CSF in the treatment of SCN in order to design an optimal therapy for this fatal disease as there were no preclinical models for this condition.

METHODS

Thirty patients (14 girls, 16 boys; aged between two months and 21 years) with SCN were treated in a Phase I/II clinical trial with rhG-CSF. Seven patients had been pretreated with rhGM-CSF [13] up to one to three months prior to rhG-CSF. The diagnosis of SCN was established on the following basis: 1) absence of blood neutrophils ($< 200/\mu l$), 2) maturation arrest in the neutrophil lineage at the promyelocyte stage with morphological abnormalities in bone marrow with normal cellularity and 3) history of frequent severe bacterial infections starting during the first 12 months of life. In general, these patients also experience absolute increases in both monocyte and eosinophil counts [13]. The WBC prior to rhG-CSF treatment ranged between 3200 and $10\,600/\mu l$.

All patients were started with $3\,\mu g/kg/d$ rhG-CSF subcutaneously (s.c.). If no response was observed by day 14, patients were moved to the next dose level ($5\,\mu g/kg/d$) and then by increments of $5\,\mu g/kg/d$ up to $20\,\mu g/kg/d$, and by increments of $10\,\mu g/kg/d$ to a maximal dose of $60\,\mu g/kg/d$. Patients with complete responses (ANC $> 1000/\mu l$) at the end of the dose escalation were eligible for enrolment into a maintenance course of treatment. RhG-CSF was provided by Amgen (Thousand Oaks, CA). It was expressed in *Escherichia coli* and purified to homogeneity. The rhG-CSF has a specific activity of approximately 10^8 U/mg protein [10]. It was endotoxin-free as judged by the rabbit pyrogen test and by the limulus amoebocyte lysate assay.

RESULTS

Effects of rhG-CSF on blood cells

The effects of rhG-CSF on blood neutrophil counts are shown in Fig. 1 and in detail for patient No. 3 in Fig. 2. RhG-CSF administration led in 29 of 30 patients to an increase in ANC to levels above $1000/\mu l$ (Fig. 1). The dosages needed to achieve an ANC of 1000 were between $3\,\mu g/kg/d$ and $60\,\mu g/kg/d$. Patient No. 9 showed only a minor response even at the highest dose ($60\,\mu g/kg/d$) with an increase in ANC to about $200/\mu l$. The dosage required to maintain an ANC of above $1000/\mu l$ was different in each patient. Sixteen patients required rhG-CSF dosages between 3 and $10\,\mu g/kg/d$, nine patients between 10 and $20\,\mu g/kg/d$, and four patients between 40 and $60\,\mu g/kg/d$. Mean and standard deviation of all patients at days 0, 28, 84, 180, and 365 of rhG-CSF treatment are shown in Fig. 1. Due to the daily oscillation of neutrophil counts observed in all patients (see also Fig. 2) the standard deviation at a given point in time is high. However, this oscillation did not affect the beneficial clinical responses. The neutrophils did show normal functions as judged by phagocytosis, intracellular killing of staphylococci, and reactive oxygen production [14]. The absolute eosinophil counts (AEoC) did not change significantly during rhG-CSF therapy in all patients. The absolute monocyte counts (AMC) increased two to eight-fold in the majority of patients during rhG-CSF treatment. The most dramatic increase in AMC has been seen

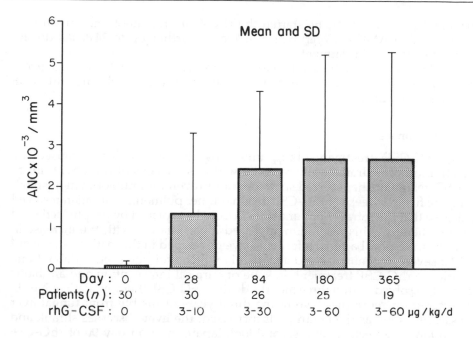

Figure 1 *Mean and standard deviation of absolute neutrophil counts of all patients prior to (day 0) and at day 28, 84, 180 and 365 of rhG-CSF treatment. To date, 26 patients have been treated for more than 84 days, 25 for more than 180 days, and 19 for more than one year. The dosage administered was 3 µg/kg/d in the first two weeks. In patients who did not respond at this dosage, rhG-CSF was increased bi-weekly to 5 or 10, 20, 30, 40, or 60 µg/kg/d, until they showed an ANC of above 1000/µl.*

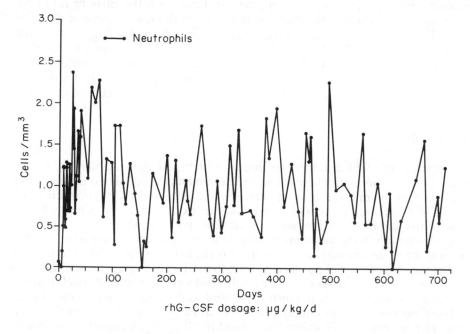

Figure 2 *Absolute neutrophil counts of patient No. 3 during maintenance treatment.*

in patient No. 3. However, he started the rhG-CSF treatment with an already excessively high AMC (3438/μl) which increased further up to 24 800/μl during the first six weeks of treatment.

The number of CFU-GMs, myeloblasts and promyelocytes in the bone marrow during rhG-CSF treatment did not change significantly during rhG-CSF maintenance treatment.

Clinical responses

During rhG-CSF treatment, lung infiltrates in patient No. 1 caused by peptostreptococcus dramatically resolved within six weeks of therapy. Prior to rhG-CSF treatment she received six weeks of intravenous antibiotics in hospital. During the first six weeks of rhG-CSF treatment, her pulmonary situation resolved to a degree that the intravenous antibiotics could be replaced by prophylactic oral antibiotic therapy. This resolution appeared in association with the increase in neutrophils. No new bacterial infections have developed in this patient. In patient No. 12 a severe anal abscess and anal fistula which had persisted for about one year prior to rhG-CSF treatment, in spite of surgical intervention and antibiotic treatment, resolved within three months during rhG-CSF therapy. Patient No. 13 had suffered for more than two of the three years of his life from fungal liver abscesses. As soon as the neutrophils increased, the liver abscesses shrank and were no longer detectable at a second-look-laparotomy on day 90 of rhG-CSF treatment.

Adverse events

The adverse events included necrotizing cutaneous vasculitis (Case 5)), generalized vasculitis (Case 17), mesangioproliferative glomerulonephritis (Case 22), all associated with a prompt increase in ANC and not with the dose of rhG-CSF. All three patients suffered from these side effects at the lowest dose of rhG-CSF (3 μg/kg/d). Patient No. 5 now receives rhG-CSF at a dose of 0.8 μg/kg/d. At this dose, she has ANC of 500–1000/μl without further re-occurrence of the vasculitis. In patients No. 17 and 22, rhG-CSF was discontinued. Two patients suffered from mild haematuria and one patient from mild thrombocytopenia. In these three patients, rhG-CSF treatment could be continued without further clinical problems.

DISCUSSION

In this study, rhG-CSF induced an increase of blood neutrophils in 29 of 30 patients. The dose necessary to reach and maintain an ANC of above 1000/μl varied from patient to patient and ranged between 3 and 60 μg/kg/d. The neutrophils in the rhG-CSF treated patients had normal functional activities as judged by *in vitro* functions and by clinical parameters. In three patients, there was a resolution of severe bacterial infections (pneumonitis, liver abscess, anal abscess) which had been resistant to intravenous antibiotic treatment prior to rhG-CSF therapy. The maintenance treatment did not lead to an exhaustion of myelopoiesis: nineteen patients have now been treated for 12 months and longer. The ANC of all patients were stable during the maintenance treatment and no increases in the dosage have been necessary to maintain the ANC during long-term treatment. The number and severity of infections decreased in all patients significantly during rhG-CSF treatment as compared with a similar time period prior to therapy.

Additional SCN patients have been treated with rhG-CSF by Bonilla *et al.* [15] showing similar increases in ANC.

The hypotheses for the immunopathogenesis of the underlying disease include defective production of G-CSF or defective response of neutrophil precursors to G-CSF or other haematopoietic growth factors. Defective G-CSF production does not seem likely in light of new data which show that serum from these patients contain normal or elevated levels of G-CSF as judged by Western blot analysis and *in vitro* bioassays [16]. The second, more attractive, hypothesis for the genetic disposition affecting these patients could involve a defective G-CSF response, either by reduced binding affinity of G-CSF to its receptor, low G-CSF receptor numbers, or defective intracellular signal transduction. Different mutations in the G-CSF receptor could explain the variations from patient to patient in response to rhG-CSF and the dose needed (3–60 µg/kg/d) to achieve an ANC of 1000.

There were side effects from rhG-CSF treatment in these patients. Two patients experienced a vasculitis, one a mesangioproliferative glomerulonephritis. Since these side effects were clearly associated with ANC of above 1000/µl and not with the dose of rhG-CSF, the relatively increased numbers of neutrophils have to be considered as a possible cause for these adverse events. The pathogenetic mechanisms of the vasculitis could be explained by infiltration of inflamed vessel walls with neutrophils and mononuclear cells and subsequent disruption of the small superficial cutaneous vessels. Deposits of immunoglobulins, complement components or circulating unspecific immune complexes, all compensatively elevated in the blood of this patient, may have potentiated this process.

These findings demonstrate that rhG-CSF is the most promising of all available treatments for SCN. The correction of neutropenia with resultant improvement of clinical status can dramatically change the high morbidity and therefore the quality of life in these patients. The risk of mortality from severe bacterial infections will most likely be diminished. These results show also the feasibility of maintenance treatment with rhG-CSF for up to two years, without exhaustion of myelopoiesis as well as the beneficial effects of rhG-CSF in patients with SCN.

REFERENCES

(1) Kostmann R. Infantile genetic agranulocytosis. *Acta Paediatr Scand* 1956; **45** (suppl 105): 1.

(2) Kostmann R. Infantile genetic agranulocytosis: a review with presentation of ten new cases. *Acta Paediatr Scand* 1975; **64**: 362.

(3) Wriedt K, Kauder E, Mauer, AM. Defective myelopoiesis in congenital neutropenia. *N Engl J Med* 1970; **283**: 1072.

(4) Barak Y, Paran M, Levin S, Sachs L. *In vitro* induction of myeloid proliferation and maturation in infantile genetic agranulocytosis. *Blood* 1971; **38**: 74.

(5) L'Esperance P, Brunning R, Good RA. Congenital neutropenia; *In vitro* growth of colonies mimicking the disease. *Proc Natl Acad Sci USA* 1973; **70**: 669.

(6) Amato D, Freedman MH, Saunders EF. Granulopoiesis in severe congenital neutropenia. *Blood* 1976; **47**: 531.

(7) Pahwa RN, O'Reilly JR. Partial correction of neutrophil deficiency in congenital neutropenia following bone marrow transplantation (BMT). *Exp Hematol* 1977; **5**: 45.

(8) Rappeport JM, Parkman R, Newburger P, Camitta BM, Chusid M. Correction of infantile agranulocytosis by allogeneic bone marrow transplantation. *Am J Med* 1980; **68**: 605.

(9) Welte K, Platzer E, Lu L, *et al.* Purification and biochemical characterization of human pluripotent hematopoietic colony stimulating factor. *Proc Natl Acad Sci USA* 1985; **82**: 1526.

(10) Souza LM, Boone TC, Gabrilove J, *et al.* Recombinant human granulocyte colony stimulating factor: effects on normal and leukemic myeloid cells. *Science* 1986; **232**: 61.

(11) Welte K, Bonilla MA, Gillio AP, *et al.* Recombinant human granulocyte colony stimulating factor: effects on hematopoiesis in normal and cyclophosphamide-treated primates. *J Exp Med* 1987; **165**: 941.

(12) Gabrilove JL, Jakubowski A, Scher H, *et al.* Granulocyte colony stimulating factor reduced the neutropenia and associated morbidity of chemotherapy for transitional cell carcinoma of the urothelium. *N Engl J Med* 1988; **318**: 1414.

(13) Welte K, Zeidler C, Reiter A, *et al.* Differential effects of granulocyte-macrophage stimulating factor (GM-CSF) in children with severe congenital neutropenia. *Blood* 1990; **75**: 1056–63.

(14) Rösler J, Emmendörfer A, Elsner J, *et al. In vitro* functions of neutrophils induced by treatment with rhG-CSF in five boys suffering from severe congenital neutropenia. *Eur J Haematol* 1991 (in press).

(15) Bonilla MA, Gillio AP, Ruggiero M, *et al.* Effects of recombinant human granulocyte colony-stimulating factor on neutropenia in patients with congenital agranulocytosis. *N Engl J Med* 1989; **320**: 1574.

(16) Mempel K, Menzel T, Pietsch T, Zeidler C, Welte K. Increased serum levels of G-CSF in patients with severe congenital neutropenia. *Blood* 1991 (in press).

Successful treatment of congenital agranulocytosis (Kostmann's Syndrome) with recombinant human granulocyte colony stimulating factor (rhG-CSF)

E. G. Davies, A. Laurie and E. Gordon-Smith

Departments of Child Health and Haematology, St George's Hospital Medical School, London, UK

(POSTER)

Severe congenital neutropenia of Kostmann's type [1], is characterized by extremely low absolute neutrophil counts (ANC) in peripheral blood with maturation arrest of granulopoiesis resulting in severe recurrent infections during the first year of life and often early death from infection. Until recently the only curative option was bone marrow transplantation. However, recombinant human granulocyte colony stimulating factor (rhG-CSF), an 18.8 KD glycoprotein that induces specific granulocyte lineage growth and differentiation and is a potent activator of neutrophils [2], is now a potential alternative therapy [3,4] (See also Welte, this volume p. 197).

CASE HISTORY

A 13-month-old male child of consanguineous parentage was referred to us with neutropenia and a severe pneumonia not responding to antibiotics. He also had acute varicella infection complicated by a large superficial abscess due to *Staphylococcus aureus* on the anterior abdominal wall. From the age of two months he had suffered recurrent infections, mainly affecting the oropharynx and respiratory tract, including four episodes of pneumonia. He had severe neutropenia [0.106×10^9/l], platelets 821×10^9/l, haemoglobin 8.3 g/l with an iron deficiency picture. Review of his previous records revealed neutropenia on several occasions with neutrophil counts $<0.2 \times 10^9$/l. Bone marrow examination showed reduced granulopoiesis with maturation arrest at the promyelocyte/early myelocyte stage. Vacuolation was present in many promyelocytes. Extensive investigation, including bronchoscopy, failed to identify the pneumonic pathogen. After 10 days empirical treatment with broad spectrum antibiotics, there was failure of resolution of the pneumonia; rhG-CSF was commenced at that stage.

Treatment with rhG-CSF

Daily subcutaneous injections (5 μg/kg) of rhG-CSF (Chugai Pharmaceuticals) were given on a compassionate basis with parental informed consent. The dose was increased to 10 μg/kg after 10 days because of failure of response. Thereafter, ANC rose progressively to 3.7×10^9/l and the bone marrow showed an improved appearance with mature forms in the granulocyte series. There was accompanying clinical improvement with resolution of the pneumonia. After one month the dose frequency was reduced to alternate day injections (10 μg/kg) given by the parents at home. This schedule was maintained for eight months. During this period the ANC was usually in the range $0.5–3.0 \times 10^9$/l but showed irregular intermittent drops to $<0.1 \times 10^9$/l without clinical deterioration. The patient remained well with only one episode of mild pneumonia responding promptly to antibiotics and no further oral or skin infections even after stopping prophylactic antibiotics. No side effects were observed and, after seven months, serum anti-rhG-CSF antibodies could not

Progress in immune deficiency III, edited by H. M. Chapel, R. J. Levinsky and A. D. B. Webster, 1991; Royal Society of Medicine Services International Congress and Symposium Series No. 173, published by Royal Society of Medicine Services Limited.

be detected by ELISA. Recently rhG-CSF has been stopped and ANCs have promptly fallen to $<0.2\times10^9$1.

DISCUSSION

This case report confirms that clinical and haematological improvement can be achieved in Kostmann's Syndrome using rhG-CSF. The treatment over several months was well tolerated and no neutralizing antibodies developed. The fact that clinical well being was maintained despite several drops of ANC to very low levels suggests that clinical parameters may be a better guide to response than ANC when evaluating dose and frequency of injections. Alternate day treatment with rhG-CSF merits further evaluation, particularly in young children.

REFERENCES

(1) Kostmann R. Infantile agranulocytosis. *Acta Paediatr Scand* 1956; **45** (suppl 105): 1.
(2) Souza LM, Boone TC, Gabrilove J, *et al.* Recombinant human granulocyte colony stimulating factor: effects on normal and leukemic myeloid cells. *Science* 1966; **232**: 61.
(3) Bonilla MA, Gillio AP, Ruggiero M, *et al.* Effects of recombinant human granulocyte colony-stimulating factor on neutropenia in patients with congenital agranulocytosis. *N Engl J Med* 1989; **320**: 1574.
(4) Welte K. Differential effects of granulocyte-macrophage colony-stimulating factor and granulocyte colony-stimulating factor in children with severe congenital neutropenia. *Blood* 1990; **75**: 1056.

Efficacy of recombinant human interferon-γ in chronic granulomatous disease

R. A. Seger and T. J. Mühlebach
representing the International CGD Study Group

Division of Immunology-Haematology, Children's Hospital, University of Zürich,
Switzerland

INTRODUCTION

Chronic granulomatous disease (CGD) is a group of congenital phagocyte disorders characterized by recurrent pyogenic infections with catalase-positive bacteria and fungi. Due to a defect in one of the four components of the NADPH-oxidase system (two cytosol factors, p47 and p67-phox, and cytochrome b heavy and light chains, gp91 and p22-phox), the phagocytic cells of these patients are unable to generate reactive oxygen metabolites upon stimulation and to kill ingested micro-organisms properly.

Interferon-γ (IFN-γ) is a lymphokine which has been shown to activate macrophages. Pretreatment of normal monocytes and neutrophils also enhances the production of reactive oxygen metabolites and improves the capacity of microbial killing [1]. In addition IFN-γ promotes non-oxidative killing by little known pathways, e.g. by down-regulating transferrin receptors and limiting iron-availability [2] and by enhancing the fusion of phagosomes with lysosomes [3].

A recent pilot study [4] demonstrated a partial correction of the phagocyte defect in four patients with X-linked CGD by subcutaneous recombinant human IFN-γ (rh-IFN-γ). Treatment resulted in increased cytochrome b_{558} content, superoxide production and bactericidal activity. Subsequently a randomized, double blind, placebo-controlled phase III multicentre trial of rh-IFN-γ in CGD patients was performed, the detailed results of which will be published separately [5]. Here we will summarize the clinical efficacy and describe our analyses of the NADPH-oxidase activity in 16 patients enrolled in this study.

Supported by Swiss National Science Foundation Grant numbers 3.921-0.85 and 32-255 28.88.

Progress in immune deficiency III, edited by H. M. Chapel, R. J. Levinsky and A. D. B. Webster, 1991; Royal Society of Medicine Services International Congress and Symposium Series No. 173, published by Royal Society of Medicine Services Limited.

PATIENTS AND METHODS

Study design

The complete study protocol is described elsewhere [5]. In brief, the patients received either rh-IFN-γ 50 μg/m^2 subcutaneously (s.c.) three times a week or placebo (the IFN-γ-diluent) for an average of 8.9 months. Various neutrophil functions were assayed on days 0 (twice), 4, 90 and 180.

Patients

We enrolled 12 patients with complete X-linked cytochrome b_{558} deficiency, two patients with autosomal-recessive (a/r) cytochrome$_{558}$ deficiency and two patients with a/r cytosol factor (p47 and p67-phox) deficiencies. The diagnosis of CGD was established by an abnormal neutrophil NBT-slide test and by abnormal superoxide release upon maximal stimulation with phorbol-myristate-acetate (PMA) and formylmethionylleucylphenylalanine (FMLP).

Laboratory evaluations

Superoxide formation was measured at 37°C as the SOD sensitive reduction of cytochrome c with PMA and FMLP as stimuli. Cytochrome b_{558} was measured by determination of the reduced-minus-oxidized spectrum in a Triton x-100 cell extract. For all calculations of cytochrome b_{558}-content, an extinction coefficient

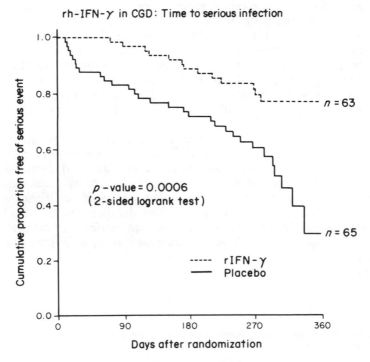

Figure 1 *Cumulative proportion of CGD patients treated with placebo or rh IFN-γ who remained free of serious infections versus time in study (n = number of patients analysed in each treatment group).*

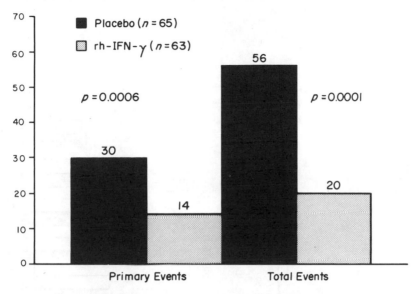

Figure 2   *Occurrence of serious infections in each treatment group.*

of 106 mM/cm for the Soret band was used [6]. The killing assay with
Staphylococcus aureus 502A was performed according to the standardized study
protocol.

RESULTS AND DISCUSSION

The final analysis of the phase III study of rh-IFN-γ for infection prophylaxis in
CGD was conducted on data collected up to the final blinded visit for each patient,

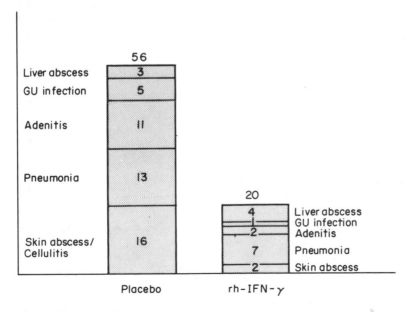

Figure 3   *Sites of serious infections in each treatment group.*

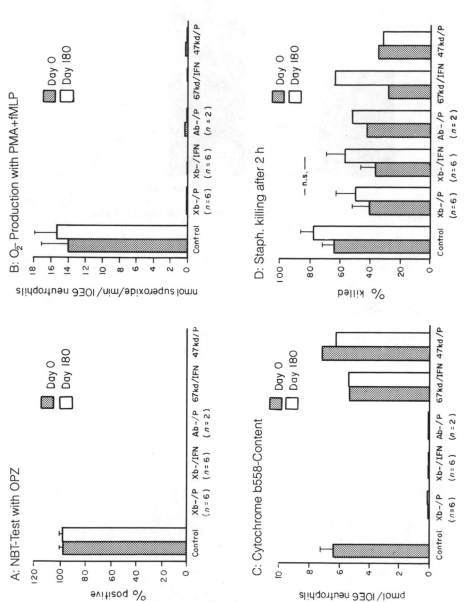

Figure 4 *Neutrophil functions and cytochrome b_{558} content of study patients on days 0 and 180. (see text for legend)*

the average duration of treatment being 8.9 months [5]. Figure 1 shows a Kaplan-Meier curve displaying the time to first serious infection after randomization for each treatment arm. Seventy seven percent of patients in the IFN-γ group were free of serious infection 12 months after randomization compared to only 30% in the placebo group. Thirty of 65 patients in the placebo group versus 14 of 63 patients in the IFN-γ group experienced at least one serious infection. Several patients had multiple serious infections. Fifty six total serious infections were observed in the placebo group versus 20 in the IFN-γ group (Fig. 2). Analysis of the nature of serious events revealed that rh-IFN-γ was most effective in reducing skin abscesses, pulmonary infections and adenitis (Fig. 3). No serious or life-threatening toxicities could be directly attributed to the study drug.

In our patient group, six of the X-linked cytochrome b_{558} deficient patients and one patient with a/r p67-phox deficiency were treated with rh IFN-γ. The other nine patients received placebo. As can be seen from Fig. 4 none of the observed parameters of neutrophil oxidative metabolism changed in the rh-IFN-γ treated patients compared to the placebo-treated controls. In the cytochemical NBT-test (Fig. 4A) all the cells remained formazan-negative. The deficient superoxide production (Fig. 4B) was not improved and the cytochrome b_{558}-content (Fig. 4C) remained below detection limit. The killing of Staphylococcus aureus 502 A (Fig. 4D) was not significantly increased in rh-IFN-γ treated patients.

In conclusion, rh-IFN-γ at $50 \mu g/m^2$ subcutaneously three times per week is effective and safe therapy for CGD. It reduces the frequency of serious infections and is not accompanied by toxic effects. The mode of action of rh-IFN-γ remains unknown. In contrast to published reports it does not increase O_2-production, cytochrome b_{558} content nor short-term bacterial killing in neutrophils and monocytes (latter data not shown) in six classical X-linked and one p67-phox-deficient CGD-patients. Clearly more study is needed to define the mechanisms by which rh-IFN-γ augments host response, work that should probably concentrate on oxygen-independent microbicidal pathways still intact in CGD.

ACKNOWLEDGMENTS

The authors wish to extend special thanks to the following paediatricians for referral of their patients: A. Campelli (Genova), R. Dopfer (Tübingen), R. Geib-König (Saarbrücken), H. Graf (Homburg-Saar), F. Hallé (Zürich), E. Keller (Leipzig), G. Souillet (Lyon), V. Wahn (Düsseldorf), H. Wiesemann (Essen).

REFERENCES

(1) Edwards SW, Say JE, Hughes V. Gamma Interferon enhances the killing of Staphylococcus aureus by human neutrophils. J Gen Microbiol 1988; 134: 37–42.
(2) Byrd TF, Horwitz MA. Interferon gamma-activated human monocytes downregulate transferrin receptors and inhibit the intracellular multiplication of Legionella pneumophila by limiting the availability of iron. J Clin Invest 1989; 83: 1457–65.
(3) Kagaya K, Watanabe K, Fukazawa Y. Capacity of recombinant gamma interferon to activate macrophages for salmonella-killing activity. Infect Immun 1989; 57: 609–15.
(4) Ezekowitz RAB, Dinauer MC, Jaffe HS, Orkin SH, Newburger PE. Partial correction of the phagocyte defect in patients with x-linked chronic granulomatous disease by subcutaneous interferon gamma. N Engl J Med 1988; 319: 146–51.

(5) The International Chronic Granulomatous Disease Cooperative Study Group: A phase III study establishing efficacy of recombinant human interferon gamma for infection prophylaxis in chronic granulomatous disease. Unpublished observations.
(6) Lutter R, van Schaik ML, van Zwieten R, Wever R, Roos D, Hamers MN. Purification and partial characterization of the b-type cytochrome from human polymorphonuclear leucocytes. *J Biol Chem* 1985; **260**: 2237–44.

Chronic granulomatous disease of childhood: A review of 25 years' experience

A. Finn, N. Hadžić, G. Morgan, S. Strobel and R. J. Levinsky

Department of Immunology, Institute of Child Health, London, UK

INTRODUCTION

Chronic granulomatous disease (CGD) was first described in 1957 [1], and later shown to be due to an inborn inability of the patients' phagocytes to kill ingested microbes [2]. The main clinical features are lymphadenitis, superficial and deep abscesses, dermatitis, organomegaly and pneumonitis leading to chronic lung damage [3]. The condition is not universally fatal in childhood and it affects predominantly, but not solely, males [4,5]. The diagnosis is confirmed by performing the phorbol-myristate acetate-stimulated nitroblue tetrazolium (NBT) test which gives percentage values of stained neutrophils near zero in affected cases, near 100% in normals and intermediate values (usually 20–80% due to lyonization) in females heterozygous for the X-linked form.

A number of different metabolic defects of the phagocyte respiratory burst could produce the CGD phenotype. The commonest is a deficiency of a phagocyte cytochrome b seen in the X-linked recessive form [6] due to mutation in the gene for the larger β-subunit of this haemoglycoprotein [7,8]. The gene has been mapped to the Xp21.1 region of the X chromosome and has been cloned [9]. Some patients with autosomal recessive, cytochrome b positive CGD have an abnormality of one or a group of neutrophil cytoplasmic proteins involved in the regulation of the respiratory burst [10]. This work provides a rational basis for the range of clinical severity seen in CGD.

Curative therapy for CGD is limited to a little experience with bone marrow transplantation and the results have shown at best partial success [11–13]. Palliative therapy has involved use of antimicrobial agents both prophylactically and for infections as they occur. Retrospective studies have suggested that regular cotrimoxazole in particular improves the clinical course [5,14] although a controlled prospective study has never been performed. Antenatal diagnosis has only been available by performing the NBT test on fetal blood obtained at the late gestational age of 18–20 weeks [15].

Important progress is now being made in all three of the areas of management mentioned above. Cure, in the form of somatic gene therapy, has not been achieved but is under investigation in several centres. Palliative treatment with interferon-γ is being studied; the cytokine has been shown to ameliorate

Progress in immune deficiency III, edited by H. M. Chapel, R. J. Levinsky and A. D. B. Webster, 1991; Royal Society of Medicine Services International Congress and Symposium Series No. 173, published by Royal Society of Medicine Services Limited.

defective phagocyte function when given sub-cutaneously to some patients with both cytochrome b-positive and cytochrome b-negative CGD in two small studies [16,17]. Multicentre prospective controlled trials are currently in progress to assess whether the cytokine has concordant clinical benefits. Finally, first trimester antenatal diagnosis by chorionic villous biopsy is now possible for the proportion of mothers informative for at least one of two polymorphisms within the X-linked CGD gene which have recently been described [18,19].

In this study we recorded our previous clinical experience of CGD.

RESULTS

Demographics

The patients were born over a 32-year period from 1955 to 1987. There were two sibling pairs, the remainder were unrelated. There were 26 male and two female patients. The racial pattern was predominantly white, reflecting that of our referral population.

Onset and diagnosis

The age of onset of symptoms is shown in Fig. 1. The mean interval between

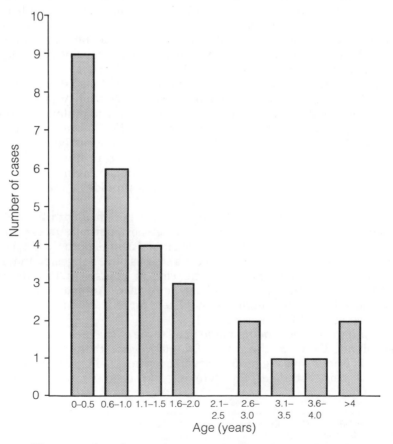

Figure 1 *Age of onset of symptoms in 28 patients with CGD.*

onset and diagnosis fell with growing experience of the disease from 4.6 years in the 1960s to 1.5 years in the 1980s.

Inheritance

The two female cases were presumed to have autosomal recessive inheritance. In both, parental NBT tests were normal and one had confirmatory studies demonstrating a lack of phosphorylation of a 47 kDa cytoplasmic protein but neither had affected siblings. Six male cases whose mothers had normal NBT tests were designated 'autosomal or new mutation'. Nineteen male cases whose mothers had abnormally low NBT test and/or bactericidal assay results were presumed to have X-linked inheritance, of these seven had pedigrees suggestive of this pattern. In one case no family data were available.

Clinical and laboratory features

The symptoms, signs and complications recorded are summarized in Table 1. The recorded weights and heights at presentation were usually below the 50th centile and often very low (Fig. 2). Many patients were found to be anaemic 9/24 (38%) (haemoglobin < 10 g/l) and hypergammaglobulinaemic 11/20 (55%) at the time of presentation. In four families, a family history of systemic lupus erythematosus had been noted, in two of these and three others the patients' mothers had a history of photosensitive facial rash (discoid lupus) [20].

Survival

At the time of study, 16 patients were alive (five aged 0–9 years, five aged 10–19 years and six aged 20–30 years, see Fig. 3), nine had died and three were lost

Table 1 *Clinical features recorded in 28 cases of CGD*

	Number (%)
Common symptoms	
Superficial abscesses & lymphadenitis	27 (96)
Persistent fevers	20 (71)
Chest infections	17 (61)
Failure to thrive	15 (54)
Common signs	
Lymphadenopathy	24 (86)
Dermatitis	23 (82)
Hepatomegaly	19 (68)
Respiratory signs	15 (54)
Splenomegaly	12 (43)
Uncommon features	
Diarrhoea	5 (18)
Otitis	4 (14)
Gingivitis	3 (11)
Fungal nail infection	1 (4)
Apthous ulcers	1 (4)
Invasive infections	
Septicaemia	11 (39)
Osteomyelitis	10 (36)
Liver abscess	7 (25)
Brain abscess	2 (7)

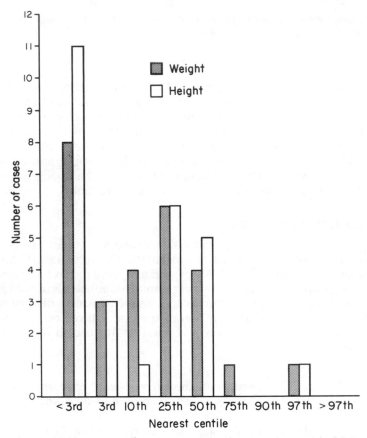

Figure 2 *Nearest centiles at presentation in 27 patients with CGD.*

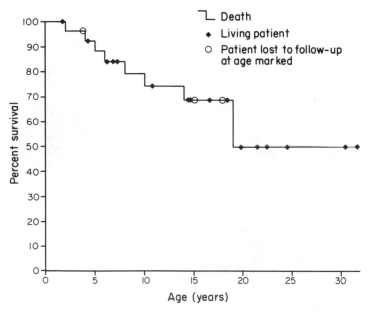

Figure 3 *Actuarial survival curve for 28 patients with CGD.*

to follow up. Six of the nine deaths were due to progressive suppuration of the lung and/or multiple other organ sites. One death was due to liver failure following partial hepatectomy for chronic liver abscess, one was during an exploratory laparotomy for intestinal obstruction and one of unknown cause in a patient who had had an attempted bone marrow transplantation seven years previously. The majority of patients had received some form of antibiotic prophylaxis at some time but data were inadequate to correlate this treatment with outcome. Recent patients had consistently been given oral cotrimoxazole prophylaxis.

Aspergillus infection occurred in eight patients. Three developed progressive infection of lung and/or bone and died, two of these received amphotericin. Two patients, one with an infected buttock haematoma and one with sternal osteomyelitis remain on treatment at the time of study. Two patients, one with empyema and one with infection of the chest wall were successfully treated. One patient was lost to follow up.

An actuarial survival curve was computed and is shown in Fig. 3. Six deaths occurred in the first decade of life and three in the second. Six patients had survived into the third decade. There was greater than 70% survival at 10 years of age and 50% survival from 20 years of age onwards.

DISCUSSION

It is to be expected that a spectrum of clinical severity will be seen in patients with CGD. Our experience bears this out. A milder clinical course among patients with the autosomal recessive cytochrome b-positive type of CGD has been reported [21]. As in another recent report [5], our series showed no apparent difference in clinical severity or mortality between the different inheritance groups. However, the two female cases, who almost certainly have autosomal recessive type CGD, both had late-onset illness (four and six years), are alive at the time of study (aged seven and 22 years) and have had a relatively mild clinical course with no growth failure, organomegaly or serious deep-seated infection.

When patients who developed symptoms for the first time before their first birthday were compared with those who developed them later, a significant difference in the long-term survival was found between the two groups (see Table 2). This suggests that onset in infancy may be an adverse prognostic indicator in CGD.

Most previous reports have suggested a poor prospect of long-term survival for children with CGD [3] although adults with CGD have been reported [22]. One report of 48 paediatric patients showed a 50% survival rate maintained from 10–20 years of age [5]. Although there were some deaths in the second decade

Table 2 Survival correlated with age of onset in 17 patients with CGD

	Alive and > 14 years old	Death before 14th birthday
Onset before 1st birthday	2	6
Onset aged 1 or more	8	1
Totals	10	7

$P = 0.01$ by Fisher's exact test
(Note: patients alive and < 14 years ($n = 6$), lost to follow up ($n = 3$) and who died aged > 14 years ($n = 2$) are excluded.)

in our group, we demonstrate a similarly encouraging 50% survival rate extending into the third decade of life. The impression that CGD is a 'less severe' disease now than when it was first recognized may in part reflect the use of prophylactic antibiotics and the diagnosis of less severely affected individuals. However, our data show 50% long-term survival rates among individuals diagnosed in childhood more than 20 years ago.

Our patients were without exception troubled by recurrent and/or chronic symptoms and their lifestyles and those of their families severely disrupted by the threat or occurrence of serious illness. The frequency of the various features and complications was comparable with previous reports [3–5]. Although bacterial suppuration was the commonest infectious problem, invasive Aspergillus infection carried a particularly high mortality when it occurred. The extreme difficulty of eradicating fungal infection in CGD patients, particularly when it affects the lungs or is disseminated, has been observed previously [23].

This study confirms the main clinical features of CGD but suggests that there is reasonable hope of long-term survival in paediatric cases, particularly those with onset of symptoms after the first birthday.

ACKNOWLEDGMENTS

We wish to thank A. W. Segal for performing the confirmatory assay for autosomal-type CGD. AF is funded by a grant from the British Shoe Corporation. NH was a British Council Research fellow.

REFERENCES

(1) Berendes H, Bridges RA, Good RA. A fatal granulomatosis of childhood. The clinical study of a new syndrome. *Minn Med* 1957; **40**: 309.
(2) Holmes B, Quie PG, Windhorst DB, Good RA. Fatal granulomatous disease of childhood. An inborn abnormality of phagocyte function. *Lancet* 1966; **i**: 1225–8.
(3) Johnston RB, McMurry JS. Chronic familial granulomatosis: report of five cases and review of the literature. *Am J Dis Child* 1967; **114**: 370–8.
(4) Johnston RB, Newman SL. Chronic granulomatous disease. *Pediatr Clin North Am* 1977; **24**: 365–76.
(5) Mouy R, Fischer A, Vilmer E, Seger R, Griscelli C. Incidence, severity, and prevention of infections in chronic granulomatous disease. *J Pediatr* 1989; **114**: 555–60.
(6) Segal AW, Cross AR, Garcia RC, *et al.* Absence of cytochrome b-245 in chronic granulomatous disease. A multicenter European evaluation of its incidence and relevance. *N Engl J Med* 1983; **308**: 245–51.
(7) Dinauer MC, Orkin SH, Brown R, Jesaitis AJ, Parkos CA. The glycoprotein encoded by the X-linked chronic granulomatous disease locus is a component of the neutrophil cytochrome b complex. *Nature* 1987; **327**: 717–20.
(8) Teahan C, Rowe P, Parker P, Totty N, Segal AW. The X-linked chronic granulomatous disease gene codes for the B-chain of cytochrome b$_{-245}$. *Nature* 1987; **327**: 720–1.
(9) Dinauer MC, Orkin SH. Molecular genetics of chronic granulomatous disease. *Immunodef Rev* 1988; **1**: 55–69.
(10) Okamura N, Curnette JT, Roberts RL, Babior BM. Relationship of protein phosphorylation to the activation of the respiratory burst in human neutrophils. Defects in the phosphorylation of a group of closely related 48-kDa proteins in two forms of chronic granulomatous disease. *J Biol Chem* 1988; **263**: 6777–82.
(11) Westminster hospitals bone-marrow transplant team. Bone marrow transplant from an unrelated donor for chronic granulomatous disease. *Lancet* 1977; **i**: 210–3.

(12) Kamani N, August CS, Campbell DE, Hassan NF, Douglas SD. Marrow transplantation in chronic granulomatous disease: an update, with 6-year follow-up. *J Pediatr* 1988; **113**: 697–700.

(13) Rappeport JM, Newburger PE, Goldblum RM, *et al.* Allogeneic bone marrow transplantation for chronic granulomatous disease. *J Pediatr* 1982; **101**: 952–5.

(14) Gonzalez LA, Hill HR. Advantages and disadvantages of antimicrobial prophylaxis in chronic granulomatous disease of childhood. *Pediatr Infect Dis J* 1988; **7**: 83–5.

(15) Levinsky RJ, Harvey BAM, Rodeck CH, Soothill JF. Phorbol-myristate acetate stimulated NBT test; a simple method suitable for antenatal diagnosis of chronic granulomatous disease. *Clin Exp Immunol* 1983; **54**: 595–8.

(16) Ezekowitz RAB, Dinauer MC, Jaffe HS, Orkin SH, Newburger PE. Partial correction of the phagocyte defect in patients with X-linked chronic granulomatous disease by subcutaneous interferon gamma. *N Engl J Med* 1988; **319**: 146–51.

(17) Sechler JMG, Malech HL, White CJ, Gallin JI. Recombinant human interferon-gamma reconstitutes defective phagocyte function in patients with chronic granulomatous disease of childhood. *Proc Natl Acad Sci USA* 1988; **86**: 4874–8.

(18) Battat L, Francke U. NsiI RFLP at the X-linked chronic granulomatous disease locus (CYBB). *Nucleic Acids Res* 1989; **17**: 3619.

(19) Pelham A, O'Reilly MJ, Malcolm S, Levinsky RJ, Kinnon C. RFLP and deletion analysis for X-linked chronic granulomatous disease using the cDNA probe: potential for improved prenatal diagnosis and carrier determination. *Blood* 1990; **76**: 820–4.

(20) Schaller J. Illness resembling Lupus Erythematosus in mothers of boys with chronic granulomatous disease. *Ann Intern Med* 1972; **76**: 747–50.

(21) Weening RS, Adriaansz LH, Weemaes CMR, Lutter R, Roos D. Clinical differences in chronic granulomatous disease in patients with cytochrome b-negative or cytochrome b-positive neutrophils. *J Pediatr* 1985; **107**: 102–4.

(22) Dilworth JA, Mandell GL. Adults with chronic granulomatous disease of "childhood". *Am J Med* 1977; **63**: 233–43.

(23) Cohen MS, Isturiz RE, Malech HL, *et al.* Fungal infection in chronic granulomatous disease. The importance of the phagocyte in defense against fungi. *Am J Med* 1981; **71**: 59–66.

RFLP and deletion analysis for X-linked chronic granulomatous disease

A. Pelham[1], S. Malcolm[2], R. J. Levinsky[1] and C. Kinnon[1]

[1]Department of Immunology and [2]Mothercare Department of Genetics, Institute of Child Health, London, UK

INTRODUCTION

Chronic granulomatous disease (CGD) is a rare inherited disorder of granulocyte function which is characterized by recurrent severe bacterial and fungal infections from early childhood. Several different underlying molecular defects have now been identified, but the clinical presentation does not vary as a result of these. In all forms of the disease the functional defect is in granulocyte killing capacity, with normal phagocytosis. The inheritance pattern in approximately 65% of families is X-linked, the remainder being autosomal recessive. Affected individuals and carrier females (in the X-linked form) may be identified by the phorbol myristate acetate (PMA)-stimulated nitroblue tetrazolium (NBT) reduction test [1]; this provides a functional assessment of the NADPH oxidase system in neutrophils, which is defective in all forms of CGD. Prenatal diagnosis for CGD has until recently only been possible by fetal blood sampling and NBT testing at 18 weeks gestation, which has meant second trimester abortion of affected fetuses.

The gene responsible for X-linked chronic granulomatous disease (X-CGD) was localized to Xp21 in 1985 by cytogenetic analysis of a patient with a complex syndrome including CGD and an interstitial deletion of this region [2]. Subsequently the gene has been isolated [3] and found to code for the 90 kilodalton β-subunit of cytochrome b$_{-245}$, a component of the membrane bound NADPH oxidase system [4]. Since then several additional patients have been described with X-CGD and cytogenetically detectable deletions, and one patient with a deletion detectable only by complete absence of hybridization to X-CGD cDNA. Each of these patients has a complex syndrome including one or all of the McCleod syndrome, Duchenne muscular dystrophy and retinitis pigmentosa. Following an extensive search for polymorphisms within the X-CGD gene, with 40 different restriction enzymes, a restriction fragment length polymorphism (RFLP) has recently been described [5] using the enzyme NsiI and the X-CGD cDNA as a probe. This will allow first trimester prenatal diagnosis in a small proportion of families. We have identified a second RFLP, also detected using NsiI, and have shown that the two polymorphisms do not appear to be in linkage

Progress in immune deficiency III, edited by H. M. Chapel, R. J. Levinsky and A. D. B. Webster, 1991; Royal Society of Medicine Services International Congress and Symposium Series No. 173, published by Royal Society of Medicine Services Limited.

Table 1   *Allele frequencies for two* NsiI *RFLPs detected by X-CGD cDNA in unrelated individuals*

Allele	Size	No. of chromosomes	%	
A1	2.9	6/32	19	} 13 females, 6 males
A2	2.5	26/32	81	
B1	1.7	26/29	90	} 12 females, 5 males
B2	1.3	3/29	10	

Genomic DNA was digested with NsiI, *size separated on agarose gels and blotted onto nylon membranes, which were then hybridized with the X-CGD cDNA probe labelled with* ^{32}P dCTP. *Allele sizes are in kilobases.*

disequilibrium. The existence of these two separate RFLPs will increase the proportion of families to whom prenatal diagnosis will be available by chorionic villous sampling. In two situations we have also found discrepancies between the assessment of carrier status by PMA-stimulated NBT testing and RFLP analysis. In informative families the use of RFLP analysis will ensure unambiguous carrier detection. One family affected by X-CGD, whose members are not informative for either polymorphism, was found to carry a deletion involving the X-CGD gene. This was revealed by altered band patterns on hybridization with the X-CGD cDNA probe in affected and carrier family members, none of whom have any other clinical abnormalities. This appears to be a smaller deletion than any previously described. On the basis of the altered band pattern, prenatal diagnosis and carrier detection will also be available to this family.

RESULTS

*Nsi*I RFLP

Genomic DNA from members of eight families affected by X-CGD and seven normal unrelated females was digested with *Nsi*I and hybridized with X-CGD cDNA. In addition to several invariant fragments, two pairs of polymorphic bands were seen, of 2.9 and 2.5 kb (A1 and A2), and 1.7 and 1.3 kb (B1 and B2). The latter polymorphism has previously been described (5). The allele frequencies in our population for each polymorphism are shown in Table 1. The predicted heterozygote frequencies from these are 31% for polymorphism A and 18% for polymorphism B. The observed haplotype distribution is not significantly different from that expected on the basis of the allele frequencies (Table 2), which implies that there is no strong linkage disequilibrium between the two RFLPs, although the size of the sample is small. On this basis, approximately 50% of families may

Table 2   *Haplotype distribution for two* NsiI *X-CGD RFLPs*

Haplotype	Frequency (%) Observed	Expected
A1, B1	20	17
A2, B1	69	73
A1, B2	0	1.9
A2, B2	10	8.1

therefore be expected to be informative for one or other of the RFLPs. Of our eight affected families studied, four were informative for polymorphism A and three for polymorphism B (one was informative for both). Mendelian X-linked inheritance was demonstrated in three generations in four of the families (two for each polymorphism). In two families inconsistency was found between carrier prediction made on the basis of PMA-stimulated NBT testing and RFLP analysis. In one case the grandmother of an affected child showed 83% NBT reduction (which lies on the borderline for carrier status) but on RFLP analysis was shown clearly not to possess the allele associated with the disease in that family; in this case the disease must have arisen as a result of a new mutation in the mother of the affected boy, who showed 20% NBT reduction. In another family the sister of an affected boy had been labelled normal on the basis of an NBT result of 93%, but she clearly carries the same allele as her affected brother. In this case paternity was confirmed using the minisatellite probe pλG3 [6] hybridized to *Hin*fI digested genomic DNA from this family (F. Katz, unpublished observations). The certainty of carrier prediction should therefore now be much improved in informative families.

X-CGD deletion

One family of the eight investigated in this study was found to carry a deletion involving the X-CGD gene. This was demonstrated by altered band patterns, seen in both affected and carrier family members, after digestion of genomic DNA with a variety of restriction enzymes and hybridization with the X-CGD cDNA probe. Following *Nsi*I digestion of genomic DNA from the affected boy (PT), an additional fragment of 11 kb was seen on hybridization with X-CGD, but he lacked most of the other invariant and polymorphic bands. DNA from two carriers (NBT results 27% and 38%) revealed all the normal bands, but also the extra 11 kb band. Further analysis of the deletion was performed using fragments of the X-CGD cDNA from the 5' and 3' ends (represented in Fig. 1). Hybridization patterns seen using the X-CGD5' and X-CGD3' probes in normal individuals and PT are shown in Fig. 2. From these results it is possible to conclude firstly that both of the *Nsi*I polymorphisms lie within the central portion of the X-CGD gene, since neither X-CGD5' nor X-CGD3' detects either of the RFLPs. Secondly the extent of the deletion in PT must encompass most of the X-CGD gene, from within the first 500 bp of the cDNA to beyond the 3' end of the coding region and into the 3' untranslated region. The minimum size of the deletion is estimated to be about 11 kb. This family exhibits no other clinical abnormalities, which implies that the closest flanking disease genes (McLeod red cell phenotype on the telomeric side

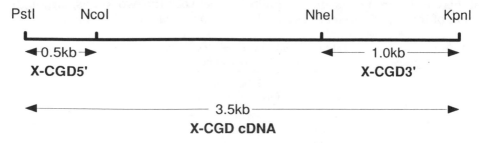

Figure 1 *Schematic representation of X-CGD cDNA probes used in mapping the deletion in PT. X-CGD5' and X-CGD3' are fragments of X-CGD cDNA digested with restriction enzymes as shown.*

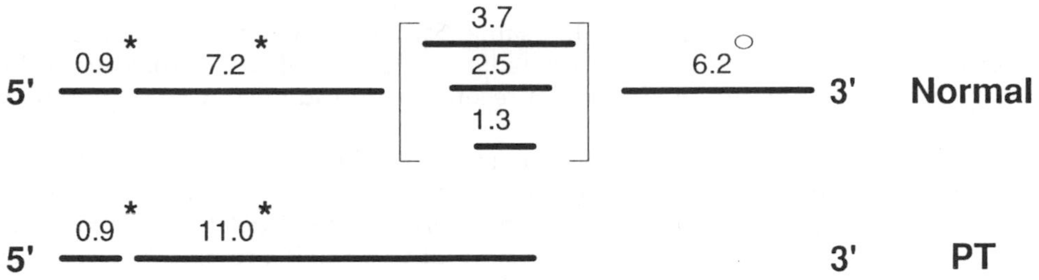

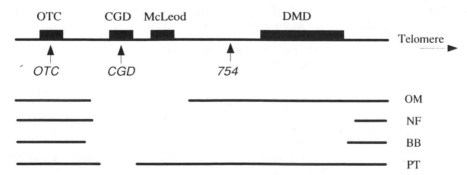

Figure 2 *Schematic representation of NsiI fragments detected with X-CGD, X-CGD5' and X-CGD3' probes in normal DNA and DNA from PT. All bands shown hybridize with X-CGD; an asterisk indicates hybridization with X-CGD5' and o indicates hybridization with X-CGD3'. No signal was seen at any time with X-CGD3' in PT. Identical bands were always seen in PT with X-CGD and X-CGD5'. Bands for which the order has not been determined are enclosed in brackets.*

and ornithine transcarbamylase (OTC) deficiency on the centromeric side; Fig. 3) are unaffected by this deletion. Normal hybridization patterns were seen in the affected boy using the closely linked probe 754, which also lies telomeric to X-CGD. The exact extent of the deletion has however not been defined, but further studies are in progress.

DISCUSSION

Prenatal diagnosis and carrier detection in X-linked CGD has been possible for some time using the NBT reduction test on fetal blood samples taken at around 18 weeks gestation or on peripheral blood of possible carriers. However, this has meant second trimester abortions of affected fetuses, and, as we have demonstrated, establishment of carrier status using the NBT test may not always be certain. The identification of RFLPs within the X-CGD gene represents a major advance, allowing first trimester prenatal diagnosis by chorionic villus sampling for informative families. One case of prenatal diagnosis has previously been reported using linked polymorphic probes [7], but the use of RFLPs within the cDNA will allow prediction of 100% accuracy. The two polymorphisms do not appear to be in linkage disequilibrium, which means that approximately 50% of families should benefit from this advance. In addition, unequivocal identification

Figure 3 *Schematic map of Xp21 including the region around the X-CGD locus and the approximate extent of deletions described: OM [9], NF [10], BB [2] and PT (this study). The positions of probes OTC, X-CGD and 754 are indicated by arrows.*

of carriers will be possible in the same families. We have demonstrated discrepancies between assessed carrier status on the basis of NBT results and RFLP analysis in two cases, although another recent report found complete agreement between the two methods [8].

Several patients with deletions involving the X-CGD gene have previously been described [2,9,10], but all of these cases have been associated with complex syndromes (Fig. 3), and most with cytogenetically detectable deletions. Our patient (PT) appears to have a smaller deletion than any of those previously described, probably extending from close to the 5' end of the cDNA to beyond the 3' untranslated region, although the precise extent of the deletion has not been defined. This family is not informative for either of the above polymorphisms, but prenatal diagnosis and carrier detection will be possible for them on the basis of the altered band patterns caused by the deletion. In addition, since the affected boy retains the 5' end of the gene it may be possible to orientate the X-CGD gene on the X-chromosome using more closely linked probes.

ACKNOWLEDGMENTS

AP is an Action Research Training Fellow. CK is supported by the Wellcome Trust.

REFERENCES

(1) Levinsky RJ, Harvey BAM, Rodeck CH, Soothill JF. Phorbol myristate acetate stimulated NBT test; a simple method suitable for antenatal diagnosis of chronic granulomatous disease of childhood. *Clin Exp Immunol* 1983; **54**: 595–8.
(2) Francke U, Ochs HD, de Martinville B, *et al.* Minor Xp21 chromosome deletion in a male associated with expression of Duchenne muscular dystrophy, chronic granulomatous disease, retinitis pigmentosa and McLeod syndrome. *Am J Hum Genet* 1985; **37**: 250–67.
(3) Royer-Pokora B, Kunkel LM, Monaco AP, Goff SC, Orkin SH. Cloning the gene for an inherited human disorder—chronic granulomatous disease—on the basis of its chromosomal location. *Nature* 1986; **322**: 32–8.
(4) Teahan C, Rowe P, Parker P, Totty N, Segal AW. The X-linked chronic granulomatous disease gene codes for the α-chain of cytochrome b_{-245}. *Nature* 1987; **327**: 720–1.
(5) Battat L, Francke U. *Nsi*I RFLP at the X-linked chronic granulomatous disease locus (CYBB). *Nucleic Acids Res* 1989; **17** (9): 3619.
(6) Wong Z, Wilson V, Jeffreys AJ, Thein SL. Cloning a selected fragment from a human DNA fingerprint: Isolation of an extremely polymorphic minisatellite. *Nucleic Acids Res* 1986; **14**: 4605–16.
(7) Lindlof M, Kere J, Ristola M, *et al.* Prenatal diagnosis of X-linked chronic granulomatous disease using restriction fragment length polymorphism analysis. *Genomics* 1987; **1**: 87–92.
(8) Francke U, Ochs HD, Darras BT, Swaroop A. Origin of mutations in two families with X-linked chronic granulomatous disease. *Blood* 1990; **76** (3): 602–6.
(9) Frey D, Machler M, Seger R, Schmid W. Orkin SH. Gene deletion in a patient with chronic granulomatous disease and McLeod syndrome: Fine mapping of the Xk gene locus. *Blood* 1988; **71** (1): 252–5.
(10) Koussef B. Linkage between chronic granulomatous disease and Duchenne muscular dystrophy? *Am J Dis Child* 1981; **135**: 1149.

Modulation of superoxide production by cytokines in monocytes from patients with chronic granulomatous disease

V. Jendrossek[1], A. M. J. Peters[1], S. Buth[1], B. H. Belohradsky[2] and M. Gahr[1]

[1]Universitätskinderklinik Göttingen, Robert-Koch-Straße, Göttingen and
[2]Universitätskinderklinik München, Lindwurmstraße, München, Germany

INTRODUCTION

Chronic granulomatous disease of childhood (CGD) represents a group of genetically and biochemically distinct disorders characterized by reduced or deficient production of reactive oxygen species of phagocytes. About 60% of the CGD-patients have an X-linked inheritance pattern with absence of one component of the NADPH-oxidase, the cytochrome b_{558}, in their phagocyte membrane (X$^-$ CGD); other patients have an autosomal recessive inheritance pattern lacking the cytochrome b_{558} (AR$^-$ CGD) or some cytosolic factors (AR$^+$ CGD) [3,4]. Interferon-γ (IFNγ), a potent monocyte and macrophage activator, has recently been shown to enhance superoxide production of monocytes from healthy donors but also from some patients with CGD after stimulation of the NADPH-oxidase with a second stimulus, a phenomenon called priming [2,5–10,13]. The aim of our study was to determine if other cytokines involved in monocyte maturation, differentiation and activation prime cultured human peripheral blood monocytes from CGD patients for enhanced respiratory burst activity.

MATERIAL AND METHODS

Patient population

The CGD patients were characterized by inheritance pattern and NBT test (nitroblue tetrazolium test), superoxide production as well as cytochrome b content of the polymorphonuclear neutrophils (PMN) from the patients and their mothers (see Table 1). X-linked CGD patients are males whose mothers showed a mosaic of cells with normal and deficient formazan formation in the NBT test and had intermediate superoxide production. AR-CGD patients are males and females whose mother's phagocytes had normal NBT reduction and superoxide

Progress in immune deficiency III, edited by H. M. Chapel, R. J. Levinsky and A. D. B. Webster, 1991; Royal Society of Medicine Services International Congress and Symposium Series No. 173, published by Royal Society of Medicine Services Limited.

Table 1

Patient No.	1	2	3	4	5	6	7	8	9	10	11	12	13
Inheritance	AR	AR	AR	AR	AR	AR	AR	X	X	X	X	X	X
NBT [%]	2	2–48	3–11	6	76	3	80	14	11	5	0	0	0
O_2^-	r.a.	r.a.	r.a.	r.a.	r.a.	r.a.	r.a.	r.a.	r.a.	r.a.	—	—	—
Cytochr. b_{558}	+ (a)	+ (b)	+ (a)	+ (a)	+ (a)	+ (a,b)	nd	- (a)	- (a)	nd	- (a)	- (b)	- (a)

r.a. = residual activity   — = absent   nd = not determined

formation. All seven AR-CGD patients had cytochrome b_{558} in their phagocyte membranes (AR$^+$ CGD) and residual superoxide production. The six X-CGD patients lacked cytochrome b_{558} (X-CGD); three were 'classical' X$^-$ CGD patients without residual superoxide producing capacity; the three other X$^-$ CGD patients had residual NADPH-oxidase activity.

The patient population is characterized by the inheritance mode, the reactivity of PMN in the NBT-test, the stimulated superoxide production and the cytochrome b_{558} content of PMN, determined as sodium dithionite induced difference spectrum (a) or by FACS-analysis with the monoclonal antibody 7D5 against the cytochrome b_{558} light chain (b) (kindly provided by M. Nakamura, Tokyo). Residual NADPH-oxidase activity was presumed if the patient's PMN showed more than 3% NBT-positive cells and/or measurable cytochrome c reducing activity (Table 1).

Reagents and chemicals

Tissue culture reagents were obtained from Biochrom, Berlin; all other chemicals were from Sigma, Deisenhofen. Human recombinant cytokines were obtained as follows:

Cytokine	Manufacturer	Specific act. [10^6 U/mg]	Source	EU/$2*10^7$ U	Test conc. [U/ml]
IFNγ	Bioferon	20	E. coli	100	500
TNFα	Boehringer M.	20	yeast	—	500
IL-1β	Boehringer M.	10	E. coli	20	100
IL-3	Genezyme	350	yeast	—	100

EU = endotoxin units (1 ng LPS = 5–200 EU)

Cell isolation, cell culture and superoxide assay of cultured monocytes

Human peripheral blood monocytes from healthy volunteers and CGD patients were isolated from heparinized blood by one-step density centrifugation over Ficoll-Paque [1] (Pharmacia Fine Chemicals, Uppsala, Sweden). Mononuclear cells to be cultured were washed three times with phosphate buffered saline (PBS) pH 7.4 without calcium and magnesium at 4°C to remove remaining platelets, suspended in RPMI 1640 medium supplemented with 2 g/l sodium bicarbonate, 2 mmol glutamine, 100 U/ml penicillin, 100 μg/ml streptomycin and 10% heat-inactivated pooled human AB–serum at a concentration of 10^6 cells/ml (determined by nonspecific esterase stain—Technikon, Terrytown, New York) and plated at 10^5 cells/well (100 μl) in each well of a 96 well microtitre plate (LINBRO flat bottom 96 well tissue culture plates. Flow, Meckenheim). Cells were allowed to adhere for 1–2 h at 37°C before vigorously washing away non-adhering lymphocytes twice with RPMI 1640 medium and adding 100 μl of culture medium with or without cytokines. The remaining cells were greater than 90–95% monocytes and more than 99% viable (as determined by trypan blue exclusion test). Cells were cultured in 5% CO_2 at 37°C for three days. The superoxide production of cultured monocytes was measured as superoxide dismutase (SOD) inhibitable cytochrome c reduction by a modified Pick and Mizel method [11]. Stimulation was performed with phorbol-12-myristate-13-acetate (PMA), 2 ng/ml, or formylmethionylleucylphenylalanine (FMLP), 100 nmol/l. The cumulative superoxide production was measured 120 min after the addition of the reaction mixture at 550 nm in a Dynatech Microtitre reader MR 600 (Dynatech, Denkendorf) using absorbance at 490 nm as reference. The superoxide production was calculated from the difference of the optical densities between the wells with and without SOD in nmol $O_2^-/10^5$ cells/120 min.

NBT-test

The nitroblue tetrazolium reduction of isolated PMN's was determined by using the method of Preisig and Hitzig [12].

RESULTS AND DISCUSSION

The *in vitro* effects of recombinant human cytokines on the stimulated superoxide production of cultured monocytes from 13 CGD patients were tested. In preliminary experiments with monocytes from healthy volunteers we established standard culturing conditions (see Material and Methods). Monocytes from healthy volunteers were primed by IFNγ, TNFα, IL-1β, IL-3, IL-6 and GM-CSF for enhanced stimulated superoxide production after 48–96 h of monocyte culture (unpublished observations).

We tested seven AR$^+$ CGD patients with residual NADPH-oxidase activity of their PMN. With one exception, we could also find residual superoxide producing capacity in monocytes after three days of monocyte culture.

Figure 1 show the results of the cytokine pretreatment on the stimulated superoxide production of AR$^+$ CGD-monocytes: Monocytes from 6/7 AR$^+$ CGD patients were primed by at least one cytokine for PMA-stimulated and from 4/6 for FMLP-stimulated superoxide production. Cells from most patients reacted to IFNγ, TNFα and IL-3. One patient did not react to any of the tested cytokines. No patient reacted to all cytokines.

We also tested six X$^-$ CGD patients; three of them had residual superoxide-producing activity characterized by NBT-test. After three days of monocyte culture without cytokines all three patients with residual NADPH-oxidase activity, but also two (PMA) and one (FMLP) of the patients without residual activity showed detectable superoxide production. The residual superoxide production of these X$^-$ CGD patients was always lower than that of AR$^+$ CGD patients.

Cytokine treatment primed monocytes from X$^-$ CGD-patients for enhanced stimulated superoxide production (Fig. 1): 4/6 X$^-$ CGD were primed by at least one cytokine for enhanced PMA, 5/6 for enhanced FMLP stimulated superoxide production. One 'classical' X$^-$ CGD patient without residual activity (patient 12; Table 1) did not react to any of the cytokines tested. After cytokine treatment the patient's superoxide production reached values between 5–80% of untreated control cells from healthy volunteers.

nmol O2–/IE+5 cells/120 min

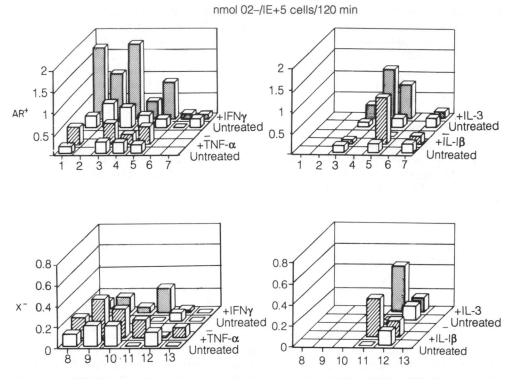

Figure 1   *PMA stimulated cytochrome c reduction in cytokine (IFNγ, TNFα, IL-3, IL-1) primed peripheral blood monocytes from our patients (see Table 1).*

Cytokine priming was not dependent on the inheritance mode, the presence of cytochrome b_{558} in the phagocyte membrane or residual superoxide-producing capacity of the patients' phagocytes, because patients of all subtypes of CGD were sensitive or insensitive to cytokine treatment. Only the extent of the residual superoxide-producing capacity is dependent on the inheritance modes and/or cytochrome b_{558} content of the phagocyte membranes: it was always higher in AR+ CGD-patients.

The increase of superoxide production after cytokine treatment was higher with PMA (2–6 fold) than with FMLP (1.5–3.5 fold). Some patients showed a different pattern of reactivity to cytokines when tested for PMA- or FMLP-stimulated superoxide production: e.g. patient 10 was only primed for FMLP but not for PMA-stimulated superoxide production. When tested for PMA-stimulated superoxide production, patients sensitive to IFNγ always reacted to TNFα and IL-3, suggesting a similar effect of these three cytokines on the PMA stimulated NADPH-oxidase activating pathway.

We have shown that not only IFNγ but also other cytokines increase the stimulated superoxide production in cultured CGD monocytes. Testing various cytokines in monocytes of individual patients *in vitro* could give information about possible therapeutic use of other cytokines than IFNγ. In addition, an effect of various cytokines on stimulated superoxide production, cytochrome b_{558} and cytosolic cofactor expression in healthy volunteers and patients with CGD could help to elucidate the molecular mechanism of cytokine priming in phagocytes.

ACKNOWLEDGMENTS

This work was supported by grants from the Deutsche Forschungsgemeinschaft (AZ Ga 148/7-1) and the Nordwestdeutsche Gesellschaft für Kinderheilkunde. We thank M. Nakamura, Tokyo, Japan, for kindly providing us the monoclonal antibody 7D5 and J. Roesler, Hannover, FRG for helpful advice.

REFERENCES

(1) Böyum A. Isolation of mononuclear cells and granulocytes from human blood. *Scand J Clin Lab Invest* 1976; **21**: 77–89.

(2) Cassatella MA, Capelli R, Della Bianca V, Grezkowiak M, Dusi S, Berton G. Interferon-gamma activates human neutrophil oxygen metabolism and exocytosis. *Immunology* 1988; **63**: 499–506.

(3) Clark CA, Malech HL, Gallin JI, *et al*. Genetic variants of chronic granulomatous disease: prevalence of deficiency of two cytosolic components of the NADPH oxidase system. *N Engl J Med* 1989; **321**: 647–52.

(4) Dinauer MC, Orkin SH. Molecular genetics of chronic granulomatous disease. *Immunodef Rev* 1988; **1**: 55–69.

(5) Ezekowitz RAB, Orkin SH, Newburger PE. Recombinant interferon gamma augments phagocyte superoxide production and X-chronic granulomatous disease gene expression in X-linked variant chronic granulomatous disease. *J Clin Invest* 1987; **80**: 1009–16.

(6) Murray HW. Interferon γ, the activated macrophage and host defense against microbial challenge. *Ann Intern Med* 1988; **108**: 595–608.

(7) Murray HW, Cohn ZA. Macrophage oxygen dependent antimicrobial activity III: Enhanced oxidative metabolism as an expression of macrophage activation. *J Exp Med* 1980; **152**: 1596–1609.

(8) Nathan CF, Murray HW, Wiebe ME, Rubin BY. Identification of interferon γ as the lymphokine that activates human macrophage oxidative metabolism and antimicrobicidal activity. *J Exp Med* 1983; **158**: 670–89.

(9) Nathan CF, Prendergast TJ, Wiebe ME, *et al*. Activation of human macrophages: Comparison of other cytokines with interferon-γ. *J Exp Med* 1984; **160**: 600–5.

(10) Newburger PE, Ezekowitz RAB, Whitney C, Wright J, Orkin SH. Induction of phagocyte cytochrome b heavy chain gene expression by interferon γ. *Proc Natl Acad Sci USA* 1988; **85**: 5215–19.

(11) Pick E, Mizel D. Rapid microassays for measurement of superoxide and hydrogen peroxide production by macrophages in culture using an automatic enzymeimmunoassay reader. *J Immunol Methods* 1981; **46**: 211–26.

(12) Preisig E, Hitzig WH. Nitroblue—tetrazolium test for the detection of chronic granulomatous disease—technical modification. *Eur J Clin Invest* 1971; **1**: 409–10.

(13) Sechler JMG, Malech HL, White CJ, Gallin JI. Recombinant human interferon-γ reconstitutes defective phagocyte function in patients with chronic granulomatous disease of childhood. *Proc Natl Acad Sci USA* 1988; **85**: 4874–8.

Chronic granulomatous disease:
The role of imaging

M. von Planta, U. Willi and R. Seger

Division of Immunology/Radiology, University Children's Hospital, Zurich, Switzerland

(POSTER)

The recognition of characteristic imaging patterns of serious infections, their complications and residual effects should lead to appropriate laboratory evaluation to diagnose or exclude chronic granulomatous disease (CGD) as the underlying condition. Although infections appear mostly within the first year of life, diagnosis of CGD was made on an average of 6.25 years in 40 CGD patients. The early identification of characteristic imaging features in CGD could improve prognosis by immediate introduction of adequate therapeutic measures.

A retrospective analysis of the X-rays, ultrasonograms, CT-scans and scintographies of 40 CGD patients showed the following characteristic imaging features:

Bone: multifocal osteomyelitis with extensive bone destruction and minimal local inflammatory signs; osteomyelitis of the ribs, spondylitis and vertebra plana due to an Aspergillus infection extending locally from the lung; osteomyelitis of the small bones of the hands and feet. *Lungs*: invasive pneumonia with involvement of the thoracic wall, ribs, vertebrae and vertebral canal always associated with an Aspergillus infection; chronic nodular pneumonia as the manifestation of pulmonary aspergillosis; slow resolving or persistence of consolidations despite appropriate antimicrobial therapy; calcified pulmonary granulomas. *Gastrointestinal tract*: single or multiple liver abscesses mainly involving the right liver lobe; calcified liver granulomas secondary to a known liver abscess or without previous apparent clinical liver infection; granulomatous hepatitis with portal hypertension; oesophageal narrowing due to mediastinal lymphadenitis; gastric antral narrowing, anal stenosis and perianal fistulas as signs of a granulomatous gastro-enterocolitis. *Urinary tract*: granulomatous cystitis; hydroureter and hydronephrosis due to granulomatous infiltration of the bladder wall and/or ureter or due to calcifications; calcified renal granulomas.

The combination of certain imaging patterns (liver abscesses and hepatic granulomas) seems to be pathognomonic of CGD. Other combinations (multifocal osteomyelitis and granulomatous cystitis) or even a single particular manifestation (invasive pneumonia) are highly suggestive of the diagnosis of CGD and require definitive laboratory work-up.

Progress in immune deficiency III, edited by H. M. Chapel, R. J. Levinsky and A. D. B. Webster, 1991; Royal Society of Medicine Services International Congress and Symposium Series No. 173, published by Royal Society of Medicine Services Limited.

Expression of human adenosine deaminase in mice and rhesus monkeys following transplantation of bone marrow cells infected with recombinant retroviruses

D. Valerio and V. W. van Beusechem

Institute of Applied Radiobiology and Immunology, Rijswijk, The Netherlands

(ABSTRACT)

Amphotropic recombinant retroviruses were generated carrying sequences encoding human adenosine deaminase (hADA). Transcription of the hADA gene was under control of a hybrid long terminal repeat in which the enhancer from the Moloney murine leukemia virus was replaced by an enhancer from the F101 host range mutant of polyoma virus. Haemopoietic stem cells present in murine bone marrow were infected with this virus under defined culture conditions. As a result, 59% of day-12 CFU-S became infected without any *in vitro* selection. Preselection experiments showed that infected CFU-S expressed hADA prior to transplantation and this expression was sustained upon *in vivo* maturation. Mice transplanted with infected bone marrow exhibited hADA expression in lymphoid, myeloid and erythroid cell types. Moreover, hADA expression persisted in secondary and tertiary transplanted recipients showing that hADA expressing cells were derived from pluripotent stem cells.

To extend these studies into a model more relevant for the clinical situation we also performed autologous transplantation in rhesus monkeys using bone marrow that was co-cultured with the hADA-virus-producing cells. We showed that our culture procedures required to infect the bone marrow do not result in a loss of the quality of the graft. This was measured by CFU-C content as well as by regenerating capacity *in vivo*. Preliminary data indicate that the results achieved in the murine system can also be achieved in our rhesus monkey model. Human ADA was detectable at significant levels (2–3% of human control in one animal tested) in four out of four animals tested. In two out of three evaluable monkeys human ADA expression was sustained for approximately 60 days before it dropped below detection levels ($\pm 0.5\%$).

We hold the characteristics of our viruses to be promising for their possible application in gene therapy protocols for the treatment of severe combined immunodeficiency caused by ADA deficiency. In this respect it is also of relevance that the retrovirus that served as the backbone for the ADA vector was previously shown to be non-leukaemogenic.

Progress in immune deficiency III, edited by H. M. Chapel, R. J. Levinsky and A. D. B. Webster, 1991; Royal Society of Medicine Services International Congress and Symposium Series No. 173, published by Royal Society of Medicine Services Limited.

Marked clinical improvement and immune reconstitution in adenosine deaminase (ADA) deficiency after treatment with polyethylene glycol-conjugated ADA (PEG-ADA)

E. Mazzolari [1], L. D. Notarangelo[1], O. Parolini[1], A. Avanzini[2],
A. Plebani[1], P. Servida[3], M. Eibl[4], C. Bordignon[3], A. Ugazio[1]
and M. Hershfield[5]

[1]Department of Paediatrics, University of Brescia, [2]Department of Paediatrics, University of Pavia,
[3]IRCCS S. Raffaele, Milan, Italy; [4]Department of Immunology, University of Vienna, Austria, and
[5]Department of Biochemistry, Duke University Medical Center, Durham, NC, USA

Adenosine deaminase (ADA) deficiency is a rare, autosomal recessive form of severe combined immunodeficiency characterized by recurrent and severe infections, failure to thrive, rapid and profound decrease of immune function, and frequent association with bone abnormalities and neurological involvement. From the biochemical point of view, ADA deficiency leads to accumulation of toxic deoxyadenosine derivatives, with secondary inhibition of other enzyme reactions. In the absence of proper treatment, ADA deficient children often die within a few years of life. Besides supportive therapy with prophylactic antibiotics, treatment of choice is by bone marrow transplantation, when an HLA-identical donor is available. Irradiated red cell transfusions have been used in the past with unsatisfactory results [1].

In 1987, Hershfield and co-workers proposed substitution therapy with polyethylene glycol-conjugated ADA (PEG-ADA) in the treatment of children with ADA deficiency. Preliminary results in three patients demonstrated rapid detoxification of deoxyadenosine derivatives [2]. However, few data have been published on the clinical and immunological outcome of the few patients treated with PEG-ADA so far. We report on one child with ADA deficiency, who has been treated with PEG-ADA for the past two years. Dramatic clinical and immunological improvements are described.

G. B. was admitted to the hospital at the age of one year in poor clinical condition, with a history of severe, recurrent infections, interstitial pneumonia, failure to thrive, and hepatosplenomegaly. Laboratory evaluation revealed lymphopenia ($520/mm^3$) and extremely low ADA activity (1.3 μKat/Kg Hb; n.v. 17 ± 8). In the absence of an HLA-identical sibling, when PEG-ADA became available, treatment was started with intramuscular (i.m.) weekly injections of 20 U/Kg PEG-ADA in conjunction with prophylactic cotrimoxazole and ketoconazole,

Progress in immune deficiency III, edited by H. M. Chapel, R. J. Levinsky and A. D. B. Webster, 1991; Royal Society of Medicine Services International Congress and Symposium Series No. 173, published by Royal Society of Medicine Services Limited.

and intravenous immunoglobulin (IVIg) at the dosage of 300 mg/kg/month. Stable normalization of plasma ADA, with concurrent removal of deoxyadenosine derivatives were rapidly achieved. Clinical condition improved, and no infections were recorded.

After two months, *in vitro* production of IgG by a lymphoblastoid cell line was first demonstrated. Furthermore, one month later, the total number of mature, CD3+ lymphocytes reached normal values (1368/mm³). Vaccination with an animal viral meningoencephalitis antigen (FSME-IMMUN) followed by a boosting injection resulted in marked production of specific antibodies (up to 1790 Units/ml) eight weeks later (his basal serum sample did not contain detectable anti-FSME antibodies). Administration of IVIg was discontinued 10 months after PEG-ADA had been started. Serum levels of IgG have remained normal (15 months since then), with a mean value of 733 mg/dl (lowest value recorded: 675 mg/dl). Vaccination with tetanus toxoid (TT) resulted in marked *in vivo* production of specific antibodies, with a maximal value of 1600 IU/ml at eight weeks after a boosting injection.

The immune reconstitution has been further demonstrated by *in vitro* specific T cell responses to FSME and TT antigens.

The child is currently in good general condition, his growth parameters have normalized. He receives i.m. PEG-ADA at home, and is seen once every five weeks. No side-effects have been reported throughout the period of treatment with PEG-ADA.

As a whole, this study represents the first complete report on a marked clinical and immunological improvement of an ADA-deficient child, after treatment with PEG-ADA. While additional data on other patients are needed, these results confirm and strengthen previous observations that administration of PEG-ADA is a safe and efficient therapy in this form of severe combined immunodeficiency.

REFERENCES

(1) Hirschorn R, Vawter GF, Kirkpatrick Ja Jr, Rosen FS. Adenosine deaminase deficiency: frequency and comparative pathology in autosomally recessive severe combined immunodeficiency. *Clin Immunol Immunopathol* 1979; **14**: 107–20.
(2) Hershfield MS, Buckley RH, Greenberg ML, *et al*. Treatment of adenosine deaminase deficiency with polyethylene glycol-modified adenosine deaminase. *N Engl J Med* 1987; **316**: 589–96.

Vector-mediated expression of the ADA gene *in vivo*, in PBL derived from ADA-SCID patients

C. Bordignon[1], G. Ferrari[1], S. Rossini[1], D. Maggioni[1], N. Nobili[1], M. Soldati[1], R. Giavazzi[2], F. Mavilio[1] and E. Gilboa[3]

[1]Istituto Scientifico H. S. Raffaele, Milan, [2]Istituto 'Mario Negri', Bergamo, Italy and [3]Memorial Sloan-Kettering Cancer Center, New York, NY, USA

(ABSTRACT)

Deficiency of the enzyme adenosine deaminase (ADA) results in a variant of severe combined immunodeficiency (SCID). A new retroviral vector called double-copy vector (DCA) was utilized to introduce the human ADA minigene into bone marrow cells and peripheral blood lymphocytes (PBL) obtained from patients affected by ADA-deficient SCID.

Freshly isolated PBL were subjected to multiple infection cycles with cell-free vector containing supernatants at high vector to cell ratio (2–5 cfu/cell) under antigen stimulation, and then maintained in culture or injected intraperitoneally into immunodeficient *bg/nu/xid* (BNX) mice. Vector-mediated expression of human ADA in the obtained T cell line reached levels of approximately 10% of normal controls. Subcloning of the cell line in limiting dilution gave rise to 144 individual clones. Approximately 80% of the clones tested (46) were positive for ADA activity as measured by adenosine to inosine conversion. DNA obtained from all ADA-positive clones tested positive for vector sequences in PCR analysis. *In vivo*, survival of human cells in the recipient BNX mice was demonstrated by the presence of Alu sequences in the DNA extracted from the spleen of three animals. In their peripheral blood and spleen, human cells were detected at low frequency by FACS analysis with monoclonal antibodies directed against human CD20 and CD3, four weeks after reconstitution. Cellogel analysis of recipient spleen cell lysates demonstrated the typical band of vector-derived human ADA.

When tested for the production of human IgG, the reconstituted animals showed levels comparable with those of BNX mice reconstituted with normal human PBLs. Furthermore, allospecific T cell clones were obtained from the spleens of BNX recipients reconstituted with DCA vector-transduced PBLs, but not from non-infected ADA-deficient PBLs.

Progress in immune deficiency III, edited by H. M. Chapel, R. J. Levinsky and A. D. B. Webster, 1991; *Royal Society of Medicine Services International Congress and Symposium Series No. 173, published by Royal Society of Medicine Services Limited.*

Sensitive methods for the demonstration of chimaerism early after allogeneic bone marrow transplantation

J. M. Vossen[1], J. Labadie[1], H. van den Berg[1], J. E. M. van Leeuwen[1], E. J. A. Gerritsen[1], M. J. D. van Tol[1] and P. Meera Khan[2]

[1]Department of Paediatrics, Leiden University Hospital, and [2]Department of Human Genetics, Sylvius Laboratory, Leiden, The Netherlands

INTRODUCTION

Following allogeneic bone marrow transplantation (BMT) one or more haemato-poietic cell lineages may engraft. This depends on the nature of the original disease, the type of pretreatment of the graft recipient, matching between graft donor and recipient for HLA antigens, composition of the graft, i.e. the number of T lymphocytes in the graft, and immunosuppressive treatment after BMT. Documentation of chimaerism in the follow-up period of BMT is important in order to determine whether the procedure was successful or not. Failure may consist of no or transient engraftment followed by autologous haematopoietic reconstitution, engraftment of a single haematopoietic cell lineage, or rejection of the graft. The risk to obtain an incomplete engraftment or an early rejection has increased lately, as a result of the use of partially HLA-matched donor-recipient combinations and the almost complete T cell depletion of the graft. The documentation of chimaerism early after BMT is hampered by the low numbers of circulating peripheral blood cells, the masking effect of transfusion of red blood cells, platelets and plasma or immunoglobulins, and the poor proliferative capacity of blood lymphocytes following mitogenic stimulation. Three sensitive methods, providing distinct information but circumventing the problems mentioned, were developed in our laboratory for the demonstration of early chimaerism after BMT.

METHODS

PCR of VNTR in genomic DNA of FACS-sorted cell populations

Peripheral blood lymphocytes (PBL) were sorted by FACS according to their membrane markers, using appropriate monoclonal antibodies for e.g. CD4$^+$, CD8$^+$ T lymphocytes, CD20$^+$ B lymphocytes and CD16$^+$ natural killer (NK) cells. Sorted cells were lysed by heating to 95°C for 10 min, followed by proteinase K

Progress in immune deficiency III, edited by H. M. Chapel, R. J. Levinsky and A. D. B. Webster, 1991; Royal Society of Medicine Services International Congress and Symposium Series No. 173, published by Royal Society of Medicine Services Limited.

treatment. The informative genomic DNA marker, known as variable number of tandem repeats (VNTR), i.e. different in bone marrow donor and recipient, was amplified by polymerase chain reaction (PCR) according to standard techniques and alleles were separated by agarose gel electrophoresis, followed by Southern analysis. The pattern of VNTRs used was 33.6, APOB, HRAS, INS, and YNZ22.1 (for details see [1]).

In situ hybridization of Y-chromosome in immunofluorescent-marked mononuclear cells

Peripheral blood mononuclear cells (PBMC), isolated by Ficoll-Isopaque sedimentation, were stained by indirect immunofluorescence using appropriate monoclonal antibodies, and developed by a TRITC-labelled conjugate. PBMC were spun on to slides, air dried and fixed with methanol/glacial acetic acid, washed and fixed with formaldehyde, washed and dehydrated in rising concentrations of ethanol. Y-chromosome specific RPN.1305 probe (Amersham Lab., Amersham, UK), nick modified with biotin-dUTP, was applied under DNA denaturing conditions and developed with avidin-FITC. Two hundred TRITC-labelled cells per slide were examined for the presence of the FITC-labelled Y-probe (for details see [2]).

Immunoglobulin allotype determination of H-Ig components in serum

Transient homogeneous immunoglobulin (H-Ig) components, mostly of IgM or IgG class, can be demonstrated in the serum of almost 100% of BMT recipients using agar gel electrophoresis combined with immunoblotting. The subclass of IgG-H-Ig's was determined with appropriate monoclonal antibodies (for IgG1 BAM15 Unipath, Bedford, UK, for IgG2 NI6014, for IgG3 NI86 and for IgG4 NI315 Nordic Immunological Lab., Tilburg, The Netherlands). Allotyping of IgG-H-Ig's was performed with the following monoclonal antibodies: 5 A1 for G1m (z), 5 F10 for G1m (f), 12 D9 for G3m (b1/u), 8 D10 for G3m (g1) (all monoclonals were kindly provided by Dr G. G. de Lange, [3]), and SH 21 (Bio Makor, Rehovot, Israel) for G2m (n).

RESULTS

This section will focus on the methodological aspects of the different techniques, i.e. sensitivity, specificity, detection limit and degree of information provided.

PCR or VNTR in FACS-sorted PBL

The sensitivity of the finding of allotypic differences in VNTRs for the panel of five VNTRs used in this study was dependent on the length of the repeats and proved to be 98%. The specificity was 100% when a sufficient number of $\geqslant 5 \times 10^3$ PBL could be investigated under standard conditions, i.e. applying 20 to 23 amplification cycles. When less PBL were available following sorting and a higher number of amplification cycles was necessary, spurious bands could be observed on the Southern blots. The detection limit was shown by mixing experiments to be between 1 and 5% of a minor allelic cell population (see Fig. 1). With the panel of five different VNTRs used, this test was informative in 95% of the 34 donor-recipient couples tested before allogeneic BMT.

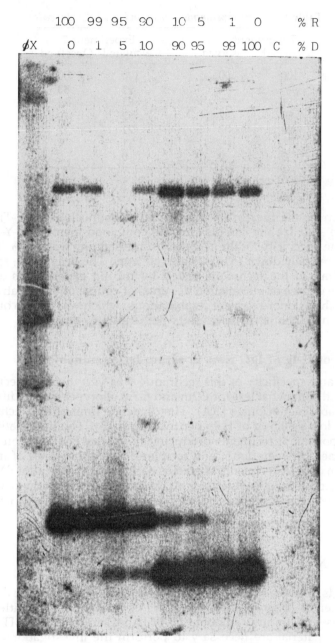

Figure 1 *PCR of INS-VNTR in reconstruction mixing experiments. PBMC of a bone marrow recipient (R) and a donor (D) were mixed in different proportions as indicated (%). The INS-VNTR was amplified in approx. 5×10^3 cells ϕX: phage ϕX 174 digested with Hae III. C: negative control.*

Combined Y-chromosome-membrane antigen staining of PBMC

The mean sensitivity of this technique was 99% for the different PBMC populations investigated so far, i.e. CD3$^+$, CD14$^+$, CD16$^+$, CD19$^+$ and CD20$^+$ cells. The B cell-specific monoclonals (anti-CD19 and anti-CD20) needed sandwich-

Table 1   *Mixing experiments of male and female CD3+ cells*

Experiment 1		Experiment 2	
Calculated	Observed	Calculated	Observed
100[a]	100	100	100
—	—	91	83
81	75	81	72
50	52	52	49
20	22	21	17
—	—	11	8
0	0	0	0

[a]% of Y-probe positive cells

amplification of the membrane signal with a monoclonal anti-TRITC/GAMm Ig-TRITC to stabilize the complex for the combined membrane-Y-chromosome staining. The specificity for the Y-chromosome staining was 100%. The detection limit is theoretically down to the single cell level. The sensitivity, specificity and detection limit of the technique tested by mixing experiments are shown in Table 1. The degree of information depends of course on the relative number of sex-mismatched donor-recipient combinations, which was 47% in our population of more than 150 bone marrow grafts performed to date.

Allotyping of H-Ig of IgG class in serum by immunoblotting

Sensitivity and specificity of this technique was very high, especially for G1m allotypes and somewhat less for G2m and G3m allotypes due to differing quality of the available monoclonals [3,4]. The detection limit of this technique is very low, i.e. as low as 0.5 μg of H-Ig per ml serum [5]. The informativity depends on the proportion of recipients producing H-Ig after BMT and on the disparity of Ig allotypes between donor and recipient. The appearance of transient H-Ig in the serum of graft recipients started as early as six weeks after BMT and could be observed in up to 100% of recipients. The frequency of informative Gm allotype differences between donor and recipient was 65% in 20 donor-recipient pairs tested so far.

DISCUSSION

The methods described in this paper are very well suited for the demonstration of the allogeneic origin of small numbers of nucleated cells within distinctive cell lineages and minute amounts of H-Ig in serum after BMT. Only small amounts of material are necessary to perform the investigations. Transfusion of blood components did not interfere with the interpretation of the findings in a dozen donor-recipient transplant couples investigated so far. The detection of nucleated blood cells transferred from mother to fetus during pregnancy or *vice versa*, is also obtainable by PCR amplification of VNTR in genomic DNA of sorted cell populations. Allotyping of H-Ig may indicate the origin of Ig-secreting cells not only in the recipient of a bone marrow graft, but also in newborn babies and young infants, despite the presence of maternal IgG. Extension of the latter technique to allotyping of restricted specific antibodies is feasible.

REFERENCES

(1) Leeuwen JEM van, Tol MJD van, Bodzinga BG, *et al*. Detection of mixed chimerism in flow sorted cell subpopulations by PCR-amplified VNTR markers after allogeneic bone marrow transplantation. Manuscript submitted for publication.

(2) Berg H van den, Vossen JM, Langlois van den Bergh R, Bayer J, Tol MJD van. Detection of Y-chromosome by in situ hybridization in combination with membrane antigens by two-color immunofluorescence. *Lab Invest* (in press)

(3) Lange GG de, Leeuwen AM van, Vlug A, *et al*. Monoclonal antibodies against IgG allotypes G1m(z), G1m(a), G1m(f), G3m(b1/u) and G3m(g1): their usefulness in HAI and capture ELISA. *Exp Clin Immunogenet* 1989; **6**: 18–30.

(4) Tol MJD van, Gerritsen EJA, Lankester AC, *et al*. Allotypes of homogeneous immunoglobulins after allogeneic bone marrow transplantation. In: Radl J, Camp B van, eds. *Monoclonal gammapathies II. Clinical significance and basic mechanisms*. Rijswijk: Eurage, 1989: 203–6.

(5) Radl J. Monoclonal gammapathies in immunodeficient adults. In: Radl J, Camp B van, eds. *Monoclonal gammapathies II. Clinical significance and basic mechanisms*. Rijswijk: Eurage, 1989: 45–50.

The antibody response against tetanus toxoid: A longitudinal study in healthy infants and adults

C. M. Jol-van der Zijde[1], M. van der Kaaden[1], H. C. Rümke[2],
E. J. A. Gerritsen[1], J. M. Vossen[1] and M. J. D. van Tol[1]

[1]Department of Paediatrics, Leiden University Hospital, Leiden, and [2]National Institute of Public Health and Environmental Protection (RIVM), Bilthoven, The Netherlands

(POSTER)

INTRODUCTION

The contribution of IgM, IgG and IgG subclasses to the antibody response against tetanus toxoid (TT) was determined with a TT-specific ELISA in sera of healthy infants and adults. The diversity of the anti-TT antibodies (IgG and IgG subclasses) was evaluated by Isoelectric-focusing (IEF) combined with TT-specific immuno-blotting. The results of this study will be used as reference for the investigation of the recovery of the humoral immune response after allogeneic bone marrow transplantation.

MATERIALS AND METHODS

Sera were collected from 20 healthy infants, who received five DTP vaccinations according to the Dutch National Immunization Programme (see Fig. 1), and from 20 healthy adults, before and after two TT boosters with a one-year interval.

Anti-TT ELISA

PVC-microtitre plates were coated with 3.75 μg TT/ml for the quantification of TT-specific total IgG, IgG1, IgG3 and IgG4 and with 18.75 μg TT/ml for IgG2 and IgM. The IgG total and IgM plates were developed with GAHu IgG/AP and GAHu IgM/AP (TAGO, Burlingame, USA), respectively.

Anti-TT antibodies within the IgG subclasses were detected with MoAbs, MH 161–2 (CLB, Amsterdam, The Netherlands) for IgG1 and NI 6014, NI 86 and NI 315 (Nordic Immunological Laboratories, Tilburg, The Netherlands) for IgG2, IgG3 and IgG4, followed by a second incubation with RAM/AP (Dakopatts, Glostrup, Denmark).

Isoelectric-focusing (IEF) and TT-immunoblotting

Sera, diluted to contain the same amount of antibodies, were focused on IEF gels (0.8% agarose containing 12% of a mixture of Ampholine 3.5–10 and Pharmalyte 3–10) for 1200 Vh at 0°C. After the focusing was completed, the gel was overlayered with the TT-coated

Progress in immune deficiency III, edited by H. M. Chapel, R. J. Levinsky and A. D. B. Webster, 1991; Royal Society of Medicine Services International Congress and Symposium Series No. 173, published by Royal Society of Medicine Services Limited.

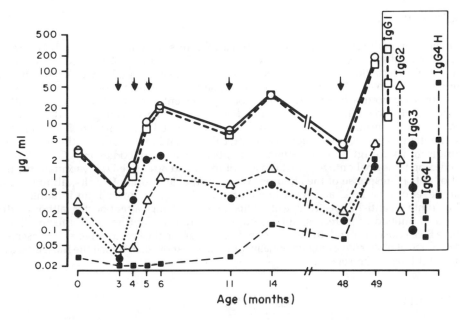

Figure 1 *Geom. mean of anti-TT response of 20 infants after five DTP vaccinations (↓). The range of the adult response (geom. mean ± 2 SD) one month after the first booster immunization is shown at the right. ○——○ = IgG total.*

(3 μg/cm²) and BSA-blocked nitrocellulose membrane and transfer was obtained by pressure. The membrane was washed and incubated with IgG subclass specific MoAbs, AP-conjugate, as described for ELISA and colour developed with substrate for AP. For detection of the spectrotype of total IgG anti-TT a combination of two MoAbs NI 335 and NI 343 (Nordic) was used.

RESULTS

The anti-TT response of adults after booster and of children after five DTP vaccinations was similar; IgG1 was the major constituent of the response, but also the ranges of the antibody response within the other subclasses were comparable. One year after the first booster 40% of the amount of antibodies was still present in the sera of adults. After primary immunization, generally very low levels of IgM anti-TT could be detected; only in one infant was there was an obvious IgM anti-TT response. After the first vaccination of infants only the increase of IgG3 anti-TT was significant ($p < 0.01$). In infants levels of IgG3 anti-TT above 5 μg/ml (highest level 35 μg/ml) were frequently measured, whereas in adults IgG3 anti-TT was always below 3 μg/ml. A response in IgG4 (1–30 μg/ml)(IgG4H in Fig. 1) was found in 12 of 20 adults, whereas eight adults did not (< 0.2 μg/ml)(IgG4L in Fig. 1) respond in IgG4; IgG2 anti-TT is significantly higher in the group with a high IgG4 response. In sera of infants IgG4 anti-TT was very low after the first immunizations, started to rise after the fourth and was comparable to that of adults after the fifth immunization, i.e. 12 of 17 children produced IgG4 anti-TT antibodies (above 1 μg/ml). None of the adults in the group of low IgG4 responders produced IgG4 anti-TT after the second booster immunization.

Longitudinal study of the anti-TT spectrotypes of adults showed no major changes in the pattern after booster. The IgG1 spectrotype always showed a more heterogeneous pattern than that of the other subclasses. In infants the spectrotype changed from month to month especially after the first immunizations.

DISCUSSION

The major part of the anti-TT antibody response in adults and children was in IgG1. Forty per cent of adults had almost exclusively IgG1 anti-TT, in 60% IgG4 and IgG2 antibodies were also detectable. In contrast to other investigators [1,2] we used affinity chromatography to isolate anti TT-antibodies for quantification instead of myeloma proteins. In addition we used a five times higher coating concentration for IgG2 than for other isotypes, so that low affinity anti-TT antibodies (e.g. IgG2 anti-TT) might be detected. In infants, after the primary immunization the sera contained IgG1 and IgG3 anti-TT, but only the increase of IgG3 was significant; after the second immunization there was also a significant rise of IgG1. This sequence of appearance of antibodies in IgG subclasses is according to normal ontogeny. At the age of four, and after five DTP vaccinations, the level of anti TT-response of the children was comparable to that of adults, although the serum level of total IgG2 and IgG4 in children of that age is lower than in adults.

The dominant anti-TT spectrotype of adults does not change after booster, although the amount of antibodies increases, suggesting that only existing (the most effective?) TT-reactive B-cell clones expand. In infants, dynamic changes in the spectrotypes were observed in the course of time, suggesting an initially immature response, in which the most effective clones still have to be selected.

REFERENCES

(1) Dengrove J, Lee EY, Heiner DG, *et al.* IgG and IgG subclass specific antibody responses to Diphtheria and Tetanus Toxoids in newborns and infants given DTP immunization. *Pediatr Res* 1986; **20**: 735–9.
(2) Rubin RL, Tang FL, Lucas AH, Spiegelberg HL, Tan EM. IgG subclasses of anti-TT antibodies in adult and newborn normal subjects, and in patients with systemic lupus erythematosus, Sjogren's syndrome, and drug-induced autoimmunity. *J Immunol* 1986; **137**: 2522–7.

Bone marrow transplantation for immunodeficiencies and osteopetrosis in Europe

The EBMT/EGID working party on bone marrow transplantation for inborn errors

INSERM U 132, Hôpital des Enfants-Malades, Paris, France

(ABSTRACT)

A retrospective analysis of the outcome of bone marrow transplantation (BMT) performed between 1968 and February 1989 in 314 children with immunodeficiencies or osteopetrosis has been conducted. One hundred and eighty-three patients have been transplanted because of severe combined immunodeficiency. The probability of survival for recipients of HLA-identical BMT was 75.9%, reaching 96.9% for those treated since 1983. Recipients of T cell depleted, HLA non-identical BMT had a probability of survival of 52.2%. Four parameters have been found significantly to influence the outcome of HLA non-identical BMT, i.e. presence of a lung infection prior to BMT (relative risk (RR) 9.3), absence of protection (RR 11.07), female to male transplant (RR 3.4) and absence of conditioning regimen (CR) (for patients treated since 1986) (RR 3.3). Use of a CR was associated with an increased engraftment rate and with a more frequent development of full immunological function. Favourable combination of the three modifiable factors led to a probability of survival of 76%.

One hundred and thirty-one patients have received a BMT because of T cell deficiency, Wiskott-Aldrich syndrome ($n=32$), phagocytic cell diseases ($n=30$) or osteopetrosis ($n=29$). The probability of survival after HLA-identical BMT ($n=60$) was 68% with a probability of 89% for patients treated since 1986. It was 35% after HLA non-identical BMT. Older age at BMT, female to male combination and absence of use of monoclonal antibody for prevention of graft failure were associated with a poorer outcome.

Progress in immune deficiency III, edited by H. M. Chapel, R. J. Levinsky and A. D. B. Webster, 1991; Royal Society of Medicine Services International Congress and Symposium Series No. 173, published by Royal Society of Medicine Services Limited.

The spectrum of humoral immunoreconstitution in SCID following HLA-non-identical bone marrow transplantation

W. Friedrich, Ch. Knobloch, W. Hartmann, P. Bartmann, A. Wölpl,
S. F. Goldmann

Department of Paediatrics and Transfusion Medicine, University of Ulm, Ulm, Germany

(POSTER)

Following HLA-identical bone marrow transplantation (BMT), severe combined immunodeficiency (SCID) B cells have the potential to mature fully, with humoral immunity being reconstituted by host B cells. In contrast, following HLA non-identical BMT with T-cell depleted marrow, prolonged and persistent antibody deficiency has frequently been observed, indicating abnormal host B cell maturation.

We have analysed 11 patients with B+ SCID surviving at least three years after HLA-non-identical BMT. A significant variation of B cell functions was noted, which normalized only in a minority, while the majority of patients showed persistent hypo- and dys-gammaglobulinaemia even years after BMT. There was no obvious correlation to HLA mismatch, number of grafted cells and complications of treatment such as mild GvHD and infections. In two cases, conditioning treatment was given prior to BMT using low-dose Busulfan (8 mg/kg); both patients reconstituted B cell functions promptly. Surprisingly, as in non-conditioned cases, engraftment of donor cells was limited to T cells, while B cells and haemopoietic cells were exclusively of host origin.

The basis of the observed incomplete and highly variable maturation of SCID B cells remains unclear. Since maturation proceeded normally following T-depleted, HLA- haplo-identical BMT when using myelosuppressive conditioning (in two of our cases), we assume that transitory engraftment of other haemopoietic cells such as macrophages may be important to provide necessary signals to induce functional maturation of SCID B cells.

Progress in immune deficiency III, edited by H. M. Chapel, R. J. Levinsky and A. D. B. Webster, 1991; Royal Society of Medicine Services International Congress and Symposium Series No. 173, published by Royal Society of Medicine Services Limited.

Failure to thrive after haploidentical bone marrow transplantation for severe combined immunodeficiency disease (SCID): Due to an autoimmune gut disease?

S. Strobel[1], G. Morgan[1], R. Mirakian[2] and R. J. Levinsky[1]

[1]Department of Immunology, Institute of Child Health and The Hospital for Sick Children and
[2]Department of Immunology, Middlesex Hospital, London, UK

(POSTER)

INTRODUCTION

In the absence of an HLA-matched donor, parental (haploidentical), T cell-depleted bone marrow transplantation (BMT) is the treatment of choice for severe combined immuno-deficiency (SCID). Clinical complications, despite successful long-term engraftment in ~ 60%, are frequently related to acute and/or chronic graft-versus-host disease (GvHD). The development of autoimmune phenomena after allogeneic BMT frequently leads to the production of autoantibodies (auto-ab) without a clear correlation to acute or chronic GvHD [1,2].

Our experience shows that autoantibodies which bind to intestinal epithelial cells are associated with significant gut symptoms and failure to thrive (FTT) in the absence of 'overt' GvHD and/or gastrointestinal infections.

AIM

To investigate the aetiology of FTT after BMT we studied patients during the pre- and post-transplant period for the presence of intestinal infections, GvHD and autoimmunity. The study population comprised infants undergoing BMT for SCID and severe CID ($n = 18$; 7 ADA-deficient).

MATERIALS AND METHODS

Patient sera were screened by routine immunofluorescence for antibodies to gut (epithelium, brushborder), CD25, DR, nuclear antigens, microsomes, liver-kidney-microsomes, basement membrane, parietal cells, erythrocytes, platelets and thyroid epithelium.

RESULTS

Serum auto-ab were only detected after BMT (3–6 months) and persisted for up to four years (Table 1).

DISCUSSION

Our study demonstrates the presence of gut-specific auto-ab in all children with FTT and mucosal atrophy. Associated immunohistochemical findings in these patients included

Progress in immune deficiency III, edited by H. M. Chapel, R. J. Levinsky and A. D. B. Webster, 1991; Royal Society of Medicine Services International Congress and Symposium Series No. 173, published by Royal Society of Medicine Services Limited.

Table 1 *Autoantibodies in individual patients*

Diagnosis		GvHD	Gut-ab	Auto-ab	Histology	Therapy
1	ADA-	no	+ + +	Erythrocyte	Mild PVA	P
2	ADA-	II,*c*	+ + +	Mitochond. Platelets	SPVA	P/Cya
3	CID	I–II	+ +	ND	PVA	None
4	ADA-	II,*c*	+ + +	Platelets	PVA	P/CyA
5	SCID[a]	I–II	ND	ND	Mild PVA	None
6	ADA-	I	+	Parietal cell Erythrocytes	Minor Changes	None
7	SCID	II–III	ND	Parietal cell	Normal Platelet	P/CyA
8	ADA-	I,liver,*c*	+	ND	NB	P/A
9	ADA-	I,liver,*c*	+	None	NB	P/A
10	ADA-	II–III,*c*	+ +	Platelet	SPVA	P/CyA
11	Omenn	I–II	+ +	ND	NB	P
12	SCID	I	+	ND	NB	None

and 6 additional patients (SCID) with GvHD I–II(skin) without auto-ab.

[a] Matched transplant; ADA-=SCID due to adenosine deaminase deficiency; *c*=chronic GvHD; ND=not detected; NB=no biopsy; A=Azathioprin; CyA=Cyclosporin A; P=Prednisolone; SPVA=severe partial villus atrophy; PVA=partial villus atrophy.

aberrant (increased) HLA-DR and CD25 (IL-2 receptor) expression. The autoimmune profile after BMT differs from those of collagen vascular diseases. There is no clear correlation between clinical GvHD and the development of autoimmunity. The specificity of the gut auto-ab is unclear; there is, however, no cross-reactivity with the above-mentioned antigens (Material and Methods) or rotaviral proteins.

SPECULATIVE CONCLUSION

The *in vivo* administration of anti IL-2-receptor antibodies or IL-2-toxins after BMT to eliminate recently-activated (auto-reactive) T lymphocytes may prevent significant morbidity and mortality after transplantation [3,4].

REFERENCES

(1) Rouquette-Gally AM, Boyeldieu D, Prost AC, Gluckman E. Autoimmunity after allogeneic bone marrow transplantation. A study of 53 long-term-surviving patients. *Transplantation* 1988; **46**: 238–40.
(2) Shulman HM, Sullivan KM. Graft-versus-host disease: allo- and autoimmunity after bone marrow transplantation. *Concepts Immunopathol* 1988; **6**: 141–65.
(3) Strom TB, Kelley VE. Toward more selective therapies to block undesired immune responses. *Kidney Int* 1989; **35**: 1026–33.
(4) Kelley VE, Gulton GN, Hattori M, Ikegami H, Eisenbarth G, Strom TB. Anti-interleukin 2 receptor antibody suppresses murine diabetic insulitis and lupus nephritis. *J Immunol* 1988; **140**: 59–61.

T cell reconstitution of SCID recipients grafted with T-depleted bone marrow

A. R. Hayward[1], S. Schiff[2] and R. H. Buckley[2]

[1]Departments of Paediatrics, University of Colorado Health Sciences Center, Denver, Colorado, and [2]Duke University, Durham, NC, USA

(POSTER)

Naive and memory human T cells have different isoforms of the 220 kDa common leucocyte antigen (CD45) on their surface [1]. Naive cells as they leave the thymus express the 200 kDa CD45RA and this is the predominant subset at birth and in infancy [2]. Memory T cells express the 180 kDa CD45RO which is bound by the monoclonal antibody UCHL1 [3]. T cell reconstitution of infants with SCID is likely to be dependent on the recipient's thymus for the production of CD45RA cells and on peripheral antigen stimulus for the conversion of these cells to the CD45RO phenotype. We examined blood from 15 infants who had received T-depleted grafts from one to five years previously to obtain an indication of the rate at which T cell subsets were reconstituted.

Figure 1 shows the percentage of T cells in the blood following transplantation, and the percentage of these cells which were positive for CD45RO. In this cross sectional analysis it is clear that high percentages of CR45RO cells were found in the six months following transplantation, and that these subsequently fell to control values. Serial data were available on four subjects in the first year following transplantation which confirm the trend seen in the cross-sectional study. Explanations for the high frequency of CD45RO cells in the first three months following grafting include the possibility of escape from the thymus or a rapid response to antigen stimulus.

The frequency of T cells in the blood using the Vβ5 or Vβ8 families as part of the T cell receptor was studied in the transplanted children and in healthy adults by fluorescence with monoclonal antibodies as previously described [4]. The results (Fig. 2) show a wide scatter during the first seven months following transplantation with values subsequently approximating to the adult controls. These data are reminiscent of the imbalances of immunoglobulin production which have been reported in post-transplant situations [5,6].

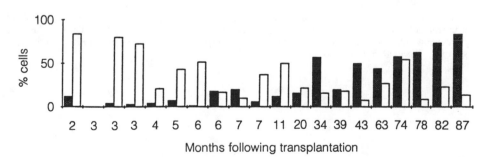

Figure 1 *Percentage of CD3 (hatched columns) and CD45RO⁺ T cells (open columns) in blood after T-depleted bone marrow transplantation.*

Progress in immune deficiency III, edited by H. M. Chapel, R. J. Levinsky and A. D. B. Webster, 1991; Royal Society of Medicine Services International Congress and Symposium Series No. 173, published by Royal Society of Medicine Services Limited.

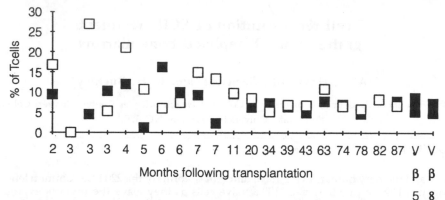

Figure 2 *Percentage of blood T cells (identified as CD3+) expressing Vβ5 (closed symbols) and Vβ8 (open symbols) after T-depleted bone marrow transplantation. Control bars for Vβ5 and Vβ8 show the ±1SD range for 25 adult controls.*

The initially high frequency of CD45RO+ cells we found, together with the transient imbalances of Vβ5 and Vβ8 use, suggest that T cell reconstitution following grafting of T-depleted marrow is subject to environmental pressures and does not simply recapitulate ontogeny.

REFERENCES

(1) Beverley PC, Merkenschlager M, Terry L. Phenotypic diversity of the CD45 antigen and its relationship to function. *Immunology* (Suppl) 1988; **1**: 3.
(2) Hayward A, Lee J, Beverley PCL. Ontogeny of expression of UCHL1 antigen on TcR1+ (CD4/8) and TcRd+ T cells. *Eur J Immunol* 1989; **19**: 771–3.
(3) Terry LA, Brown MH, Beverley PCL. The monoclonal antibody, UCHL1, recognizes a 180,000 MW component of the human leucocyte common antigen, CD45. *Immunology* 1988; **64**: 331.
(4) Hayward A, Clarke RJ, Cosyns M. $V_β5$ and $V_β8$ memory T cells in adults and infancy: coordinated increase in response to early antigen stimulus. *Clin Exp Immunol* 190; **81**: 475–9.
(5) Kent EF, Crawford J, Cohen HJ, Buckley RH. Development of multiple monoclonal serum immunoglobulins (multiclonal gammopathy) following both HLA-identical unfractionated and T-depleted haploidentical bone marrow transplantation in severe combined immunodeficiency. *J Clin Immunol* 1990; **10**: 106–14.
(6) Lum LG, Seigneuret MC, Orcutt-Thordarson N, Noges JE, Storb R. The regulation of immunoglobulin synthesis after HLA-identical bone marrow transplantation. VI. Differential rates of maturation of distinct functional groups within lymphoid subpopulations after human marrow grafting. *Blood* 1985; **64**: 1422–33.

A 16-year follow up of bone marrow transplantation for severe combined immunodeficiency

J. Begley[3], P. Hindocha[1], J. Henderson[1], S. Strobel[2] and C. B. S. Wood[1]

[1]Joint Academic Department of Child Health, Medical Colleges of St Bartholomew's and the London Hospitals, [2]Institute of Child Health, London, and [3]Family practitioner, Frome, UK

(POSTER)

Unless immunological reconstitution can be achieved, severe combined immunodeficiency (SCID) is usually fatal in the first year of life. Its presentation in infancy is characteristic—with gross failure to thrive, diarrhoea, repeated viral and fungal infections (usually candidiasis). Obviously different from hypogammaglobulinaemia as described by Bruton, antibody deficiency in SCID is characteristically associated with grossly deficient T cell function shown by severely depressed lymphocyte transformation. Neither immunoglobulin replacement, thymic extracts, nor lymphocyte extracts (transfer factor) affect the disease or its gloomy prognosis and bone marrow transplantation was attempted in the 1960s. HLA typing at two loci was available and HLA identity in host and donor was sought by typing siblings. HLA identical but unrelated donors were not satisfactory and, like mismatched first-degree relatives, their use resulted in graft versus host disease (rash, diarrhoea, fever, pneumonia and other infections) and bone marrow failure preceding a fatal outcome. High dose steroids and the use of anti-lymphocyte serum specific for the host HLA antigens not present in the donor (to render them 'invisible') was not successful.

With HLA identity, success was reported by Gatti in 1968 [1] and the young person now described after a 16-year follow-up is believed to be one of the earliest recorded [2] successful cases in Britain. His presentation and investigation were typical in the terms described and he received a small graft (5×10^7 nucleated cells) from his HLA-identical and MLC non-reactive, four-year-old brother. Recovery was uneventful, apart from a napkin area dermatitis (perhaps due to hypersensitivity to Candida) and was marked by steady weight gain and the restoration of lymphocyte numbers and transformation. IgM and IgG levels rose rapidly (IgM seven times normal) but homeostasis was asserted after a few weeks.

Regular follow-up ceased at four years and childhood and adolescence have been normal. Recently common warts on the hands have been a problem. Immunological reassessment at the age of 17 years is normal (PHA Transformation Index 68; lymphocyte numbers: CD2 78%, CD3 62%, CD4 35%, CD8 33%, CD14 24%, CD57 18%, CD19 12%; normal serum immunoglobulins).

This boy's transplantation was conducted in an ordinary hospital cubicle constructed in the early part of this century and not modified. Reverse barrier nursing was employed and his diet was sterilized at first. The cost of his transplant was probably of the same order or possibly less than that of a blood transfusion.

REFERENCES

(1) Gatti A, Meuwissen HJ, Allen HD, Hong R, Good RA. Immunological reconstitution of sex-linked lymphopenic immunological deficiency. *Lancet* 1968; ii: 1366–9.
(2) Robinson JE. Severe combined immunodeficiency treated with bone marrow graft. *Proc Roy Soc Med* 1975; 68: 583–4.

Progress in immune deficiency III, edited by H. M. Chapel, R. J. Levinsky and A. D. B. Webster, 1991; Royal Society of Medicine Services International Congress and Symposium Series No. 173, published by Royal Society of Medicine Services Limited.

Bone marrow transplantation in Costa Rica

O. Porras[1,2], A. Fasth[3], A. Baltodano[1], C. Odio[1], M. de Los Angeles Umana[1], L. Gonzalez[2] and L. Del Valle[1]

[1]BMT Team, National Children's Hospital, San Jose, [2]INCIENSA, Costa Rica and [3]Department of Pediatrics, Gothenburg University, Gothenburg, Sweden

(POSTER)

A bone marrow transplantation (BMT) programme began at The National Children's Hospital, San Jose, Costa Rica (NCH) in December 1985. Its main aim is the treatment of non-malignant disorders.

The European conditioning protocol is used. Standard busulfan (BU) 16 mg/kg + cyclophosphamide (CY) 200 mg/kg were used for HLA-identical MLC-negative donors. For mismatched BMT we used BU + CY + IV monoclonal antibodies (anti-LFA or CAMPATH 1G) and *in vitro* T cell depletion with CAMPATHL 1M. A short course of methotrexate and cyclosporin was given to patients receiving non-T cell-depleted marrow. Intravenous immunoglobulin, acyclovir, S-TMP and ketoconazole were used to prevent infections.

Ten patients have been transplanted: one with severe combined immunodeficiency (SCID), one with combined immune deficiency, one with Wiskott-Aldrich syndrome, three with osteopetrosis, three severe aplastic anaemia and one acute lymphocytic leukaemia CR2. Four children had an HLA-identical MLC-negative BMT and all were engrafted. Three patients had acute graft-versus-host-disease (GvHD) with one death, one had mild chronic GvHD. Three children are living 50 days to two years after BMT.

Of the six mismatched BMT, four patients died, one of candidiasis and venous occlusive disease before engraftment could be evaluated. None experienced GvHD. Two children (one SCID and one osteopetrosis) are long-term survivors.

Overall BMT children showed a 50% mortality. All the survivors live with BMT-associated complications. Three cases had nephropathy.

Progress in immune deficiency III, edited by H. M. Chapel, R. J. Levinsky and A. D. B. Webster, 1991; Royal Society of Medicine Services International Congress and Symposium Series No. 173, published by Royal Society of Medicine Services Limited.

The effect of vitamin A supplementation on the immune response in measles

D. W. Beatty, M. E. Tilders, R. Allin, F. Pocock

Institute of Child Health, Red Cross War Memorial Children's Hospital and the University of Cape Town, Rondebosch, South Africa

The aim of this study was to measure the effects of Vitamin A supplementation on the immune function in children with measles infection. During and following acute measles cell-mediated immunity is significantly depressed and secondary infections are common complications [1]. Vitamin A supplementation has been shown to improve the morbidity and mortality in acute measles infection, especially in areas where Vitamin A deficiency is present [2,3].

The clinical effects of Vitamin A may be due to three mechanisms: (i) Regeneration, growth and maintenance of epithelial cells and tissues; (ii) restoration of impaired immune function. Animal studies have shown this effect [4] but there are no studies in human diseases; (iii) antioxidant properties which would neutralize free radicals and thereby minimize cell damage.

Children between the ages of six months and 10 years with severe measles infection who were admitted to the infectious disease wards were randomly allocated to receive either 200 000 IU Vitamin A or placebo orally on the first and second day of admission. Blood was taken for investigation on the day of admission before receiving Vitamin A or placebo and seven days later. Investigations included: Serum proteins, T cells and subsets, lymphocyte transformation to PHA and ConA, B cells, immunoglobulins, measles antibody, vitamin A, retinol binding protein and serum antioxidant activity (measured by luminol chemiluminescence in an oxygen generating system).

Twenty patients received Vitamin A and 19 placebo and the results were analysed using non-parametric statistics.

RESULTS

The groups were no different on admission. Both groups had low levels of total protein, albumin, Vitamin A, retinol binding protein, lymphocyte numbers and lymphocyte transformation on admission. Both groups showed significant rises in total protein, IgG, measles antibody, vitamin A, retinol binding protein, white cell count, platelets, monocytes, lymphocytes, CD3 cells, CD4 cells, CD8 cells and B cells on day 7.

Progress in immune deficiency III, edited by H. M. Chapel, R. J. Levinsky and A. D. B. Webster, 1991; Royal Society of Medicine Services International Congress and Symposium Series No. 173, published by Royal Society of Medicine Services Limited.

Vitamin A levels were low in both groups on admission ($<20\,\mu g/dl$ is significantly low). After one week both groups showed an increase in vitamin A. The low levels on admission can be explained by increased utilization, impaired release from liver stores and decreased intake, all of which have been reported in acute infection. The rise in vitamin A in the control group suggests adequate stores in our population. Retinol-binding protein showed the same trend as vitamin A.

No significant differences were seen in B cell function (B cells, immunoglobulins, measles antibody), or T cell function (lymphocyte transformation). There was a trend towards a greater increase in CD3 cells, CD4 cells and the opposite in CD8 cells in the vitamin A supplemented group. The only statistically significant immunological difference found was the increase in the CD4/CD8 ratio seen in the vitamin A group which was absent in the control group. Anti-oxidant production was significantly higher in the control group on day 7, whereas the vitamin A-supplemented group did not show a significant increase. Vitamin A levels showed a positive correlation with serum antioxidant activity. There were no statistically significant differences between the two groups on day 7. No correlations were found between vitamin A levels and measures of immune function. A correlation was found between the change in vitamin A levels and the change in serum antioxidant activity.

CONCLUSION

Vitamin A supplementation in acute measles infection resulted in minimal but not significant improvement in immune function. The observed trends in improved immunity may have become more significant if larger groups had been studied.

REFERENCES

(1) Coovadia HM, Wesley A, Brain P. Immunological events in acute measles influencing outcome. *Arch Dis Child* 1978; **53**: 861–7.
(2) Barclay AJG, Foster A, Sommer A. Vitamin A supplements and mortality related to measles: a randomised clinical trial. *BMJ* 1987; **294**: 294–6.
(3) Hussey GD, Klein M. A randomised controlled trial of Vitamin A in children with severe measles. *N Engl J Med* 1990; **323**: 160–4.
(4) Jurin M, Tannock IF. Influence of Vitamin A on immunological response. *Immunology* 1972; **23**: 283–7.

Hyper IgE syndrome and IgG subclass deficiency, a family association. Response to IVIg therapy

N. Matamoros, J. Milá, M. Hernández, F. Perona, A. Serra and J. Buades

Immunology Section and Department of Medicine, Son Dureta Hospital, Palma de Mallorca, Spain

(POSTER)

The hyper IgE syndrome (HIE) is a rare disorder characterized by markedly elevated serum IgE and recurrent bacterial sinopulmonary and skin infections. The cause of the recurrent infections and increased serum IgE levels is poorly understood [1,4]. Few reports of familial occurrence exist and since males and females may be affected in successive generations, inheritance in autosomal dominant form with incomplete penetrance is suspected [2,3]. Recently, IgG$_2$ subclass deficiency associated with HIE has been described [3].

We report here, nine family members (father and eight children, aged 26–62 years) with heterogeneous immunodeficiency. Two sisters met the criteria of hyper IgE syndrome, presenting with eosinophilia, elevated serum IgE levels, absent delayed type hypersensitivity reactions to *Candida albicans* and tetanus toxoid and low numbers of CD8 cells. IgG$_2$ subclass deficiency was also present. The patient's father presented only with CD8 deficiency. Two brothers and two other sisters presented with IgG$_2$ deficiency only.

Lately, in the offspring of hyper IgE patients we have found a girl with IgG$_2$ subclass and CD8 deficiency, and a boy with hyper IgE, low levels of CD8 and IgG$_2$ deficiency. At the moment both are asymptomatic. The clinical findings in all adult patients were chronic eczema, recurrent cold staphylococcal abscesses, recurrent otitis media/externa and multiple caries. One IgG$_2$ deficient brother had chronic mastoiditis and recurrent oral ulcers. The two HIE patients had recurrent staphylococcal pneumonia and vaginal Candida infection. None have coarse facies.

The HLA A,B,DR typing studies performed in eight patients are too limited to draw conclusions. However, our results together with those published by Buckley *et al.* [4], suggest no remarkable incidence of any HLA haplotype.

Our HIE patients were doing poorly on antibiotics and one year ago we started intravenous gammaglobulin therapy (IVIg), (250 mg/Kg/21 days). In both patients the infections remitted within several days of IVIg. They now present with minor infectious problems only in the last months and do not require much antibiotic therapy. Intravenous gammaglobulin replacement therapy may be effective in HIE patients, especially in those who present with IgG$_2$ subclass deficiency.

REFERENCES

(1) Donabedian H, Gallin J. The hyperimmunoglobulin E, recurrent infection (Job's) syndrome. A review of the NIH experience and literature. *Medicine* 1983; **62**: 195–208.
(2) Blum R, Geller G, Fish LA. Recurrent severe staphilococcal infections, eczematoid rash, extreme elevations of IgE, eosinophilia and divergent chemotactic responses in two generations. *J Pediatr* 1977; **90**: 607–9.
(3) Leung DYM, Geha RS. Clinical and immunological aspects of the hyperimmunoglobulin E syndrome. *Hematol Oncol Clin N Am* 1988; **2**: 81–100.
(4) Buckley RH, Becker WG. Abnormalities in the regulation of human IgE synthesis. *Immunol Rev* 1978; **41**: 288–96.

Progress in immune deficiency III, edited by H. M. Chapel, R. J. Levinsky and A. D. B. Webster, 1991; Royal Society of Medicine Services International Congress and Symposium Series No. 173, published by Royal Society of Medicine Services Limited.

Hyper IgE syndrome—is H_2 receptor blockade of clinical benefit?

T. Hansel[1], R. A. Thompson[1] and D. S. Kumararatne[2]

Departments of Immunology, [1]East Birmingham Hospital and [2]Dudley Road Hospital, Birmingham, UK

(POSTER)

INTRODUCTION

The term 'hyper IgE syndrome' (HIE) was first introduced by Buckley [1] in 1972 to describe a group of patients with high IgE levels and undue susceptibility to infection. The term has since been used in the medical literature [1,2] to describe an uncommon group of patients characterized by: (1) serious recurrent bacterial infections of the skin and sinopulmonary tract, usually commencing from childhood; these infections are usually caused by *Staphylococcus aureus* although infections caused by *Haemophilus influenzae*, Gram-negative rods and fungal infection have been documented; (2) high serum IgE levels (>2000 ku/l); (3) chronic (eczematoid) dermatitis. Other variable clinical features are described in ref. [2]. The distinction of HIE syndrome (as strictly defined) from severe atopic dermatitis is worthwhile as clinical improvement characterized by significant reduction in infective episodes has been observed in patients with HIE when treated with H_2 receptor blockers [3].

MATERIALS AND METHODS

We present a retrospective analysis of patients with the hyper IgE syndrome, seen in the West Midlands region of the UK (population about 2 million) over the past decade.

RESULTS

We have identified nine patients with the above disorder within the past 10 years; 8/9 patients were treated with cimetidine or ranitidine (alone or in combination with H_1 receptor antagonists) in standard dosage as recommended for peptic ulcer therapy in the *British National Formulary*. The H_1 receptor antagonist was added for symptomatic relief of pruritus caused by the associated dermatitis. The results of therapy are summarized in Table 1.

Table 1 *H_1/H_2 receptor antagonist therapy for hyper IgE syndrome*

Therapy	No. of subjects	Hospital admissions for infection	
		Pre-treatment	During treatment
Cimetidine	4	11	2
Ranitidine[a]	2	8	1
Ranitidine & terfenadine	2	8	0

[a]One patient became non-compliant after one year of therapy. Following this she developed two episodes of staphylococcal pneumonia, requiring hospital admission.

Progress in immune deficiency III, edited by H. M. Chapel, R. J. Levinsky and A. D. B. Webster, 1991; Royal Society of Medicine Services International Congress and Symposium Series No. 173, published by Royal Society of Medicine Services Limited.

CONCLUSIONS

Our results indicate that patients with the hyper IgE syndrome as defined above show striking clinical improvement, characterized by a significant reduction of infective episodes, when treated with H_2 receptor antagonists, alone or in combination with H_1 receptor blockers. Admittedly, our experience is anecdotal, but it could be the basis for a multi-centre, placebo-controlled study.

REFERENCES

(1) Buckley RH, Wray BB, Belmaker Z. Extreme hyperimmunoglobulin E and and undue susceptibility to infections. *Paediatrics* 1972; **49**: 59.
(2) Donabdin H, Gallin JI. The hyper IgE, recurrent infection (Job's) syndrome. *Medicine* 1983; **62**: 195.
(3) Mawhinney H, Killen M, Fleming WA, Roy AD. The hyperimmunoglobulin E syndrome—a neutrophil chemotactic defect reversible by histamine H2 receptor blockade? *Clin Immunol Immunopathol* 1980; **17** (4): 483–91.

Effects of recombinant interferon (IFN)-γ *in vivo* in a patient with hyper IgE syndrome

R. Paganelli[1], E. Scala[1], E. Fanales-Belasio[1], A. Giannetti[2], M. Fiorilli[1] and F. Aiuti[1]

[1]Department of Allergy and Clinical Immunology, University 'La Sapienza', Rome, and [2]Department of Dermatology, University of Modena, Italy

(POSTER)

The hyper IgE syndrome is characterized by eczema with atypical distribution and onset in early childhood, recurrent pyogenic infections of the skin, mainly due to *Staphylococcus aureus*, muco-cutaneous candidiasis, respiratory infections and visceral abscesses. Immunological abnormalities include hyperimmunoglobulinaemia E, low T cells with decreased CD8+ lymphocytes, low or absent production of IFN-γ, defective chemotaxis, circulating immune complexes, hypereosinophilia and activation of osteoclasts. Treatment is mainly aimed at prevention of abscesses and sinopulmonary infections, and control of symptoms (itching).

Souillet *et al.* [1] reported a beneficial effect of r-IFN-α in a patient with hyper IgE, based on their finding of the antagonistic action of IFN-α on *in vitro* IgE synthesis. Since we could not confirm this action, and IFN-γ is defective in these patients and it has a proven strong inhibitory effect on IgE production, we attempted treatment of a case of hyper IgE with r-IFN-γ (Boehringer Ingelheim, Germany).

The patient, aged four years at admission, was diagnosed at one year of age, having had eczema since four months of age, growth impairment, diarrhoea, chest infections, subcutaneous abscesses, cutaneous candidiasis, diffuse lymphadenopathy, eosinophilia, hyper IgE. Treatment (antifungal, steroids, antihistamines) was discontinued two weeks before starting IFN-γ injections. Measurements of biochemical and immunological parameters were made six months before and immediately prior to receiving the first dose. Two consecutive doses of 1 MU/m² of body surface were administered subcutaneously, then the patient was monitored for one month. Therapy was resumed after this time, with r-IFN-γ at the same dosage three times a week for three months. Blood samples were taken every other week. Paracetamol was given before and after the injections to reduce the fever induced by IFN-γ. The patient continued to ⸱ ₌ceive a semiliquid, very restricted diet to avoid diarrhoea, and bronchodilators. The clinical condition persisted unchanged for four weeks, then cutaneous candidiasis reappeared and needed fluconazole treatment. After 10 weeks pneumonia developed and was treated with antibiotics intramuscularly. At 11 weeks severe exfoliating dermatitis prompted discontinuation of treatment and hospitalization.

Leukocytosis doubled during IFN-γ treatment, with lymphocytosis and hyper-eosinophilia. CD4+ cells increased, as well as B lymphocytes. Platelets also doubled. IgE levels increased three times, whilst IgG, IgA and IgM persisted at the same level. No sign of toxicity was noted from biochemical and other investigations (EKG, etc), apart from increases of LDH and serum eosinophil cationic protein.

REFERENCE

(1) Souillet G, Rousset R, deVries JE. Alpha-interferon treatment of patient with hyper-IgE syndrome. *Lancet* 1989; **ii**: 1384.

Progress in immune deficiency III, edited by H. M. Chapel, R. J. Levinsky and A. D. B. Webster, 1991; Royal Society of Medicine Services International Congress and Symposium Series No. 173, published by Royal Society of Medicine Services Limited.

Primary membrane T cell immunodeficiencies

F. Le Deist, G. de Saint-Basile, F. Mazerolles, G. Thoenes,
J-P. de Villartay, N. Cerf-Bensussan, B. Lisowska-Grospierre,
C. Griscelli and A. Fischer

INSERM U 132, Hôpital Necker-Enfants Malades, Paris, France

In this review, we will summarize recent findings on three primary immuno-deficiencies characterized by membrane T cell defects, namely leucocyte adhesion deficiency (defective expression of LFA-1 on T cells), immunodeficiency with low expression of the T cell receptor/CD3 complex, and immunodeficiency with eosinophilia (possible limited diversity of the T cell receptor).

LEUCOCYTE ADHESION DEFICIENCY (LAD)

LAD is characterized by a defective expression of three related leucocyte adhesion molecules, i.e. LFA-1, Mac-1 and p150.95. These molecules are heterodimers that share a common β-subunit (CD18) and have specific α-subunits (CD11a, b, c respectively) [1]. They represent a subgroup of the integrin family. The disease has an autosomal recessive inheritance, the affected locus being mapped on chromosome 21q22.3 [2,3]. There are about 80 known cases which have been described throughout the world i.e. Europe, Middle East, Japan and America.

Moderate and severe phenotypes have been characterized according to the level of expression of all three heterodimers on leucocytes [2,4]. A residual expression is found in the moderate phenotype. Affected patients are suffering from repeated infections that usually do not lead to death before adulthood. In contrast, in the complete type that is characterized by an undetectable expression of the adhesion molecules, life-threatening bacterial infections often cause death within the first years of life. It is worth noting that most of the infections are of bacterial origin and that the hallmark of these infections is the absence of pus, i.e. the consequence of a defective adhesion and migration of phagocytic cells [2].

Evidence has been given that the primary defect affects the β-subunit encoding gene. Indeed, biosynthetic studies have revealed that patients' leucocytes normally synthesize the α-subunit precursors while the β-subunit is often not synthesized [2,5]. In some patients, the β-subunit can be detected, but there is no α–β subunit association. Similarly the β-subunit specific mRNA is either present or not [6–8]. Hibbs *et al.* have demonstrated that a β-subunit-encoding gene anomaly is causal since transfection of normal β-subunit encoding cDNA into patients' B cells

Progress in immune deficiency III, edited by H. M. Chapel, R. J. Levinsky and A. D. B. Webster, 1991; Royal Society of Medicine Services International Congress and Symposium Series No. 173, published by Royal Society of Medicine Services Limited.

resulted in a rescue of LFA-1 expression [9]. There exist at least five classes of mutations according to the detectable level of β-chain mRNA, the presence of a β-subunit precursor and the level of membrane α β complex expression [4,7]. In a small number of patients, mutations have been characterized as either a single point mutation or as the creation of an alternative splice site leading to the deletion of a 90 nucleotide exon [11].

Although the *in vivo* immune deficiency does not evoke a functional T cell deficiency, *in vitro* and *in vivo* T cell dysfunctions have been observed. T cell activation by antigens or allogeneic cells as well as delayed type hypersensitivity can be initiated, whereas anti-CD3-mediated T cell activation has been found impaired [12]. Cytotoxic T and non-T cell functions are defective [4,13]. This does not lead to an increased susceptibility to viral infections. The disease may however be associated with an absence of rejection of HLA non-identical marrow resulting in efficient use of BMT as a therapy for LAD [14].

In some patients, it was found that antibody responses after immunizations were absent, chronic infections, however, being able to induce an antibody response [15]. *In vitro* LFA-1⁻ T cells were found to help HLA-identical B cells from a healthy sibling to produce an inadequate antibody response to influenza virus [16]. It is very likely that the partial deficiency of T cell effector functions (cytotoxicity and help) is due to defective adhesion, as found for T to B cell binding [2,4]. Moreover, Dustin *et al.* have shown that a transient upregulation of T cell adhesion that is triggered by T cell activation relies on an alteration of LFA-1 affinity [17]. Such upregulation does not occur for LFA-1⁻ T cells. However, LFA-1⁻ T cells can be induced to bind normally to B cells by hyperactivation with ionomycin, phorbol esters and IL-2 [16]. Together with the CD2-LFA-3 adhesion pathway and possibly others (involving VLA molecules), these findings may account for the moderate consequences on T cell functions of the absence of LFA-1. The absence of expression of LFA-1 may also diminish the migration pattern of lymphocytes since lymphoid organs from patients with LAD, were found to be hypoplasic *post mortem* [18].

IMMUNODEFICIENCY WITH LOW EXPRESSION ON THE T CELL RECEPTOR (TCR)/CD3 COMPLEX

The TCR/CD3 complex is composed of the α/β or γ/δ subunits of TCR associated with the CD3 γ, δ, ξ subunits, the CD3-ζ homodimer of CD3-ζ/η heterodimers [19]. CD3 subunits are supposedly involved in signal transduction. Regueiro *et al.* have described a low expression of the TCR/CD3 complex in two siblings with a mild immunodeficiency [20]. They have found a defective biosynthesis of the CD3-ζ chain and proposed that patients' T cells express an immature form of the CD3/TCR complex not associated with CD3-ζ and poorly glycosylated [20]. We have recently observed a third patient who is a three-year-old boy with mild bacterial lung infections. The TCR/CD3 complex was found poorly expressed on all types of T lymphocytes (TCR αβ or γδ) whether T cells were in a resting or activated state. There was residual expression of the TCR/CD3 complex that did not exceed 10% of normal. Biosynthetic studies have shown a quantitatively normal synthesis of CD3-ζ [21] which suggests that the primary defect is due to a general regulatory anomaly or a defective synthesis of another subunit, limiting thereby the number of complexes formed. Studies of the CD3 subunits mRNA expression are presently ongoing.

Immunological consequences of the defect are worth analysing. T cell differentiation appeared normal since there is no gross anomaly either in T cell numbers or in membrane molecule expression excluding TCR/CD3. Self to non-self discrimination is normal since patients' T cells are fully activated by allogeneic cells but not by their own cells. However, antibodies to CD3 and also to CD2 were unable to trigger T cell activation as measured by both calcium flux and cell proliferation. This confirms that the CD3 complex is required for the transduction of CD2-mediated activation [22]. Surprisingly, it was found that antigens such as Candida and tetanus toxoid could induce patients' T cell proliferation following infection and immunization respectively. Antigen-activated T cell blasts still expressed the TCR/CD3 complex poorly. This observation indicates that the ag/MHC complex may be a more efficient ligand of the TCR/CD3 complex than anti CD3 antibodies for triggering T cell activation. It is also not known how T cell differentiation occurs in the thymus in the context of a partial CD3/TCR expression defect.

IMMUNODEFICIENCY WITH EOSINOPHILIA (OMENN'S SYNDROME)

In 1965, Omenn reported a syndrome observed in several infants in a large pedigree, which was characterized by a diffuse erythrodermia associated with alopecia, protracted diarrhoea, failure to thrive and life-threatening infections [23]. Other patients have since been found and a profound T and B cell immunodeficiency were observed in these patients [24–26]. Skin and gut biopsies revealed infiltration by T lymphocytes with a graft versus host-like reaction. Finally, the syndrome has been found to be curable by allogeneic bone marrow transplantation.

We have further characterized T lymphocytes in five patients we have studied recently. The number of blood T lymphocytes is increased to 10 000–20 000/μl. These T cells were not of maternal origin thus ruling out the hypothesis of a materno-fetal graft-versus-host disease. Blood T cells were found to express activation antigens such as the p55 subunit of the IL-2 receptor or HLA class II molecules. They may be activated to some extent by lectins and antibodies to CD3 and CD2 while no antigen-induced activation could be induced. Interestingly, it was found that in each patient, there was a predominant T cell subset, i.e. TCR $\alpha\beta^+$ CD4+, TCR$\alpha\beta^+$ CD8+, TCR $\alpha\beta^+$ CD4$^-$ CD8$^-$ as found in a recently published case [27] or TCR$\gamma\delta^+$. Similar findings were made on skin and gut biopsies in two patients.

By studying the rearrangement of the T cell receptor of the blood T cells, using Cβ, Jγ and Jδ probes it was found that discrete bands could be detected in four patients (1–4 bands) which suggest, together with the previous findings, the existence of only a limited number of T cell clones in some of these patients. They may correspond to a leakiness in a context of SCID as observed in nude and severe combined immunodeficient (SCID) mice [28,29].

This hypothesis is further supported by the observation in a same family of one patient with classical SCID (i.e. with alymphocytosis) and of a sibling with Omenn's syndrome. In this setting, one may envisage that the limited number of T cell clones which dramatically expand, exert autoimmune responses directed at skin and gut epithelia.

REFERENCES

(1) Springer TA, Dustin ML, Kishimoto TK, Marlin SD. The lymphocyte function-associated LFA-1, CD2 and LFA-3 molecules. Cell adhesion receptors of the immune system. *Ann Rev Immunol* 1987; **5**: 223.

(2) Anderson DC, Springer TA. Leukocyte adhesion deficiency: an inherited defect in the Mac-1, LFA-1 and p150.95 glycoproteins. *Ann Rev Med* 1987; **38**: 176.

(3) Corbi AL, Larson RS, Kishimoto TK, *et al.* Chromosomal location of the genes encoding the leukocyte adhesion receptors LFA-1, Mac-1 and p150.95. Identification of a gene cluster involved in cell adhesion. *J Exp Med* 1988; **67**: 1597.

(4) Fischer A, Lisowska-Grospierre B, Anderson CD, Springer TA. Leukocyte adhesion deficiency: Molecular basis and functional consequences. *Immunodef Rev* 1988; **1**: 39.

(5) Dimanche MT, Le Deist F, Fischer A, *et al.* LFA-1 β chain synthesis and degradation in patients with LAD. *Eur J Immunol* 1987; **17**: 417.

(6) Dana N, Clayton LK, Tenen DG, *et al.* Leukocytes from four patients with complete or partial leu-Cam deficiency contain the common beta subunit precursor and beta subunit messenger RNA. *J Clin Invest* 1987; **79**: 1010.

(7) Kishimoto TK, Hollander N, Roberts TM, Anderson DC, Springer TA. Heterogeneous mutations in the β-subunit common to the LFA-1, Mac-1 and p150.95 glycoproteins cause LAD. *Cell* 1987; **50**: 193.

(8) Dimanche-Boitrel MT, Guyot A, de Saint-Basile G, *et al.* Heterogeneity in the molecular defect leading to the LAD. *Eur J Immunol* 1988; **18**: 1575.

(9) Hibbs ML, Wardlaw AJ, Stacker SA, *et al.* Transfection of cells from patients with leukocyte adhesion deficiency with an integrin β-subunit (CD18) restores LFA-1 expression and function. *J Clin Invest* 1990; **85**: 674.

(10) Arnaout MA, Dana N, Gupta SK, *et al.* Point mutations impairing cell surface expression of the common β-subunit (CD18) in a patient with leukocyte adhesion molecule deficiency. *J Clin Invest* 1990; **85**: 977.

(11) Kishimoto TK, O'Connor K, Springer TA. Leukocyte adhesion deficiency. Aberrant splicing of a conserved integrin sequence causes a moderate deficiency phenotype. *Biol Chem* 1989; **264**: 3588.

(12) Van Noesel C, Miedema F, Brouwer M, *et al.* Regulatory properties of LFA-1 α and β chains in human T lymphocyte activation. *Nature* 1988; **333**: 850.

(13) Mentzer SJ, Bierer BE, Anderson DC, Springer TA, Burakoff SJ. Abnormal cytolytic activity of LFA-1 deficient human cytolytic T lymphocyte clones. *J Clin Invest* 1986; **78**: 1387.

(14) Le Deist F, Blanche S, Keable H, *et al.* Successful HLA non identical bone marrow transplantation in three patients with LAD. *Blood* 1989; **74**: 512.

(15) Fischer A, Durandy A, Sterkers G, Griscelli C. Role of LFA-1 in antigen-specific helper T lymphocyte–B lymphocyte interaction. *J Immunol* 1986; **136**: 3198.

(16) Mazerolles F, Lumbroso C, Lecomte O, Le Deist F, Fische A. The role of LFA-1 in the adherence of T lymphocytes to B lymphocytes. *Eur J Immunol* 1988; **18**: 1229.

(17) Dustin ML, Springer TA. T cell receptor cross-linking transiently stimulates adhesiveness through LFA-1. *Nature* 1989; **431**: 619.

(18) Nunoi H, Yanabe Y, Higushi S, *et al.* Severe hypoplasia of lymphoid tissues in Mo1 deficiency. *Hum Pathol* 1988; **19**: 753.

(19) Clevers H, Alarçon B, Wileman T, Terhorst C. The T-cell receptor/CD3 complex: a dynamic protein ensemble. *Ann Rev Immunol* 1988; **6**: 629.

(20) Alarçon B, Regueiro JR, Arnaiz-Villena A, Terhorst C. Familial defect in the surface expression of the T-cell receptor-CD3 complex. *N Engl J Med* 1988; **319**: 1203.

(21) Thoenes G, Le Deist F, Fischer A, *et al.* Defect in expression of TCR/CD3 complex not due to lack of the CD3 zeta chain. *N Engl J Med* 1990, in press (Letter).

(22) Breitmeyer J, Daley J, Levine N, Schlossman SF. The T11 (CD2) molecule is functionally linked to the T3/Ti T cell receptor in the majority of T cells. *J Immunol* 1987; **139**: 2899.

(23) Brown MH, Cantrell DA, Brattsand G, Crumpton MJ, Gullberg M. The CD2 antigen associates with the T cell antigen receptor/CD3 antigen complex on the surface of human T lymphocytes. *Nature* 1989; **339**: 551.

(24) Omenn GS. Familial reticuloendotheliosis with eosinophilia. *N Engl J Med* 1965; **273**: 427.
(25) Barth RF, Vergara GG, Khurana SK, *et al.* Rapidly fatal familial histiocytosis associated with eosinophilia and primary immunological deficiency. *Lancet* 1972; **ii**: 503.
(26) Cederbaum SD, Niwayama G, Stiehm ER, *et al.* Combined immunodeficiency and reticuloendotheliosis with eosinophilia. *J Pediatr* 1974; **85**: 466.
(27) Le Deist F, Fischer A, Durandy A, *et al.* Déficit immunitaire mixte et grave avec hyperéosinophilie. Etude immunologique de cinq observations. *Arch Franç Pediatr* 1985; **42**: 11.
(28) Wirt DP, Brooks EG, Vaidya S, *et al.* Novel T-lymphocyte population in combined immunodeficiency with features of graft versus host disease. *N Engl J Med* 1989; **321**: 370.
(29) MacDonald HR, Lees RK, Bron C, *et al.* T cell antigen receptor expression in athymic (nu/nu) mice. Evidence for an oligoclonal β chain repertoire. *J Exp Med* 1987; **166**: 195.
(30) Bosma GC, Fried M, Custer RP, *et al.* Evidence of functional lymphocytes in some leaky scid mice. *J Exp Med* 1988; **167**: 1016.

Impaired lymphocyte function in a patient with deficient expression of leucocyte adhesion molecules

D. Lilić[1], M. Abinun[2], N. Pejnović[1], Lj. Popović[1] and A. Dujić[1]

[1]Institute for Experimental Medicine, Military Medical Academy, and
[2]Mother and Child Health Institute, Beograd, Jugoslavia

Interaction of cell surfaces with other cells or extracellular matrix is essential in the immune response, as well as in a variety of other functions (cell migration, organogenesis etc.) [1]. The complexity and diversity of adhesion molecules is becoming evident through recent rapid progress in this field [2]. Surface molecules involved in adhesion can be divided into three families: *the immunoglobulin superfamily* (antigen-specific receptors on T and B lymphocytes, CD4, CD8, MHC class I and II, CD2(LFA2), CD58(LFA3), CD54(ICAM-1), ICAM-2, VCAM-1); *the integrin family* (see below) and *the selectins* (Mel-14, LAM-1, ELAM-1 and CD62(PADGEM)) which are prominent in interactions with vascular endothelium.

The versatile family of integrins is comprised of glycoprotein molecules each consisting of an α and β-subunit. Three families of integrins can be distinguished by their β-subunit, known as: $\beta1$(CD29), $\beta2$(CD18) and $\beta3$(CD61) integrins. Perhaps the best studied group to date is the $\beta2$ integrin family, also known as leucocyte adhesion molecules or leucocyte integrins because their expression is limited to white blood cells [3]. The common $\beta2$(CD18) subunit associates with three different α subunits: CD11a(αL), CD11b(αM) and CD11c(αx) forming LFA-1, Mac-1(Mo1, CR3) and p150,95. LFA-1 is expressed on all lymphocytes, some monocytes and granulocytes and is the receptor for ICAM-1 and 2, while Mac-1 and p150,95 are particularly important in adhesion of myeloid cells, certain lymphocytes (LGL) and monocytes and serve as receptors for C3bi, fibronectin and factor X. The importance of the leukocyte integrins is illustrated in congenital leucocyte adhesion deficiency (LAD) [4] where different mutations of the $\beta2$ chain [5] significantly reduce or completely prevent formation of the $\alpha\beta$ heterodimer on cell surfaces, resulting in deficient expression of all leucocyte integrins (LFA-1, Mac-1 and p150,95) and severe, often fatal susceptibility to infection [6].

We report a 1.5 month-old male infant, third child of non-consanguinous healthy parents. His older brother (the second child) had died of sepsis in the second month of life after an identical clinical presentation. The first child is a healthy three-year-old girl.

Progress in immune deficiency III, edited by H. M. Chapel, R. J. Levinsky and A. D. B. Webster, 1991; Royal Society of Medicine Services International Congress and Symposium Series No. 173, published by Royal Society of Medicine Services Limited.

The child presented with delayed umbilical cord separation (10 days), omphalitis, suppurative otitis and deep-seated necrotizing skin infections with absence of pus formation, localized in the left axilla, both inguinal regions and in the palate. Cultures of the infected sites grew *Candida albicans*, *Pseudomonas aeruginosa*, *Klebsiella pneumoniae*, *Acinetobacter calcoaceticus* and *Escherichia coli*. He had persistent and overwhelming Candida infection of the oropharynx causing dysphonia. The skin infections healed poorly. The infant showed some improvement with antibiotics, ketoconazole and supportive measurements. The parents rejected the possibility of bone marrow transplantation.

The patient had marked neutrophilic leucocytosis (55–105 × 10^9/l, 80% neutrophils), elevated IgG, IgA and IgM levels, normal C3 concentrations and haemolytic complement activity, normal IgE, normal yeast phagocytosis and a normal nitroblue tetrazolium (NBT) test. Delayed hypersensitivity skin tests were positive to candida antigen and negative to PPD.

Lymphocyte function was studied in assays where leucocyte adhesion molecules are known to be involved: mitogen-induced proliferation (3H-TDR uptake) was assessed on density gradient-separated peripheral blood mononuclear (PBM) cells employing two mitogens (PHA and ConA) at four concentrations. The response to ConA was diminished (stimulation indices from 5.10–11.00, normal above 30.00) while PHA-induced proliferation was on the lower limit for normal values (19.00–36.00). NK cell cytotoxicity of PBM cells, evaluated in a standard 4h ^{51}Cr release assay on K562 target cells with a target : effector cell ratio from 1 : 100–1 : 12, was undetectable. Phorbol myristate acetate (PMA) (200 ng/ml)-induced aggregate formation [7] of PBM cells was totally absent (score 0 compared to score 4+ of control PBM cells as described by Rothlein and Springer) [7] while PHA (40 μg/ml)-induced aggregate formation was markedly impaired (score 2+ compared to 5+). Membrane marker analysis of peripheral blood leucocytes (density gradient-separated PBM cells and isolated granulocytes [8] was performed on the EPICS-C flow cytometer, employing indirect immunofluorescence with various monoclonal antibodies (Coulter, Ortho, Behring) (Table 1). Results demonstrated normal numbers of CD3, CD4, CD8 lymphocytes, CD14, CD33 mononuclear cells and CD15 (separated) granulocytes. In all cell populations CD11b (CR3) cells were absent (normally >95% monocytes and granulocytes positive) while CD11c (p150/95) cells were absent from lymphocytes and

Table 1 *Leucocyte phenotype (%)*

	Lymphocytes	Mononuclear cells	Granulocytes
CD3	68.72	—	—
CD4	54.08	—	—
CD8	20.42	—	—
CD11b[a]	0	0	0
CD11c[b]	0	8.67	0
CD13	—	—	14.50
CD14	3.22	55.47	19.38
CD15[c]	—	2.55	38.36
CD16	14.60	—	—
CD33	—	30.17	—
CD45	91.62	52.91	41.17

[a] CD11b = Mo1 (Coulter)
[b] CD11c = BMA 0320 Ki/M2 (Behring)
[c] CD15 = BMA 0200 VIM-C 6 (Behring)

granulocytes and reduced among mononuclear cells (normally >95% granulocytes positive).

Based on these findings a diagnosis of LAD was reached. Clinical presentation, family history, markedly impaired lymphocyte function and total absence or marked decrease of CD11b and CD11c suggest the severe phenotype of this disease.

REFERENCES

(1) Hemler ME. Adhesive protein receptors on hematopoietic cells. *Immunol Today* 1988; **9**: 109–13.

(2) Springer TA. Adhesion receptors of the immune system. *Nature* 1990; **346**: 425–34.

(3) Kuypers TW, Roos, D. Leucocyte membrane adhesion proteins LFA-1, CR3 and p150,95: a review of functional and regulatory aspects. *Res Immunol* 1989; **140**: 461–86.

(4) Springer TA, Thompson WS, Miller LJ, Schmalstieg FC, Anderson D. Inherited deficiency of the Mac-1, LFA-1, p150,95 glycoprotein family and its molecular basis. *J Exp Med* 1984; **160**: 1901–18.

(5) Kishimoto TK, Hollander N, Roberts TM, Anderson DC, Springer TA. Heterogeneous mutations in the β subunit common to LFA-1, Mac-1 and p150,95 glycoproteins cause leucocyte adhesion deficiency. *Cell* 1987; **50**: 193–202.

(6) Hayward AR, Leonard J, Wood CBS, Harvey BAM, Greenwood MC, Soothill JF. Delayed separation of the umbilical cord, widespread infections and defective neutrophil motility. *Lancet* 1979; **i**: 1099–101.

(7) Rothlein R, Springer TA. The requirement for lymphocyte function-associated antigen 1 in homotypic leucocyte adhesion stimulated by phorbol ester. *J Exp Med* 1986; **163**: 1132–49.

(8) Eggleton P, Gargan R, Fisher D. Rapid method for the isolation of neutrophils in high yield without the use of dextran or density gradient polymers. *J Immunol Methods* 1989; **121**: 105–13.

Leucocyte adhesion deficiency in a Chinese girl

Y. L. Lau, L. Low, B. Jones and J. Lawton

Departments of Paediatrics and Pathology, Queen Mary Hospital, Hong Kong

(POSTER)

We report a Chinese girl with the moderate phenotype of leucocyte adhesion deficiency (LAD), presenting with persistent omphalitis and recurrent infections. She had subnormal adhesion-dependent neutrophil functions, such as chemotaxis and chemiluminescence response to a particulate stimulant (opsonized zymosan). Despite her adequate humoral

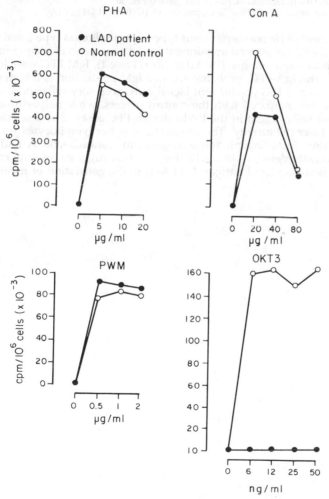

Figure 1 *Proliferative responses of blood MNC to lectins and to OKT3.*

Progress in immune deficiency III, edited by H. M. Chapel, R. J. Levinsky and A. D. B. Webster, 1991; Royal Society of Medicine Services International Congress and Symposium Series No. 173, published by Royal Society of Medicine Services Limited.

Table 1 *PWM-stimulated PFC/10^6*

Cells cultured	PFC/10^6 : IgG	IgA	IgM
Normal values (unfractionated)	>3000	>3000	>2500
[C]^a unfractionated	14 250	18 000	8250
[P]^b unfractionated	100	100	1800
[C]B+[C]CD4+[C]AC^c	10 640	6560	4800
[P]B+[C]CD4+[C]AC	1170	1450	2690
[C]B+[P]CD4+[C]AC	0	80	80
[C]B+[C]CD4+[P]AC	2640	2200	1560
[C]B+[C]CD4+[C]AC+[C]CD8^d	3720(65)^e	2254(66)	1890(61)
[C]B+[C]CD4+[C]AC+[P]CD8	6100(43)	4350(34)	4280(11)

^{a} Control.
^{b} Patient.
^{c} [C]B+[C]CD4, [C]CD4+[C]AC and [C]B+[C]AC gave 0 PFC/10^6.
^{d} CD8 added at final concentration of 22%. ^{e} % suppression cf [C]B+[C]CD4+[C]AC

response to documented *Herpes simplex* virus type 1, parainfluenza type 2 and adenovirus infection *in vivo*, there was marked impairment in the generation of plaque-forming cells (PFC) driven by pokeweed mitogen (PWM) *in vitro* (Table 1). IgM-PFC were less severely affected than IgG and IgA-PFC, probably because IgM production is less dependent on T cell help than IgA and IgG production. Her B cells, accessory cells and CD8$^+$ cells all had reduced function compared with the control subsets, while helper function of her CD4$^+$ cells was virtually absent in the PWM driven PFC assay. She also had a marked defect in natural killer cell activity. The proliferation of her lymphocytes was normal to several plant lectins, including phytohaemagglutinin, concanavalin A and pokeweed mitogen, but markedly defective to OKT3 (Fig. 1). This suggests an important role for lymphocyte function-associated antigen 1 (LFA-1) in the generation of memory T cells.

A 19 year old male with leucocyte adhesion deficiency— *In vitro* and *in vivo* studies of leucocyte function

K. A. Davies, V. J. Toothill, J. Savill, N. Hotchin, A. M. Peters, J. D. Pearson, C. Haslett, M. Burke, S. K. A. Law, M. J. Walport and A. D. B. Webster

Immunodeficiency Disorders Research Group, Clinical Research Centre, Harrow, UK

(POSTER)

We describe a male patient with leucocyte adhesion molecule deficiency (LAD) of moderate phenotype. Although the diagnosis was made only two years before his death, the patient survived until 19 years of age. Recurrent infections and widespread ulcerated skin lesions were the primary clinical problems. The patient died of a severe Pseudomonas infection. A number of novel investigations were performed, both *in vivo* and *in vitro*, relating to the patient's leucocyte biology. CD11a expression on leucocytes was 11–13% of normal, while CD11b/c expression was also reduced (3–8% of normal). CD11/18 expression in one healthy sibling, and the patient's parents was 45–55% normal, suggesting that they were heterozygotes for the defect. Preliminary genetic investigation by RFLP analysis, using a specific CD18 β-chain probe, confirmed this observation. Monocytes cultured *in vitro* matured into morphologically normal phagocytically capable macrophages, which were able to recognize aged 'apoptotic' neutrophils—a process mediated by another specific β-3 integrin molecule. There was a persistent neutrophilia in the patient's blood (typical of the condition). By injection of Indium-labelled autologous neutrophils we were able to demonstrate a prolonged neutrophil half-life (13.2 h [normal=6.7 h]), but normal margination, de-margination on exercise, and splenic pooling. Adherence of the patient's neutrophils *in vitro* to human umbilical vein endothelial cells was normal, and could be partially blocked by an anti-CD18 monoclonal antibody. Histological examination of the patient's lungs at *post-mortem* showed intravascular aggregation of PMN, but a paucity of cells in the interstitium and alveolar spaces, suggesting defective emigration from the vessels. Skin grafts attempted just prior to the patient's death were unsuccessful. Donor skin failed to adhere, and histological examination of the tissues revealed a grossly subnormal inflammatory response adjacent to the sloughing donor skin. These studies demonstrate the highly selective nature of the adhesion molecule defect in these patients, and our *in vivo* observation of a prolonged neutrophil survival may provide an explanation for the persistent neutrophilia often found in these patients.

Progress in immune deficiency III, edited by H. M. Chapel, R. J. Levinsky and A. D. B. Webster, 1991; Royal Society of Medicine Services International Congress and Symposium Series No. 173, published by Royal Society of Medicine Services Limited.

RFLP linkage and X chromosome inactivation analysis in X-linked immunodeficiency with hyperimmunoglobulinaemia M

R. W. Hendriks[1], L. A. Sandkuijl[2], M. E. M. Kraakman[1], T. Español[3] and R. K. B. Schuurman[1]

[1]Division of Immunobiology and Genetics, Department of Immunohaematology, University Medical Centre, Leiden, [2]Department of Cell Biology and Genetics, Erasmus University, Rotterdam, The Netherlands and [3]Immunology Unit R.S. Valle Hebrón, Barcelona, Spain

INTRODUCTION

X-linked immunodeficiency with hyperimmunoglobulinaemia M (XHM) is thought to be due to impairment of the immunoglobulin heavy chain (IgH) class switch of B lymphocytes from IgM to IgG or IgA production. The patients have elevated IgM levels, normal or elevated IgD and decreased IgG, IgA and IgE levels in the serum. The proportions of surface IgM and/or IgD expressing B lymphocytes in peripheral blood are normal or increased, whereas the numbers of IgG or IgA expressing B lymphocytes and plasma cells are severely decreased in peripheral blood, lymph nodes and bone marrow. T lymphocyte (sub)populations and T cell responses to antigens, mitogens and allogeneic cells are normal [1–3]. Patients have frequent or chronic bacterial infections, are susceptible to autoimmune haemolytic anaemia and have an increased risk of developing B cell neoplasms [1,4]. In addition to XHM, autosomal recessive and acquired forms of immunodeficiency with hyper IgM have been described.

Originally, it was proposed that the defect was intrinsic to the B lymphocyte since allogeneic T lymphocytes did not correct the defect [1–3]. However, in vitro addition of T lymphoblasts obtained from a patient with a Sezary-like syndrome induced IgG and IgA production by hyper-IgM B lymphoblasts, suggesting that the IgH chain class switch system in XHM B lymphocytes is intact [5].

If leucocyte subpopulations are intrinsically affected in X-linked immunodeficiencies, they manifest a unilateral X chromosome inactivation in female carriers [6–8]. If XHM originates from a defect that is intrinsic to the B lymphocyte, only those B cells with the intact gene on the active X chromosome will switch to IgG or IgA production. We demonstrated random X chromosome inactivation patterns in separate IgM, IgG and IgA expressing B cell populations from two obligate female carriers within a single XHM pedigree [9]. Moreover, the heterogeneity of Ig heavy chain rearrangements and the Ig light chain usage

Progress in immune deficiency III, edited by H. M. Chapel, R. J. Levinsky and A. D. B. Webster, 1991; Royal Society of Medicine Services International Congress and Symposium Series No. 173, published by Royal Society of Medicine Services Limited.

in the IgA- or IgG-expressing B cell clones that had inactivated the X chromosome, which carries the intact XHM gene, and in B cell clones with the homologous X chromosome inactivated were similar. This implied that the IgH chain class switch mechanism is intact and that the XHM gene may code for a factor that can be transferred to the B lymphocyte. In view of the induction of switch of XHM B cells by Sezary-like T lymphoblasts, the XHM factor could well be produced by T lymphocytes [9].

The immunological manifestations of XHM may show some overlap with other X-linked B lymphocyte deficiencies (i.e. X-linked agammaglobulinaemia). However, XLA carriers have a unilateral X chromosome inactivation pattern in the B lymphocyte population [8]. Moreover, in a multi-point linkage analysis on the XHM pedigree using nine RFLPs, XHM was found to be linked to the DXS42 locus, known to be located within the Xq24-q25 region [10,11], whereas XLA is localized at the Xq22 region [12]. Thus, in spite of some phenotypic heterogeneity, XLA and XHM involve different genes and gene products.

X-inactivation and RFLP linkage studies in XLA provide evidence that in a considerable number of families the gene defect is introduced by healthy males, due to an X-chromosomal mosaicism [13]. Paternal introduction of genetic defects does not only occur in XLA but also in other X-linked recessive diseases such as the Wiskott Aldrich Syndrome (WAS), Duchenne muscular dystrophy and haemophilia A [13,14]. This phenomenon led us to evaluate the possibility of paternal introduction of XHM in the pedigree, in particular because the mother of the XHM carriers had no sons definitely proven to have XHM, and the X inactivation patterns in the B lymphocyte subpopulations of these carriers precluded assignment of the defect to either the paternal or the maternal X chromosome [9]. An extended RFLP linkage analysis within the pedigree was performed using 16 RFLP loci.

MATERIAL AND METHODS

Within a three-generation pedigree, three surviving boys (III.2, III.4 and III.6) suffered from immunodeficiency with hyper IgM and one boy (II.1) had died at three years of age, probably due to the same disease (Fig. 1).

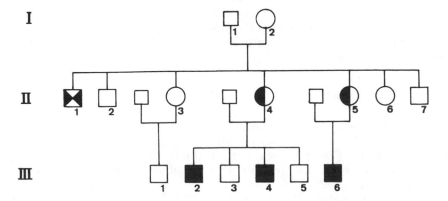

Figure 1   XHM Pedigree. (□ = male; ○ = female; ■ = XHM patient; ⊠ = boy who died at three years of age, ◐ = obligatory XHM carrier).

Table 1 *RFLPs and their lod scores in the XHM pedigree analysis*

Genetic Distance (cM)[a]	Physical localization	Locus	Probe	Restriction enzyme	Lod score
10.0	Xp22.32	DXYS75	P9	Taq I	−INF
21.0	Xp22.3–p22.2	DXS85	L782	Eco RI	−0.07
43.7	Xp22.1	DXS41	p99–6	Pst I	−INF
60.5	Xp21.1	DXS84	L754	Pst I	−INF
81.4	Xp11.22	DXS255	M27B	Pst I	−INF
93.6	Xp11.21	DXS14	p58.1	Msp I	−INF
97.9	Xq12	DXS159	cpx289	Pst I	−INF
107.2	Xq21.31	DXYS1	pDP34	Taq I	+0.08
115.0	Xq21.3	DXS3	p19–2	Taq I	−INF
121.8	Xq22	DXS94	pXG–12	Pst I	−INF
124.5	Xq22	DXS17	S9	Taq I	−INF
128.9	Xq24–q25	DXS11	p22–33	Taq I	+1.37
155.5	Xq24–q25	DXS42	p43–15	Bgl II	+2.29
174.6	Xq27.1–q27.2	DXS105	55E	Pst I	+1.88
200.5	Xq28	DXS15	DX13	Bgl II	−INF
211.5	Xq28	DXS134	cpx 67	Msp I	−INF

[a]Genetic distance from Xpter (XG=0.0 cM) [15]; probes are listed in Kidd *et al.* [11].

For RFLP linkage analysis, high molecular weight DNA was isolated from B lymphoblastoid cell lines established from peripheral blood mononuclear cell fractions. DNA (10 μg) was digested with the appropriate restriction endonuclease (Table 1) and further processed by Southern blotting [9,10].

The RFLP markers used for the multi-point linkage analyses were assumed to constitute a known genetic map with distances from the Xg marker at Xpter [15] given in Table 1. A complete penetrance of the XHM gene was assumed. The allele frequencies of the RFLPs were taken from Kidd *et al.* [11]. The likelihood of the pedigree was calculated for every possible location on the X chromosome, using version 5.03 of the MLINK program [16]. Four contiguous submaps of 4–5 RFLP loci were defined with boundaries formed by RFLP loci that were completely informative for all meioses in the pedigree. These submaps comprised the RFLP loci DXYS75 to DXS255, DXS255 to DXS3, DXS3 to DXS42 and DXS42 to DXS134, respectively (Table 1).

For calculations on the assumption of introduction of the XHM defect by the grandfather, I.1 was designated as affected in the multi-point linkage analysis. This analysis was independent of the fraction of grandpaternal germ cells that were assumed to carry the XHM mutation, i.e. independent of the carrier status of female II.3 or II.6.

RESULTS AND DISCUSSION

The segregation of X chromosomal segments in the XHM pedigree (Fig. 1) was examined using 16 RFLP loci, six on the short arm and 10 on the long arm of the X chromosome (Table 1). In the multi-point linkage analysis the likelihood of the pedigree was calculated for 180 possible locations for XHM on the X chromosome (Fig. 2A).

Several recombinations between the XHM locus and RFLP markers on the short arm of the X chromosome were found, leading to negative lod scores with the exception of the Xp segment between the DXS84 and

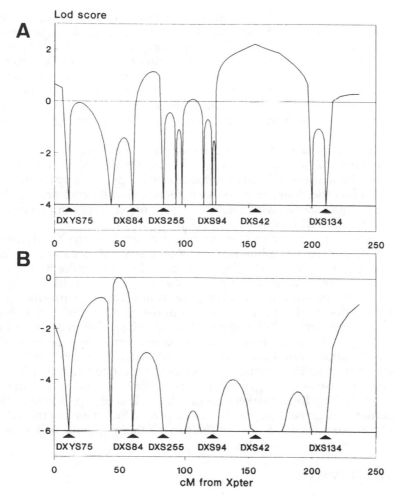

Figure 2 *(A) Multi-point linkage for XHM at map distances in cM (centimorgans) from Xg at Xpter; (B) the multi-point linkage for XHM, on the assumption of introduction of the XHM defect by the grandfather I.1 (see Fig. 1). The positions of a number of RFLP loci utilized are indicated.*

DXS255 loci, whereas a maximum lod score of $+1.15$ was detected (at $d = 75$ cM; Xp11.22–Xp21.1).

On the long arm of the X chromosome, the RFLP markers DXS11, DXS42 and DXS105 in the Xq24–Xq27 region showed no recombination with the XHM locus (Table 1, Fig. 2A). A maximum lod score of 2.29 was reached at $d = 155$ cM from Xpter at the DXS42 locus (Xq24–Xq25). Therefore, the most likely localization of the XHM locus is in the region between the DXS17 and DXS13 loci ($124.5 < d < 200.5$). Localization of XHM at $d = 155.5$ cM is 12 times more likely than localization at $d = 75$ cM. The likelihood for linkage of XHM to DXYS1 ($d = 107.2$; Xq21.13), previously found to be five times lower compared with linkage to DXS42 [10], was now 162 times lower.

From the two obligate female carriers II.4 and II.5, B lymphoblastoid cell populations that either expressed exclusively IgM or exclusively IgG or IgA had been analysed for X chromosome inactivation patterns. A differential methylation analysis using the highly polymorphic DXS255 locus, detected with the M27B probe, exposed random X chromosome inactivation patterns, irrespective of the Ig isotype produced in both obligate XHM carriers [9]. However, the X-inactivation analysis in the IgG or IgA expressing B cell population of carrier II.4 exposed a preference for inactivation of the paternal X chromosome [9]. As this preference was not found in the IgG or IgA B cells of carrier II.5 this phenomenon does not appear to be relevant for the studies on the pathogenesis of XHM, but it nevertheless leaves a theoretical possibility of an incomplete primary involvement of the XHM B cells, assuming grandpaternal introduction of XHM.

As only circumstantial evidence for the diagnosis of XHM in II.1 was available, the grandmother I.2 was not proven to be an XHM carrier. The possibility remained that the XHM defect was introduced into the pedigree by the grandfather I.1. As shown for other X-linked recessive defects with full penetrance such males are X chromosomal mosaics with a defective gene in germ cells but an intact gene in the primary affected lymphocyte subpopulation [13,14].

In a multi-point linkage analysis, assuming introduction of the XHM gene defect by the grandfather I.1, recombination between the XHM locus and all 16 RFLP loci was found. As negative lod scores were found for the entire X chromosome (Fig. 2B), paternal transmission of the XHM defect was very unlikely. Therefore, the skewed X chromosome inactivation pattern in IgG or IgA producing B cells in carrier II.4 reflected the normal variation in distribution that is also found in females that do not carry an X-linked lymphocyte differentiation disorder [17,18].

The unilateral X chromosome inactivation patterns in various peripheral blood leucocyte populations found in females carrying XLA, WAS and X-linked severe combined immune deficiency enable carrier detection in females at risk [13–15]. As this is not the case in XHM, genetic risk calculations in XHM are still dependent on analysis of flanking RFLP markers. To provide a clinically applicable method for carrier detection and prenatal diagnosis, a more precise localization of the XHM gene on the X chromosome by RFLP linkage analysis of other pedigrees will be required.

ACKNOWLEDGMENTS

These studies were supported in part by the Dutch Prevention Fund (Grants Nos. 28.1102 and 28.1607) and the Dutch Foundation for Science (Grant No. 504.102).

REFERENCES

(1) Geha RS, Hyslop N, Alami S, Farah F, Schneeberger EE, Rosen FS. Hyper immunoglobulin M immunodeficiency (dysgammaglobulinemia). *J Clin Invest* 1979; **64**: 385–91.
(2) Levitt D, Haber P, Rich K, Cooper MD, Hyper IgM immunodeficiency. A primary dysfunction of B lymphocyte isotype switching. *J Clin Invest* 1983; **72**: 1650–7.
(3) Mensink EJBM, Schuurman RKB. Immunodeficiency disease genes on the X chromosome. *Dis Markers* 1987; **5**: 129–40.
(4) Rosen FS, Janeway CA. The gamma globulins III. The antibody deficiency syndromes. *N Engl J Med* 1966; **275**: 709–15.
(5) Mayer L, Kwan SP, Thompson C, *et al.* Evidence for a defect in "switch" T cells in patients with immunodeficiency and hyperimmunoglobulinemia M. *N Engl J Med* 1986; **314**: 409–13.
(6) Prchal JT, Carroll AJ, Prchal JF, *et al.* Wiskott-Aldrich Syndrome: Cellular impairments and their implication for carrier detection. *Blood* 1980; **56**: 1048–54.

(7) Puck JM, Nussbaum RL, Conley MA. Carrier detection in X-linked severe combined immunodeficiency based on patterns of X chromosome inactivation. *J Clin Invest* 1987; **79**: 1395–1400.

(8) Conley ME, Brown P, Pickard AR, *et al.* Expression of the gene defect in X-linked agammaglobulinemia. *N Engl J Med* 1986; **315**: 564–7.

(9) Hendriks RW, Kraakman MEM, Craig I, Español T, Schuurman RKB. Evidence that in X-linked immunodeficiency with hyperimmunoglobulinemia M the intrinsic immunoglobulin heavy chain class switch mechanism is intact. *Eur J Immunol* 1990 (in press).

(10) Mensink EJBM, Thompson A, Sandkuijl LA, *et al.* X-linked immunodeficiency with hyperimmunoglobulinemia M appears to be linked to the DXS42 RFLP locus. *Hum Genet* 1987; **76**: 96–9.

(11) Kidd KK, Bowcock AM, Schmidtke J, *et al.* Report of the DNA committee and catalogue of cloned and mapped genes and DNA polymorphisms. *Cytogenet Cell Genet* 1989; **51**: 622–947.

(12) Timmers E, De Weers M, Alt FW, Hendriks RW, Schuurman RKB. X-linked agammaglobulinemia. *Clin Immunol Immunopathol* 1991 (in press).

(13) Hendriks RW, Mensink EJBM, Kraakman MEM, Thompson A, Schuurman RKB. Evidence for male X chromosomal mosaicism in X-linked agammaglobulinemia. *Hum Genet* 1989; **83**: 267–70.

(14) Arveiler B, De Saint-Basile G, Fischer A, Griscelli C, Mandel JL. Germ-line mosaicism simulates genetic heterogeneity in Wiskott-Aldrich syndrome. *Am J Hum Genet* 1990; **46**: 906–11.

(15) Keats B, Ott J, Connealy M. Report of the committee on linkage and gene order. *Cytogenet Cell Genet* 1989; **51**: 459–502.

(16) Lathrop GM, Lalouel JM. Efficient computation in multilocus linkage analysis *Am J Hum Genet* 1988; **42**: 498–505.

(17) Boyd Y, Fraser NJ. Methylation patterns at the hyper-variable X-chromosome locus DXS255 (M27B): correlation with X-inactivation status. *Genomics* 1990; **7**: 182–7.

(18) Brown RM, Fraser NJ, Brown GK. Differential methylation of the hypervariable locus DXS255 on active and inactive X chromosomes correlates with the expression of a human X-linked gene. *Genomics* 1990; **7**: 215.

Localization of three of the X-linked immunodeficiency related genes: Where do we stand?

G. de Saint-Basile[1], B. Arveiler[2], M. Caniglia[1],
K. Cohen-Solal[1], C. Griscelli[1] and A. Fischer[1]

[1]INSERM U 132, Hôpital des Enfants-Malades, Paris,
and [2]INSERM U 184, Strasbourg, France

(ABSTRACT)

In the recent past, five human immunodeficiency disease-associated loci have been mapped on the X chromosome, i.e. severe combined immunodeficiency disease (SCID), X-linked agammaglobulinaemia (XLA), Wiskott-Aldrich syndrome (WAS), hyper IgM, low IgG and IgA and X-linked lymphoproliferative syndrome. Several groups, including ours, have localized genes more precisely by the use of new probes and by X-deletion studies. Present data for the three most frequent diseases are as follows:

Diseases	Probes	Heterozygosity	Lod scores	0
SCID	DXS159	0.33	7.45	0.05
(de Saint-Basile et al., 1987)	PGK1	0.21	5.13	0.00
(Puck J et al., 1989)	DXS72	0.45	7.58	0.05
(Goodship J HGM10)				
Probable locus order: DXS159–(PGK1, SCID)–DXS72				
XLA	DXS3	0.38	9.83	0.05
(Kwan SP et al., 1990)	DXS178	0.30	10.74	0.00
(Malcolm S et al., 1987)	DXS94	0.48	8.57	0.05
(Giuoli S et al., 1989)	DXS17	0.35	6.39	0.05
Probable locus order: DXS3–(DXS178, XLA)–DXS94–DXS17				
WAS	DXS7	0.38	8.35	0.05
(de Saint-Basile et al., 1989)	DXS255	>90%	15.61	0.00
(Green WL et al., 1990)	DXS146	0.36	2.50	0.00
(Kwan SP et al., 1988)	DXS14	0.35	12.20	0.05
Probable locus order: DXS7–(DXS255, WAS, DXS146)–DXS14				

Associated with X-inactivation studies, these data make prenatal diagnosis and carrier detection feasible in a large proportion of at-risk families.

Progress in immune deficiency III, edited by H. M. Chapel, R. J. Levinsky and A. D. B. Webster, 1991; Royal Society of Medicine Services International Congress and Symposium Series No. 173, published by Royal Society of Medicine Services Limited.

Investigation of X chromosome use in an obligate carrier of hyper IgM syndrome

J. Goodship[1], R. Callard[2], S. Malcolm[2] and R. J. Levinsky[2]

[1]Department of Human Genetics, Newcastle-upon-Tyne, and
[2]Department of Immunology and Genetics, Institute of Child Health, London, UK

(POSTER)

X-linked hyper IgM syndrome is characterized by absence of serum IgG and IgA with normal or elevated levels of IgM. The underlying defect is not known. The failure to class switch from IgM to IgG production may be intrinsic to the B cell or may be due to absence of a switch factor produced by another cell. We have investigated the underlying defect by studying X chromosome use in an obligate carrier of the hyper IgM syndrome.

In any cell population from a normal female a proportion of cells will have the paternal X active and the remainder will have the maternal X active. If hyper IgM syndrome is an intrinsic B cell defect then in female carriers all IgG producing B cells will have the normal gene on the active X chromosome. In females who have inherited the disorder, the maternal X chromosome would be inactive in all IgG-producing B cells. However, if the primary defect is absence of an extrinsic switch factor, then B cells with the defective gene on the active X chromosome should be able to switch to IgG production when the factor is present; in carrier females one would find IgG-producing B cells with the maternal X active, as well as IgG-producing B cells with the paternal X active.

X chromosome use was investigated by Southern blotting and hybridization with the X chromosome probe M27B which detects both a polymorphism and methylation differences between the active and inactive X [1]. Seven independent Epstein Barr virus (EBV) lines from the subject were studied. Four EBV lines used predominantly the paternal X as the active X chromosome and the remaining three lines used predominantly the maternal X chromosome. DNA from these lines was Southern blotted and probed with an immunoglobulin heavy chain J_H region probe. The IgG rearrangements seen confirmed that none of these lines had become clonal during culture.

The results suggest that there are IgG-producing B cells with the defective gene on the active X chromosome in obligate carrier females, and support the theory that hyper IgM syndrome is due to absence of an extrinsic switch factor. Further EBV lines have been subcultured from this subject by limiting dilutions after IgM depletion using dynabeads. Quantitation of IgM and IgG by ELISA in the supernatants from all lines so far shows that they are producing both IgG and IgM. Further subcloning is in progress to produce lines secreting only IgG to test this hypothesis further.

REFERENCE

(1) Boyd Y, Fraser NJ. Methylation patterns at the hypervariable X-chromosome locus DXS255 (M27B): correlation with X-inactivation status. *Genomics* 1990; **7**: 182–7.

Progress in immune deficiency III, edited by H. M. Chapel, R. J. Levinsky and A. D. B. Webster, 1991; Royal Society of Medicine Services International Congress and Symposium Series No. 173, published by Royal Society of Medicine Services Limited.

Hyper IgM with combined immunodeficiency

E. A. Goddard, D. W. Beatty and E. J. Hughes

Institute of Child Health, Red Cross War Memorial Children's Hospital and
the University of Cape Town, Rondebosch, South Africa

(POSTER)

Hyper IgM immunodeficiency is extremely rare, may be X-linked or acquired and presents as failure to thrive, chronic lymphadenopathy, recurrent or chronic infections and an increased risk of malignancy. It is characterized by very high serum IgM and very low or absent levels of IgG and IgA. The primary defect is unknown but failure of isotype switching from IgM to IgG and IgA has been suggested. It was originally thought that B cell dysfunction was not related to abnormal T cell regulation [1].

More recently abnormal T cell function has been reported: including excessive T suppressor cells [2], deficient T helper cells [3] and decreased lymphocyte transformation. This evidence suggests that abnormal T cell function may be responsible for impaired isotype switching.

This report describes a girl with an unusual immunodeficiency characterized by hypogammaglobulinaemia, hyper IgM and a severe T cell defect. Since two years of age the patient has had chronic massive and fluctuating lymphadenopathy, failure to thrive and recurrent infections. There is no family history of immunodeficiency.

Investigations have shown persistent hypogammaglobulinaemia. The maximum IgG attained was 1.5 g/l ($n = 7.7-15.1$ g/l) despite 400 mg/kg of monthly intravenous gammaglobulin infusions. In contrast the IgM has been consistently raised with levels up to four times normal. Increases in lymphadenopathy were accompanied by further rises in IgM suggesting that IgM production may be an ineffective but partial response to chronic infection. B cell numbers were low as were antibody responses to tetanus immunization. Qualitative in vitro synthesis of immunoglobulins by pokeweed mitogen-stimulated lymphocytes showed only IgM heavy and light chain secretion. Total T cell (CD3) numbers were normal but the T helper (CD4) cells were low and T suppressor (CD8) cells were high. Lymphocyte transformation responses to phytohaemagglutin, pokeweed mitogen and Concanavalin A were all decreased to between 30–50% of the control. Human immunodeficiency virus antibodies were absent. The patient died at 14 years of age from presumed overwhelming septicaemia accompanied by gross lymphadenopathy and an extremely high IgM (12.5 g/l). Lymph node biopsy prior to death showed no malignancy but diffuse infection of the glands by *Haemophilus influenzae*. This case of hypogammaglobulinaemia with hyper IgM, severe T cell defects and chronic lymphadenopathy is similar to the report of Fiorelli *et al.* [4]. The hyper IgM syndrome may in some cases be more complex and involve other cellular abnormalities.

REFERENCES

(1) Levitt D, Haber P, Rich K, Cooper MD. Hyper IgM immunodeficiency. A primary dysfunction of B lymphocyte isotype switching. *J Clin Invest* 1983; **72**: 1650–7.
(2) Krantman HJ, Stiehm ER, Stevens RH, Saxon A, Seeger RC. Abnormal B-cell differentiation and variable increased T-cell suppression in immunodeficiency with hyper IgM. *Clin Exp Immunol* 1980; **40**: 147–56.
(3) Pascual-Salcedo D, de la Concha EG, Garcia Rodriguez MC, Zabay JM, Sainz T, Fontán G. Cellular basis of hyper IgM immunodeficiency. *J Clin Lab Immunol* 1983; **10**: 29–34.
(4) Fiorilli M, Russo G, Paganelli R, *et al.* Hypergammaglobulinaemia with hyper-IgM, severe T-cell defect, and abnormal recirculation of OKT$_4$ lymphocytes in a girl with chronic lymphadenopathy. *Clin Immunol Immunopathol* 1986; **38**: 256–64.

Progress in immune deficiency III, edited by H. M. Chapel, R. J. Levinsky and A. D. B. Webster, 1991; Royal Society of Medicine Services International Congress and Symposium Series No. 173, published by Royal Society of Medicine Services Limited.

Non-random X chromosome inactivation and advantage of the mutated allele in carriers of X-linked immunodeficiency with hyper IgM

L. D. Notarangelo, O. Parolini, F. Candotti, M. Lusardi,
E. Mazzolari, M. Duse, A. Plebani and A. G. Ugazio

Department of Paediatrics, University of Brescia, Brescia, Italy

(POSTER)

X-linked immunodeficiency with hyper IgM (HIGM1) is a rare primary immunodeficiency characterized by recurrent bacterial and opportunistic infections, autoimmune-like disorders, neutropenia, and increased susceptibility to neoplasms in the affected males [1]. The immunological picture includes absence of serum IgG and IgA, with increased or normal levels of IgM and IgD. The pathogenesis of the disease is still unknown. While some authors have focused on a possible defect of the B cells to switch from IgM to IgG–IgA production [2], others have proposed that a regulatory defect of the T cells might play a major role [3]. The basis for the neutropenia is also largely unknown.

Obligate carriers of HIGM1 are both clinically and immunologically normal. In other X-linked primary immunodeficiencies, selective inactivation of the X chromosome carrying the mutation has been demonstrated in the cell types involved by the disease [4], thus opening the possibility for carrier detection.

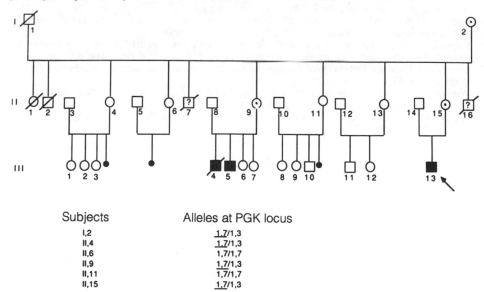

Subjects	Alleles at PGK locus
I,2	1.7/1,3
II,4	1.7/1,3
II,6	1,7/1,7
II,9	1.7/1,3
II,11	1,7/1,7
II,15	1.7/1,3

Figure 1 *Pedigree with HIGM1. The bottom of the figure lists the respective 1.7 and 1.3 kb polymorphic alleles at the PGK locus inherited by the females investigated. The underlined allele identifies the X chromosome which is non-randomly inactivated in peripheral blood cells.*

Progress in immune deficiency III, edited by H. M. Chapel, R. J. Levinsky and A. D. B. Webster, 1991; Royal Society of Medicine Services International Congress and Symposium Series No. 173, published by Royal Society of Medicine Services Limited.

In an attempt to better characterize the pathogenesis of HIGM1, we have evaluated the randomness of X chromosome inactivation in such a pedigree. The methodology involved analysis of the methylation pattern at the 5′, polymorphic region, of the phosphoglycerate kinase (PGK) gene, as revealed by hybridization with probe pSPT-PGK of DNA samples digested in the absence or presence of the methylation-sensitive enzyme HpaII [5].

Figure 1 shows the pedigree analysed and the results of randomness of X chromosome inactivation.

In obligate carriers 1,2, II,9 and II,15, non-random X chromosome inactivation was demonstrated in T cells, B lymphocytes and granulocytes. As a control, random X chromosome inactivation was present in fibroblasts, thus ruling out the possibility of extreme lyonization in these females. Similarly, non-random X chromosome inactivation was demonstrated in blood-derived DNA from at-risk individual II,4. As a whole, these data suggest that different cell lineages are primarily involved in the pathogenesis of clinical and immunological manifestations of HIGM1.

Analysis of inheritance of alleles at the PGK locus demonstrated that females II,4, II,9, and II,11 non randomly inactivate the paternally-derived allele. Such a finding had been never previously reported in carriers of X-linked primary immunodeficiencies, and might indicate an advantage conferred by the HIGM1 mutation.

These data confirm and extend previous observations by Conley *et al.* [6], who had reported a non-random pattern of X chromosome inactivation in B cells from an HIGM1 carrier.

REFERENCES

(1) Eibl M, Griscelli C, Seligman M, *et al.* Primary immunodeficiency diseases. Report of a WHO sponsored meeting. *Immunodef Rev* 1989; **1**: 173–205.
(2) Levitt D, Haber P, Rich K, Cooper MD. Hyper IgM immunodeficiency. A primary dysfunction of B lymphocyte isotype switching. *J Clin Invest* 1983; **72**: 1650–3.
(3) Mayer L, Kwan SP, Thompson C, *et al.* Evidence for a defect in "switch" T cells in patients with immunodeficiency and hyperimmunoglobulinemia M. *N Engl J Med* 1986; **314**: 409–14.
(4) Conley ME, Puck JM. Definition of the gene loci in X-linked immunodeficiencies. *Immunol Invest* 1988; **17**: 425–63.
(5) Vogelstein B, Fearon ER, Hamilton SR, *et al.* Clonal analysis using recombinant DNA probes from the X-chromosome. *Cancer Res* 1987; **47**: 4806–13.
(6) Conley ME, Brown P, Pahwa S, Puck JM. An intrinsic B cell defect in X-linked hyper IgM syndrome. *Pediatric Res* 1988; **23**: 353A.

Is Omenn's syndrome a leaky form of SCID?

G. de Saint-Basile, F. Le Deist, J. P. de Villartay, C. Griscelli and A. Fischer

Immunology and Rheumatology Paediatrics, INSERM U 132,
Hôpital des Enfants-Malades, Paris, France

(ABSTRACT)

Severe combined immunodeficiency with hypereosinophilia (Omenn's syndrome) is characterized by the presence of large numbers of activated HLA DR$^+$ T lymphocytes that also infiltrate the skin and the gut mucosa. No antigen-specific T cell response can be elicited *in vitro*. The origin of these functionally deficient T cells is not known. Expression of T cell subsets in this syndrome was found to be abnormal since one given subset (TCR $\alpha\beta^+$ CD4$^+$ or TCR $\alpha\beta^+$ CD8$^+$ or TCR $\gamma\delta^+$) was predominant in five different patients tested. Moreover, evidence was given for restricted heterogeneity of TCR rearrangements (one to four discrete bands) in blood T lymphocytes from the five patients as shown by Southern blot analysis using Cβ, Jγ and Jδ probes. In addition, we observed in the same family the occurrence in one child of the alymphocytose-type of SCID and, in his brother, of the Omenn's syndrome. We therefore propose that this syndrome may correspond to the emergence of a limited number of T cell clones as a leakiness in the context of defective T cell differentiation (SCID). Such clones could be further expanded by recognition of epithelial autoantigens.

[See review by F. Le Deist *et al.* p. 255]

Progress in immune deficiency III, edited by H. M. Chapel, R. J. Levinsky and A. D. B. Webster, 1991; Royal Society of Medicine Services International Congress and Symposium Series No. 173, published by Royal Society of Medicine Services Limited.

Immunological, histological and clinical features of familial reticuloendotheliosis (Omenn's syndrome) contrasted with materno-fetal engraftment with graft versus host disease

A. J. Cant[1], R. J. Levinsky[1], S. Strobel[1], F. Katz[2], M. Sheehan[3], D. J. Atherton[3] and G. Morgan[1]

Departments of [1]Immunology, [2]Haematology, and [3]Dermatology, The Hospitals for Sick Children and The Institute of Child Health, London, UK

(POSTER)

Familial reticuloendotheliosis (Omenn's syndrome) is an autosomal recessive condition. Affected infants develop eczematous skin, diarrhoea, failure to thrive, hepatosplenomegaly, massive lymphadenopathy and multiple infections. Lymph node histology shows a lymphocytic, histiocytic, and eosinophilic infiltrate with loss of follicular architecture. Skin histology reveals a similar infiltrate. Immune function may initially be normal, but then there is a marked lymphocytosis, eosinophilia, high IgE levels, and severe combined immunodeficiency (SCID) then ensues. It has been suggested that Omenn's syndrome (OS) is a form of Langerhans' cell histiocytosis (LCH), but the histology is very different. OS shares many features with materno-fetal graft versus host disease (GvHD) but maternal cells are not usually found. Low levels of the purine salvage enzyme, 5'nucleotidase, have been found in OS but also in immature normal lymphocytes. High IgE levels, eosinophilia, poor mitogen responses (variably corrected with IL-2) and raised proportions of CD8+ lymphocytes in patients' first degree relatives suggest an immunoregulatory defect. Three patients with OS are contrasted with two others with different forms of SCID suffering maternal engraftment.

The infants studied had an eczematous rash, lymphadenopathy, failure to thrive and diarrhoea. The two infants with two maternal haplotypes (proven materno-fetal engraftment) did not have hepatosplenomegaly, unlike those with OS. All had low levels of immunoglobulin and absent B cells. Four had a lymphocytosis, and eosinophilia with a poor PHA response. Skin histology showed a lymphocytic infiltrate with parakeratosis, and acanthosis in all. Neither of the cases who had GvHD had an eosinophilic infiltrate but all three cases of OS did. One OS patient was treated with cyclosporin A with some skin improvement but no change in the other clinical features or in the mononuclear cell studies.

High molecular weight DNA was extracted from circulating cells from one OS patient and hybridized with locus-specific minisatellite probes. T cell receptor β and γ chain rearrangement was examined in a similar manner. No evidence for maternal engraftment was found and the TCRβ and γ genes were present in the germ-line configuration with no evidence of clonal rearrangements.

The rash in our patients was exfoliative and erythrodermatous with an infiltrate of activated T lymphocytes and few CD1+ cells. By contrast in LCH there is a seborrhoeic dermatitis with an infiltrate of CD1+ Langerhans' cells. Clinically and immunologically OS and GvHD are similar. No features clearly distinguish one from the other, although an eosinophilic infiltrate was only found in the OS. Massive lymphadenopathy and hepatosplenomegaly with a marked lymphocytosis and severe skin rash may favour the diagnosis of OS. The similarities may be related to the T lymphoctye activation and cytokine release which occur in GvHD in response to host antigens, and in OS due to unspecified stimuli. The failure of DNA probes to detect maternal cells in case 5 suggests OS is not due to GvHD. T lymphocyte receptor gene rearrangements were polyclonal. Studies in other patients have detected oligoclonal rearrangements suggesting heterogeneity in this disorder. OS may result from an immunoregulatory disorder allowing variable numbers of T lymphocyte clones to undergo uncontrolled activation and proliferation due to a lack of negative feedback or a failure to clear the stimulus. The partial response to cyclosporin supports this notion.

Progress in immune deficiency III, edited by H. M. Chapel, R. J. Levinsky and A. D. B. Webster, 1991; Royal Society of Medicine Services International Congress and Symposium Series No. 173, published by Royal Society of Medicine Services Limited.

Combined immunodeficiency with defective expression in MHC Class II genes

C. Griscelli and B. Lisowska-Grospierre

Hôpital Necker—Enfants Malades, Paris, France

Primary immunodeficiencies (ID) in humans are a heterogenous group of diseases mostly characterized by abnormal differentiation of T and/or B lymphocytes. In the 1980s, several patients with inherited immunodeficiencies, with a normal number of T and B lymphocytes, were described. Among them, an autosomal recessive combined immunodeficiency syndrome characterized by an abnormal expression of HLA Class II antigens and a complete lack of cellular and humoral responses to foreign antigens was described [1–3]. This disease was named major histocompatibility complex (MHC) Class II deficiency by the WHO [4]. It had already been established that the MHC plays a central role in all specific immune responses and this allowed a prediction of a relationship between the observed cellular defect and the susceptibility to infections. The proper recognition of foreign antigens depends on their presentation, together with HLA Class II molecules, on the cell membrane of antigen-presenting cells (APC). MHC Class II-deficient combined immunodeficiency (CID) confirmed the important role of MHC gene products in immune defence mechanisms, since all patients lacking these molecules have abnormal cellular and humoral responses to specific antigen and suffer from repeated, severe infections, frequently causing death.

The so-called 'Bare lymphocyte syndrome' reported by Touraine et al. [5] in immunodeficient children, is characterized by abnormal HLA Class I antigen expression while HLA Class II expression is normal. The same membrane abnormalities were described by Payne et al. [6] and Maeva et al. [7] in non-immunodeficient or normal individuals. Studies performed at protein and RNA levels showed that the defect involves HLA Class I gene expression. The syndrome we described is thus different from the 'Bare lymphocyte syndrome'.

Thirty-one patients with HLA Class II deficient ID are described. They suffered from severe infections that occurred within the first year of life: bacterial (opportunistic infections, Pneumocystis carinii), fungal and viral infections of respiratory and intestinal tracts. Chronic diarrhoea is responsible for failure to thrive. Adenovirus, herpes simplex virus, syncytial respiratory virus and cytomegalovirus (CMV) were the most frequent cause of respiratory manifestations and, for CMV, of hepatitis. Coxsackie virus, adenovirus and poliovirus may be responsible for meningoencephalitis. Some patients developed an autoimmune cytopenia (anaemia, neutropenia and/or thrombocytopenia) of a severe nature. Progression of the disease is very severe and 17 out of the 31 patients have died.

Progress in immune deficiency III, edited by H. M. Chapel, R. J. Levinsky and A. D. B. Webster, 1991; Royal Society of Medicine Services International Congress and Symposium Series No. 173, published by Royal Society of Medicine Services Limited.

The eldest of the deceased patients was 17 years old but most of them died between six months and five years. Eight of our patients are still alive. Because of the severity of the disease, bone marrow transplantation (BMT) was performed in 13 patients.

MHC Class I antigens and $\beta2$ microglobulin ($\beta2$m) were detected on the membrane of leucocytes and platelets of all patients but were reduced in several. In all patients studied, correction in HLA Class I expression was obtained by *in vitro* treatment of blood leucocytes by α, β or γ interferon (IFN) [8,9].

HLA Class II expression was abnormal on all cells which express them physiologically: B lymphocytes, monocytic cells, and PHA-activated T blast cells were DR, DQ and DP negative. HLA Class II molecules were also absent on the membrane of Epstein Barr virus (EBV)-derived or IL-2-dependent B or T cell lines. Endothelial cells, as well as epithelial cells of the intestinal mucosa and of thymus, also had abnormal membrane expression of these molecules. The abnormal expression of Class II molecules was not changed by cell incubation in presence of IFN or IL-4.

The most striking and constant feature of HLA Class II-negative CID is a combined cellular and humoral deficiency of specific immune responses. The absence of delayed type hypersensitivity, correlated with an absence of T cell responses *in vitro* in the presence of antigens (tetanus and diphtheria toxoid or PPD) [10,11]. In contrast, most patients have a normal allogeneic response as measured by mixed lymphocyte reaction (MLR) and the capacity of a normal allogeneic-induced cytotoxicity (CTL) [10]. Study of the capacity of patients' leucocytes to stimulate allogeneic cells gave variable results. These results do not correlate even with the degree of HLA Class II antigen expression and are difficult to understand. Either residual HLA Class II molecules are sufficient in number to allow allo-reactivity, or HLA Class I molecules are involved instead of Class II molecules under such circumstances. The mitogen-induced proliferations were generally found to be normal as well as activation by anti-CD3 Mab or by two anti-CD2 Mabs.

As judged from the level of serum immunoglobulins (Ig), there was a variable expression of the humoral immunity from patient to patient. While most of them were hypogammaglobulinaemic (or almost agammaglobulinaemic) [12], some have normal concentrations of immunoglobulins and even elevated IgM levels. Antibody responses to immunization antigens (tetanus and diphtheria toxoids and polioviruses) were never observed, even in patients with normal Ig levels. Antibody responses after infection were dissociated; some patients had antibodies to viruses and/or to *Candida albicans* when chronically infected.

Further studies were performed in order to characterize mechanisms responsible for the defective expression of HLA-DR, -DQ or -DP molecules. It was first shown that patients' lymphocytes did not contain mRNA corresponding to α or β chain of DR, DQ and DP specificity. Even PHA-activated lymphocytes were totally negative. Furthermore, the expression of HLA Class II mRNA could not be restored by stimulation with interferon [13]. However, patients' cells contained mRNA for the HLA-associated invariant chain (Inv), which is normally co-regulated with Class II genes. The level of mRNA for HLA Class I (H chain) was either normal or slightly reduced in certain patients [13,14].

This lack of mRNA for all HLA Class II products suggested a genetic defect in gene expression, affecting the entire family of Class II genes and an abnormal regulation that occurs at the gene level. This was formally established in family studies, where the inheritance of HLA Class I alleles was followed and shown to segregate independently of the disease [14]. Thus, we could conclude that the genetic defect of MHC Class II deficiency must be located outside of the MHC and probably outside chromosome 6. Accordingly, it was also shown that no major deletion in the HLA Class II region had taken place in these patients [15].

In order to define better the molecular defect responsible for the lack of HLA Class II gene expression, analysis of specific binding of nuclear proteins from patients' cell lines to the HLA Class II promoter was performed by B. Mach and co-workers. Two specific nuclear proteins from normal B lymphocytes, RF-X and RF-Y that bind to specific target sequences on HLA Class II promoters, the X and the Y boxes, were described. These two proteins interact to form a large molecular weight complex, easily identified in DNA-binding assays performed with DNA fragments containing both the X and the Y boxes. RF-X and RF-Y can also be bound to specific X or Y DNA fragments [16]. When these experiments were performed with nuclear extracts from CID B cell lines, a remarkable difference was observed. There was no protein binding to the X sequence of the HLA Class II A promoter and, consequently, in the 'band shift' assays the bands resulting from the binding of RF-X to DNA, either close to or in association with RF-X, were absent. From these experiments, it was concluded that a specific protein RF-X, which normally binds to a regulatory sequence common to Class II promoters, is affected in the hereditary defect in HLA Class II regulation [16].

However, the DNA binding assays performed using patients' cells in different laboratories working on the other nuclear regulatory factors: NFX1.1, NFX1.2, hXBP-1, NFX, gave conflicting results. Their appearance in gel retardation assays was clearly different and, most importantly, they were not affected in CID cell lines [19–21].

This contradiction may not be as important as it first appeared. It now seems, on the basis of experiments with the cloned RF-X gene and its product, that CID lines do contain RF-X mRNA and protein in normal abundance, size and sequence [22, W. Reith and B. Mach, personal communication]. It is conceivable that RF-X is not affected by the genetic lesion in CID patients and that the retarded band found to be missing in CID extracts [16] was really an altered form of a nuclear regulatory factor due either to post-translational modification or to association with another factor. The CID defect would then lie in another factor which binds to or modifies RF-X, not in RF-X proper; this hypothesis is now being tested. Whatever the answer will be, the MHC Class II-deficiency represents the first genetic disease involving a regulatory DNA-binding protein.

REFERENCES

(1) Griscelli C, Durandy A, Virelizier J. Impaired cell to cell interaction in partial immuno-deficiency with variable expression of HLA antigens. In: Seligmann M, Hitzig WH, eds. *Primary immunodeficiencies*. Amsterdam: Elsevier/North-Holland, 1980: 499–503.
(2) Griscelli C, Fischer A, Grospierre B, *et al*. Clinical and immunological aspects of combined immunodeficiency with defective expression of HLA antigens. In: Griscelli C, Vossen J, eds. *Progress in immunodeficiency research and therapy I*. Amsterdam: Excerpta Medica, 1984: 19–26.
(3) Lisowska-Grospierre B, Durandy A, Virelizier JL, Fischer A, Griscelli C. Combined immunodeficiency with defective expression of HLA: modulation of an abnormal HLA synthesis and functional studies. *Birth Defects* 1983; **19**: 87–92.
(4) Report of World Health Organisation Committee. *Clin Immunol Immunopathol* 1986; **40**: 166–70.
(5) Touraine JL, Betuel H, Souillet G. Combined immunodeficiency disease associated with absence of cell-surface HLA A and B antigens. *J Pediatr* 1978; **93**: 47–51.

(6) Payne R, Brodsky FM, Peterlin BM, Young LM. "Bare lymphocytes" without immunodeficiency. *Hum Immunol* 1983; **6**: 219–27.

(7) Maeva H, Hirata R, Chen RF, Suzaki H, Kudoh S, Tohyama H. Defective expression of HLA class I antigens: a case of the Bare lymphocyte without immunodeficiency. *Immunogenetics* 1985; **21**: 549–58.

(8) Durandy A, Virelizier JL, Griscelli C. Enhancement by interferon of membrane HLA antigens in patients with combined immunodeficiency with defective HLA expression. *Clin Exp Immunol* 1983; **52**: 173–8.

(9) Rijkers GT, Roord JJ, Koning F, Kuis W, Zegers BJM. Phenotypical and functional analysis of B lymphocytes of two siblings with combined immunodeficiency and defective expression of major histocompatibility complex (MHC) class II antigens on mononuclear cells. *J Clin Immunol* 1987; **7**: 98–106.

(10) Griscelli C, Fischer A, Lisowska-Grospierre B, *et al.* Defective synthesis of HLA class I and II molecules associated with a combined immunodeficiency. In: Aiuti F, Rosen F, Cooper MD, eds. *Recent advances in primary and acquired immunodeficiencies*. Vol. 28. New York: Raven Press, 1985: 176–83.

(11) Zegers BJM, Rijkers GT, Roord JJ, *et al.* Defective expression of MHC antigens on mononuclear cells in two siblings with combined immunodeficiency: delineation of the class II antigen defect. In: Vossen J, Griscelli C, eds. *Progress in immunodeficiency research and therapy II*, Amsterdam: Elsevier Science, 1986.

(12) Hadam MR, Dopfer R, Peter HH, Niethammer D. Congenital agammaglobulinemia associated with lack of expression of HLA D-region antigens. In: Griscelli C, Vossen J, eds. *Progress in immunodeficiency research and therapy*. Amsterdam: Excerpta Medica, 1984: 19–24.

(13) Lisowska-Grospierre B, Charron DJ, de Préval C, Durandy A, Griscelli C, Mach B. A defect in the regulation of major histocompatibility complex class II gene expression in human HLA DR negative lymphocytes from patients with combined immunodeficiency syndrome. *J Clin Invest* 1985; **26**: 381–5.

(14) de Préval C, Lisowska-Grospierre B, Loche M, Griscelli C, Mach B. A trans-acting class II regulatory gene unlinked to the MHC controls expression of HLA class II genes. *Nature* 1985; **318**: 291–5

(15) Marcadet A, Cohen D, Dausset J, Fischer A, Durandy A, Griscelli C. Genotyping with DNA probes in combined immunodeficiency syndrome with defective expression of HLA. *N Engl J Med* 1985; **312**: 1287–92.

(16) Reith W, Satola S, Sanchez CH, *et al.* Congenital immunodeficiency with a regulatory defect in MHC class II gene expression lacks a specific HLA-DR promoter binding proteins, RF-X. *Cell* 1988; **53**: 897–906.

(17) Gladstone P, Pious D. Stable variants affecting B cell alloantigens in human lymphoid cells. *Nature* 1978; **271**: 459–61.

(18) Accolla RS. Human B cell variants immunoselected against a single Ia antigen subset have lost expression of several Ia antigen subsets. *J Exp Med* 1983; **157**: 1053–8.

(19) Hume CR, Lee JS. Congenital immunodeficiencies associated with absence of HLA class II antigens on lymphocytes results from distinct mutations in trans-acting factors. *Hum Immunol* 1989; **26**: 288.

(20) Liou HC, Boothby MR, Finn PW, *et al.* A new member of the leucine zipper class of proteins that binds to the HLA DR promoter. *Science* 1990; **247**: 1581.

(21) Kouskoff V, Mantovani RM, Candéias SM, *et al.* NF-X, a transcription factor implicated in MHC class II gene regulation. *J Immunol* in press.

(22) Reith W, Barras E, Satola S, *et al.* Cloning of the major histocompatibility complex class II promoter binding protein affected in a hereditary defect in class II gene regulation. *Proc Natl Acad Sci USA* 1989; **86**: 4200.

Recent advances in MHC Class II deficiency

M. R. Hadam[1], J. Lohmeyer[2], C. Fonatsch[3], M. Voges[1], B. Mach[4], G. Dammer[5] and R. Dopfer[6]

[1]Abteilung Kinderchirurgie, Kinderklinik, Medizinische Hochschule Hannover, [2]Medizinische Klinik, Giessen, [3]Institut für Humangenetik, Lübeck, Germany, [4]Département de Microbiologie, Genéva, Switzerland, [5]Rudolf-Virchow-Krankenhaus, Berlin, and [6]Universitäts-Kinderklinik, Tübingen, Germany

MHC Class II deficiency has been recognized as an experiment of nature whereby the lack of a gene regulatory element, in trans and in common to all Class II genes, results in the inability to express MHC Class II antigens [1–3]. Apart from immunodeficiency, patients typically suffer from intractable diarrhoea and failure to thrive [4], suggesting the involvement of additional cellular targets in this disorder. The defect may be complemented by cell fusion between patients or apparently identical mutant cell lines derived *in vitro* [5,6] and hence, at least three complementation groups are proposed [7]. Gel retardation assays have revealed the absence of an HLA-DRA promoter binding protein (RF-X) in (some) patients [8]; the gene coding for RF-X has been cloned [9] and localized to chromosome 19p13 [10]. When tested for the presence of RF-X protein, an apparently intact molecule was found in all patients. This was also verified by sequence analysis (unpublished observations). Moreover, cells from complementation group 1 (RJ-2.2.5, BLS2 [7]) have been shown to contain RF-X which binds normally to the DRA-promoter (unpublished observations). We are thus left with the hypothesis, that (i) other (defective) trans-acting factors must exist and (ii) RF-X alone is not sufficient to explain the Class II negative phenotype in our patients and it is those additional factors that are missing or defective in MHC Class II deficiency.

We describe here for the first time the lack of expression of a surface molecule (defined by CDw78 [11]), which is not encoded by the MHC and which is absent in 4/4 patients with MHC Class II deficiency (Fig. 1). Though not well characterized at present, it is clearly distinct from Class II in terms of tissue distribution, workshop clustering and immunoprecipitation [6]. Also little is known about its functional role as a B cell-specific membrane structure, except for its expression being markedly increased upon transformation with Epstein Barr virus (EBV). In our patients' lymphoblastoid cell lines (LCL), it is neither found in the cytoplasm nor after incubation with interferon-γ (IFN-γ). Like HLA-DQ, it is not detected in sublines which re-express Class II antigens [12]. That CDw78 is in fact controlled by the same MHC-regulatory gene requires formal proof by cell fusion. This is currently being done.

Progress in immune deficiency III, edited by H. M. Chapel, R. J. Levinsky and A. D. B. Webster, 1991; Royal Society of Medicine Services International Congress and Symposium Series No. 173, published by Royal Society of Medicine Services Limited.

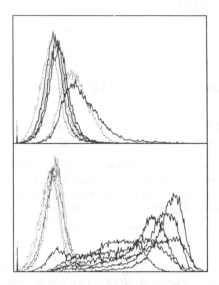

Figure 1 *Expression of CDw78 on LCL from four patients with MHC Class II deficiency (top) and six randomly selected controls (bottom).*
Methods: *The patients' cell lines have been characterized previously [2]; control cell lines were established in our laboratory. Cell suspensions were labelled with mAb at saturating concentrations after blocking Fc-receptors with excess human IgG. Mouse IgG was detected using FITC-labelled rabbit-F(ab')₂-anti-mouse-IgG (Dako). 20 000 cells were evaluated after scatter gating on live cells using a FACS 440 (Becton Dickinson) with three-decade logarithmic amplification. Data were analysed on a Consort 40 computer system (Becton Dickinson). All data shown were assayed on the same day with the same instrument settings. Both panels display the reactivity of CDw78 antibody 1588 (solid line) versus controls without mAB (dotted line). Note the increased autofluorescence in the LCL from one patient (FH). Antibodies were obtained from the 4th WS.*

We also present evidence for a second B cell-specific molecule (defined by monoclonal antibody 2-7 [13–15] which is lacking in MHC Class II deficiency [16]. This structure is not well defined biochemically though clearly different from Class II by workshop results. There is some additional complexity since this antibody apparently detects a polymorphic site [13]; in our hands eight out of 60 controls were negative. However, no negative reactions were found in the families of our patients. Rather, its expression is lost upon transition to the class II negative phenotype, as exemplified in the B cell tumour described below.

Third, we describe a non-MHC surface marker abnormality in MHC Class II deficiency which segregates with the disease in one informative family. Using 15 different monoclonal antibodies against the low-affinity receptor for IgE as defined by CD23 [15], all LCL from our patients and their relatives stained strongly with one notable MAb exception (Fig. 2): antibody Tü1 did not react with LCL from patients AH and FH [17]. However, it stained all LCL from the remaining healthy family members as well as all other patients. Antibodies crossblocking Tü1 on normal cells [18] reacted normally with both AH and FH. Since surface molecules are usually expressed in a co-dominant fashion, lack of a single epitope requires homozygosity at that locus. Screening more than 60 control LCL has not revealed a similar phenomenon; there are no reports of polymorphic epitopes on the CD23-antigen in the literature. Our results are best explained by an extremely rare polymorphism in the CD23-gene (CD23+ Tü1-) which is found in a homozygous state just in those two patients. Plausibility

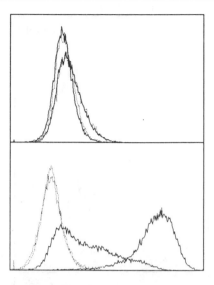

Figure 2 *Lack of CD23-epitope defined by antibody Tü1 in siblings AH and FH (top) with MHC Class II deficiency, as compared to patients SM and RS (bottom).*
Methods: *Cell lines and immunofluorescence staining were as in Fig. 1. Patients are identified in reference [2] as follows: AH (No 1), FH (No 4), SM (No 3) and RS (No 2). Monoclonal antibody Tü1 was kindly provided by Dr A. Ziegler, Berlin. The negative control (dotted line) is virtually superimposed by the histogram for Tü1 (solid line) in patients AH and FH. The low expression of CD23, including Tü1, in patient RS (bottom panel) resulted from a freshly thawed ampoule; its level of expression normalized upon further culture.*

dictates that this very rare event (CD23+ Tü1−) is linked to the defective gene in MHC Class II deficiency. CD23 was mapped recently to chromosome 19q13.1–19pter or 19q13.4 [19].

Fourth, we report on the lymphoid blast crisis in a 40-year-old patient with chronic myelogenous leukaemia without overt immunodeficiency (Fig. 3). His tumour lymphoblasts were unique since they expressed all constitutive B-cell markers (including sIgM) but were negative for all MHC Class II antigens. In addition, tumour cells displayed distinctly lower levels of Class I antigens compared with normal peripheral blood lymphocytes which is characteristic of MHC Class II deficiency [1]. B cells from the patient in remission or his EBV-transformed LCL were Class II positive. These cells allowed us unequivocally to define a polymorphic non-MHC molecule (assayed by antibody 2–7; see above) which is lacking from all our MHC-defective cells. The exclusive loss of all Class II antigens from the patients' tumour cells is probably caused by one defective allele of the Class II regulatory gene in germ-line, which may be undetectable in normal cells. Upon transformation, the second (normal) allele is lost, resulting in the extinction of the Class II positive phenotype. Cytogenetic analysis of the Ph-negative blast cells revealed three informative deletions at Chromosome 1q21–1qter, 7p and 9p which may be considered as candidates for the chromosomal localization of a MHC-regulatory molecule. Since the lack of CR2 (mapped to chromosome 1q32) has been observed once in MHC Class II deficiency [20], we favour 1q21–1qter.

The absence of CDw78 and the antigen defined by antibody 2–7 in all our patients, regardless of ethnic origin, provides the first evidence for a pleiotropic effect in MHC Class II deficiency. Previously only the receptor for EBV has been

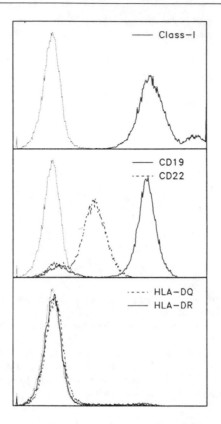

Figure 3 *CML blast crisis with Class II defect; Class I (top panel), B cell markers (middle panel) and HLA Class II (bottom panel).*
Methods: *Peripheral blood mononuclear cells were isolated during relapse and freshly stained and evaluated as described in Fig. 1. Antibodies were as indicated in the panels; dotted lines indicate negative controls.*

reported absent in a single patient [9]. Since we have already shown that the primary defect in MHC Class II deficiency may be found in any somatic cell [2], searching for additional marker abnormalities seems warranted. Furthermore, the functional role of those newly defined molecules deserves clarification.

The unusual polymorphism (CD23+ Tü1-) in the CD23 gene in combination with the CML blast crisis provides some intriguing and novel insights into the primary genetic lesion involved: RF-X has been mapped to chromosome 19p13 [10]; CD23 is on the same chromosome, but not yet localized [19]. Data from our patient with CML suggest involvement of chromosome 1q, 7p or 9p. Reports from the literature suggest a specific translocation t(1;19)(q23;p13.3) in a significant proportion of patients with pre-B ALL [21,22]. Both breakpoints are consistent with our findings. Careful review of the published data reveals one exceptional case (out of seven) with a t(1;19) translocation [21] with the phenotype cIg+ CALLA+ HLA-DR- which is somewhat comparable to the CML-patient described here. We thus propose hat both chromosomes 1q and 19p are involved in the pathogenesis of MHC Class II deficiency.

REFERENCES

(1) Hadam MR, Dopfer R, Dammer G, et al. Defective expression of HLA-D region determinants in children with congenital agammaglobulinemia and malabsorption: A new syndrome. In: Albert ED, Baur MP, Mayr WR, eds. Histocompatibility testing 1984. Heidelberg: Springer, 1984: 645.

(2) DePréval C, Hadam MR, Mach B. Regulation of genes for HLA class II antigens in cell lines from patients with severe combined immunodeficiency. N Engl J Med 1988; 318: 1295.

(3) Griscelli C, Lisowska-Grospierre B, Mach B. Combined immunodeficiency with defective expression in MHC class II genes. Immunodef Rev 1989; 1: 135.

(4) Hadam MR, Dopfer R, Peter HH, Niethammer D. Congenital agammaglobulinaemia associated with lack of expression of HLA-D-Region antigens. In: Griscelli C, Vossen J, eds. Progress in immunodeficiency research and therapy, Vol I. Amsterdam: Elsevier, 1984: 43.

(5) Yang Z, Accolla RS, Pious D, Zegers BJM, Strominger J. Two distinct genetic loci regulating class II gene expression are defective in human mutant and patient cell lines. EMBO J 1988; 7: 1965.

(6) Hume CR, Lee JS. Congenital immunodeficiencies associated with absence of HLA class II antigens on lymphocytes result from distinct mutations in transacting factors. Hum Immunol 1989; 26: 288.

(7) Benoist C, Mathis D. Regulation of major histocompatibility complex class-II genes: X, Y and other letters of the alphabet. Ann Rev Immunol 1990; 8: 681.

(8) Reith W, Zatola S, Sanchez CH, et al. Congenital immunodeficiency with a regulatory defect in MHC class II gene expression lacks a specific HLA-DR promoter binding protein, RF-X. Cell 1988; 53: 897.

(9) Reith W, Barras E, Satola S, et al. Cloning of the major histocompatibility complex class II promoter binding protein affected in a hereditary defect in class II gene regulation. Proc Natl Acad Sci USA 1989; 86: 4200.

(10) Pugliati I, Reith W, Fey S, Mach B. Mapping the RF-X gene, encoding a DNA-binding protein controlling HLA class II gene expression, to 19p13. Cytogenet Cell Genet 1989; 51: 1061.

(11) Dörken B, Möller P, Pezzutto A, Schwartz-Albiez R, Moldenhauer G. B-cell antigens: CDw78. In: Knapp W, Dörken B, Gilks W, et al. eds. Leukocyte typing IV. Oxford: Oxford University Press, 1989: 122.

(12) Hadam MR, Dopfer R, Dammer G, Derau C, Niethammer D. Expression of MHC-antigens in MHC class II deficiency. In: Vossen J, Griscelli C, eds. Progress in immuno-deficiency research and therapy II. Amsterdam: Elsevier, 1986: 89.

(13) Nadler LM. B cell leukemia panel workshop: Summary and contents. In: Reinherz EL, Haynes BE, Nadler LM, Bernstein ID, eds. Leukocyte Typing II. New York: Springer, 1986: 3.

(14) Ling NR, MacLennan ICM, Mason DY. B-cell and plasma cell antigens: new and previously defined clusters. In: McMichael A, ed. Leukocyte typing III. Oxford: Oxford University Press 1987: 302.

(15) Dörken B, Möller P, Pezzutto A, Schwartz-Albiez R, Moldenhauer G. B-cell antigens: Section report. In: Knapp W, Dörken B, Gilks W, et al, eds. Leukocyte typing IV. Oxford: Oxford University Press, 1989: 15.

(16) Hadam MR, Dopfer R, Dammer G. Pleiotropic effects in cell lines from patients with MHC class-II-deficiency. Tissue antigens 1989; 33: 154.

(17) Hadam MR, Heerwagen C, Ziegler A. Aberrant expression of a CD23 epitope (Tü1) on lymphoblastoid cell lines from two siblings with MHC class II deficiency. In: Knapp W, Dörken B, Gilks W, et al, eds. Leukocyte typing IV. Oxford, Oxford University Press, 1989: 74.

(18) Schwartz-Albiez R, Moldenhauer G. Immunochemistry and epitope analysis using CD10, CD19, CD20, CD21, CD23, CD24, CD37, CD38, CD39, and CD40 mAb. In: Knapp W, Dörken B, Gilks W, et al. eds. Leukocyte typing IV. Oxford: Oxford University Press, 1989: 142.

(19) Wendel-Hansen V, Riviere M, Uno M, *et al.* The gene encoding CD23 leukocyte antigen (FCE2) is located on human chromosome 19. *Somat Cell Mol Genet* 1990; **16**: 283.
(20) Clement LT, Plaeger-Marshall S, Haas A, Saxon A, Martin AM. Bare lymphocyte syndrome. Consequences of absent class II major histocompatibility antigen expression for B lymphocyte differentiation and function. *J Clin Invest* 1988; **81**: 669.
(21) Williams DL, Look AT, Mrlbin SL, *et al.* New chromosomal translocations correlate with specific immunophenotypes of childhood acute lymphoblastic leukemia. *Cell* 1984; **36**: 101.
(22) Carroll AJ, Crist WM, Parmley RT, Roper M, Cooper MD, Finley WH. Pre-B cell leukemia associated with chromosome translocation 1;19. *Blood* 1984; **63**: 721.

Analysis of the peripheral T cell compartment in an MHC Class II deficiency patient

M. Lambert[1], M. van Eggermond[1], M. Andrien[2], F. Mascart[3], C. Vannus[4], E. Dupont[1] and P. van den Elsen[1]

[1]Department of Immunohaematology and Bloodbank, University Hospital, Leiden, The Netherlands, [2]Department of Immunohaematology, Erasme Hospital, Brussels, [3]Department of Immunohaematology, Hospital St Pierre, Brussels, and [4]Department of Immunohaematology, Brugman Hospital, Brussels, Belgium

(POSTER)

INTRODUCTION

The MHC Class II deficiency syndrome is mainly characterized by a lack of membrane expression of the MHC Class II antigens on somatic cells, including those involved in T cell development [1,2]. Studies in the mouse have shown that disruption of the TCR/(self)peptide/MHC Class II interaction during T cell development by treatment of neonatals with anti-I-A antibodies resulted in a greatly diminished number of peripheral CD4+ CD8- T cells [3]. In man, the MHC Class II deficiency syndrome provides a model to study the impact of alterations in the TCR/(self)peptide/MHC Class II interaction on the peripheral T cell compartment.

RESULTS

To study the composition of the peripheral T cell population, peripheral blood lymphocytes (PBLs) and polyclonal activated T cell lines and clones were stained with several monoclonal antibodies. No MHC Class II expression could be detected on activated T cells and, in addition, MHC Class I expression was lowered compared to a healthy control (Fig. 1). No differences in the TCR/CD3 antigen expression could be observed. In the PBLs of the patient, a distinct CD4+ CD8- population could be observed, albeit the number of CD4+ CD8- T cells was diminished (31% compared with 58% in the control). After two weeks of culture, the percentage CD4+ T cells decreased dramatically (6% compared with 40% in the control) and an increase in cells with a double positive phenotype (CD4+ CD8+) was observed. Only two (15%) single CD4+ clones could be established from the T cell culture of the patient whereas about half of the clones derived from a healthy family member bear this phenotype. Isolation of the single CD4+ CD8- population by FACS sorting and limiting dilution resulted in the establishment of several single CD4+ CD8- clones exhibiting a stable phenotype. This finding points to an *in vitro* growth disadvantage of the CD4+ CD8- T cells in this patient compared with the CD4- CD8+ cells.

The proliferative response of T cells that have matured in an MHC Class II-deficient environment was tested by activation via the TCR/CD3 pathway. Normal proliferative responses were found with anti-CD3 and PMA. Also activation of the T cells with several enterotoxins, PHA and rIL-2 resulted in normal proliferative responses.

Progress in immune deficiency III, edited by H. M. Chapel, R. J. Levinsky and A. D. B. Webster, 1991; Royal Society of Medicine Services International Congress and Symposium Series No. 173, published by Royal Society of Medicine Services Limited.

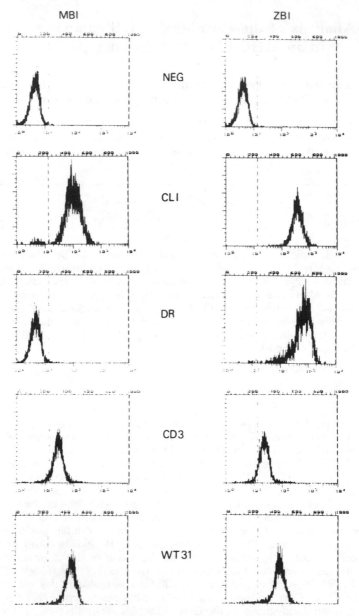

Figure 1 *Flow cytometric analysis of antigen expression on activated T cells of a patient with the MHC Class II deficiency syndrome (MBI) and a healthy control (ZBI).*

DISCUSSION

The PBLs and T cell lines and clones derived from an MHC Class II-deficient patient did not manifest MHC Class II expression and exhibited a lowered MHC Class I expression despite their activated state as determined by CD25 expression (data not shown). Triggering of the T cells via the TCR/CD3 complex in this patient appears to be normal. Despite the absence of detectable MHC Class II expression, a single CD4$^+$ CD8$^-$ population could be observed in the PBLs of the patient. The presence of these CD4$^+$ CD8$^-$ T cells in the periphery is in marked contrast with murine studies where disturbance of the TCR/(self)peptide/MHC Class II or Class I resulted in a greatly diminished number of peripheral T cells expressing the CD4, or CD8 antigen respectively [3,4]. In this human model it cannot be excluded that the CD4+ CD8− T cell population is the result of residual thymic MHC Class II expression during fetal development. Alternatively it is possible that these CD4+ CD8− cells are mainly MHC Class I restricted through selection via a low but sufficient affinity for MHC Class I. The existence of such CD4+ MHC Class I restricted T cells in man has been demonstrated [5,6].

REFERENCES

(1) Schuurman RKB, van Rood JJ, Vossen JM, et al. Failure of lymphocyte membrane HLA-A and -B expression in two siblings with combined immunodeficiency. Clin Immunol Immunopathol 1979; 14: 418–34.
(2) Schuurman HJ, van de Wijngaert FP, Huber J, et al. The thymus in 'Bare lymphocyte' syndrome: Significance of expression of major histocompatibility complex antigens on thymic epithelial cells in intrathymic T-cell maturation. Hum Immunol 1985; 13: 69–82.
(3) Kruisbeek AM, Mond JJ, Fowlkes BJ, Carmen JA, Bridges S, Longo DL. Absence of the Lyt-2− L3T4+ lineage of T cells in mice treated neonatally with anti-I-A correlates with absence of intrathymic I-A-bearing antigen-presenting cell function. J Exp Med 1985; 161: 1029–47.
(4) Zijlstra M, Bix M, Simister NE, Loring JM, Raulet DH, Jaenisch R. Beta-2-microglobulin deficient mice lack CD4− + cytolytic T cells. Nature 1990; 344: 742–6.
(5) Strassman G, Bach FH. OKT4+ cytotoxic T cells can lyse targets via class I molecules and can be blocked by monoclonal antibody against T4 molecules. J Immunol 1984; 133: 1705–9.
(6) Spits H, Borst J, Terhorst C, de Vries JE. The role of T4 cell differentiation markers in antigen specific and lectin dependent cellular cytotoxicity mediated by T8+ and T4+ human cytotoxic T cell clones directed at class I and class II MHC antigens. J Immunol 1982; 129: 1563–9.

Bone marrow transplantation in a patient with MHC Class II deficiency

M. M. Eibl[1], J. W. Mannhalter[1], Ch. Peters[2] and H. Gaadner[2]

[1]Institute of Immunology, University of Vienna, and
[2]St Anna's Children Hospital, Vienna, Austria

(ABSTRACT)

MHC Class II deficiency results in a functional defect of both cell-mediated and humoral immunity. Most of the patients suffer from intractable diarrhoea, failure to thrive and severe recurrent infections. Long term prognosis is usually poor. Bone marrow transplantation (BMT) appears to be difficult in this type of immunodeficiency. We now report the results obtained in a patient, a boy born in 1984 in whom the diagnosis of MHC Class II deficiency was made 1987. In April 1989 the patient received a marrow transplant from his histioidentical brother. The post-transplant period was uneventful without graft versus host disease. Sixty days post-transplant the following results could be obtained: Ery 3.2, Hb 9.9, Thrombo 388000, White cells 6300, Diff. 1 meta, Neutrophils 59, Ly 13, Mo 23, Eo 4.

Immunological investigation five months after BMT revealed: Leucocytes 10400, Ly 17%, CD2 61% (1082), CD4 22% (384), CD8 31% (545), Mo2 2% (31), HLA-DR 20%. T cells expressing HLA-DR were <5%. Measurements performed on monocytes demonstrated that 64% of the circulating monocytes expressed HLA-DR.

Progress in immune deficiency III, edited by H. M. Chapel, R. J. Levinsky and A. D. B. Webster, 1991; Royal Society of Medicine Services International Congress and Symposium Series No. 173, published by Royal Society of Medicine Services Limited.

The murine model of severe combined immunodeficiency

G. J. Bancroft

Department of Clinical Sciences, London School of Hygiene and Tropical Medicine, London, UK

Models of primary immunodeficiency in inbred mice have yielded important information on the development and function of the mammalian immune system. Some, such as the beige and nude mutations, share immunological characteristics with established human immunodeficiency syndromes (Chediak-Higashi and DiGeorge syndromes respectively). However, the majority have no known human homologue, but provide unique insights into the pathways which control immune development [1]. In this paper I will review the characteristics and uses of one of the more recently described immunodeficiency models, that of murine severe combined immunodeficiency (SCID). This mutation was first described by Bosma et al. in 1983 [2] and segregates as an autosomal recessive mutation in mice of the CB17/Icr strain. It has since been mapped to chromosome 16, and has no effect on adenosine deaminase expression which in the mouse is encoded on chromosome 2.

While initially identified by the absence of serum immunoglobulins, the SCID defect is now known to result in deficiency of both T and B lymphocyte lineages. Such mice do not mount antibody responses to foreign antigens, and do not reject skin grafts or develop proliferative or cytotoxic T cell responses in vitro. The absence of functional lymphocytes is the result of an arrest in the differentiation of both T and B lymphocyte subsets. T cell development is blocked at a point phenotypically equivalent to day 14–15 of thymic ontogeny, with 98% of thymocytes being $CD4^-/CD8^-$, lacking CD3 and expressing low levels of CD2. B cell development is arrested at the pro-B cell stage prior to expression of intracellular or cell surface immunoglobulin. However, expression of natural killer (NK) cells ($J11d^-$, $CD3^-$, $CD4^-$, $CD8^-$, TcR^-) and their precursors is normal in the SCID mutant, suggesting that NK cell development is independent of mature T cell differentiation.

In contrast to the blockade in lymphoid development, myeloid and erythroid cell lineages are apparently unaffected by the SCID mutation. Macrophages, granulocytes and mast cells can be identified in SCID tissues (see below). Histologically, the SCID mutation impairs lymphoid development but retains the stromal and reticular networks found in normal lymphoid organs. Furthermore, lymphoid function can be reconstituted in these mice by adoptive transfer of fetal liver or bone marrow stem cells from their coisogenic partner strain CB-17. The extent of engraftment is often variable and incomplete, but this can be overcome

Progress in immune deficiency III, edited by H. M. Chapel, R. J. Levinsky and A. D. B. Webster, 1991; Royal Society of Medicine Services International Congress and Symposium Series No. 173, published by Royal Society of Medicine Services Limited.

by using newborn recipients or by prior sublethal irradiation. In contrast, SCID bone marrow can reconstitute irradiated normal recipients for myeloid but not lymphoid function, again illustrating the intrinsic arrest of lymphoid development characteristic of this mutation [3].

These results suggested that the SCID defect affected a developmental process unique to lymphoid cells and common to both T and B cells. It has since been demonstrated that the hallmark of the SCID mouse is the absence of lymphocytes bearing antigen specific receptors and that the molecular events involved in rearrangement and expression of these molecules constitute the primary target of the SCID mutation. Transformed lymphoid cells, spontaneous thymomas and cells derived from long term bone marrow cultures all demonstrate a high incidence of abnormal T cell receptor or immunoglobulin gene rearrangements. This is characterized by extensive deletions involving V(D)J gene segments. Studies with exogenous recombination substrates transfected into SCID cells demonstrate normal cleavage of DNA strands, with some abnormalities in signal joint formation, but failure to properly ligate the coding ends and thus generate a functional receptor. Thus, the SCID mutation is believed to disrupt the 'recombinase system' responsible for productive rearrangement of antigen receptor genes [3].

ANALYSIS OF MACROPHAGE FUNCTION IN SCID MICE

The specificity of the SCID defect for lymphoid rather than myeloid development provided a unique opportunity to study macrophage function in the absence of T and B cells. In experiments performed in the laboratory of Prof. E. R. Unanue and in collaboration with Prof. R. D. Schreiber (Washington University Medical School, St Louis USA) we analysed the effect of the SCID mutation on macrophage development. Our initial experiments compared uninfected CB-17 and SCID mice for the number, phenotype and functional characteristics of resident macrophages. Despite the loss of all measurable T and B cell function, normal numbers of macrophages were obtained from the liver, spleen and peritoneal cavity of SCID mice. Moreover, these cells expressed similar levels of MHC Class II (Ia) molecules as immunocompetent control mice and could be activated with purified T cell-derived cytokines such as IFNγ for tumour cytotoxicity and enhanced Ia expression *in vitro*. To date, we have no evidence for any intrinsic abnormality in macrophage function as a result of the SCID defect [4].

These results allowed further analysis of macrophage function during infection with the facultative intracellular bacterium *Listeria monocytogenes* (Listeria). Infection of CB-17 mice with Listeria resulted in a peak of bacterial load in the spleen by day 4 followed by resolution of the infection by day 12. In contrast, infected SCID mice were unable to clear the bacteria from the liver and spleen, such that by day 12, bacterial loads in the spleen were 6000-fold higher in the immunodeficient strain than CB-17 controls. The influence of infection on macrophage activation was analysed by expression of Ia antigens. Infection of normal mice resulted in the expected increase in Ia bearing macrophages in the peritoneal cavity. Despite the absence of T cells, SCID mice also demonstrated an increase in macrophage number and Ia expression in the liver, spleen and peritoneal cavity (21% vs 95% Ia positive peritoneal macrophages at day 12). This was not mediated by the re-emergence of lymphoid function in infected SCID mice during infection, and was also observed in similar experiments using T cell-deficient athymic mice. Other microbial stimuli such as BCG and *Corynebacterium parvum* (but not T cell mitogens such as Con A) also activated SCID macrophages *in vivo* for enhanced Ia expression and tumourolytic capacity. These results therefore suggested the existence of a T cell independent pathway of macrophage activation *in vivo* [4].

Previous studies of macrophage activation have demonstrated the pivotal role of T cell-derived IFNγ. The importance of IFNγ in the T cell independent responses of SCID mice *in vivo* was examined by administration of the IFNγ neutralizing hamster monoclonal antibody H22. Pretreatment with 100 µg of H22 Mab completely inhibited Ia induction *in vivo* and enhanced Listeria growth in the spleens of SCID mice 60-fold. Furthermore, naive SCID spleen cells secreted IFNγ *in vitro* following coculture with heat killed Listeria but not the T cell stimulus ConA. Thus, in the absence of functional T cells, SCID mice produce IFNγ in response to microbial stimuli *in vitro* and utilize this cytokine for macrophage activation *in vivo* [5].

Finally, we examined the mechanism of IFNγ production in the SCID mouse. The previous experiments demonstrated the presence of a non-T cell source of IFNγ. Since natural killer (NK) cells are present in SCID spleens and have previously been shown to secrete IFNγ *in vitro*, we examined the effect of depleting NK cells *in vivo* on SCID macrophage function. Pretreatment of SCID mice with rabbit anti-ASGM1 sera ablated NK cell cytolytic function and inhibited induction of macrophage Ia expression by Listeria *in vivo* (uninfected SCID, 19% Ia+; Listeria infected SCID, 69% Ia+; anti-ASGM1 plus Listeria, 26% Ia+).

IFNγ secretion by SCID cells *in vitro* was also abolished by prior removal of adherent macrophages which themselves did not produce IFNγ. This suggested that following ingestion of Listeria, macrophages secreted a soluble product(s) required for initiation of IFNγ synthesis by NK cells. Assay of SCID cell supernatants following addition of Listeria *in vitro* demonstrated the early release of tumour necrosis factor (TNF) prior to secretion of IFNγ. Addition of a neutralizing monoclonal antibody to TNF (TN3-19.12) abolished SCID IFNγ secretion *in vitro*. Finally, injection of this antibody prior to infection of SCID mice also inhibited Ia induction and enhanced replication of Listeria *in vivo* [6].

Together, these experiments suggest that IFNγ synthesis can occur in a T cell independent manner in response to microbial challenge. This pathway, mediated by NK cells and involving an obligate requirement for TNF, provides the host with a rapid source of macrophage activating cytokine prior to the development of antigen specific T cells. It is likely that activation of host macrophages via this pathway represents an important early step in resistance to microbial infection.

OTHER USES OF THE MURINE SCID MODEL

The loss of both T and B lymphocyte subsets in the SCID mutation results in increased susceptibility to infection and the inability to reject foreign tissue. Other immunodeficient mouse strains (e.g. motheaten) also have severe deficits in immune function but are difficult to study due to their short lifespans. The SCID mouse, which can be maintained for over one year under barrier conditions, has now provided a unique model to study (i) the course of infection with opportunistic pathogens and (ii) the potential transfer of xenogeneic lymphoid/myeloid cells *in vivo*.

Infection of immunodeficient mouse colonies with opportunistic pathogens such as mouse hepatitis virus and *Pneumocystis carinii* can present severe problems. However, these observations also provide the possibility of studying opportunistic infection in a model immunocompromised host. *Pneumocystis* infection is an important source of morbidity and mortality in patients with AIDS and previous animal models were limited to reexpression of endogenous infections following corticosteroid treatment of experimental rodents. In contrast, SCID mice which have acquired the organism from the environment show progressive pulmonary and systemic signs of infection which is invariably lethal. This can be ablated by prior transfer of normal lymphoid tissue and resistance is dependent upon the presence of CD4+ T cells [7]. It is still uncertain whether healthy SCID mice can be electively infected with either mouse derived *Pneumocystis*, or more importantly, isolates of the organism from AIDS patients. If this can be achieved, then more extensive studies of host resistance and the possibility of *in vivo* drug screening may be feasible.

Infections with Listeria, Candida, Reovirus, Rotavirus and Borrelia have also been examined in SCID mice as models of disease in the immunocompromised host and to help define the pathways of resistance to infection in the normal host.

The SCID mutant also provides a useful *in vivo* recipient for the adoptive transfer of lymphoid or myeloid tissue. This has been utilized to study the transfer of murine cells for resistance to infection (as described above), to identify and enumerate lymphoid stem cell populations and to study the regulated development of T or B lymphocytes subsets *in vivo*. The inability of SCID mice to reject foreign tissue is also being used to promote the growth and development of human cells in the murine *in vivo* environment. Initial experiments described the transient expression of human lymphocytes or immunoglobulins in SCID mice following injection with human peripheral blood cells or with subcapsular kidney grafts of human fetal thymus, lymph node and/or liver [8,9]. The maintenance and/or growth of human lymphoid cells in SCID-hu chimaeras has now been used to establish an experimental model of HIV infection. Direct intra-graft injection of HIV resulted in progressive infection of the human cells over several months. In this model, direct injection of AZT reduced the number of infected cells although protection was not complete [10]. This model may allow further studies on novel antiviral drugs or the effects of cytolytic T cells in controlling viral replication. Nevertheless, the similarity of this system to the human disease is still unclear and further efforts should determine whether this is a widely applicable system to study the immunobiology of HIV.

The establishment of SCID-hu chimaeras also provides potential models of infection with other human pathogens. Transfer of human lymphocytes into SCID recipients followed by injection of purified Epstein-Barr virus now provides the first non-primate *in vivo* model of EBV-mediated tumourigenesis. Infected mice develop fatal aggressive lymphoid tumours of human B cell origin which possess EBV DNA sequences, providing a unique opportunity to study the mechanisms of EBV-induced lymphoproliferative disease in an experimental animal [11]. This is particularly important since patients with congenital immunodeficiencies have a high risk of B lymphocyte neoplasia, and EBV-derived tumours can cause lethal complications in patients undergoing bone marrow transplantation.

Finally, recent attempts to mimic aspects of human autoimmune diseases have used lymphoid cells from autoimmune individuals to generate SCID-hu chimaeras.

Injection of PBL from patients with primary biliary cirrhosis results in detectable human antibodies reactive to mitochondrial antigens characteristic of PBC and signs of biliary pathology [12]. In conclusion, the loss of both T and B lymphocyte function in the SCID mouse provides a unique system for studying resistance to a variety of infections and the exciting potential of studying human immune responses in an experimental host.

ACKNOWLEDGMENT

This work was supported by grants from the National Institutes of Health, Eli Lilly Research Laboratories, Monsanto Company, Genentech Inc and the Wellcome Trust.

REFERENCES

(1) Schultz LD, Sidman CL. Genetically determined murine models of immunodeficiency. *Ann Rev Immunol* 1987; **5**: 367–80.

(2) Bosma GC, Custer RP, Bosma MJ. A severe combined immunodeficiency mutation in the mouse. *Nature* 1983; **301**: 527–9.

(3) Schuler W. The scid mouse mutant: biology and nature of the defect. In: Sorg C, ed. *Molecular biology of B cell developments. Cytokines.* Karger: Basel, 1990; vol 3: 132–53.

(4) Bancroft GJ, Bosma MJ, Bosma GC, Unanue ER. Regulation of macrophage Ia expression in mice with severe combined immunodeficiency: induction of Ia expression by a T cell independent mechanism. *J Immunol* 1986; **137**: 4–9.

(5) Bancroft GJ, Schreiber RD, Bosma GC, Bosma MJ, Unanue ER. A T cell independent mechanism of macrophage activation by interferon gamma. *J Immunol* 1987; **139**: 1104–6.

(6) Bancroft GJ, Sheehan KCF, Schreiber RD, Unanue ER. Tumor necrosis factor is involved in the T cell independent pathway of macrophage activation in scid mice. *J Immunol* 1989; **143**: 127–30.

(7) Harmsen AG and Stankiewicz M. Requirement for CD4+ cells in resistance to Pneumocystis carinii pneumonia in mice. *J Exp Med* 1990; **172**: 937–45.

(8) Mosier DE, Gulizia RJ, Baird SM, Wilson DB. Transfer of a functional human immune system to mice with severe combined immunodeficiency. *Nature* 1988; **335**: 256–9.

(9) McCune JM, Namikawa R, Kaneshima H, Shultz LD, Lieberman M, Weissman IL. The SCID-hu mouse: murine model for the analysis of human haematolymphoid differentiation and function. *Science* 1988; **241**: 1632–39.

(10) McCune JM, Namikawa R, Shih CC, Rabin L, Kaneshima H. Suppression of HIV infection in AZT-treated SCID-hu mice. *Science* 1990; **247**: 564–6.

(11) Cannon MJ, Pisa P, Fox RI, Cooper NR. Epstein-Barr virus induces aggressive lymphoproliferative disorders of human B cell origin in scid/hu chimeric mice. *J Clin Invest* 1990; **85**: 1333–7.

(12) Krams SM, Dorschkind K, Gershwin ME. Generation of biliary lesions after transfer of human lymphocytes into severe combined immunodeficient (scid) mice. *J Exp Med* 1989; **170**: 1919–30.

Fine mapping the ataxia-telangiectasia gene complex to a 4 cM region at chromosome 11q23

R. A. Gatti

University of California at Los Angeles, Department of Pathology, Los Angeles, CA, USA

In 1988, we localized the gene for ataxia-telangiectasia (AT) Group A to chromosome 11q22–23 [1] by linking it to two genetic markers, THY1 and pYNB3.12 (now called D11S144) using eight families with Group A AT. We further noted that the statistical significance of our linkage data was actually strengthened when we included all AT families, regardless of complementation groups. This suggested either that the genes for the other complementation groups (groups C, D, E and V1) were linked to this same region or that Group A was far more common than the 55% found by Jaspers *et al.* [2]. The AT Group A gene was most probably located centromeric to the two markers, THY1 and D11S144, and not in between them (a distance of approximately 10 cM). The results were analysed using the linkage analysis computer package MENDEL, developed by Lange and colleagues [3]. Progress since 1988 is reviewed below.

In order to localize the AT gene(s) to a region small enough to clone, it has been necessary to develop a higher resolution map of the 11q22–23 region. This is being accomplished using not the AT families but instead the families established by a Paris-based consortium CEPH [4]. The CEPH families are ideal for linkage mapping because they include many children and, often all four grandparents. Many laboratories contribute new genetic markers to the CEPH database, allowing each new marker to be mapped with regard to all previously existing ones [5–7]. Table 1 lists the genetic markers in the 11q22–23 region that were tested on the 40 CEPH families. These experiments involved making Southern blots with the appropriate restriction enzymes. In some cases, such as for CD3 and ETS-1, probes for functional genes were obtained and screened for polymorphism by testing against DNAs of racially diverse individuals that had been digested with eight enzymes [7–11]. Polymorphic probe/enzyme combinations were then tested on all informative CEPH families.

The order of the various DNA polymorphisms on chromosome 11q22–23 was further clarified by testing two somatic cell hybrids containing derivative human chromosomes 11. These hybrids, '11;X' and '4;11', established whether each of the markers we used was proximal or distal to their respective breakpoints [12]. Figure 1 shows a map of the 11q22–23 region based on our studies of the CEPH families and the hybrid cell lines.

Progress in immune deficiency III, edited by H. M. Chapel, R. J. Levinsky and A. D. B. Webster, 1991; Royal Society of Medicine Services International Congress and Symposium Series No. 173, published by Royal Society of Medicine Services Limited.

Table 1 *Polymorphic loci in chromosome region 11q22–23*

Locus (probe)	Enzyme	Allele size (kb)	Allele frequency	Observed hetero-zygosity	Individuals typed
CD20 (p81–21A–29)	MspI	9.0	0.43	0.31	413
		6.0	0.57		
TYR (pmel 34)	TaqI	2.8	0.42	0.58	226
		2.0	0.42		
		2.4	0.16		
D11S84 (p2–7–1D6)	TaqI	6.4	0.24	0.40	661
		4.3	0.76		
CJ.75M1 (S385)	MspI	5.5	0.87	0.17	755
		3.5, 2.0	0.13		
STMY (psp 64)	TaqI	4.6	0.54	0.46	453
		2.1, 1.0	0.46		
D11S132 (CRI–L424)	haplotype		0.58	0.58	372
			0.30		
			0.06		
			0.06		
DRD2 (HD2G1)	TaqI	6.6	0.11	0.24	265
		3.7, 2.9	0.89		
CJ52.208 (D11S351)	haplotype		0.58	0.52	644
			0.36		
			0.05		
D11S144 (MCT128.1)	MspI	2.9	0.53	0.56	619
		2.6	0.47		
APO (apolipoprotein)	haplotype		0.55	0.82	491
			0.28		
			0.17		
D11S29 (L7)	TaqI	10.9	0.79	0.30	322
		13.9	0.21		
CD3	haplotype		0.62	0.54	412
			0.29		
			0.08		
PBGD (pUSE109)	MspI	3.0	0.43	0.52	683
		2.2	0.57		
THY1 (pcr502–505)	MspI	0.9	0.28	0.45	447
		0.8	0.72		
D11S133/D11S138 (CRI-L451/CRI-R548)	haplotype		0.70	0.53	199
			0.20		
			0.05		
			0.05		
D11S147 (HBI18P1)	MspI	5.2	0.43	0.48	585
		4.8	0.57		
ETS1	haplotype		0.62	0.57	396
			0.36		
			0.02		
D11S83	MspI	4.3	0.22	0.49	240
		3.2, 1.1	0.78		

Using the same probe/enzyme combinations, we then returned to an analysis of the AT families. By three-point mapping, we were able to exclude the AT gene(s) from the region distal to THY1 [7,13]. By trisecting the 10 cM region between THY1 and D11S144 with a trio of markers at the CD3 complex (CD3G, CD3D and CD3E) and the more proximal S29 marker, we excluded the AT gene(s) from

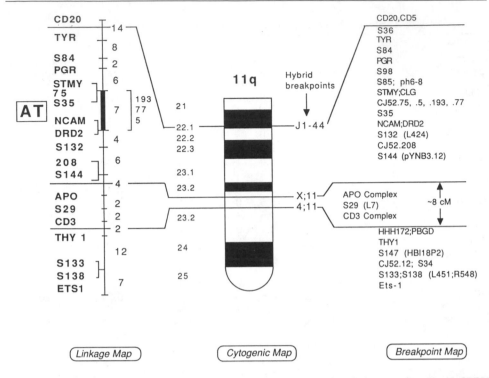

Figure 1 *Maps of the human chromosome 11q22–23 region, based on linkage analyses in 40 CEPH families (left) and breakpoints of three somatic cell hybrids (right). Distances shown are sex-averaged. The AT locus is confined to a 7 cM region flanked proximally by STMY, CJ75 and S35, and distally by NCAM and DRD2.*

each of the segments defined by these markers as well [13]. We localized the gene(s) to the region between STMY and D11S144.

The distance between STMY and D11S144 was originally estimated as 31 cM. When additional markers were characterized in the region, this distance decreased to 17 cM (sex averaged). Three-point location scores excluded the AT gene(s) from the intervals between D11S144 and DRD2, D11S144 and NCAM, CJ208 and DRD2 and CJ208 and NCAM. They also excluded the AT gene(s) from the region centromeric to STMY. They localized it to the 7 cM (sex averaged) region flanked centromerically by STMY and CJ75 and telomerically by NCAM and DRD2. The marker D11S132 (formerly called L424) further confirmed this localization. By pulsed field gel analysis, S132 is located very near to the NCAM gene. Thus, the AT gene(s) is flanked by two genetic markers proximally, STMY and CJ75, and by at least two markers distally, NCAM and DRD2 [14].

The distances shown in Fig. 1 are based on the *average* of male and female recombination fractions. Reports by Leppert *et al.* [15] and Gatti *et al.* [16] suggest a 2 : 1 female : male distance ratio for this region of the genome, further decreasing the estimated male-specific distance between STMY/CJ75 and NCAM/DRD2 to 4.5 cM.

The resolution of linkage analysis can be improved by increasing the number of meioses characterized. However, this presents a serious challenge to the capability of most computer programs for linkage analysis since disease-affected families are usually less than ideal, with key members often unavailable for genetic testing. To circumvent this problem we have both improved the efficiency of our computer analyses and added additional families to the AT database [14]. Five centres have contributed to the 132 families included in the Los Angeles-based International AT Consortium.

An Israeli pedigree, known to be complementation group C, has shown significant linkage to the same 11q23 probes as those that link to Group A [17]. Recently, Komatsu et al. [18] have corrected the radiosensitivity of a fibroblast stain from a Group D AT patient by fusing it with a hybrid cell containing a normal human chromosome 11. Taken together, these data strongly suggest that the genes for Groups C and D also link to 11q23. Together, Groups A, C and D account for 97% of all tested AT families.

REFERENCES

(1) Gatti RA, Berkel I, Boder E, et al. Localization of an ataxia-telangiectasia gene to chromosome 11q22–23. Nature 1988; 336: 577–80.

(2) Jaspers NGJ, Gatti RA, Baan C, Linssen PCML, Bootsma D. Genetic complementation analysis of ataxia-telangiectasia and Nijmegen breakage syndrome: a survey of 50 patients. Cytogenet Cell Genet 1988; 49: 259–63.

(3) Lange K, Weeks DE, Boehnke M. Programs for pedigree analysis: MENDEL, FISHER and dGENE. Genet Epidem 1988; 5: 471–2.

(4) Dausset J, Cann H, Cohen D, Lathrop M, Lalouel J-M, White R. Centre d'Etude du Polymorphisme Humain (CEPH): Collaborative genetic mapping of the human genome. Genomics 1990; 6: 575–7.

(5) Charmley P, Foroud T, Wei S, et al. A primary linkage map of the human chromosome 11q22–23 region. Genomics 1990; 6: 316–23.

(6) Julier C, Nakamura Y, Lathrop M, et al. A detailed genetic map of the long arm of chromosome 11. Genomics 1990; 7: 335–45.

(7) Concannon P, Malhotra U, Charmley P, Reynolds J, Lange K, Gatti RA. Ataxia-telangiectasia gene (ATA) on chromosome 11 is distinct from the ETS-1 gene. Am J Hum Genet 1990; 46: 789–94.

(8) Charmley P, Wei S, Sanal O, et al. Human T-cell receptor CD3-gamma (CD3G)/MspI DNA polymorphism. Nucleic Acids Res 1989; 17: 2372.

(9) Charmley P, Sanal O, Wei S, Chou A, Terhorst C, Gatti RA. Human T-cell receptor CD3-epsilon (CD3E)/TaqI DNA polymorphism. Nucleic Acids Res 1989; 17: 2374.

(10) Malhotra U, Concannon P. Human T-cell receptor CD3-delta (CD3D)/MspI DNA polymorphism. Nucleic Acids Res 1989; 17: 2373.

(11) Mietus-Snyder M, Charmley P, Korf B, Ladias JAA, Gatti RA, Karathanasis SK. Genetic linkage of the human apolipoprotein AI-CIII-AIV gene cluster and the neural cell adhesion molecule (NCAM) gene. Genomics 1990; 7: 633–7.

(12) Wei S, Rocchi M, Archidiacono N, Sacchi N, Romeo G, Gatti RA. Physical mapping of the human chromosome 11q23 region containing the ataxia-telangiectasia locus. Cancer Genet Cytogenet 1990; 46: 1–8.

(13) Sanal O, Wei S, Foroud T, et al. Further mapping of an ataxia-telangiectasia locus to the chromosome 11q23 region. Am J Hum Genet 1990; 47: 860–6.

(14) Foroud T, Wei S, Ziv Y, et al. Localization of the AT locus to an 8 cM interval defined by STMY and S132. Am J Hum Genet (submitted).

(15) Leppert M, O'Connell P, Nakamura Y, et al. A partial primary genetic linkage map of chromosome 11. Cytogenet Cell Genet 1987; 46: 648.

(16) Gatti RA, Lathrop GM, Salser W, et al. Location of Thy-1 with respect to a primary linkage map of chromosome 11q. Cytogenet Cell Genet 1987; 46: 618.

(17) Ziv Y, Rotman G, Frydman M, et al. The ataxia-telangiectasia (Group C) locus localizes to 11q22–23. Genomics (in press).

(18) Komatsu K, Kodama S, Okumura Y, Oshimura M. Restoration of radiation resistance in ataxia-telangiectasia cells by the introduction of normal human chromosome 11. Mutation Res 1990; 235: 59–63.

Bromodeoxyuridine-induced SCE in ataxia-telangiectasia heterozygous lymphocytes

A. L. Pawlak[1] and R. Ignatowicz[2]

[1]Institute of Genetics, Polish Academy of Sciences, Poznań and
[2]Centre for Child Health, Warsaw, Poland

(POSTER)

Normal frequency of sister chromatid exchanges (SCEs) was found in lymphocytes of AT patients [1]. Genotoxic agents effective in inducing chromosomal aberrations in AT cells induced SCE to the same extent in AT and in normal cells [2]. The agents used in these studies (X-rays, ethylmethanesulphonate, adriamycin) were, however, not typical inducers of SCEs. Bromodeoxyuridine (BrdU) is known to induce SCEs [3] and its effects were characterized in human lymphocyte cultures [4]. Therefore, we studied the sensitivity of AT heterozygous cells to induction of SCE by BrdU.

MATERIALS AND METHODS

Frequencies of SCE were studied in mitogen-stimulated lymphocytes of whole blood cultures from obligatory heterozygotes of AT ($n=3$) and control persons ($n=5$), as described [4] at BrdU concentrations 2.5 and 25.0 μg/ml.

RESULTS AND DISCUSSION

An increased frequency of SCE was found at higher concentrations of BrdU in both groups. The increase was, however, smaller in AT-heterozygous lymphocytes ($+2.64$), as compared with that in the controls ($+6.81$). This difference was found mainly in the number of cells with the highest frequency of SCE (high frequency cells (HFC), SCE $\geqslant 16$). The number of HFC was significantly higher in high-BrdU control cultures (43.8%) as compared with that in low-BrdU control cultures (2.4%) and high-BrdU AT-heterozygous cultures (7.8%). The BrdU-induced increase in the percentage value of HFC was significantly smaller in AT-heterozygotes ($+1.9$) compared with that in control cultures ($+41.4$). Different responses to BrdU may be displayed by lymphocytes differing in intracellular nucleotide pools, proliferation kinetics and/or requirements for minimal BrdU concentration for sister chromatid differentiation [5]. It is suggested that the relative deficiency in AT-heterozygous persons of cells displaying high frequency of SCE in high BrdU cultures may be due to a lower content of a specific population of lymphocytes. Low inducibility of HFC (SCE $\geqslant 16$) can be considered as a criterion for diagnosis of heterozygotes of AT.

REFERENCES

(1) Taylor AMR. Cytogenetics of ataxia-telangiectasia. In: Bridges BA, Harnden DG, eds. *Ataxia-telangiectasia. A cellular and molecular link between cancer, neuropathology, and immune deficiency.* Chichester: J Wiley & Sons, 1982: 53–81.
(2) Galloway SM. Ataxia-telangiectasia: the effects of chemical mutagens and X-rays on sister chromatid exchanges in blood lymphocytes. *Mutation Res* 1977; **45**: 343–9.
(3) Zwanenburg TSB, van Zeeland AA, Natarajan AT. Influence of incorporated bromo-deoxyuridine on the induction of chromosomal alterations by ionizing radiation and long-wave UV in CHO cells. *Mutation Res* 1985; **150**: 283–92.
(4) Kotecki M, Pawlak AL. Estimation of BrdUrd-independent sister chromatid exchanges and proliferation rate of human lymphocytes *in vitro*. *Bull Polish Acad Sci (Ser Sci Biol)* 1989: **38**: 243–7.
(5) Das BC. Factors that influence formation of sister chromatid exchanges in human blood lymphocytes. *Crit Rev Toxicol* 1988; **19**: 43–86.

Progress in immune deficiency III, edited by H. M. Chapel, R. J. Levinsky and A. D. B. Webster, 1991; Royal Society of Medicine Services International Congress and Symposium Series No. 173, published by Royal Society of Medicine Services Limited.

Ataxia-telangiectasia presenting as hyper IgM syndrome

O. Sanal, F. Ersoy, I. Tezcan, S. Gögüs

Hacettepe Children's Hospital, Ankara, Turkey

(POSTER)

INTRODUCTION

The hyper IgM syndrome is a primary immunodeficiency disease characterized by very low or absent IgG and IgA, with normal or elevated IgM levels. Associated T cell abnormalities have been reported [1,2]. Thymus atrophy with decreased or absent Hassall's corpuscles has also been reported in some patients [3].

The most common humoral immune defect in patients with ataxia-telangiectasia (AT) is diminished or absent serum IgA, IgE and IgG2 and the presence of low molecular weight serum IgM [4]. Decreased IgG or IgG, IgM and IgA or IgG and IgA have also been reported [5]. The thymus shows various abnormalities; in some cases it is atrophic, in others it is hypoplastic with absence of Hassall's corpuscles and corticomedullary differentiation [5]. Lymphoid tissue is variably hypoplastic. Pathological studies of the central nervous system (CNS) reveal a loss of the Purkinje cell and granular cell layer in the cerebellum [6].

CASE REPORT

The patient was admitted to hospital at the age of 26 months with frequent pulmonary infections, recurrent otitis and diarrhoea since the early months of age. On physical examination he had growth retardation (height and weight were below the fifth percentile) and otitis. The immunological findings are shown in Table 1.

Since the clinical history and immunological findings were compatible with hyper IgM syndrome, gammaglobulin was given monthly and he did well.

During follow up he developed bulbar telangiectasia and ataxia around the age of 4–5 years and alpha-feto protein (AFP) was found to be high.

FAMILY HISTORY

The patient is the product of the sixth pregnancy of parents who are first degree relatives.

The first child (male) was hospitalized at the age of 16 months with frequent infections and chronic diarrhoea. He had severe malnutrition along with pneumonia and gastroenteritis. The serum IgG was 150 mg/dl, IgM 27 mg/dl, and IgA undetectable. Delayed type skin tests were negative. He died on the fifth hospital day. *Post mortem* examination revealed the presence of pneumonia, meningitis and gastroenteritis. The thymus showed severe atrophy suggesting dysplasia or dysinvolution with very few, and calcified, Hassall's corpuscles and the secondary lymphoid tissues showed severe lymphoid depletion. The spleen lacked lymphoid follicles and periarteriolar lymphoid sheets. Mesenteric lymph nodes showed lymphoid depletion in the cortical and paracortical areas. Lymphoid follicles were devoid of germinal centres in the intestine. The cerebellum did not show any noticeable pathology with haematoxylin and eosin (Bielschowsky staining was not performed).

The second child (female) died at the age of one week. The third, fourth, fifth and seventh pregnancies terminated by spontaneous abortion. The eighth child is an eight-month old boy whose physical examination and serum immunoglobulin levels are normal. AFP level was 49 ng/ml at the age of three months.

Progress in immune deficiency III, edited by H. M. Chapel, R. J. Levinsky and A. D. B. Webster, 1991; Royal Society of Medicine Services International Congress and Symposium Series No. 173, published by Royal Society of Medicine Services Limited.

Table 1 *Immunological findings*

Serum Igs (mg/dl)				
IgG	IgM	IgA	IgD (iu/ml)	IgE
100–110	290–402	0[+]	0[+]	NT[++]

Isohaemagglutinin titres: Anti-A 1/1024, anti-B 1/1024

Lymphocytes positive for surface antigens (%)					
SIgG	SIgM	SIgA	CD3	CD4	CD8
8	11	0	78	27	41

In vitro response to PHA:
   80% of normal with high PHA concentration. 13% of normal with low PHA concentration

Delayed hypersensitivity skin tests:

PHA	Candida	SKSD	PPD
+	+	−	−

Lymph node biopsy, obtained after antigenic stimulation, revealed severe lymphoid depletion. Aggregates of lymphocytes in cortical and paracortical areas without follicle formation; germinal centres were observed.

+Undetectable
++Not tested

DISCUSSION

When first evaluated the clinical presentation and the laboratory findings of the patient were found to be compatible with hyper IgM syndrome and he did well on gammaglobulin therapy. At the age of 4–5 years he developed ataxia and telangiectasia and AFP was found to be high.

Severe lymphoid depletion observed at *post mortem* examination of his brother who had panhypogammaglobulinaemia and severe malnutrition was compatible both with severe combined immunodeficiency (SCID) or malnutrition [7]. When the clinical and laboratory features of the propositus are taken into consideration, these findings may also be attributed to hyper IgM syndrome or AT [3–5]. He did not have any noticeable cerebellar pathology with haemotoxylin and eosin staining (Bielschowsky staining was not performed). Thus the histopathological findings in his brother were not helpful for the definitive diagnosis of AT.

The patient seems interesting in respect of the findings in the first 3–4 years which were compatible with hyper IgM syndrome, his sibling history and the development of the classical AT phenotype.

REFERENCES

(1) Ochs HD, Wedgwood RJ. Disorders of the B cell system. In: Stiehm ER, ed. *Immunologic disorders in infants and children*. Philadelphia: WB Saunders, 1989: 226–56.
(2) Fiorilli , Russo G, Paganelli R, *et al.* Hypogammaglobulinemia with hyper IgM, severe T-cell defect, and abnormal recirculation of OKT4 lymphocytes in a girl with lymphadenopathy. *Clin Immunol Immunopathol* 1986; **38**: 256–64.
(3) Hong R, Schubert WK, Perrin EV, West CD. Antibody deficiency syndrome associated with beta-2 macroglobulinemia. *J Pediatr* 1962; **61**: 831–42.
(4) Boder E. Ataxia-telangiectasia. An overview. In: Gatti RA, Swifth M, eds. *Ataxia telangiectasia: Genetics, neuropathology, and immunology of a degenerative disease of childhood*. Vol. 19. New York: Alan R. Liss, 1985: 1–63.
(5) Peterson RDA, Cooper MC, Good RA. Lymphoid tissue abnormalities associated with ataxia-telangiectasia. *Am J Med* 1966; **41**: 342–59.
(6) Gatti RA, Vinters HV. Cerebellar pathology in ataxia telangiectasia: The significance of basket cells. In: Gatti RA, Swifth M, eds. *Ataxia-telangiectasia: Genetics, neuropathology, and immunology of a degenerative disease of childhood*. Vol. 19. New York: Alan R. Liss, 1985: 225–32.
(7) Gosseye S, Diebold N, Griscelli C, Nezelof C. Severe combined immunodeficiency diseases: A pathological analysis of 26 cases. *Clin Immunol Immunopathol* 1983; **29**: 58–77.

T cell receptor $\gamma\delta$ expression in healthy children and children with ataxia telangiectasia

J. J. M. Van Dongen[1], R. de Groot[2], W. M. Comans-Bitter[1,2], H. J. Neijens[2]

[1]Department of Immunology, Erasmus University/University Hospital Dijkzigt, Rotterdam, and
[2]Department of Paediatrics, Sophia Children's Hospital, Rotterdam, The Netherlands

(POSTER)

Two types of T cell receptors (TcR) have been described, the classical TcR-$\alpha\beta$ and the alternative TcR-$\gamma\delta$ [1–3]. Double immunofluorescence (IF) staining analyses of a series of blood samples ($n=92$) from healthy children (0–16 yr) revealed that 85–99% of the CD3$^+$ T lymphocytes expressed TcR-$\alpha\beta$, whereas only 1–15% expressed TcR-$\gamma\delta$. The relative distributions of TcR-$\alpha\beta$ and TcR-$\gamma\delta$ expression appeared to be age-dependent: in children younger than two years old ($n=38$) the $\gamma\delta/\alpha\beta$ ratio was <0.1, while in older children (2–16 yr) ($n=54$) the ratio was <0.2 (Table 1). Additional double IF stainings on 33 blood samples from healthy individuals (>2 yr) demonstrated that a small fraction of the TcR-$\gamma\delta^+$ cells ($1.2\pm3.3\%$) expressed the CD4 molecule and that a larger fraction ($6.9\pm5.8\%$) expressed the CD8 molecule. This implies that TcR-$\gamma\delta^+$ cells cannot be defined as CD3$^+$/CD4$^-$/CD8$^-$ T lymphocytes.

Table 1 *TcR-$\alpha\beta$ and TcR $\gamma\delta$ expression by blood T lymphocytes in healthy children and AT patients*

	Healthy children			AT patients		
	0–2 years ($n=38$)	2–8 years ($n=34$)	8–16 years ($n=20$)	J.B. 5 years	N.B. 10 years	I.D. 10 years
% CD3$^+$ T lymphocytes[a]	60 ± 12	61 ± 8	60 ± 11	27	19	47
(absolute numbers $\times10^9$/l)	(3.7 ± 1.7)	(2.5 ± 1.3)	(1.5 ± 0.6)	(0.34)	(0.32)	(1.1)
% TcR-$\alpha\beta$ per CD3$^+$ cells[b]	95 ± 4	90 ± 6	90 ± 9	88	94	75
% TcR-$\gamma\delta^+$ per CD3$^+$ cells[b]	4 ± 3	8 ± 5	7 ± 6	9	7	21
$\gamma\delta/\alpha\beta$ ratio	0.04 ± 0.03	0.10 ± 0.07	0.08 ± 0.08	0.1	0.07	0.28

[a]Percentages per mononuclear cells after ficoll (1.077 g/ml) density centrifugation.
[b]The frequency of TcR-$\alpha\beta^+$ and TcR-$\gamma\delta^+$ cells within the CD3$^+$ lymphocyte population was determined by use of double IF stainings [3,4]

In some immunodeficiency diseases with decreased numbers of blood T lymphocytes and/or decreased T cell function, relative high frequencies of TcR-$\gamma\delta^+$ T lymphocytes have been found [5,6]. In a patient with complete DiGeorge anomaly the $\gamma\delta/\alpha\beta$ ratio appeared to be >25 [6]. Recently it was reported that most patients with ataxia telangiectasia (AT) have a relative increase of TcR-$\gamma\delta^+$ cells, since in seven out of 10 AT patients the $\gamma\delta/\alpha\beta$ ratio was higher than in a control group [7]. All 10 AT patients were older than two years and the control values in the study were derived from only 14 individuals (without mentioning their age). Based on our control values only four out of the 10 AT patients had an increased $\gamma\delta/\alpha\beta$ ratio (>0.2).

Progress in immune deficiency III, edited by H. M. Chapel, R. J. Levinsky and A. D. B. Webster, 1991; Royal Society of Medicine Services International Congress and Symposium Series No. 173, published by Royal Society of Medicine Services Limited.

We studied three AT patients and found that in only one patient the $\gamma\delta/\alpha\beta$ ratio was increased to 0.28. This 10-year-old patient had normal percentages and absolute numbers of T lymphocytes. In the other two AT patients (five years and 10 years old) normal $\gamma\delta/\alpha\beta$ ratios were found. These two patients had decreased percentages and absolute numbers of T lymphocytes ($<0.4\times10^9$/l) (Table 1), as well as decreased T cell function as determined in lymphocyte proliferation assays (results not shown).

Our data indicate that one should be careful with the interpretation of $\gamma\delta/\alpha\beta$ ratios, if no appropriate normal values are available. Furthermore our data indicate that there is no direct relationship between an increase of $\gamma\delta/\alpha\beta$ ratios and decrease of blood T lymphocytes or T cell function in AT patients. It is questionable whether $\gamma\delta/\alpha\beta$ ratios as such are informative at all. We hope that the era of B/T ratios and the era of CD4/CD8 ratios will not be followed by a period in which an overwhelming series of publications about $\gamma\delta/\alpha\beta$ imbalances in all kinds of disease states. It would be more appropriate to determine absolute numbers of T lymphocytes and to study T cell function and, if possible, T cell specificity in order to obtain information about the status of the T cell immune system.

REFERENCES

(1) Strominger JL. Developmental biology of T cell receptors. *Science* 1989; **244**: 943–50.
(2) Matsunaga T, Dahl U. What was wrong with the T-cell receptor γ/δ heterodimer? Divergence of the T-cell receptor α/β and γ/δ heterodimers. *Scand J Immunol* 1989; **30**: 511–7.
(3) Borst J, Wicherink A. Van Dongen JJM, De Vries E, Comans-Bitter WM, Wassenaar F, Van Den Elsen P. Non-random expression of T cell receptor γ and δ variable gene segments in functional T lymphocyte clones from human peripheral blood. *Eur J Immunol* 1989; **19**: 1559–68.
(4) Van Dongen JJM, Adriaansen HJ, Hooijkaas H. Immunological marker analysis of cells in the various hematopoietic differentiation stages and their malignant counterparts. In: Ruiter DJ, Fleuren GJ, Warnaar SO, eds. *Application of monoclonal antibodies in tumor pathology*. Dordrecht: Martinus Nijhoff Publishers, 1987: 87–116.
(5) Borst J, Van Dongen JJM, De Vries E, Comans-Bitter WM, Van Tol MJD, Vossen JM, Kurrle R. BMA031, a monoclonal antibody specifically suited to identify the T cell receptor $\alpha\beta$/CD3 complex on viable human T lymphocytes in normal and disease states. *Hum Immunol* 1990; **29**: 175–88.
(6) Van Dongen JJM, Comans-Bitter WM, Friedrich W, *et al.* Expression of T cell receptor (TcR)-$\alpha\beta$ and TcR-$\gamma\delta$ in healthy and immunodeficient children: Evidence for peripheral expansion of TcR-$\gamma\delta^+$ T lymphocytes. Manuscript submitted.
(7) Carbonari M, Cherchi M, Paganelli R, *et al.* Relative increase of T cells expressing the gamma/delta rather than the alpha/beta receptor in ataxia-telangiectasia. *N Engl J Med* 1990; **322**: 73–6.

Abnormal biosynthesis, processing and membrane expression of the TCR/CD3 complex in an immunodeficient child

G. Thoenes, C. Soudais, F. LeDeist, C. Griscelli, A. Fischer and B. Lisowska-Grospierre

Hôpital Necker-Enfants-Malades, Laboratoire d'Immunologie et de Rhumatologie pédiatriques, Paris, France

Among T lymphocyte membrane antigens, the T cell receptor for antigens (TCR) is the crucial one for all antigen-specific responses. Normal membrane expression of the T cell receptor depends on coordinated synthesis of all seven proteins composing the complex, the TCR α and β chains, the CD3 γ, δ, and ϵ chains, and the ζ homodimer. A protein of 28 kD (ω) is expressed only intracellularly and associated with the different chains during the processing of the complex. In several experimental TCR membrane defective mutants [1] and in one patient whose lymphocytes express only a low level of the TCR/CD3 complex [2], a defect in ζ chain synthesis and/or association is thought to explain the defective membrane synthesis of the whole complex.

We report another immunodeficient patient presenting a different type from the one already described [2]. His T cells express the TCR complex only at one-tenth of normal fluorescence intensity, but such cells are found in peripheral blood almost in normal numbers. Although their *in vivo* and *in vitro* functions are severely impaired, the patient's T cell defect is partial. Most striking is the finding of conserved proliferative responses of the patient's peripheral blood lymphocytes (PBL) to *Tetanus toxoid* and to *Candida albicans* antigens *in vitro*, as if some antigen recognition could take place. This alone speaks in favour of presence on the patient's lymphocytes of some T cell receptors, leading to the question as to what structural differences the abnormally expressed (but partially functioning) receptors could have.

Analysis of the surface iodinated patient's PBL failed to detect the TCR α, β and the CD3 γ, δ and ϵ proteins but revealed the presence of the ζ homodimer (Fig. 1).

In the metabolically labelled patient's cells, the TCR α and β chains were detected (apparently not S–S bound) but only traces of the CD3 γ, δ and ϵ could be precipitated together with p28 chain (Fig. 2).

The patient's PBL have an abnormally high level of natural killer (NK) cells (38%). Since the NK cells were shown to synthesize ζ chain in the absence of other

Progress in immune deficiency III, edited by H. M. Chapel, R. J. Levinsky and A. D. B. Webster, 1991; Royal Society of Medicine Services International Congress and Symposium Series No. 173, published by Royal Society of Medicine Services Limited.

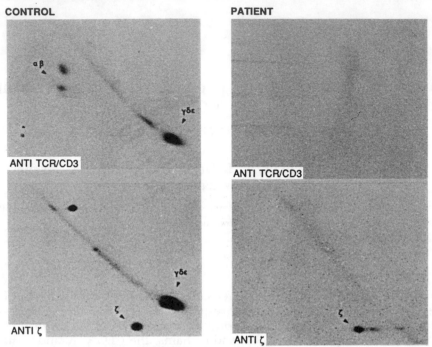

Figure 1   *2-D (NR/R) SDS-PAGE analysis of immunoprecipitated TCR/CD3 obtained with βF1 + Leu 4 mAbs of lysates from surface-iodinated cells.*

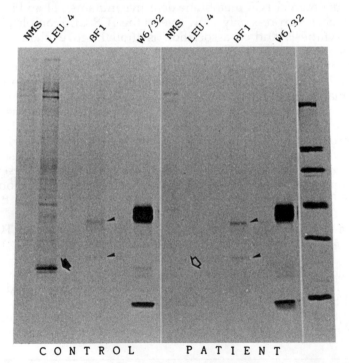

Figure 2   *Sodium dodecil sulphate PAGE analysis of precipitates obtained with normal mouse serum bF1: anti β TCR, Leu 4, anti-ε CD3, from the lysates of control and the patient's cells biosynthetically labelled with S-35 methionine for 60 min. ζ chain was normally detected (not shown).*

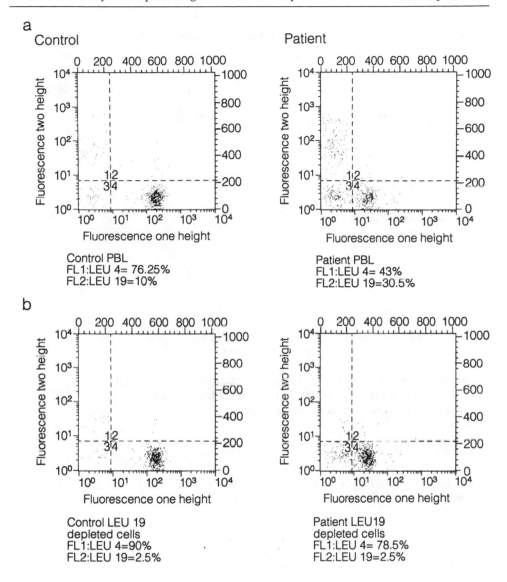

Figure 3 *FACS analysis of the patient's and control PBL before a) and after b) depletion of Leu 19+ cells.*

TCR components [3], it was essential to distinguish whether T or NK cells were synthesizing the ζ chain in the patient's PBL.

When the NK cells were eliminated from the patient's PBL, Western blot analysis of the lysate of Leu 19 depleted cells has shown that the patient's T cells do synthesize ζ chain, although in lower amounts (Figs. 3, 4).

The Northern blot analysis of the patient's mRNA has shown an important decrease of the CD3 δ gene transcripts, while the CD3 γ and ε mRNA were detected apparently at normal levels (not shown).

We believe that the patient we describe in this report presents a new type of T cell receptor/CD3 complex defect. The molecular basis underlying it could be

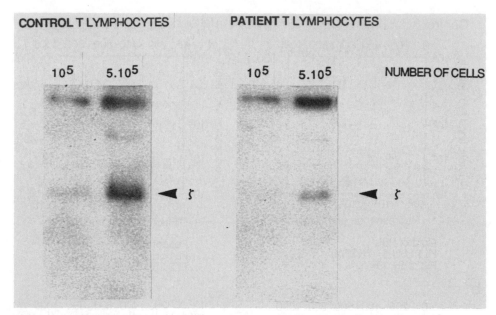

Figure 4 *Western blot analysis of the patient's Leu 19 depleted T cell lysates, rabbit anti ζ antibody revealed by I-125-Protein A was used to detect ζ chain.*

an abnormal expression of the CD3 δ gene, resulting in a defect in the CD3 γ, δ, ε assembly. Alternatively, a putative gene which controls in T cells the CD3 γ, δ, ε core assembly could be affected in this patient.

REFERENCES

(1) Sussman JL, Bonifacino JS, Lippincott-Schwartz J, *et al.* Failure to synthesize the T cell CD3-ζ chain: Structure and function of a partial T cell receptor complex. *Cell* 1988; **52**: 85–95.
(2) Alarcon B, Regueiro JR, Arnaiz-Villena A, Terhorst C. Familial defect in the surface expression of the T cell receptor-CD3 complex. *N Engl J Med* 1988; **319**: 1203–8.
(3) Anderson P, Caliguiri M, Ritz J, Schlossmann SF. CD3-negative natural killer cells express ζ TCR as part of a novel molecular complex. *Nature* 1989; **341**: 159.

Immunohistochemical analysis of lymphoid tissues in a T cell receptor (TCR) expression defect: a possible CD3γ abnormality

J. R. Regueiro[1,4], P. Perez-Aciego[1], C. Ballestin[2], T. Sotelo[2], C. Perez-Seoane[2], J. M. Martin-Villa[1] and A. Arnaiz-Villena[1,3]

Departments of [1]Immunology and [2]Pathology, Hospital 12 de Octubre, Madrid, [3]Department of Medicine, University of Alcalá, and [4]Department of Paediatrics, University of Valladolid, Spain

INTRODUCTION

The T lymphocyte $\alpha\beta$ antigen receptor (TCR) consists of a disulphide-linked heterodimer termed Ti$\alpha\beta$ or Ti$\gamma\delta$. Both are structurally and functionally associated with the monomorphic CD3 complex, which comprises the polypeptides γ, δ, ϵ and ζ [1]. It is believed that only mature complexes containing all TCR subunits are effectively exported to the cell surface, although detectable cell membrane levels of partial TCR complexes have been demonstrated in the absence of CD3ζ or normal Ti$\alpha\beta$ heterodimers [2]. We have previously reported a novel type of immunodeficiency in a patient who showed an impaired TCR expression by peripheral blood T lymphocytes [3]. The peripheral T cells of this individual (and of one of his siblings) contained in their cytoplasm a variant form of TCR which was not fully glycosylated and apparently lacked CD3ζ. As a consequence, little if any TCR reached the cell surface, and the T lymphocytes of both siblings were functionally inert. However, free CD3ζ chains were detectable, ruling out a direct involvement of CD3ζ in the disorder and pointing rather to an assembly defect. In the present work, we have tested the expression of different TCR chains (Ti$\alpha,\beta,\gamma,\delta$,CD3 γ,δ,ϵ) and of other leucocyte antigens on available autopsy lymphoid tissue obtained from the patient, in order to study the tissue distribution and the biochemical basis of the defect. Our results support the findings that CD3ϵ, CD3δ, Tiα and Tiβ are probably not involved in this type of immunodeficiency, and strongly suggest that CD3γ may rather be the affected chain giving rise to the mutant T cell phenotype.

METHODS

Tissues (spleen and lymph nodes) were obtained at autopsy from the patient and control individuals. Frozen sections, fixed in acetone, were stained with different polyclonal and monoclonal antibodies (moAbs, summarized in Table 1) using the Avidin-Biotin-Complex technique.

Progress in immune deficiency III, edited by H. M. Chapel, R. J. Levinsky and A. D. B. Webster, 1991; *Royal Society of Medicine Services International Congress and Symposium Series No. 173*, published by Royal Society of Medicine Services Limited.

RESULTS AND DISCUSSION

The lymph node and spleen sections were examined for the expression of several lymphoid antigens and TCR epitopes (Table 1). Within the observed lymphoid depletion, there were lymphocytes with a normal mature T cell phenotype in the patient's tissues (normal expression of CD2, CD4, CD8, CD11a, CD18, CD19 and CD57). The patient's lymph nodes showed occasional CD1$^+$ lymphocytes (completely absent in a control tissue). This may suggest that his thymus was 'leaky' as a result of abnormal T cell interactions through his TCR variant. HLA-DR antigens were slightly higher than controls in the patient's lymph nodes, probably due to the presence of histiocytic cells.

In the patient's tissues there were normal levels of expression for all tested CD3ϵ (Leu4, SP10, SP6, SP34), CD3δ (APA1.2, SP64) and clonotypic Tiα (αF1) and partially Tiβ (βF1) epitopes (Table 1). However the expression of the TCR epitopes recognized by OKT3 (CD3$\epsilon\delta + \epsilon\gamma$), TG5 (CD3$\gamma$), WT31 and BMA031 (framework

Table 1 *Immunostaining results on autopsy tissue*

			Expression score[b]			
			Spleen		Lymph node	
Antibody	Source[a]	CD-epitope	Control	Patient	Control	Patient
LEU6	BD	1	−	−	−	+
LEU5b	BD	2	+ + +	+ + +	+ + +	+ + +
LEU4	BD	3-ϵ	+ + +	+ + +	+ + +	+ + +
SP6	CT	3-ϵ	+ +	+ +	+ +	+
SP10	CT	3-ϵ	+ +	+ +	+ + +	+ +
SP34	CT	3-ϵ	+ + +	+ + +	+ + +	+ + +
APA1.2	SM	3-δ	+ +	+ +	+ +	+ +
SP64	CT	3-δ	+ + +	+ + +	+ +	+ + +
OKT3	O	3-$\gamma\epsilon + \delta\epsilon$	+ + +	+	+ + +	+
TG5	DA	3-γ	+ + +	−	+ + +	−
WT31	S	Ti-$\alpha + \beta$	+ + +	−	+ + +	+
BMA031	RK	Ti-$\alpha + \beta$	+ + +	−	+ + +	−
βF1	TC	Ti-β	+ + +	+ +	+ + +	+ +
αF1	TC	Ti-α	+ +	+ +	+ +	+ +
Tiγ/δ	c	Tiγ/δ	+	+	+	+
LEU3	BC	4	+ + +	+ + +	+ + +	+ + +
LEU2a	BD	8	+	+	ND	ND
TS1/11	SM	11a	+ +	+ + +	ND	+ +
TS1/18	SM	18	+ +	+ +	ND	ND
LEU12	BD	19	+ +	+ +	+ +	+ +
RIL2	CC	25	+	+	+	+
BERH2	D	30	−	−	+	+
LEU7	BD	57	−	−	+	+
OKT9	O	71	+ +	+	+ +	+
OKIa	O	HLA-DR	+ + +	+ + +	+ +	+ + +
DR	BD	HLA-DR	+ + +	+ + +	+ +	+ + +

[a] Origin of antibodies: **BD**, Becton Dickinson, CA, USA; **CT**, C. Terhorst, MA, USA; **SM**, F. Sanchez-Madrid, Spain; **O**, Ortho, NJ, USA; **S**, Sanbio, Holland; **RK**, R. Kurrle, FRG; **TH**, T. Hercend, France; **TC**, T cell Sciences, MA, USA; **CC**, Coulter Clone, FLO, USA; **D**, Dako, Denmark; **DA**, D. Alexander, UK.
[b] The semi-quantitative score for immunostaining levels (within the observed lymphoid depletion in the patient) was as follows: − absent, + present in low percentage, + + present in medium percentage, + + + present in high percentage, ND not determined.
[c] A mixture of MoAbs was used (TiγA, TH, plus TCRδ1, TC)

TCR) was severely diminished in both spleen and lymph node sections. The tissue distribution and expression of CD3γ,δ,ϵ and Tiα,β are coincidental in normal individuals [4]. Thus, the clear-cut differences in expression observed in our patient's tissues with some TCR-specific antibodies (notably TG5, OKT3, WT31, BMA031 and partially βF1, Table 1) demonstrate the presence of an abnormal TCR in this immunodeficiency. This abnormal TCR contained detectable CD3δ and ϵ chains, but it seemed to lack normal CD3γ. This chain is detected by TG5 (an antipeptide antiserum) and is involved in the epitope recognized by OKT3. WT31 and BMA031 recognize fully assembled and glycosylated TCR complexes [5], and are therefore unable to stain the abnormal TCR of this patient's T lymphocytes. βF1 clearly stains fewer cells in the patient than CD3ϵ- or δ-specific reagents, but more than OKT3, TG5, WT31 or BMA031. Therefore, Tiβ chains are present in the patient as confirmed by immunoprecipitation of peripheral blood lymphocytes [3]. The fact that αF1 shows normal staining patterns in the patient further supports that Tiα and β chains are probably not directly involved in the abnormal phenotype of these T lymphocytes. The lower expression of βF1 may be rather due to a partial loss of a conformational (glycosylation-dependent) epitope caused by the absence or abnormal structure of CD3γ. Therefore, in this immunodeficiency, normal Ti$\alpha\beta$ clonotypic molecules are probably synthesized and coupled to available CD3 proteins (CD3δ, CD3ϵ and CD3ζ) but a lack of normal CD3γ protein hinders the full CD3$\epsilon\delta\gamma\zeta$-Ti$\alpha\beta$ complex assembly. As a result, few, if any, mature assembled complexes are exported to the membrane. Residual surface expression of some TCR epitopes in a low number of peripheral T lymphocytes may be due to the presence of partial TCR complexes, as described by others [2]. This would explain all our previous phenotypic and functional results [3].

ACKNOWLEDGMENTS

We thank B. Alarcon, D. Alexander and C. Terhorst for sharing reagents and unpublished results, R. Gongora and M. D. de Juan for their technical help and J. Manzanares for referring the patient to us. This work was supported in part by FIS, CICYT and NATO grants.

REFERENCES

(1) Clevers H, Alarcon B, Wileman T, Terhorst C. The T cell receptor/CD3 complex: a dynamic protein ensemble. *Ann Rev Immunol* 1988; **6**: 629–62.
(2) Ley SC, Tan KN, Kubo R, Sy MS, Terhorst C. Surface expression of CD3 in the absence of T cell receptor: evidence for sorting of partial TCR/CD3 complexes in a post-ER compartment. *Eur J Immunol* 1990; **19**: 2309–17.
(3) Alarcon B, Regueiro JR, Arnaiz-Villena A, Terhorst C. Familial defect in the surface expression of the T-cell receptor-CD3 complex. *N Engl J Med* 1988; **319**: 1203–9.
(4) Pessano S, Oettgen H, Bhan AK, Terhorst C. The T3/T-cell receptor complex: antigenic distinction between the two 20 Kd T3 (T3-k and T3-n) subunits. *EMBO J* 1985; **4**: 337–44.
(5) Transy C, Moingeon P, Reinherz EL: Deletion of the cytoplasmic region of the CD3 epsilon subunit does not prevent assembly of a functional T-cell receptor. *Proc Natl Acad Sci USA 1989*; **86**: 7108–15.

Novel genetic immune deficiency with selective absence of thymic medullary epithelium and increased number of circulating T cells expressing γ-δT cell receptor. Correction by BMT

C. Koch[1], C. Geisler[2], G. Pallesen[4] and N. Jacobsen[3]

[1]Department of Pediatrics, [2]Tissue Typing Laboratory, [3]Department of Haematology, Risghospitalet, University of Copenhagen, [4]Laboratory of Immunohistology, Kommunehospitalet, University of Århus, Denmark

(POSTER)

CASE REPORT

An eight year old girl was followed from birth. Her older brother had died at the age of five from interstitial pneumonia and autopsy revealed absent thymus and general cellular depletion of lymphoid organs. Apart from a lobar pneumonia at four years, and period of cough with positive cultures of cytomegalovirus from urine, she developed normally with normal thorax CT scans. She was in good health at the time of bone marrow transplantation (BMT) at six years old.

Immunological findings were characterized by moderate lymphopenia, decreased serum IgA, and by gradual loss of proliferative lymphocyte responses to levels below 20% of normal. Analysis of T subsets revealed that only 24% of the CD3$^+$ cells carried the usual $\alpha\beta$T cell receptor (TCR), whereas 56% expressed $\gamma\delta$TCR (Table 1). These abnormal cells were all CD4$^-$ and their expression of CD8 and CD5 varied.

Thymic morphology and immunohistology showed poor differentiation with only a single Hassall's corpuscle. The most striking finding was the selective absence of almost all medullary epithelium [1].

BMT. In view of the fate of the brother, and the progressive loss of immune competence, the girl was transplanted with marrow from her one D locus mismatched mother. Following BMT, the lymphocyte counts are normal, the majority being of donor origin, and proliferative responses are now close to normal. The distribution of $\alpha\beta$TCR- and $\gamma\delta$TCR-carrying cells is normal.

Table 1 *Expression of cell surface molecules on lymphocytes isolated from peripheral blood before and after transplantation (3 months)*

Surface molecule	(Antibody)	Pre-BMT	Post-BMT	Normal range
CD2	(Anti-Leu-5)	85%	n.d.	73–90%
CD3	(Anti-Leu-4)	80%	86%	64–89%
$\alpha\beta$TCR	(WT-31)	24%	81%	50–81%
$\alpha\beta$TCR	(BMA-031)	24%	n.d.	54–80%
$\gamma\delta$TCR	(Anti-TCR-δ1)	56%	2%	1–10%
CD4	(Anti-Leu-3)	16%	16%	45–65%
CD8	(Anti-Leu-2)	36%	54%	21–35%
CD5	(Anti-Leu-1)	57%	n.d.	61–84%
CD16	(Anti-Leu-11)	8%	4%	3–15%
—	(Anti-Leu-7)	62%	58%	0–20%

TCR-δ1 was a kind gift from Dr M. B. Brenner (Dana-Farber Cancer Institute, Boston, USA)

Progress in immune deficiency III, edited by H. M. Chapel, R. J. Levinsky and A. D. B. Webster, 1991; Royal Society of Medicine Services International Congress and Symposium Series No. 173, published by Royal Society of Medicine Services Limited.

CONCLUSIONS

We have previously proposed that this novel syndrome may be a human analogue of the nude mouse syndrome [1]. It is of great clinical importance that immunological reconstitution could be achieved with BMT in spite of the marked thymic abnormalities, analogous to the situation in DiGeorge's syndrome [2].

REFERENCES

(1) Geisler C, Pallesen G, Platz P, *et al*. Novel primal thymic defect with T lymphocytes expressing γδT cell receptor. *J Clin Path* 1989; **42**: 705–11.
(2) Goldsobel AB, Haas A, Stiehm ER. Bone marrow transplantation in DiGeorge syndrome. *J Pediatr* 1987; **111**: 40–4.

A point-mutation in the TCR-α gene makes T cells naked

S. Caspar, E. Champagne, A. Huchenq, G. Geisler and B. Rubin

Laboratory of Cellular and Molecular Immunology CRPG-CNRS, CHU Purpan, Toulouse, France

(POSTER)

The T cell antigen receptor is composed of two variable chains (α and β, termed TCR), which confer ligand specificity, and four constant chains (γ, δ, ε and ζ, collectively termed CD3). The CD3 chains seem to be involved in cell surface expression of and signal transmission via the TCR-αβ dimer. We have used TCR/CD3 membrane negative variants of the human T cell tumour line Jurkat to explore the role of the individual TCR and CD3 components in TCR/CD3 biosynthesis, assembly, transport, membrane expression and biological function.

TCR/CD3 membrane negative Jurkat variants arose spontaneously or were induced by ethyl-methyl-sulphonate, methyl-nitro-nitrosoguanidine, or irradiation. Variant cells were isolated by immunoselection with anti-CD3 monoclonal antibody (mAb) and passage through immunoglobulin (Ig) anti-Ig coated columns followed by cloning using limiting dilution. Three different types of variants were used in the present study: 1) a TCR-α mRNA negative variant, 2) a TCR-β mRNA negative variant and 3) J79, a TCR/CD3 membrane negative clone, which produces all TCR/CD3 components (including CD3-ω chains).

Immunoprecipitation studies with anti-CD3 mAb showed that all possible TCR/CD3 proteins except CD3-ζ chains were easily detectable: in none of the three variant clones CD3-ζ chains were co-precipitated. In addition, the TCR-α or TCR-β chains remained in an immature glycosylated form, indicating that the TCR/CD3 chains in these variants stayed in the endoplasmic reticulum (RE). In contrast, immunoprecipitation with anti-CD3-ζ antiserum demonstrated that free CD3-ζ chains were synthesized and present in all three Jurkat variants. The conclusions from these experiments is that 1) TCR-β/CD3γ, δ, ε, 2) TCR-α/CD3γ, δ, ε and 3) TCR-α, β/CD3-γ, δ, ε complexes are arrested in the ER, possibly due to lack of interaction with CD3-ζ chains.

Further studies on J79 cells demonstrated that their TCR-α chains were about 1000 daltons heavier than the wild type Jurkat TCR-α chains, even when the TCR-α chains were deglycosylated enzymatically. Transfection of the mouse 2B4 TCR-α cDNA into J79 cells allowed membrane expression of the TCR/CD3 complex. The J79 TCR-α cDNA sequence showed one nucleotide exchange (T→G), which changes a Phe to a Val in position 195 of the TCR-Cα region. Based on our present data, we conclude that the interaction between CD3-ζ₂ homodimer and the TCR-α, β/CD3γ, δ, ε complex is dependent on both the presence of TCR-α, β dimeric structures and on an extracellular conformational epitope located in the constant region domain of the TCR-α chain.

The T→G nucleotide exchange also causes induction of a new restriction enzyme site. Further studies will show whether this mutation exists in the human population and in particular in immunodeficient patients with naked T cells.

Progress in immune deficiency III, edited by H. M. Chapel, R. J. Levinsky and A. D. B. Webster, 1991; *Royal Society of Medicine Services International Congress and Symposium Series No. 173*, published by Royal Society of Medicine Services Limited.

Immune haemolytic anaemia, thrombocytopenia and liver disease in a patient with DiGeorge syndrome

J. H. Passwell, O. Pinchas, M. Mandel and S. Engelberg

Department of Paediatrics, Sheba Medical Centre, Tel-Hashomer,
and Sackler School of Medicine, Tel-Aviv, Israel

(POSTER)

INTRODUCTION

The DiGeorge anomaly is now a well recognized spectrum of disease syndromes consequent on abnormal development of the third and fourth pharyngeal pouches [1]. The clinical syndromes manifest with characteristic dysmorphic facies, varying degrees of parathyroid and thymic hypofunction and congenital cardiac lesions, particularly of the aortic arch. Depending on the extent of these dysfunctions, partial and complete forms of the syndrome have been recognized [1,2].

The immunodeficiency of the thymic defect is variable and immune reconstitution by thymic hormone, thymus or bone marrow transplantation is only indicated in a small proportion of the patients [3,4,5]. In those patients who initially have moderate or normal T cell functions, late onset of cellular immunodeficiency is unlikely to occur. A single older patient with the DiGeorge anomaly, who developed autoimmune Graves disease, has been reported [6]. We report the development of autoimmune haemolytic anaemia, thrombocytopenia and chronic persistent hepatitis in a child with the DiGeorge syndrome.

MATERIALS AND METHODS

Case report

BS, a five-year-old female is the third child of non-related parents. Her siblings are healthy and there is no family history of primary immunodeficiency. She was first admitted at the age of 11 days with persistent convulsions due to hypocalcaemia (4.5 mg/dl).

Hypoparathyroidism was confirmed by a phosphorus level of 8.5 mg/dl, increased tubular reabsorption of phosphate (99%) and low parathormone concentration in the presence of hypocalcaemia (53 ng/dl [normal 50–250 ng/dl]). The diagnosis of DiGeorge syndrome was considered and subsequently confirmed by characteristic dysmorphic features of low set malformed ears, hypertelorism, micrognathia, short philtrum and resultant fish mouth. Aphonia was present at birth and persisted for 10 months. At present a distinct nasal quality of speech and unclear pronunciation of gutteral sounds is present. The vocal cords move normally on bronchoscope examination: No cardiac anomalies are present aside from a right sided aortic arch. A thymic shadow was not seen on chest X-ray and tests of cellular immune functions (Table 1) showed a normal mitogen-induced lymphocyte proliferative response, however CD1 positive lymphocytes were present in the peripheral blood and low numbers of lymphocytes with the CD8 phenotype were present, which accounted for an increased CD4/CD8 ratio.

Physical and psychomotor development have been normal. Speech therapy for her unusual speech defect and intensive dental therapy for severe caries are necessary.

This work was supported by a grant from the Samuel Jared Kushnick Foundation.

Progress in immune deficiency III, edited by H. M. Chapel, R. J. Levinsky and A. D. B. Webster, 1991; Royal Society of Medicine Services International Congress and Symposium Series No. 173, published by Royal Society of Medicine Services Limited.

Table 1 *Immunological findings*

Serum IgG (% normal)	190 ± 39
Serum IgA (% normal)	362 ± 43
Serum IgM (% normal)	425 ± 111
CD3 (%)	66 ± 16
CD4 (%)	44 ± 18
CD8 (%)	10 ± 2
CD4/8 ratio	4.6 ± 2
Con A (5 μg/ml) LPR (cpm × 10^3)	30.5
PHA (3 μg/ml) LPR (cpm × 10^3)	68.5
PHA (6 μg/ml) LPR (cpm × 10^3)	86.0
PHA (12 μg/ml) LPR (cpm × 10^3)	94.7

The hypocalcaemia has been well controlled with oral 1.25 dihydroxycalciferol and oral calcium supplements. She has not had fungal or bacterial infections but since the age of 18 months she has had five episodes of gradual onset of haemolytic anaemia associated with hypoplastic bone marrow crises. Three of these episodes have been associated with Coombs' test positive red cells; neutropenia ($1.0–1.5 \times 10^9$/l) and thrombocytopenia ($60–90 \times 10^9$/l) have been associated features. On two occasions these episodes followed what appeared to be a viral illness; on one occasion Adenovirus type 3 was isolated from the urine. The marrow showed hypoplasia; however parvo virus infection could not be documented by rising antibody titres. In addition four episodes of thrombocytopenic purpura ($30–60 \times 10^9$/l) with ecchymosis of the limbs have occurred, without haemolytic anaemia or bone marrow hypoplasia. Platelet associated antibodies were detected during one of the thrombocytopenic episodes. In each of these haematological crises, a prompt therapeutic response has been achieved with short courses of corticosteroids.

An enlarged liver (5 cm below costal margin) and spleen (6 cm below the costal margin) have been observed since the age of two years. There is no abnormality of liver function, nor evidence of hypersplenism. Liver biopsy at age four showed epithelioid granulomata with mononuclear cell infiltrate in the portal spaces and normal parenchymal cells. Smooth muscle antibodies are present, but mitochondrial antibodies were not detected.

IMMUNE FUNCTIONS

Immunoglobulins were measured by radial immunodiffusion. T lymphocyte subpopulation phenotypes and B lymphocytes were characterized by monoclonal antibodies and immunofluorescent microscopy. Mitogen-induced lymphocyte proliferative responses are expressed as a stimulation index reflecting the degree of ^{3}H thymidine incorporation in the stimulated cultures compared to the control untreated cultures. A summary of her immune functions are shown in Table 1. Coombs positive red cells were detected by an anti-Ig antibody. Platelet-associated antibodies were detected with an ELISA assay. Smooth muscle antibodies 1/20 were detected, but neither DNA antibodies, thyroid microsomal nor mitochondrial antibodies were found. The patient was immunized with DPT and Salk polio vaccine. Antibody to polio virus (1/8), by viral neutralization and tetanus (1/40) by haemagglutination were detected.

DISCUSSION

The early development of hypoparathyroidism in association with typical dysmorphic features confirmed the diagnosis of DiGeorge anomaly in this patient. A right aortic arch and aphonia were associated features. The latter symptom was not due to laryngeal cord paralysis but has been described in DiGeorge syndrome. Her clinical course and immune functions were characteristic of partial immune deficiency in that serious fungal infections have not occurred, mitogen-induced lymphocyte proliferative responses are normal, but low CD8 lymphocyte phenotype has resulted in a persistently elevated CD4/CD8 ratio.

The presence of immature T lymphocyte phenotypes in the peripheral blood (CD1) and low numbers of CD8 lymphocytes are also characteristic of this syndrome [7]. The decrease in percentage of CD8 lymphocytes accounts for defective induction of concanavalin A-induced suppressor T cell function and increased immunoglobulin synthesis *in vitro* from these patients' mononuclear cells [8,9].

There is considerable laboratory evidence supporting the role of abnormal T cell regulation in the development of autoimmune disease. For example both thymectomy or cyclosporin (which primarily inhibits CD4 lymphocyte function) ameliorate, while interferon-γ (which is produced primarily by CD4 lymphocytes) aggravates the naturally-occurring murine systemic lupus erythematosus in certain inbred mouse strains.

The presence of recurrent episodes of autoimmune haemolytic anaemia and thrombocytopenia that responded to corticosteroids, indicate that systemic autoimmune phenomena were present in this child. The precise nature of the patient's liver disease is not defined; however, epithelioid granulomata, smooth muscle antibodies and the mononuclear cell infiltrate support the diagnosis of granulomatous hepatitis, probably of autoimmune origin.

This patient, and the patient reported with DiGeorge syndrome and Graves disease, suggest that abnormal immunoregulation consequent on the primary T cell immunodeficiency is central in the pathogenesis of the autoimmune disease.

REFERENCES

(1) Bastian J, Law, S, Vogler L, Herrod H, Anderson S, Horowitz S. Prediction of persistent immunodeficiency in the DiGeorge anomaly. *J Pediatr* 1989; **115**: 391–6.
(2) Conley ME, Beckworth JB, Mancer JF, Tenckhoff L. The spectrum of the DiGeorge syndrome. *J Pediatr* 1979; **94**: 883–90.
(3) August CS, Rosen PS, Filler RM, Janeway CA, Murkowski B, Kay HE. Implantation of a fetal thymus, restoring immunological competence in a patient with thymic aplasia (DiGeorge's syndrome). *Lancet* 1968; **ii**: 1210–11.
(4) Goldsobel AB, Haas A, Stiehm ER. Bone marrow transplantation in DiGeorge syndrome. *J Pediatr* 1987; **111**: 40–44.
(5) Barrett DJ, Wara DW, Ammann AJ, Cowan MJ. Thymosin therapy in the DiGeorge syndrome. *J Pediatr* 1980; **97**: 66–71.
(6) Pong AJ, Cavallo A, Molman GM, Goldman AS. DiGeorge syndrome: Long-term survival complicated by Graves disease. *J Pediatr* 1985; **106**: 619–20.
(7) Reinherz EI, Cooper MD, Schlossman SF, Rosen FS. Abnormalities of T cell maturation and regulation in human beings with immunodeficiency disorders. *J Clin Invest* 1981; **68**: 699–705.
(8) Fizioni A, DiGeorge AM, Lischner HW. Decreased suppressor cell derivity in DiGeorge syndrome. *Pediatr Res* 1982; Abst. 855: 221A.
(9) Durandy A, Le Deist F, Fischer A, Griscelli C. Impaired T8 lymphocyte-mediated suppressive activity in patients with partial DiGeorge syndrome. *J Clin Immunol* 1986; **6**: 265.

High levels of circulating γ-δ T cells in children with malnutrition and under investigation for immunodeficiency

S. Singh[1], R. J. Levinsky[1], S. Strobel[1], O. Jobe[2], H. Whittle[2] and G. Morgan[1,2]

[1]Department of Immunology, Institute of Child Health and The Hospital for Sick Children, London, UK and [2]MRC Laboratories, The Gambia, West Africa

(POSTER)

Most human peripheral T lymphocytes express a CD3-associated T cell receptor (TCR) composed of α and β glycoprotein subunits (TCR2). This receptor is used to recognize antigens in the context of self major histocompatibility complex (MHC) molecules. A minority of T lymphocytes express a CD3-associated complex designated γ-δ (TCR1). These cells may participate in host immune surveillance and may also recognize foreign antigens in the context of restriction molecules other than MHC, but their exact role is ill-understood.

A recent study of healthy Western children has shown that the proportion of T cells bearing the γ-δ receptor rises from a mean of 1.7% at birth to 10% at 6 years of age after which the mean falls to approximately 5% in adults [1].

We studied 36 severely malnourished and 10 normally nourished children (age range 1–3 years) in the Gambia (Group 1), and 41 children (age range 3 days–17 years) in the United Kingdom under investigation for a heterogenous group of immunodeficiency disorders (Group 2). Whole blood or peripheral blood lymphocytes obtained by density centrifugation were stained by standard direct and/or indirect immunofluorescence techniques using anti-CD3 and TCR δ-1 monoclonal antibodies; analysis was done by flow cytometry. The number of γ-δ cells were expressed as a percentage of the total CD3$^+$ cells.

The mean γ-δ count in malnourished Gambian children was 12.1% while that in matched controls was 13.7%. Children in developing countries are exposed to significantly more infections and also have a higher prevalence of chronic parasitic infestation. High γ-δ counts in this situation may be participating in host immune responses against infection.

We also found that the percentage of γ-δ cells in some children under investigation for immunodeficiency was strikingly high (>15% in eight individuals). This increase is probably due to different mechanisms in that some patients had primary immunodeficiencies, but it should be noted that most of these subjects were also at high risk of infection.

Serial measurements performed over one to six months on three children in Group 2, revealed that the levels remained high in each individual.

We conclude that children who are at high risk of infection in both developing and developed countries may have increased numbers of circulating γ-δ cells. This finding of raised levels in heterogenous populations is consistent with a functional role for these cells. It is probable that γ-δ TCR may constitute part of the mature T cell repertoire.

REFERENCE

(1) Parker CM, Groh V, Band H, et al. Evidence for extrathymic changes in the T cell receptor gamma-delta repertoire. J Exp Med 1990; 171: 1597–612.

Progress in immune deficiency III, edited by H. M. Chapel, R. J. Levinsky and A. D. B. Webster, 1991; Royal Society of Medicine Services International Congress and Symposium Series No. 173, published by Royal Society of Medicine Services Limited.

Studies on sialophorin in the Wiskott-Aldrich syndrome

T. B. Wallington, P. D. J. Holt and F. A. Spring

South Western Regional Transfusion Centre, Bristol, UK

INTRODUCTION

Sialophorin (CD43) is a surface sialoglycoprotein found on leucocytes that is phenotypically defective in patients with Wiskott-Aldrich syndrome (WAS) [1].

WAS is a rare disease which varies in its severity. Like other X-linked conditions, up to 50% of cases are the first expression of the mutation and thus it can be very difficult to diagnose with certainty. Demonstration of an abnormality of sialophorin strongly supports the diagnosis. Two case studies are presented in which laboratory tests for this defect were undertaken. Firstly, using peripheral blood lymphocytes (PBL), a defect of sialophorin was demonstrated by auto-radiography after electrophoresis of radio-iodinated cell surface proteins, confirming the diagnosis of WAS in both patients. Further studies followed to answer the following questions: Could Epstein Barr virus (EBV)-transformed B lymphocytes be used to demonstrate and study the abnormality, thus decreasing the need for repeated blood samples? Would the simpler methods of western blotting or flow cytometry of whole cells reactive with CD43 Mabs demonstrate faults in the cells of such patients or their immediate relatives, particularly the putative female carriers of the disease?

CASE 1

A boy born 31.8.79; his parents are unrelated and both are well. He has a younger brother who is well. There is no significant family history. He has suffered severe eczema from the age of six weeks and infections, particularly of his skin, ear, nose, throat and foreskin, since early infancy. He also has mild thrombocytopenia, his platelet count averaging $100 \times 10^9/l$ with some bruising and occasional nose bleeds. Immunological tests, immunoglobulin isotypes, IgG subclasses, lymphocyte surface marker counts and *in vitro* lymphocyte proliferation to standard mitogens, are all normal. He is blood group A and the isohaemagglutinin anti-B is detected in neat serum only.

Progress in immune deficiency III, edited by H. M. Chapel, R. J. Levinsky and A. D. B. Webster, 1991; Royal Society of Medicine Services International Congress and Symposium Series No. 173, published by Royal Society of Medicine Services Limited.

CASE 2

A boy born 1.6.85, his parents are unrelated and both well. He has two brothers who are well. There is no significant family history. He has suffered from mild flexural eczema from the age of 10 months, also mild recurrent chest infections from infancy. His most severe problem is thrombocytopenia which presented at six weeks of age. His platelets are small. At the age of four years he developed severe autoimmune haemolytic anaemia which is transfusion-dependent. Immunological tests, as in case 1, are normal. His blood group is O, the isohaemagglutinin anti-A is detected in neat serum only; anti-B is not detected.

EBV-TRANSFORMED B LYMPHOCYTES

CD43 is expressed on most EBV-transformed B lymphocytes [2,3]. Cells were infected with the EBV B95-8 supernatant, (UKTS Bristol) and maintained in culture and not cloned. For use, cell cultures were grown to 5×10^5/ml.

MONOCLONAL ANTIBODIES (Mabs)

Several Mabs reacting with CD43 were used including DF-T1 (D. Flavell, Southampton, England).

WESTERN BLOTTING

Cell membrane molecules were solubilized by incubation of B lymphocytes harvested from the cell culture (10^8/ml) in PBS with added Triton X-100 (1%), ethanol (1%) and 2 mM phenylmethyl sulphonyl fluoride (PMSF) for 10 min at 0°C. The supernatant (after centrifugation at 3000 G for 10 min at 4°C) was assayed for protein content, and then suitably diluted in PBS containing 2 mercaptoethanol (5%) and 2mM PMSF. An aliquot containing 200 mg of protein was added to SDS polyacrylamide gel for electrophoresis by a standard technique. Molecular weight (MW) markers (SDS-6H Sigma Ltd) were included. Separated proteins were blotted on to Immobilon-P membrane and any remaining binding sites were blocked with PBS Tween containing 5% bovine milk powder. The membrane was then reacted with DF-T1, followed by horse-radish peroxidase-conjugated rabbit anti-mouse IgG and substrate to reveal the antibody-antigen interaction.

In case 1, the strong band of 115 kDa present in his mother, father and aunt was absent. Each gel was loaded with the same amount of protein and lower concentrations of sialophorin were found in the patient's father's cells than in his mother's. There were many bands of higher MW also reacting with anti-CD43; in our experience, these are unique to EBV-transformed B cells and are not present on untransformed PBL.

In case 2 complete absence of the 115 kDa band was not demonstrated in the preparation from transformed B lymphocytes. His father appeared to have higher concentrations of sialophorin than he or his mother. Many reactive lines of higher MW were also seen in this family.

FLUORESCENCE ACTIVATED CELL ANALYSIS

Freshly harvested lymphocytes were washed and re-suspended in PBS with 1% albumin to a concentration of 4×10^6/ml. The suspension was then incubated with DF-T1 for 1 h at 0°C at a previously determined optimum concentration. Mabs BRIC 125 and 162, specific to erythrocyte antigens, were used as controls. The cells were washed and incubated with fluorescein-conjugated anti-mouse IgG at previously determined optimum concentrations. The cell suspension was then analysed on a flow cytometer (data were analysed after counting 5000 cells).

Virtually all of the cells carried some surface molecules reacting with DF-T1. For each fluorescence profile, the log peak channel number (PCN) was recorded and this value was converted into a linear value using the equation

$$PCN\ LIN = anti\text{-}log\ (3 \times PCN/256).$$

The PCN and PCN LIN values give an indication of the shape of the fluorescence profile and thus the numbers of molecules on the cell population studied reacting with DF-T1. The results are shown in Table 1.

Table 1 *Results of flow cytometry of EBV-transformed B lymphocytes from each family*

Sample	Case 1			Father			Mother			Control		
	% Pos	PCN	PCN LIN	% Pos	PCN	PCN LIN	% Pos	PCN	PCN LIN	% Pos	PCN	PCN LIN
DF-TI	98.5	119	24.1	97.5	141	44.9	99	140	43.7	99	135	38.7
Sample	Case 2			Father			Mother			Control		
DF-TI	96.1	91	11.6	97.2	89	11	97.3	104	16.5	99	121	26.6

EBV-transformed B lymphocytes from case 1 showed markedly fewer cell surface molecules reacting with DF-T1 than either of his parents. The parental cells compared closely with those obtained from a healthy control. Transformed B lymphocytes obtained from case 2 and his parents did not show differences in reactivity with DF-T1 and less fluorescence than the control cells examined in the same experiment.

DISCUSSION

Cell surface molecules reacting with anti-CD43 Mabs were detected on all of the EBV-transformed lymphocytes examined, whether they were obtained from patients with putative WAS, their parents or healthy controls. These studies confirm the presence of CD43 as a major band of 115 kDa on EBV-transformed cell lines with additional CD43 reactive bands of variable and generally higher molecular size. Western blotting both of lymphocyte-derived cell lines or peripheral blood mononuclear cells has demonstrated broad CD43-reactive bands in the region of 115 kDa to 135 kDa [4,6]. The absence of sialophorin was demonstrated using transformed cells from case 1 by Western blotting. This defect is the presumed reason for reduced fluoresence when these cells were studied by flow cytometry using anti-CD43. Absence of sialophorin was not demonstrated using transformed B lymphocytes from case 2 although a fault is present on PBL by cell surface radio-iodination techniques. Case 2 was dependent on regular blood transfusion for treatment of haemolytic anaemia when a blood sample was taken for EBV-B lymphocyte transformation. Contamination by donor lymphocytes may explain the failure to show absence of sialophorin. It is also possible that the expression of sialophorin is cell-cycle dependent. No effort was made to harvest cells at a particular stage in cell culture, sufficient cell concentration for analysis being the limiting parameter.

The results also suggest that there are differences in the numbers of anti-CD43-reactive molecules between individuals. The father of case 1 appears to express less sialophorin than the mother or maternal aunt. All members of family 2 appear to express lower levels of sialophorin than family 1.

We conclude that studies of sialophorin are a useful adjunct to the diagnosis of WAS. Anti-CD43 Mabs facilitate this and flow cytometry is probably the simplest way to detect this molecule on cell surfaces so that differences in concentration can be measured. EBV-transformed B cells are not ideal, due to their expression of many anti-CD43-reactive epitopes on cell surface molecules with a higher MW than sialophorin. This produces background fluorescence, making detection of a deficiency more difficult.

REFERENCES

(1) Remold-O'Donnell E, Kenney DM, Parkman R, Cairns L, Savage B, Rosen FS. Characterisation of a human lymphocyte surface sialoglycoprotein that is defective in Wiskott-Aldrich syndrome. *J Exp Med* 1984; **159**: 1705.
(2) Cobbold S, Hale G, Waldmann H. Non-lineage, LFA-1 family and leucocyte common antigens: New and previously defined clusters. In: McMichael AJ *et al*, eds. *Leukocyte typing III*. Oxford: Oxford University Press, 1987: 788.
(3) Stoll M, Dalchau R, Schmidt RE. Cluster report CD43. In: Knapp W *et al*, eds. *Leukocyte typing IV*. Oxford: Oxford University Press, 1989: 604.
(4) Remold-O'Donnell E, Kenney D, Rosen FS. Biosynthesis of human sialophorins and analysis of the polypeptide core. *Biochem* 1987; **26**: 3908.
(5) Fukuda M, Carlsson SR, Klock JC, Dell A. Structures of o-linked oligosaccharides isolated from normal granulocytes, chronic myelogenous leukaemia cells. *J Biol Chem* 1986; **261**: 12796.
(6) Stross WP, Warnke RA, Flavell DJ, *et al*. Molecules detected in formalin fixed tissue by antibodies MT1, DF-T1 and L60 (Leu22) corresponds to CD43 antigen. *J Clin Pathol* 1989; **42**: 953.

The pathogenesis of the Wiskott-Aldrich syndrome

F. S. Rosen

Center for Blood Research, Children's Hospital, Department of Pediatrics,
Harvard Medical School, Boston, Massachusetts, USA

(ABSTRACT)

The Wiskott-Aldrich syndrome (WAS) is an X-linked immunodeficiency disease that is characterized by severe thrombocytopenia, eczema and recurrent infections. The defect appears to result from a mutation at a single locus, which maps to Xp11.2–11.3 and is defined by two flanking DNA probes, TIMP and DXS255, which are within 2 cM of the WAS locus.

Some cell membrane glycoproteins of the platelets, lymphocytes and other formed elements of the blood are unstable in the WAS. Most prominent of these is CD43, whose biosynthesis is normal in WAS but this protein is abnormally susceptible to proteolytic cleavage.

Progress in immune deficiency III, edited by H. M. Chapel, R. J. Levinsky and A. D. B. Webster, 1991; Royal Society of Medicine Services International Congress and Symposium Series No. 173, published by Royal Society of Medicine Services Limited.

Spondyloepiphyseal dysplasia associated with systemic lupus erythematosus: A new syndrome

J. H. Passwell, G. Robinson and D. Lotan

Department of Paediatric Immunology, Sheba Medical Centre, Tel-Hashomer, Israel

(POSTER)

INTRODUCTION

Spondyloepiphyseal dysplasia (SED) is a heterogenous group of inherited disorders that is usually dominantly inherited and characterized by disproportionate, short stature, varying degrees of epiphyseal involvement and flat vertebrae. The disease is due to structural defects in type II collagen and genomic analysis has confirmed the corresponding molecular defect in several relatives [1–3]. Myopia is frequently associated. A recent association with membranous glomerulonephritis has been reported in three families [4].

Primary immune deficiency and associated bone abnormalities have been reported in (i) severe combined immunodeficiency with adenosine deaminase deficiency. Both the immune deficiency and bony abnormalities are improved following bone marrow transplantation; (ii) cartilage hair hypoplasia (incompletely defined T cell deficiency results in susceptibility to varicella infection); (iii) short-limbed dwarfism and immunodeficiency [5].

We report the association of SED and systemic lupus erythematosus (SLE) in three patients from separate families.

METHODS AND RESULTS

Patients

A summary of the pedigrees and the main clinical features of each of the three patients is presented in Table 1. The three families were of Sephardic Jewish origin. None of the parents had any clinical features of the disease; in two families the parents were first cousins. Thus, at least in the families presented, inheritance appears to be autosomal recessive. In two families, there was another sibling with SED who had not developed SLE. The patients and their affected siblings were dwarfed and bone roentgenograms showed typical radiological findings of spino-epiphyseal dysplasia.

The clinical manifestations of SLE showed a varied pattern in the three patients. Onset of disease was early in life in all three. Patient DY initially presented with idiopathic thrombocytopenic purpura at the age of three and subsequently developed an inferior myocardial infarction at the age of seven. He did not show any renal, cerebral, skin or joint involvement. Patient AS presented at age 16 with fever of two months duration, arthritis of the limb joints and the small joints of the hands. Four years later, her course was complicated by pericarditis. The predominant presentation in patient YP was that of haematuria and proteinuria with mild renal dysfunction. Kidney biopsy showed diffuse lobulation and hypercellularity of the glomerular tufts with proliferation of the mesangial cells and thickening of the basement membrane with formation of wire loops. Immunohistology showed diffuse deposition of IgG and C3. The findings were characterisic of the membrano-proliferative glomerulonephritis of SLE. All three patients responded promptly to steroid therapy. Imuran was required for limited time periods so as to spare toxic steroid effects.

Progress in immune deficiency III, edited by H. M. Chapel, R. J. Levinsky and A. D. B. Webster, 1991; Royal Society of Medicine Services International Congress and Symposium Series No. 173, published by Royal Society of Medicine Services Limited.

Table 1 *Clinical features of three patients with SED associated with SLE*

Patient	DY	AS	YP
Family Tree / SED / SLE			
Ethnic origin	Iraq	Iraq	Iraq/Iran
Sex	Male	Female	Female
Age of onset (years)	3	16	10
Clinical manifestations	ITP / Inferior myocardial infarction	Arthritis / Pericardial effusion	Haemolytic anaemia / Membrano-proliferative glomerulonephritis
Treatment:	Steroids / Imuran	Steroids / Imuran	Steroids / Imuran

Table 2 *Laboratory findings in three patients with SED and SLE*

Patient	DY	AS	YP
ANF	Positive + + +	Positive + + +	Positive + + +
ds DNA Ab	73%	87%	93%
Circulating anticoagulant	30%	42%	37%
Complement total CH50%	35	70	20
C3 mg/dl	45	66	150
C4 mg/dl	6	16	11
IgG (g/l)	22.0	23.5	17.8
IgA (g/l)	4.2	3.5	1.32
IgM (g/l)	1.7	2.0	1.17
CD3 (%)	Not done	90	64
CD4 (%)	Not done	55	64
CD8 (%)	Not done	22	25
PHA LPR	Normal	Normal	Normal
ConA LPR	Normal	Normal	Normal

The laboratory findings in the three affected patients with SLE is summarized in Table 2. Mild hypergammaglobulinaemia of all isotypes was present. C3, C4 and complement haemolytic activity were decreased (though present) during active episodes of disease.

DISCUSSION

The association of SED and SLE in three patients from separate families strongly suggests that the development of autoimmune disease is related to the inherited skeletal disease. The clinical and laboratory features of the SLE were varied, but disease onset occurred at an unusually early age in all three. Although the growth failure and radiological findings were typical of SED, consanguinous marriage in two families and the fact that all parents were asymptomatic suggests that inheritance was autosomal recessive rather than the usually described dominant inheritance pattern. Interestingly, all three families were Sephardic Jews of Iraqi origin.

SED has recently been reported to be associated with other immune-mediated diseases. In three families glomerulonephritis which manifested as the nephrotic syndrome, was reported; in one family severe arthropathy in association with SED occurred [4,6]. In neither of these reports was the presence of DNA antibodies reported; however, the clinical manifestations were confined to one target organ.

The association of immune-mediated diseases and SED provides a new model for the possible link between osteocyte and lymphocyte function. The nature of this association remains speculative. A common developmental or genetic abnormality in both osteocytes and lymphocytes may result in varied effects on the skeletal and immune systems. The presence of abnormal cartilage proteins in patients with SED may predispose to the development of autoimmune disease. We speculate that an as yet undefined primary deficiency of immune regulation is responsible for the development of the autoimmune disease in patients who have both SED and SLE. Further dissection of the immune response and identification of the abnormal gene for SED in these patients are in progress.

REFERENCES

(1) Murray LW, Bautista J, James PL, Rimoin DL. Type II Collagen defects in the chondrodysplasias. 1. Spondyloepiphyseal dysplasias. *Am J Hum Genet* 1989; **45**: 5–15.
(2) Brendan L, Vissing H, Ramirez F, Rogers D, Rimoin DL. Identification of the molecular defect in a family with spondyloepiphyseal dysplasia. *Science* 1989; **244**: 978.
(3) Byers PH. Invited editorial: Molecular heterogeneity in chondrodysplasias. *Am J Hum Genet* 1989; **45**: 1–4.
(4) Ehrich JHH. Offner G, Schirg E, Hoyer PF, Helmchen U, Brodehl J. Association of spondyloepiphyseal dysplasia with nephrotic syndrome. *Pediatr Nephrol* 1990; **4**: 117–21.
(5) Hong R. Associations of the skeletal and immune systems. *Am J Hum Genet* 1989; **34**: 55–9.
(6) Miladi M, Elleuch MH, Sellami S, Douik M. Spondyloepiphyseal dysplasia tarda with progressive arthropathy. *Int Orthop* 1987; **11**(3): 271–5.

Abnormal course of Epstein Barr virus infection in two siblings of North African origin

E. R. de Graeff-Meeder, I. Hiemstra, W. Kuis,
W. Vooys, J. Middeldorp, J. le Poutre, R. C. M. Hennekam,
R. de Weger, H. J. Schuurman, G. T. Rijkers, B. A. van Oost, B. J. M. Zegers

Department of Immunology, University Hospital for Children and Youth, Utrecht, The Netherlands

(POSTER)

INTRODUCTION

Epstein Barr virus (EBV) infection may lead to several clinical syndromes including infectious mononucleosis, persistent EBV infection, so-called X-linked lymphoproliferative syndrome (XLP), and B lymphocyte malignancies [1,2]. In some of these syndromes defects in EBV specific immunity may be present together with more general disturbances of immune function. We had occasion to study two brothers of North-African origin who showed an abnormal course of an EBV infection. In-depth analysis showed clinical and immunological heterogeneity and DNA linkage studies directed to establish the possibility of XLP disclosed genetic heterogeneity.

CASE HISTORIES

The first patient, a boy, born in 1984 developed an abnormal course of an EBV infection at the age of three years, i.e. prolonged fever, severe progressive lymphadenopathy, hepatomegaly, uveitis and recurrent pneumonia. EBV serology showed the presence of VCA-IgG antibodies (up to 1:1000) and antibodies to EA (up to 1:320) whereas anti-EBNA remained negative during the follow up period of almost 1.5 years. Conventional serology was confirmed and extended by Western blot experiments [3]. Granulocytopenia and thrombocytopenia developed and gradually progressed to pancytopenia. He was treated with partial gut decontamination, acyclovir and intravenous IgG (IVIg). At the age of 4.5 years the patient died of septic shock due to infection with a multi-resistant *Streptococcus sanguinis*.

Analysis of immune function showed increases in serum IgG and in peripheral blood lymphocyte numbers. Phenotyping of the lymphocytes showed predominance of CD8+ T lymphocytes. *In vitro* T cell function, as measured in proliferation assays, appeared to be almost negative.

Analysis of EBV-specific immunity showed the presence of EBNA+ cells in a lymph node removed during life; EBV-specific cytotoxicity appeared to be intact in the peripheral blood. *Postmortem* examination showed diffuse infiltration of CD8+ T cells in all lymphoid organs and in liver, lung and endocardium. Expression of EBV antigens in *postmortem* tissues, including EBNA and EA, was negative. However, techniques using the polymerase chain reaction on cells convincingly showed the presence of EB virus.

The second patient, a younger boy born in 1987, contracted the EB virus at the age of 2.5 years. The clinical course was initially almost as severe as that of his brother. Analysis of EBV-specific immunity and general immune status showed essentially similar findings as his brother. The patient was treated with acyclovir, α-Interferon and IVIg. Nine months after the onset of the EBV infection, and five months after treatment, the patient showed marked clinical improvement, i.e. fever, lymphadenopathy and hepatomegaly had completely disappeared. However serum IgM and IgG, which initially showed levels of 0.8 and 12.1 g/l respectively, were now decreased to 0.1 for IgM and 4.4 g/l for IgG.

Progress in immune deficiency III, edited by H. M. Chapel, R. J. Levinsky and A. D. B. Webster, 1991; *Royal Society of Medicine Services International Congress and Symposium Series No. 173, published by Royal Society of Medicine Services Limited.*

GENETIC STUDIES AND CONCLUSION

Since the clinical course of EBV infection in patient 1 is suggestive of the diagnosis of XLP, DNA marker analysis was performed using several DXS probes encompassing the Xq25–26 region which comprises the XLP gene [4]. The results clearly showed that the brothers had a different X chromosome. This finding suggests that the patients cannot both have XLP based on genetic abnormalities located in the region Xq25–26. They are therefore either discordant for the XLP gene and incidentally have a similar course of EBV infection or they have another, as yet undefined, abnormality associated with EBV infection. Clinical and immunological follow-up is required to establish this assumption. We also conclude that clinical follow-up combined with studies on EBV-specific immunity are not sufficient to ensure the diagnosis of XLP. Furthermore acyclovir, α-interferon and IVIg may be used successfully in patients showing a severe course of EBV infection.

REFERENCES

(1) Sullivan JL, Woda BA. X-linked lymphoproliferative syndrome. *Immunodef Rev* 1989; **1**: 325–47.
(2) Kuis W, Roord JJ, Zegers BJM, *et al.* Heterogeneity of immune defects in three children with a chronic active Epstein-Barr virus infection. *J Clin Immunol* 1985; **5**: 377–85.
(3) Middeldorp J, Herbrink P. Epstein-Barr virus specific marker molecules for early diagnosis of infectious mononucleosis. *J Virol Methods* 1988; **21**: 133–46.
(4) Skare JC, Milunsky A, Byron KS. Mapping of X-linked lymphoproliferative syndrome. *Proc Natl Acad Sci USA* 1987; **84**: 2015–18.

Cytokines modulate glycosaminoglycan metabolism in endothelial cells

N. J. Klein, G. I. Shennan and M. Levin

Infectious Disease Unit, Hospital for Sick Children and Institute of Child Health, London, UK

(ABSTRACT)

Vascular endothelial damage is an important component of the physiological derangement seen in septicaemia. The endothelial glycosaminoglycans (GAGS) are vital to the permeability and thromboresistant properties of the vessel wall. We have investigated the influence of endotoxin and cytokines, alone and in the presence of neutrophils, on glycosaminoglycan metabolism in human umbilical vein cell cultures. Whilst endotoxin alone did not alter GAG metabolism, IL-1, IL-4 and TNF caused a significant up-regulation of one or more classes of GAGS. We observed an increased release of GAGS into the culture supernatant and a decrease of cell-associated Dermatan and Heparan sulphate. This reduction in cell surface GAGS was enhanced when neutrophils were added to the cytokine stimulated cultures. Using a cytochemical technique to visualize anionic sites we found a correlation between the loss of cellular GAGS and a decrease in surface charge. These results suggest that alteration of endothelial cell GAGS and surface charge may be important in the pathophysiology of inflammatory states.

Progress in immune deficiency III, edited by H. M. Chapel, R. J. Levinsky and A. D. B. Webster, 1991; Royal Society of Medicine Services International Congress and Symposium Series No. 173, published by Royal Society of Medicine Services Limited.

Meeting of the Primary Immune Deficiency Patient Support Groups Oxford, 1990

Approximately two years ago it was suggested that a meeting of patient support groups for the primary immune deficiency diseases be held in conjunction with the EGID meeting at Oxford. At that time it was expected that only about three or four countries would be represented. Therefore, everyone was surprised and pleased to find 21 representatives from 13 nations.

The first day's meetings consisted of presentations by the group from each country of their history, current position and their aims. The common themes were:

1. Early diagnosis is a problem.

2. Because of confidentiality, and late diagnosis, it is difficult to identify patients with primary immune deficiency diseases so that they can be included in a patient support organization.

3. Groups publish literature to educate and inform patients, GPs, nurses and members of the medical profession. Further publicity should aim to educate and inform the general public.

4. Raising funds.

5. All the groups expressed interest in promoting international cooperation in the field of primary immune deficiency diseases.

Organizational structures varied, but generally consisted of an entirely or mainly non-medical committee of up to nine people. This was supported either by a formal Medical Advisory Board or by close links with appropriate members of the medical profession who could provide medical advice and counsel.

The second day was spent on discussion topics. These included: concerns on the administration of gammaglobulin, home therapy courses, positive actions the groups could take to improve the rate of diagnosis, assistance that could be provided for patients, families and friends and how funds could be raised for research into the primary immune deficiency diseases.

On the third day the group voted unanimously to form an International organization that would represent the National organizations. After extensive discussion, an 'Organizing Committee' was formed to recommend an organizational structure and operating procedures for approval by the group. In addition, Dr Cunningham Rundles kindly gave an informative presentation on the greatly increased speed of advances in immunology over the last 15 years. This ended the proceedings on a very positive note.

Robert L. Bein

Index

abnormal biosynthesis processing and membrane expression of the TCR/CD3 complex in an immunodeficient child, 307–10

acquired immunodeficiency syndrome *see* AIDS

adenosine deaminase (ADA)
deficency, marked clinical improvement and immune reconstitution after treatment with polyethylene glycol-conjugated ADA, 230–1
vector-mediated expression *in vivo* in PBL derived from ADA-SCID patients, 232

AIDS
following mother-to-child transmission of human immunodeficiency virus type 2, 174
IgA subclasses reduced in saliva, 175–6

allogeneic marrow engrafted adults, antibody deficiency, 134

angioedema, acquired and inherited and C1q levels, 22

anti-CD43 Mabs in diagnosis of Wiskott-Aldrich syndrome, 324

anti-HB antibody in treatment of chronic hepatitis B infection, 90

anti-HCV antibodies in gammaglobulin for intravenous use, 150

anti-polysaccharide antibodies
defective response in children with recurrent respiratory tract infections, 115–17
deficiency after allogeneic bone marrow engrafted adults, 134
Haemophilus influenzae type b (Hib) vaccines in patients with recurrrent infections and/ or immune deficiences, 135
in homozygous C3 deficiency, 119–22
quantitation in human sera, 130–1
selective deficiency as risk factor for invasive disease caused by capsulated bacterial pathogens, 132–3

anti-tetanus toxoid
response, 238–40
specificity in bone marrow transplant recipients, 124–6

ataxia-telangiectasia
gene complex fine mapping to a 4.5 cM region at chromosome 11q23, 298–301
heterozygous lymphocytes, bromodeoxy-uridine-induced SCE in, 302
presenting as hyper IgM syndrome, 303–4
T cell receptor γ-δ expression in children, 305–6

autoantibodies
frequency in children with IgA deficiency, 14
occurrence and persistence in predominantly antibody defects, 87

autoimmune gut disease after haploidentical bone marrow transplantation, 243–6

B cell tumours, predictors of infection in patients, 136–7

B lymphocytes
abnormal differentiation in primary immuno-deficiencies, 279
absence in CVI, 82
defects in CVI, 61, 73–6
deficiency of lineage in SCID, 293, 294
phenotypic heterogenicity in common variable immunodeficiency, 84
SCID and defective signalling, 155–8

bare lymphocyte syndrome, 279

bone marrow transplantation
allogeneic, antibody deficiency in adults, 134
in Costa Rica, 248
HLA-non-identical, humoral reconstitution in SCID, 242
hypogammaglobulinaemia in SCID girl, 168–9
for immunodeficiencies and osteopetrosis in Europe, 241
immunological reconstitution in spite of thymic abnormalities, 315
in a patient with MHC Class II deficiency, 292
sixteen year follow-up for severe combined immunodeficiency, 247

bone marrow transplantation, allogeneic
demonstration of chimaerism, 233
restricted heterogeneity of IgG anti-tetanus toxoid antibodies, 124–6

bone marrow transplantation, haploidentical
failure to thrive after, 243–6
for SCID, 243–6

C1 inhibitor, deficiency and hereditary angi-oedema, 17

C1q levels in acquired and hereditary angioedema, 22

C3 deficiency, homozygous, association with impaired antibody responses to PCP, 119–22

candidacidal activity of monocytes and monocyte-derived macrophages: implications for immunodeficiency disease, 184–7

CD3 gene in immunodeficient child, 307–10

CD3γ abnormality, T cell receptor (TCR) expression defect, 311–13

CD43 on EBV transformed B lymphocytes, 322, 323

CD43 (sialophorin) genetic defects in Wiskott-Aldrich syndrome, 321

CD43 instability in Wiskott-Aldrich syndrome, 325